Psychopolitical Warfare

Principles, Strategies, and Tactics

By

Eric Richard Wise

Cadmus Publishing
CadmusPublishing.com

Psychopolitical Warfare:
Principles, Strategies and Tactics

Manufactured in the United States of America. Copyright 2025 by Eric Richard Wise. All rights reserved. No part of this book may be reproduced in any form, audio, digital, or in print, except excerpts by reviewers, without written permission from the copyright holder or Cadmus Publishing LLC.

DISCLAIMER:
The thoughts, opinions, and expressions herein are those of the author and do not reflect those of Cadmus Publishing LLC. "This material is intended for educational purposes only. Any similarities to actual events or people are purely coincidental. Names and distinguishing characteristics may have been changed to preserve the identities of any individuals. Published by Cadmus Publishing LLC. P. O. Box 8664. Haledon, NJ 07538

Web: Cadmuspublishing.com
Facebook.com/Cadmuspublishing
Business email: admin@cadmuspublishing.com
Author email: info@cadmuspublishing.com

ISBN# 978-1-63751-511-2

Book Catalog Info Categories:
Political Science – Intelligence & Espionage
Social Science – Criminology
Biography – Criminals & Outlaws

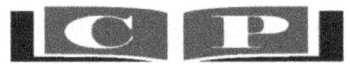

Cadmus Publishing
CadmusPublishing.com

Contents

Prologue 4

SECTION ONE: PRINCIPLES

Chapter One: Psychological Aspects of Authority 22

Chapter Two: The Official Motivation 44

Chapter Three: Fallible Officials 59

SECTION TWO: STRATEGIES

Chapter Four: The Realm of Psychopolitical Warfare 75

Chapter Five: Mind Games: 87

Chapter Six: The Faces of Deception 107

Chapter Seven: Propaganda and Persuasion 133

Chapter Eight: Anything You Say 148

Chapter Nine: The Brazen Rule 161

SECTION THREE: TACTICS

Chapter Ten: Powerful Alliances of Self-Interest 174

Chapter Eleven: A Time to Advance and a Time to Fall Back 180

Chapter Twelve: Tactical Intel 188

Chapter Thirteen: Preparation and Execution 200

Chapter Fourteen: Tales of the Unexpected 210

Chapter Fifteen: The Power of Perseverance 223

Appendix 1: DOJ Memo to Author Concerning His Letter to Attorney General Sessions 237

Appendix 2: Letter from President Biden to U.S. Citizens 239

Appendix 3: Illustrations of Poison Parasite 241

Appendix 4: Legal Minutiae Concerning Interrogations 243

Appendix 5: Abridgement from Author's Treatise *Advanced Studies in Mind Control:* Example and Analysis of Suggestive Questioning and the Implantation of False Memories 245

Appendix 6 Author's DOJ Affidavit Concerning Misconduct of Official 249

Appendix 7: Author's Email to OIG and BOP's Psychology Department Concerning Misconduct of Official 251

SOUNDTRACK 253

Author's Ancestral Arms of Achievement

Prologue

> We wrestle not against flesh and blood,
> but against the rulers,
> against the authorities,
> against the cosmic powers over this present darkness,
> against the spiritual forces of evil in heavenly places.
> — St. Paul
> Ephesians 6:12

Screams and wails shattered the silence. An iron gate stood before me. Behind me lay the burial ground of the damned, those condemned to a living death.

"Help us, Lord Wise..."

"Who are you?" I replied with rapt attention.

"No, one will challenge him Lord... all are in fear."

I couldn't hear the voices, but I understood them.

A figure in black boldly approached. I did not see him; still, I felt his presence: cold, cruel, hideous. The pleas had been silenced on his arrival. Overcome with fear, I collapsed. The monster held power beyond anything I could comprehend, yet there was something about this. The longer I lay in his presence the more I could feel it. This demon had weakness.

He noticed me studying this, and he withdrew.

I arrived at the Federal Correctional Complex—Medium in Hopewell, Virginia on the afternoon of March 13, 2008. FCC Petersburg, as it was styled due to its proximity to the city of Petersburg, was the fifteenth prison in which I'd been incarcerated since I began serving a fifty-year sentence for consensual sex with my underage girlfriend.

On the way from the Receiving and Discharge department to my housing unit, I squeezed through the human logjam. It appeared I was entering an inner-city housing project. Dirty, triangular-shaped concrete housing structures rose up above the squalid landscape. The crowding and disorder were such that there were occasions when I could not leave the building as a deadlock of human traffic clogged the sally port and outside walkways. Health and safety inspectors from subordinate jurisdictions are not permitted passage onto prison grounds to check such code violations.

A smorgasbord of substances smoked by the inmates permeated the air. Tobacco was the most prevalent, followed by marijuana, crack, meth, heroin, K2, and numerous other intoxicating agents to which I had never been exposed until I fell prey to the U.S. Government.

This perplexed me. Smoking, along with even tobacco itself had been banned years prior. Yet, inmates openly indulged in these. I was an athletic, healthy, somewhat young man who hated breathing the fumes. And as my luck had it, one of my cellmates would turn out to be the heaviest smoker of all.

Adjusting to life at this prison was extraordinarily difficult for those of my background. Studious, peaceful white men like me had been plucked straight from the sleepy neighborhoods and suburbs of Hometown USA, convicted of harmless internet-related theoretical sex offenses and thought crimes, then plunged into this dark, bloody hell with deeply disturbed rapists, drug dealers, and gang members.

I was raised in a small mostly Mennonite farm town in Iowa—700 residents.

Every day in the housing unit the gangster types, in diverse stages of intoxication from diverse substances, ran wild like little children on a playground. One might observe them screaming, cursing, howling like monkeys, barking like dogs, rolling on the floor, or swinging from the second-tier railings. For a period of six months a hunchbacked inmate emerged from cell 35 and commenced his day by yipping in delirium while flipping game tables upside down. An inmate who was part of the ultraviolent MS-13 gang lived on the top tier. He enjoyed getting drunk, dashing from cell to cell, stealing the hard plastic trash cans, then heaving them down at inmates present on the lower tier.

I began the effort to cleanse the air in my living space by speaking to my cellmate and his principal dealer, asking them to curb their harmful activities when I was in the cell. As this proved to be in vain, I spoke to unit officers and filed complaints to administration—lieutenants, associate wardens, and the unit management. No action ensued. I then escalated written administrative remedies up the entire federal Bureau of Prisons (BOP) chain of command: unit manager, warden, regional director, and national director. I protested administration's "refusal to enforce rules and laws forbidding drugs and smoking." Nothing changed.

In September 2008 I met with Officer Vaughan of the Special Investigative Section (S.I.S.). By this time, I had researched and documented the illicit network. I provided him with names of the unit's drug dealers, along with names and addresses of free world money launderers involved who lived in Virginia, Georgia, and North Carolina. I also furnished details of transactions such as the amounts, dates, and methods involved. Most of those involved payment from inmate Trust Fund accounts, as authorized by BOP officials, with checks issued by the U.S. Treasury. I sent the same information to the complex captain—the chief of security. No action resulted from these efforts and I never heard from Vaughan again.

On Christmas evening 2008 I planned to go to the recreation yard and quietly savor the solace, listening to sacred choral music via my Sony Walkman on 88.9 WCVE, Richmond's classical music station. But when I pushed open the heavy steel door to exit the building, a loud pounding assaulted my ears. I stopped on the horseshoe-shaped walkway and looked around. The noise was coming from the recreation area. I proceeded up the middle walkways and strolled past the bushes in the center circle. The percussive disturbance increased, hammering me as I drew near to the yard. Boom! Boom! ba tap! Boom! Boom! ba tap! I crossed into the recreation area and the lyrics became discernable.

> My gat screamed fire
> The bullet taught me truth
> That mutha—ka he's a liar
> I talk to my creator
> He like a b—ch on a stroll
> Niggaz wanna d-ck me
> I don't wanna play the ho
> Kill em all!

The scene unfolded before me. On the basketball court was the source of my irritation. A state-of-the-art sound system had been erected. Rouge brand loudspeakers were mounted upon stands and a booth was set up between them. Black inmates were dancing around the court, the center of which featured a painting of the mascot—The FCC Petersburg "Bearwolf." As I stepped up onto the concrete court the sweet, heady scents of marijuana and hooch wafting through the breeze rudely awakened my nostrils.

I approached the booth to confront the man responsible, only to discover he was wearing a blue uniform. Stopping in front of him I looked him over. It was Antwon Tombs, a recreation officer.

"What the hell is this all about?" I yelled at him over the pounding beat.

He returned a vacant stare.

> The Glocks, infrareds, and the Uzi things
> And if the sh-t jumps off I'm killing everything
> Don't be actin' like no bitches when the heat is on
> Cuz if them niggas catch you slippin' then you ass is gone.

A compact disc case rested next to the soundboard. I snatched it and examined the cover. This was the soundtrack to the movie "Tales from the Hood." I noted the track number by glancing at the CD player. Comparing it to the case, I decided we were listening to "Born 2 Die" by Spice 1, the "East Bay Gangsta."

I dropped the case back onto the table and accosted Tombs. "You need to shut this crap off!"

Evidently thinking I may be looking for trouble, he arose from his plastic chair, folded his massive arms and glared down at me. He was about 6'7", 400 pounds and obviously had pumped a lot of iron. I'm 5'11" and 210 pounds, but I had also pumped plenty of iron and wasn't intimidated.

The American flag adorned his shirt sleeve. On the upper left corner of his shirt was embroidered a circular seal: Department of Justice, Federal Bureau of Prisons. In the middle an eagle perched upon a red, white, and blue shield. I've always despised the seals assumed by American state and federal governments, which are inauthentic appropriations of the arms of achievement created by my ancestors.

"Don't you have any self-respect, man?" I rebuked Tombs. "You're a federal officer but you glorify drugs, violence, and a degenerate lifestyle!"

Expressionless, the giant looked down upon me. Two black inmates approached from out of the shadows and positioned themselves on each of his sides. I recognized one from a time he cut in front of me in the meal line. The inmates bobbed around, twitching nervously as their hateful grimaces spoke their thoughts.

There we stood in a staring showdown. Me on one side, the inmate/officer alliance on the other. I shook my head in disgust, pointed a finger at Tombs and announced, "You're a disgrace!" Then I turned and walked away.

I knew better than to behave in this manner. My expectations of a peaceful evening had been violated and instead of taking time to calmly assess the situation and consider a response, I emotionally reacted in the moment. While I hadn't totally lost my composure I had still displayed a bit too much aggression and said far too much. I would have to improve on this.

Mozart never figured into my Christmas.

Every few days the loud "music" was played. As time progressed it became a nightly, then daily, occurrence. On weekends the music was accompanied by parties similar to the one that kicked this all off on December 25th.

> Kill 'em off like this bye bye bye
> Sickie sickie one said I'm born to die
> Kill 'em off like this bye bye bang
> Sickie sickie one said I'm born to hang.

According to the opinion of a federal court of appeal, the BOP's much vaunted administrative remedy system has rendered lawsuits unnecessary. The BOP acts in good faith to resolve problems, the panel of jurists asserts, so there is no longer any need to turn to America's courts for forceful resolution of an issue.

By early 2009, I'd already exhausted administrative remedies on the smoking matter. I started doing the same on the "music" parties.

In my BP-9 to the warden I wrote:

> Since December 25, the Recreation staff has been playing "gangsta rap" over their loudspeakers nearly every day. The volume is so intense that when I put on my own headphones and play my radio loudly I still can't hear my radio. Everyone on the yard must listen to the rap "music." Obviously, the inmate population here is racially diverse and not everyone enjoys black gangsta rap. We all have personal radios and I'm requesting the Recreation department shut the "music" off.

The warden at the time was a black woman. Her reply read:

> Recreation activities are governed by Program Statement 5370.11. The Recreation staff strives to make recreation an enjoyable experience for all inmates. The music serves a wide range of purposes and those inmates who do not wish to listen to it may wear headphones and listen to their personal radios.

I appealed all the way up the chain of command. None of the warden's superiors countermanded her implicit decision to allow the music to continue.

It became clear, notwithstanding the court's aforementioned input concerning the efficacy of the BOP's administrative remedy system, that I was going to have to employ coercive power. But one vice at a time, I would first focus on purifying the air.

I furthered this mission by soliciting affidavits from other inmates to fully establish the extent of the issue with drugs and smoking. Some approved of what I was doing but were afraid to get involved. Others were happy to help me clean the place up and enthusiastically wrote statements.

In February 2009 my parents contacted U.S. Senator Charles Grassley (R-IA) in Washington. Senator Grassley consigned two letters to the BOP concerning the institution's problem with illicit substances. The BOP stonewalled him both times, refusing to even answer.

My parents then contacted several attorneys in the Richmond area, none of whom were willing to sue government officials. Thus, in July 2009, representing myself, I filed suit against twelve BOP officials in the U.S. District Court for the Eastern District of Virginia. Defendants ranged from A-North unit officers to director of the Mid-Atlantic region.

I charged the defendants with 1) exposing me to the dangers of Environmental Tobacco Smoke (ETS), 2) refusing to enforce policies prohibiting inmate smoking and contraband possession, 3) promulgating customs and policies that allow staff to easily and secretly transfer tobacco and illegal drugs to inmates, 4) authorizing a dangerous and disorderly prison environment, 5) receiving bribes in exchange for unlawful substances, and 6) permitting subordinates to sell hazardous chemicals to which I was unwillingly exposed.

I attached to the pleadings as exhibits copies of the relevant administrative remedy petitions and responses as well as the statements of other inmates.

(After I was placed in segregation in February 2010 by two lieutenants, whom I verbally rebuked for refusing to stop contraband transactions that took place in their presence, I added them and two retaliation counts to the pleadings.)

I directly contacted Senator Jim Webb of Virginia in March 2010, hoping an elected federal representative for that very state may have more influence than Senator Grassley had been able to exert. Senator Webb sent a Congressional Inquiry to the BOP, forwarding my complaint in so doing. The next month I received a vague modified form letter reply which did not directly respond to my allegations. The most relevant part read:

> Any type of allegation concerning staff misconduct and the ethical or unfair treatment of individuals is taken very seriously. Any and all allegations are thoroughly investigated by a neutral party and if any type of misconduct on the part of staff is discovered, the federal BOP and the FCC Petersburg complex will follow a strict disciplinary process.

Still, no changes took place. I asked my parents to try contacting Webb's office on my behalf. Free people who can vote tend to retain greater political power than incarcerated people who cannot. Webb's staff agreed to pursue the matter further, but warned my parents that BOP officials were likely to retaliate. I already knew this and didn't care; for it is a generally accepted principle of war (as well as finance) that as the potential for injury increases so does the potential for profit.

Kathleen Kinney, assistant director and general counsel for the BOP, replied to Webb's second inquiry in relevant part:

> Mr. and Mrs. Wise allege staff at FCC Petersburg are introducing drugs and tobacco into the institution in exchange for bribes. They claim their son has been trying for two years to clean up FCC Petersburg and he has provided information to investigative staff and other administrators, but they appear to not have acted on the information. The BOP takes all allegations of staff misconduct seriously... These allegations were investigated, and appropriate action was taken.

That summer I was outside talking to other white inmates when the hideous "musical" pounding started. We all agreed it *had* been a beautiful day. I suggested a petition by non-blacks to shut down the "music." Surely more inmates don't want to hear it than do, I reasoned. A peer agreed but informed me that when a few years prior some inmates presented to administration a petition seeking better medical care, they had been locked up in segregation for violating Code 212—Engaging in a Group Demonstration.

Given that the First Amendment to U.S. Constitution reads: "Congress shall make no law... abridging the freedom of speech, or of the press; or of the right of the people peaceably to assemble, and to petition the Government for a redress of grievances" this came as a bit of a surprise. But then I hadn't been able to enforce any of my so-called rights in criminal proceedings either, and it was becoming clear that, in reality, I had none.

In the early stages of my lawsuit against the officials, I'd beaten their Motion to Strike and Motion to Dismiss under FRCP 12. I'd brought an immense amount of pressure on them through all three branches of the federal government. Quietly, behind the scenes, subtle changes were finally starting to take place; changes they did not desire. Their anger was building.

One day in early 2011, "Big G," head of a Latin gang, stopped me at the bottom of the stairs when I returned from recreation. He "invited" me into his cell for a talk.

Plopping his enormous tattooed brown body into a small plastic chair that could barely sustain it, he twisted a fiendish grin and stared me up and down.

"Come on Eric, you can do better than this."

"I'm told that often these days. You'll have to be more specific, G."

"The staff—they're putting you on main street."

"I'm not fluent in urban parlance. If you would please, translate that."

"They say you're informing on business arrangements in the unit."

Big G's henchman, arms folded and a menacing cast aimed directly at me, had positioned himself in front of the door. One enters into situations like these with an outcome that is uncertain. Anything could happen. I'd learned that no matter how scared I may be, displaying that fear is a mistake. It is equally dangerous to show too much aggression. For if my opponent believes I am disrespectful or am challenging him, he will be forced to save face, which is very important in the underworld. The constant conflicts that inevitably arise when one challenges the powers that be had, by this time, toughened my mind to the point where I could remain clear-headed in nearly any confrontation.

I slowly nodded and rubbed my chin. Feigning a lack of interest, I softly replied, "From which officer are you acquiring these tidings?"

The large gangster's mischievous smirk widened. "A certain black one. Someone we both know."

There was nothing to be gained for me by discussing this, but I knew I had to satiate his obligation to get to the bottom of the issue.

"Whoever is telling you this has a motive to spin the facts to suit his perspective. Nevertheless, I assure you I mind my own business and any battles I am fighting are in self-defense against only those who are harming me."

He'd obviously been in these types of situations many times as well and displayed a tactfulness and equanimity I would've thought above such brutal types. "G" reminded me more of a polished mafia don than a crude gang boss. Still, I knew this could change in an instant with one wrong word or move on my part.

The slick smile that had been pasted on his face slowly faded and his eyes locked on mine. "Do you view me or any of my people as a cause of this harm?"

This was, of course, a loaded question. I quickly mulled it over, and issued the only correct reply, "Not to my knowledge. I would've talked to you already if that was the case."

With his piercing glare still fixed on me, he leaned back in the straining chair, silently evaluating me. Finally, he let out a deep breath and proclaimed, "That's all I wanted to know, Eric. You can go." He nodded to the goon who was blocking the door and the same stood aside. As I departed cell 18 I noticed the door had also been barricaded from the outside by Big G's crew.

Two days later I attended the mandatory biannual Inmate Program Review meeting. This waste of time constitutes the BOP's equivalent of a job appraisal; as if we had some incentive to behave, in our state of expulsion from society, as role model pariahs.

By this point my heavily smoking cellmate had been released and a few others had come and gone. I was in a cell by myself and still surrounded by smokers.

My case manager, a short, rotund black woman in her fifties, accosted me. "Wise, why don't you have a cellmate like everyone else?"

"Ms. B," I replied, "certain managers have been telling the inmates I am informing on illicit schemes here, so I am, to say the least, unpopular at the moment."

Clearly surprised that I'd verbalized this suspicion, she puffed up in her chair like an overgrown bullfrog, "Well I . . . haven't said anything if that's what you're implying."

"I never said it was you. I'm not sure why you drew that inference." I tilted my head in the direction of my correctional counselor, a massive, shady figure of grim fortitude who slouched in his chair, silently staring down at the tabletop as if he were conducting an intricate inspection of its surface.

> I felt myself falling. Darkness enveloped me. I'd never known a gloom this deep. Darker than the blackest night. Blacker than the darkest pitch. So thick I could feel it oozing over my being.
> I could see nothing, hear nothing, smell nothing, and touch nothing. Still, I knew.
> Down into the murky abyss I plunged. I was neither alive nor dead.
> "Why have they done this to me?" I asked. "Why is it so dark?"
> Something seized ahold of me, and I froze in space and time.
> I could neither see it nor feel it; yet I knew.
> I detected movement.
> Voices called to me: "Lord Wise, help us!"
> "Who are you?" I asked.
> There was no answer.
> "Help us! We are lost!" the voices implored.
> "How can I help you?" I replied. "I cannot move. I cannot see. Why is it so dark?" No answer came forth.
> "That devil can be defeated," they tempted.
> "I don't know how to defeat him. Tell me!"
> Again, there was no answer.
> The voices continued their supplications, "Help us find our way . . . save us!"
> "How can I save you?" I cried. "I cannot even save myself!"
> Sorrow overwhelmed me: a sadness unlike anything I had ever felt; drearier than the most miserable melancholy; bleaker than the most aching despair.
> I wept; not tears composed of water and salt, but droplets of my soul. Bleeding forth from the very depths of my being. They drifted off into the tenebrous void. And with each drop, a piece of my soul was forever lost.
> Something loosed and I began falling. This time spinning ever furiously into a spiral vacuum. Down I spun, deeper and deeper. Then . . . there was nothing.

I was a marked man. I knew it and so did the inmate population and staff. An Indian from Minnesota who either had no concern with the social stigma I carried or hoped to inherit my cell and meager possessions upon my disposal, asked our correctional counselor, who was a defendant in my lawsuit, if he could enter cell #3 with me. He had asked on a Monday and received the reply, "I'll let you know Wednesday." Hearing of the conversation, I was perplexed. I was told to find a cellmate and I did so. Why did the counselor need to deliberate the matter?

Over the past six months I had become acquainted with a diligent officer who worked the evening shift on weekends in my housing unit. I entered his office and complimented his work. He was surprised an inmate would appreciate his brand of enforcing strict adherence to policy, which he ascribed to his experience in the Marine Corps. I divulged that I came from a military family, and we quickly bonded. I soon began giving him information. From his perspective this meant I was doing him favors; from mine, I just wanted him to help me clean the place up. Eventually, he introduced me to his trusted associates—all of whom were former military. I gave them information and they reciprocated. One told me the warden allowed staff to transport unlimited amounts of tobacco into the secured area of the prison. He reported noticing a peer, whom he knew to be a nonsmoker, carrying two cartons of cigarettes into the prison without any question as to why he would need such a large quantity for personal use on a daily shift.

Using pseudonyms for their protection, I quoted my officer friends in the briefs I filed. To make the statements appear admissible I backed them with my own affidavits. Technically, this constitutes hearsay, but the government's attorneys never challenged them; probably because doing so would have made little difference. As one of my criminal attorneys used to say "Once a skunk has sprayed, it's really hard to clear the stink from the room."

Thus, I worked the war from both sides. While I pressured the BOP to clean up its act, I assisted the few and proud officers who actually wanted to do so.

At the head of the S.I.S. department is a position known as the special investigative agent (SIA). This is a fairly powerful office that reports to the captain—chief of security. The SIA at the time was a man whose name in Spanish translates to Dark One in English. I believed this man to be utterly corrupt and when he called me to his office to talk about the smoking/drug issue, I only stated that the matter was now being litigated and I would not comment on it. He pressed and I replied, "You'll have to speak to me through your attorney." He then asked me for the names of the officers I was working with, and I remained silent. The fact that he desired their names so badly when they were doing the right thing was a good indication of his malevolence.

I hadn't named him as a defendant because he operated in the shadows, and I could obtain no direct evidence against him. Nonetheless, my evidence indirectly showed he was, at best, not doing his job and, at worst, could be a key component of the corruption.

When he submitted to the court an affidavit in support of the defendants, he opened a door. I responded by challenging him to point to the takedown of a single inmate or officer for which he could take credit. His inability to do so was striking.

When the U.S. Attorney's office filed documents, they did so electronically. I was sent a paper copy with a list of names of officials to whom the documents had been forwarded. Those people, I later learned, had continued forwarding them. High ranking officials of the U.S. Department of Justice, the BOP's parent agency, were monitoring the proceedings, and they couldn't have been pleased.

Not one who inclines to the great indoors, I opted to spend the Tuesday night following my program review at Recreation. I packed my little battery-operated Mighty Bright book light and a textbook into my mesh bag and proceeded to the yard where I located a vacant cement table. As the loud gangsta rap pounded, I attempted to complete work for a petition under 28 U.S.C. § 2254.

I worked for two hours, during which the sun had set. When I came to a stopping point, I packed up my things and headed toward the semi-enclosed outdoor restroom. One set of curious eyes after another peered out at me. Did they know something I didn't?

I approached the urinal, then began my duty. My headphones were on and the Sony Walkman to which they were connected rested in my pocket. A song by the 70s rock band Kansas played on 96.5, Richmond's iconic rock station.

From the fuzziest edge of my peripheral vision a silhouette appeared, skulking along the fence and into the bathroom I occupied. "There's only one urinal, why is he coming in here?" I pondered.

Kerry Livgren prophetically screamed into my ears, "Carry on my wayward son. There will be peace when you are done. Lay your weary head to rest. Don't you cry no more!" Several sharp blows from behind pulverized the right side of my head. They kept coming until I fell onto the ground. The headphones I had been wearing were strewn about in pieces on the wet concrete next to my glasses. My thoughts were scattered, but I had the sense to lean up and hold my lenses in front of my eyes so I could glimpse my assailant as he crept back into the night. Large, black, long braids.

Laying back down in the pool of water and blood, my head was swimming.

> I hearkened the galloping horses; faintly, as if from across a great
> divide. A massive cloud of vermillion dust formed, and piecing
> light shone from the *mise-en-scéne*.
> Emerging from this lustrous miasma was a band of riders. As they
> drew near I beheld maces, swords, and axes descending from their waists.
> Some clutched shields. Black helmets covered their heads; tabards
> and chain mail enwrapped their bodies.
> ARMS: Sable, three chevronels argent charged with ermine.
> CREST: Demilion rampant gules guttee wielding in the dexter paw a regal mace.
> WREATH OF THE COLORS: Argent streaked with sable.
> I knew this armorial blazonry. I could not see their faces and I had not met
> these men; nonetheless I recognized them. These were my ancestors—Norman
> knights—legendary conquerors of England.
> "Eric!" called the lead rider.
> "Yes, Sir Henry?" I answered.
> "Why rest ye thither idle?"
> Confused, I did not answer.
> A second rider spoke, "Hath ye not been summoned, Eric?"
> "I've already addressed the tormented souls, Lord le Wyse. I can do nothing."
> The first again spoke, "A dreadful course from which there is no escape awaits
> ye. Lose not heart. Ye must find a way through it."
> "There must be another way."
> "There is not. Your destiny cannot be changed."
> "The demon is too strong, Lord."
> "Is not the blood which runneth through thy veins the same as that of men which
> conquered mighty armies many fold as numerous?"
> I remained silent.
> "Ye must not fail, Eric."
> The brilliant billowing mass from which the apparitions had emerged swept
> around them, whereupon they faded back into their heavenly crimson
> haze. An overwhelming weight fell upon my shoulders, and I crumpled under its burden.
> A deafening buzz filled my ears. My bones snapped. My tendons popped.
> Blood gurgled from my mouth. A pain beyond belief overtook me as I felt
> my spirit being ripped from my body.
> Then, there was silence.

The cold bit my skin as the concrete ceiling of the outdoor bathroom came into focus. I arose but fell back down. After an uncertain amount of time passed, I gathered up the pieces of my headphones and, like a newborn calf, precariously arose again. Stumbling and swaying about, I treaded the track to the gate where I departed the big field and entered the small one.

In an attempt to balance myself, I leaned against a fire hydrant. I noticed a BOP officer as he stood beside the Recreation building—hands on his hips—staring at me from the shadows. It was Tombs, one of my defendants. A small crowd of his black inmate lackeys hovered in the penumbra at his side.

I collapsed onto the ground then pushed myself into a position where my head was propped up on the hydrant. There he stood frowning: the American flag on his shoulder, Department of Justice emblem on his chest; the very embodiment of the American people.

The 8:00 p.m. activity move had not been called. Packs of dark prisoners in dark jackets lurked in dark places; necks craning so secretive sidelong glances could observe the wounded creature on the ground by the hydrant. I drifted in and out of consciousness.

"Recall!" shouted the voice over the loudspeakers. "One way move back to the housing units." Limping and staggering, I weaved along the lower walkway back to A-North.

A long scrape stretched the length of my forearm, and a huge bruise stained my hip where I fell onto the radio and light in my pocket. The right side of my head was electrified in searing pain. My jaw would not close. Fragments of bone crunched against each other as I raised and lowered my jaw. The area where the jaw hinges to the skull had been crushed.

It was up to me to reset the bones. I was accustomed to acting as my own doctor as I had attended to numerous boxing, wrestling, and motocross injuries in the short years of my pre-incarceration life. But other than popping dislocated shoulders back into place many times, I had never reset bones.

With my thumb in my mouth and index and middle fingers outside, I began aligning the fractured segments. The first attempt resulted in an orientation wherein my mouth closed less. I tried a few more arrangements until my mouth closed nearly all the way. It was the best I could do for the time being.

One witness told me I'd been hit with a piece of metal, like a pipe. The next day, Wednesday, my correctional counselor, evidently surprised that I'd survived, allowed the Indian to move into the cell with me.

I secretly met with one of my ex-military staff allies, a black Operations Lieutenant named Dean. He and I quietly investigated the attack and determined the identity of my assailant. Dean locked him up in segregation. He was later designated to USP (United States Penitentiary) Lewisburg, an old high security prison in Pennsylvania.

While I no longer needed to worry about him, the danger from his gang, known as the D.C. Blacks, remained.

A big Mexican named Ruben had, by this time, replaced Big G as the unit boss and the group had taken on a different attitude. Ruben had a transgender "girl" friend named Rachel who, even I had to concede, genuinely looked like an attractive woman. But "she" lived in a different housing unit and, as "she" stood out like a sore thumb, could not easily slip into A-North for the private time they both desired. In this predicament I saw the opportunity for a mutually beneficial arrangement.

I was already acquainted with him so one Friday as he stood idle watching Univision I approached him and offered, "The officer working second shifts on weekends now is a friend of mine. I think I could persuade him to allow Rachel to come in and spend some quiet time with you." He was fully aware that I was tight with some of the officers, and I could back this promise. Rachel knew it too, and when I obtained permission for "her" to visit, "she" relaxed completely in their visits which is, of course, exactly what Ruben wanted. Had they been caught without authorization; the penalties would have been severe. To be sure the gang leader (*jefe'* or father as one is called) knew I was an indispensable ingredient in his happiness, I came up with the idea to personally escort Rachel into the unit. In so doing we walked right past our officer. I greeted him, then walked "her" up to Ruben's cell and delivered "her" securely into his arms.

The D.C. blacks started to see I was in with this gang and backed off. When they didn't on a few occasions, I merely sent Ruben to take care of the matter. The blacks couldn't risk a war with this large Mexican gang. To show how much influence I had, if one of the latter's members got into trouble I would merely take him to one of my officers and ask the officer to dismiss the incident report. He'd make a few phone calls and it was usually taken care of. Thus, I became sort of the gang consigliere. I protected them from political harm, and they protected me from physical harm.

Eventually, this relationship caused intra-gang issues as some of the more traditional members thought it inappropriate for them to depend on a white man known to be a quasi-cop. A rift developed between factions supporting and opposing me. After two very tense meetings between myself and the overall complex *jefe'*, I decided it was time to resign. By this point many changes had taken place and I was no longer in any danger. The relationship with the gang had served its purpose and when it turned into a liability I dropped it like a bad habit.

The BOP officials who were involved in my war were, like the gang, divided into two factions. On my side, of course, was the small tight clique of about 15 military veterans. Our collective enemy consisted of the Recreation staff, the Dark One and his staff, and an uncertain fringe of crooked ghettoish cops.

As harassment, threats of violence, and actual violence had failed to accomplish their intended purpose, the enemy soon resorted to other tactics.

In a search to discover my weakness, the Dark One located medical records indicating I had difficulty urinating. He then scheduled me for a flurry of urine analyses for drugs. At first, I was unable to urinate, and his minion locked me up in segregation under the guise I had refused to provide a urine specimen. But I enlisted Dean as my staff representative, and he talked with the Disciplinary Hearing Officer behind closed doors. I was released from seg the same day. The Dark One, however, quickly rescheduled me.

At the next test I brought along a urinary catheter I had borrowed from a friend. I used it to easily provide a sample which, of course, tested clean. The enemy thus had to do a little work. The Dark One checked with Medical and discovered I was not technically authorized to use a catheter. This gave his minions sufficient grounds to stretch reason a bit by claiming that because I'd used an unauthorized catheter the test results were not authentic. They administratively nullified the result and locked me up in seg again for refusing to provide a sample.

As I stood in the holding cell waiting to be assigned a seg cell, I heard a pounding on the plexiglass window. "Wise! Wise! What happened? Ha ha ha ha!" It was the Dark One himself. Pretending I didn't care, I turned my back on him. Yet, he lingered, pounding on the window and laughing.

While I languished in the hole, the Government attorneys who were litigating against me insisted their officials had done nothing wrong. But quietly, behind the scenes, the Government's actions were speaking otherwise.

Dean had done as much as he could for the time being. I suspected I was in the red in our quid pro quo exchange and when he failed to show up for my hearing this was confirmed. Nonetheless, the case was finally heard by the DHO, and even she could see it was illegitimate. The charge was thrown out.

When I emerged back onto the sunlit compound after two months in darkness, I discovered some changes had taken place. Nowhere was there smoke to pollute my lungs. The pressure I'd brought had been too intense for my enemies to withstand. Washington had forced them into line. Their time was short. The Dark One knew it and so did I.

A few weeks later I received notice that Judge Becky Smith had granted the defendants' Motion for Summary Judgment, thus dismissing my lawsuit. Richard Posner, an illustrious Seventh Federal Circuit Court of Appeals judge (ret.) before whom I've litigated, admits U.S. judges make decisions in a manner designed to "advance their political goals," rather than to advance justice. After making their self-serving decisions, judges rationalize them by cherry picking legal grounds from America's broad, vague, and elastic legal database. Because prison officials can vote and prisoners can't, it is rare for a judge to award judgment to the latter when he sues the former. If properly executed, however, such a lawsuit can serve as a platform to draw the attention necessary to correct an issue. Thus, although a judge's words may *say*, "You are wrong," the Government's actions may *show* "You are right." This is how the Government acknowledges error—nearly always through actions, seldom through words.

Emboldened by my success in ridding the prison of its tobacco, drugs, and correlative fumes, I composed a series of letters in 2013 reporting the loud rap "music" and inappropriate relationships between the inmates and staff in the Recreation Department. I sent them to anyone I thought could be of influence. This included two U.S. senators, the U.S. House representative for my district, the Office of Professional Responsibility, and the Office of the Inspector General.

Senator Tim Kaine of Virginia refused to get involved, stating he could not "intervene in staffing matters at FCC Petersburg."

In a letter to House Representative Scott, I asked for an inquiry into incidents of staff misconduct. I had logged the exact date, time, and location of each act, many of which concerned inappropriate interactions between the Recreation staff and their inmate flunkies. All had occurred within the range of the complex's VICONET video surveillance system.

Representative Scott, showing surprising tenacity, wrote to the BOP twice asking for an explanation of the alleged misconduct. The warden, struggling with the English language, concluded his reply, "FCC Petersburg maintain a zero-tolerance policy toward staff misconduct, subsequently a review of Mr. Wise's claim is unfounded." He neither admitted nor denied whether the video footage revealed what I asserted. He simply avoided addressing it.

The Office of Professional Responsibility, similarly struggling with English, replied, "We have reviewed your complaint and have determined that the matter lies within the jurisdiction of the Office of the Inspector General. We are forwarding you're correspondence, by copy of this letter to that office." Continuing with the linguistic travail, the OIG then concluded, "We have determine that the BOP management should review your complaint. Therefore, your compliant has been forwarded to the BOP Office of Internal Affairs." The latter, as it had in 2010, took no action.

My ally Dean was promoted from Operations Lt. to S.I.S. Lt. around this time. This gave him authority over the kinds of problems I was trying to eradicate. Better yet, he was now directly beneath the S.I.A. Like so many, the Dark One likely misinterpreted my war against the vicious, disrespectful ghettoish blacks as a war against all blacks and viewed me as a racist who would never ally myself with anyone of a race not my own. He was, at any rate, clueless as to my association with his new black Lt.

In the spring of 2015 my correctional counselor, about to retire, moved me in with a retired U.S. Army lieutenant colonel who had trouble getting along with other inmates. I'd requested the move and was surprised he'd granted it. I wondered if he did so figuring the old solider would kill me. But I usually get along with military types as 1) I come from a military family and 2) we share a common complex of mental characteristics known as the *authoritarian personality*.

The colonel hated the loud rap as much as I and was speaking to a lieutenant named Garcia after lunch one day outside the cafeteria. They were discussing the issue and the Lt., well aware that I'd been fighting against the "music" for years, but unaware that the colonel and I were cellmates, suggested he team up with me. "You guys are going about this the wrong way," the Lt. further advised. "You should approach it from the perspective of security. Force the captain to shut if off." I'd already been down that path years earlier in some of my administrative remedies. I'd reasonably argued the music escalated racial tensions and was likely to provoke violence. But obviously this logic had been unpersuasive. So, I ruminated on the matter and concluded what I hadn't done is provide an actual instance where this had happened. Why hadn't I thought of this? I'd seen many other situations in which tensions had risen to an intolerable head; then, after an explosion established that a problem existed, the Government corrected it. It's unfortunate that violence often has to occur to get them to take action when it is evident such is a highly probable outcome. This is, nonetheless, how the BOP functions.

Fights frequently erupted in the rec yard and they usually went unreported. Staff generally preferred this as it meant less work for them. I would have to bite the bullet and stay out on the yard, enduring the so-called music long enough to witness an appropriate skirmish.

Luck quickly arrived. One evening as I relaxed on the small field, as far away from the noise as I could get, a scuffle broke out between a white and a black about ten yards from me. I logged the time and location. Then, when I returned to the unit, I reported to the captain via e-mail that a racial fight had broken out over the "music." I'd noticed the black had just walked away from the DJ area and I'd been at the prison long enough to know this area was in view of the video cameras. All of this supported my testimony. I was also reasonably sure neither of the fighters would talk, which would leave me as the only cooperative witness.

Two days later the music ceased. Garcia was right. The captain ordered the Recreation staff to shut it off on the grounds it caused security breaches. For the remainder of the spring, I walked the track finally listening to only my own music or even savoring the sweet chirping of the local bird population as it fluttered about.

For the past five years I had been feeding Dean a steady supply of information, behind which lay blended motives: to clean up the prison and increase my own power. The latter happened via the norm of quid pro quo. By giving him accurate information, he could effect busts for which he was credited. He then owed me favors. It also happened when he removed inmates who were causing me problems. I'd catch them slipping and he'd lock them up. I tried to act as a neutral witness in this so 1) the information was more credible and 2) the takedown didn't count as a favor to me on the informal balance sheet. Finally, my power would greatly increase by these methods if I helped Dean show the powers that be that it was he, rather than the Dark One, who should be heading S.I.S., and he was promoted. That is, with an increase in his power came a correlative increase in mine.

One sunny May morning that year I noticed inmates of a particularly rotten variety being pulled out of their cells and sent to the Lieutenant's Office. They were not returning. This purge continued for the next two days as one lowlife after another permanently disappeared. On Wednesday, at lunch, I noticed Dean standing at the front of the cafeteria. Instead of the usual crisp blue uniform with a bar on each collar, he wore black slacks, a red shirt, and a black tie. I glanced at the radio attached to his waist. Marked upon its holster were three letters: S.I.A. After consuming the hamburger and fries customarily served on this day, I approached him. "Was somebody we know promoted recently?"

"Yep," he answered.

"I see you've been doing a little housecleaning."

He smiled.

I nodded, "Congrats, Mr. S.I.A."

"Thank you."

With the Dark One gone (forced into early retirement) and Dean in his office, my life became much easier. The harassment from the Dark One's former minions ceased, and I was able to perform my power tactics in shaping the prison complex to suit my tastes much more efficiently and effectively. I could e-mail Dean directly, to obtain swift and conclusive action. Things were looking up.

In mid-August, however, my aggravation reignited when the thumping returned. My cellie, the colonel, spoke to Garcia who informed him the captain's order had only been temporary. When he came to believe racial tensions had relaxed, he allowed the Rec staff to do as it wished.

I didn't understand it. By this point in my war against hostile government officials, I'd figured out ways to manipulate the system beyond what I'd ever thought possible for someone of my lowly status. I had placed more officials on the unemployment line than I could count (with more yet to come). My efforts had even led to the FBI's arrest and conviction of one of the recreation specialists. And as for the inmates, I could cut them down like a hot knife through butter. Any who gave me problems were locked up and transferred. I had brought my enemies to heel over and over again, yet I could not get the obnoxious "music" terminated.

I decided to put the matter out of my head for awhile so I could concentrate on writing *Uncivilized Nation*. Clearly, the time was not at hand to win the battle against the blacks over the recreation "music," and there was nothing to be gained by continuing to invest my time and energy into the matter.

By early 2017 the first edition of *Uncivilized Nation* was out, and my schedule had relaxed a bit.

Newly inaugurated president Donald Trump had announced the nomination of Jeff Sessions as attorney general. From the turmoil of the confirmation hearings a rumor surfaced that he had once been a member of the Ku Klux Klan. While I presumed this to be liberal propaganda, it gave me an idea.

I had tried utilizing powerful figures before, such as senators and representatives, and while this may have yielded some fruit with the smoking issue, it failed to produce any where the "music" was concerned. Fresh blood, however, had arrived in the Executive Branch. The attorney general is the head of the Department of Justice, under which the BOP lies. Whereas Congress retained only oblique authority over the BOP, the attorney general held direct authority. He had the ability to whip these intransigent BOP officials around like ragdolls.

I debated the matter for a few weeks. Could the time be right to get rid of the warden and his whole regime altogether? (This particular method of conflict resolution can be considered one to which military doctrine refers as an *annihilation strategy*—the direct application of unrelenting force to thoroughly destroy the enemy, usually in a single campaign or action. This was more complicated for me, however, as I could not destroy the enemy but had to convince one who could to do so.) I further considered that the attorney general of the United States is the nation's highest ranking law enforcement official. He reports directly to the president. Was this a giant I wanted to awaken?

Would the FBI start snooping around and come up with some excuse to put new charges on me? Would I be transferred to a dungeon in Siberia? The man who held such a position could do nearly anything. Then again, I was already serving a life sentence on a first offense for consensual sex with my teen girlfriend. What more could he do to me? This is a rarely considered facet of the power dynamic between convicts and officials that works to the advantage of the former. While officials have far greater power, conversely they also have much more to lose. I decided to roll the dice.

Investing several days in the careful crafting of a letter, I wrote draft after draft. Knowing what I did about Sessions and he who appointed him, I laid out the problem exactly as it was. I also adduced other race-related issues, such as black domination of the TV rooms. Each day I would awaken and read the letter with fresh eyes to see if it had any flaws and met my high standards. When I was finally satisfied, I extracted documents from my records to serve as exhibits that supported my assertions. These comprised administrative remedy forms, affidavits, and e-mails I'd submitted over the years to no profit. I copied the exhibits and had the colonel type the letter.

On Monday June 12, 2017, the "music" abruptly ceased. I noticed a particular solemnity among the black staff that day. It extended over the next few days. They just weren't as cocky as usual—silently going about their duties as if they were in mourning. They weren't wearing the black bands indicating the death of a fellow officer and I could see from the southeast corner of the recreation yard that the flag was flying at full staff.

On Thursday a memo issued from the warden's office: all of the prison's TV rooms would be shut down. That evening the unit officer handed me an internal letter. See Appendix One.

While it suggested the Government saw itself as right and me as wrong, this is typical. The Government seldom admits error. Statements from the Government concerning accusations it has acted wrongly give little guidance as to what it has actually decided. The Government speaks through actions, not words.

Much later I was surprised to learn Attorney General Sessions himself had actually read my letter and exhibits and forwarded the information to Major General Mark Inch, the newly appointed national director of the BOP. Director Inch dispatched my packet, along with several direct orders, to the regional director who forwarded them on to the warden.

For the remainder of my time at this prison there would be no more music played on the recreation yard. Officer Tombs, an unrepentant black supremacist, resigned rather than obey his superior's orders. As the TV rooms began closing, a fight broke out in the C-South unit between DC blacks and Virginia blacks over control of TVs in the main unit area, and the security issue caused the TV room closure to be suspended indefinitely. The inmates involved were, nonetheless, locked up and transferred.

Two months later the chief warden, and his associate warden, both of whom I believe to be black supremacists, were transferred.

Over the remainder of the year "ghettoish" black administrators were replaced in droves by whites, or honorable blacks who were conducive to my way of thinking. Anti-social inmates again began transferring out with civilized ones replacing them.

In the late evening hours of Sunday, December 31, 2017, I rested on my beige plastic chair, feet propped up on the metal seat of the cell desk on which I had so fiercely worked. The colonel had gone to bed early and I'd shut the light off. *Drift* by Emily Osment played on my iPod. Wind gusts blew flakes from a snowbank that had accumulated atop the adjacent building into a drizzle that speckled the inky sky. Gazing out of the window at this winter wonderland, I reflected on the year's key accomplishment.

Through my creative energy and intense effort, I'd put to an end a problem that had plagued my associates and me for nearly a decade. I'd finally concluded my task of transforming one of the largest federal prison complexes from a drug infested ghetto lockup into an establishment where the scores of aging white men imprisoned in America's self-destructive War Against Sex could at least serve their unjustly imposed sentences in peace. I'd converted it from a gangsta's paradise into a semi-respectable institution.

As Emily cooed softly in my ear, I reclined and deeply inhaled the satisfaction that only a righteous victory can provide. It was, indeed, a very productive year.

SECTION I: THE PRINCIPLES OF PSYCHOPOLITICAL WARFARE

Then the Lamb broke open the second seal; and I heard the second living creature proclaim, "Come forth!" Another horse, fiery red, went out. It was granted to he who sat thereon the power to bring war to the earth, so that people would slaughter one another. And there was given unto him a great sword.

— Revelations to Saint John
Chapter vi
Verses iii and iv

Chapter One

Psychological Aspects of Authority

> The realities of power ensure that government
> will never truly be democratic.
> — Samuel Huntington

First Case in Point

In composing and arranging the Nazi Sozi (National Socialist) party's rise to dominance, leader Adolf Hitler applied a thoroughly studied method of mass psychology. This began in the early 1920s as he and his associate Ernst Rohm, who was a captain in the Reichswehr (German army), established the party's security force—the Sturmabteilung (Storm Troops, also known as the SA). Most of the men recruited for this detail were former Reichswehr soldiers who had been discharged at the conclusion of World War I. As such they were disciplined men accustomed to obeying commands and executing violent acts.

Events featuring Hitler were produced like a modern-day rock concert. Prior to one, party members plastered posters throughout the city announcing the great man would be speaking. He was, after all, endorsed by the nation's illuminati: nobles, scientists, business magnates, and military officers. All concurred he was about to restore the nation to the lofty status it had reached prior to the first World War.

As an event unfolded an intense buildup preceded the leader's appearance. Uniformed SA soldiers stood at attention monitoring the audience while a band blared out patriotic German music. A series of subordinate party officers delivered short speeches which were just interesting enough to hold the audience's attention, but not enough so as to upstage the main attraction.

When the cascading fervor reached its pinnacle, a dazzling retinue of German luxury cars, clearly meant to portray the wealth and power of their occupants, slowly cruised up to the front entrance. Mystical swastika flags flapping from their front corners projected overwhelming authority. The front doors of the auditorium burst open. Heads turned. Military commands were barked. The SA, in response, parted the crowd like God parted the Red Sea for Moses.

One-by-one, a group of impeccably fashioned and fitted middle-aged men entered, then strolled through the protective human corridor. When the crowd recognized Hitler, especially striking in the type of royal blue uniform worn by a military commander, it erupted into applause and salutations of "Heil!" Banners flew. Fires leaped from great braziers. Multi-colored searchlights sprayed shimmering brilliance upon band instruments, metallic flag fringes, and golden swastikas.

The audience jumped and cheered as the leader raised his right arm in his famous salute, then confidently strode to the front.

He spoke with absolute conviction on the shame wrongly imposed on his nation at Versailles and the great heritage of the German people. Under his leadership, he asserted, they would purify the nation of insalubrious elements, rise up from the ashes of defeat, and vindicate themselves.

He concluded his rapturous sermon by leading the audience in a unifying oath of allegiance then dismissing them into the streets of the city to sing the national anthem amidst a sea of Nazi flags and pennants.

This man, who less than twenty years earlier had been an unemployed artist living in a homeless shelter, was about to become the most powerful figure in Europe.

If ever there was one who understood how to influence beliefs and behavior it was Adolf Hitler. And it may impress us as unusual that while he educated himself in the full spectrum of general knowledge, the field he most deeply savored was not politics but fine arts. Because of this, however, he came to appreciate the effects of appearances. He discovered that when he invoked what was pleasing to his audiences' senses, they became pliable.

At the time of his rise, Germany's economy and self-esteem lay in ruins. The nation had suffered a humiliating defeat in the prior world war and the victorious nations (Britain, France, U.S.A., et al.) had myopically added insult to injury by imposing unbearable sanctions on Germany in the Treaty of Versailles.

Hitler had already learned he could not use brute force to overthrow the existing power structure and thus now seduced and manipulated influential Germans and eventually their ailing president, Paul von Hindenburg, into accepting he was the one best suited to resurrect the fatherland. He exploited the nation's vulnerable condition by presenting arguments based more on emotion than logic and replacing their perception of being a rejected, beaten people with feelings of hope, reassurance, and dignity. His party, he promised, would restore the security, structure, and prestige of the superior Germanic people.

As we will later examine, that which is dramatic and vivid makes an impression, especially when integrated with a sense of importance as to the audience's self-interest. And this certainly applies to Hitler himself who had been profoundly inspired in his youth by a performance of Richard Wagner's opera Lohengrin. So affected by the experience was he that it led him into a life-long study of the arts, including theatre, dramatics, and oration. He later came to integrate these with pageantry, ceremony, symbolism, and mythology into a larger formula of aesthetic and emotional seduction.

The Nazi leader enjoyed visiting backstage areas of musical productions to learn how the stage mechanics operate. Baldur von Schirach, governor of Vienna, accompanied him in one such episode and later remarked, "He was familiar with all sorts of lighting systems and could discourse in detail on the proper illumination for certain scenes."

In the early 1770s George Washington was frequently spotted about Virginia astride his horse, drumming up support for a revolution. He was no longer in the military and had yet to be selected to lead the Continental Army, yet he clothed himself in a military uniform during these public support campaigns. In 1775 the Second Continental Congress unanimously handed him the position he so earnestly craved. Hitler, in the same manner, approximated the dress of a military officer or political official while campaigning to become one. This showed he had the appearance of those types of leaders and eased the process of visualizing him in their roles. Hitler, however, one-upped Washington by enlisting his own private army until he was appointed Chancellor and inherited the public one.

Hitler and Rohm designed the SA to correspond with the Reichswehr national army, exactly following points of military regulations and regimentation. The SA "soldiers" were, for example, clothed in uniforms and assigned ranks. Nazi leaders regularly marched the SA through the streets of German cities to show their countrymen the party was massive, orderly, serious, and able to carry out its agenda with force—all of which are prerequisites of an actual government. The German people and their president merely needed to acquiesce, and the Nazis ready-made political and military machinery would take command to carry out its agenda.

Hitler also cited as influential boyhood religious rituals which appealed to the irrational aspects of the mind. Quoth the Fuhrer: "The artificial and yet mysterious twilight in Catholic churches—the burning lamps, incense, censors, etc. created an entrancing mood among the participants." Hitler, this is to say, was less a political scientist than a political artist. He delivered his speeches more like an evangelist than a politician—enticing and converting his audience below the conscious level. The man spent years perfecting his oratorical skills and had an enigmatic ability to merge with his audience and hold it spellbound. Such was the artistic, rather than scientific, element at work. J. Michael Sproul, emeritus professor of communications studies at San Jose State University, explains:

> People let down their critical guard when they are being entertained. Like a kitten mesmerized by a dangling pocket watch, citizens are likely to miss much of what is happening to them when they are focused on a commercial spectacle or political amusement. Further, when citizens are fed a steady diet of charming, but empty, public communication, the nation's collective economic and political intelligence may be cumulatively weakened.

In *Mein Kamph*, Hitler likened an audience to "the woman, whose psychic state is determined less by grounds of abstract reason than by an indefinable longing." Thus, instead of asking them what they thought, he took charge and told them what to think. "The masses love a commander more than a petitioner," he observed.

Shortly after launching his career in politics, Hitler began experimenting with the types of circumstances that optimized an audience's reception to his ideas. As he noticed, "There are halls which leave people cold, for reasons that are hard to discern," he learned to evaluate each auditorium on characteristics such as aesthetics, acoustics, location, and size. He decided, among other things, it should be just small enough to overflow with attendees and, to this end, strategically placed party members throughout so they would fill every vacant space while leading the cheers.

The time of day the event occurred, Hitler determined, was also a crucial factor, "The same lecture, the same speaker, the same theme have an entirely different effect at ten o'clock in the morning, at three o'clock in the afternoon, or at night." He preferred addressing the people after the sun had fallen for the day as he believed this to be the period when "they succumb more easily to the dominating force of a stronger will." And recent research suggests people are in fact more likely to make impulsive, rather than rational or deliberative, decisions when they 1) carry a heavy cognitive load (that is, have a lot on their mind), or 2) are exhausted from making decisions and resisting temptations (such as when the night comes down after a long work day). Night was also the time when his artificial lighting (e.g., searchlights and pyrotechnics) produced their most exciting effects and a magical ambiance could be maximized.

It was all a calculated presentation meant to reinforce the individual's desire to unify with his countrymen and yield the self to the authority of a higher power: Adolf Hitler's National Socialist state.

♦ ♦ ♦ ♦ ♦

Perception is paramount. In the eyes of the world, it is far more important than reality. Perception is so important in politics that illusions can actually transform into reality. John F. Kennedy understood this, and it was the reason why he was determined to force the Soviet Union to remove its missiles from Cuba in October 1962. Kennedy and his defense secretary, Robert McNamara, both believed stationing those missiles closer to the U.S. than America's Asian-based missiles were to Russia, gave the latter little, if any, military advantage. But Kennedy knew "it would have appeared to, and appearances contribute to reality." In fact, Kennedy himself demonstrated this. His successful resolution of the Cuban Missile Crisis (about which we will learn more in Chapter Five), rendered him a hero in the eyes of the American people. This is true notwithstanding the facts that his failed attempt to depose Cuban ruler Fidel Castro caused the crisis in the first place and Castro remained in power even after it was resolved.

When a man conquers, his agenda conquers with him. When he fails, of course, the inverse occurs. In his classic literary work *The Winter of Our Discontent* John Steinbeck well illustrated this point via a political struggle taking place in a fictitious New England community:

> Now a slow, deliberate encirclement was moving on New Baytown, and it was set in motion by honorable men. If it succeeded they would be thought not crooked but clever. And if a factor they overlooked had moved in, would this be immoral or dishonorable? I think it would depend on whether or not it was successful. To most of the world, success is never bad. I remember how when Hitler moved unchecked and triumphant, many honorable men sought and found virtues in him. And Mussolini made the trains run on time. Vichy collaborated for the good of France, and whatever else Stalin was, he was strong. Strength and success—they are above morality, above criticism. It seems then that it is not what you do, but how you do it and what you call it. Is there a check in men, deep in them, that stops or punishes? There doesn't seem to be. The only punishment is for failure.

Hitler himself was well aware of this and spoke on the topic: "The victor is not asked afterward whether or not he told the truth. What matters in beginning and waging a war is not righteousness, but victory." In making the same point, Ronald Reagan quoted Lincoln: "If it turns out right, the criticism will not matter. If it turns out wrong, ten angels swearing I was right will make no difference." The oft cited mantra, "History is written by the victors" aptly sums up the matter.

♦ ♦ ♦ ♦ ♦

Following a recipe used by rulers throughout history America's state and federal governments project power in establishing dominion over the people. If you are summoned to one of the sacred seats of power you will behold a scenario that evolves along the lines of the following.

It is situated high, appearing to be the supreme influence on the surrounding territory. To emphasize the potency, it may have been built upon a hill or a gigantic stone platform known as a plinth. The building itself is an enormous edifice whose visage is resplendent in columns and sculptures. It is likely topped with an impressive dome, perhaps even enameled in gold. The grounds are breathtaking. Benches, statues, and landmarks rest amidst meticulously maintained trees, shrubbery, and grass that is green throughout the year.

Accessing the building requires you to ascend the outer stairs and pass through an imposing security gauntlet. Once in the inner sanctum you will notice everything around you is large, ornate, and expensive—granite floors, spacious corridors, carved reliefs, massive windows and furnishings.

As you go about your business, you will encounter representatives of the government. Civilian officials dazzle with designer suits and ties. Paramilitary officers impress in their dress uniforms inundated in flashy accoutrements such as ribbons, badges, and rank insignia.

If the building houses a judicial branch you may encounter officials who inspire awe as they, like cardinals, popes, and emperors of yore are seated high upon their thrones of piety while clothed in luxurious flowing robes. Upon these thrones rest the Holy Bible, believed by Judeo-Christians to be the very words and laws of God. Standing tall in the rear flanks are symbols—the flags of the sovereigns. Emblazoned upon the throne itself or directly behind is another emblem of ancient origin—the seal of the sovereign.

If you are to formally meet with powerful officials, they will not come to you. You must go to them. When you arrive at one's office you can plan on waiting, and when finally seen, you will address him by a lofty title. You may stand while the official reclines in a luxurious leather chair. If he is gracious, he will invite you to sit. He will sit behind an enormous desk, bench, or table which serves both as a protective barrier and a psychological demarcation point between he who holds the power and he who does not. Among the items hanging from the wall are certificates and photos of the official with other very important people. His position of power is no accident. He retains credentials and is well connected with other elites.

Lesser officials may hover near him, likely behind and to the sides. They are present to assure either his political or personal safety, usually both. He will show he is the dominant agent by opening the discussion, controlling its direction, and terminating it when he sees fit. His tone of voice, linguistic syntax, and parlance will predominate.

When the business at hand is complete you will depart, descending and blending back into the mass of peons against whom you compete for space on the long trip home.

What you experience in your prospective day at the government command and control center is not the product of an uncertain course of events. Rather, every piece in the assemblage has been assiduously designed for a specific purpose: to subordinate the individual by radiating the perception of credible, potent, and genuine authority.

A lavish array of covert psychological schemes are at work in this. We've already noted some. Let's evaluate the others.

First, by making you go to him, the official establishes a power dynamic. You may have noticed, generally speaking, that when you want to see someone more than she wants to see you, you go to her, and vice versa. This is because the one with less power does the traveling. The postman, policeman, and census taker may stop by your house because practicality and custom necessitate it, but these are not what we consider to be powerful officials. And this is evident by the fact that they travel to you. You can be sure that if a meeting is to take place between yourself and someone high in their scalar chain of authority, such as the postmaster, chief of police, or Census Bureau manager, you will do the driving.

All animal species lose strength, confidence, and sexual potency in unfamiliar environments. And as the distance from one's home base increases, his willingness to fight, and ability to do so effectively, decreases. This is commonly manifested in athletic competitions, which is why the player or team who competes in his home area is known to have the "home field advantage." Heads of state are well aware of the power imbalance involved in this and often have to negotiate meetings with their foreign counterparts in neutral territory—to which all must travel and in which none will have a home field advantage. Winston Churchill (Great Britain), Joseph Stalin (USSR), and Franklin Roosevelt (USA) agreed to hold a post World War II conference in the country they had collectively defeated (Germany), rather than in any of their own nations. U.S. President Donald Trump met with his chief antagonist, North Korean Chairman Kim Jong Un, three times, but always in a different neutral territory: Singapore (May 2018), Hanoi (February 2019), and the DMZ separating North and South Korea (June 2019). (Trump's father Fred understood the principle and insisted suppliants come to him—either at his Brooklyn office or his mansion in Queens.)

Structures such as buildings, monuments, statues, and pillars have throughout the history of organized societies served as expressions of significance. Usually they glorify a god, ruler, or aristocratic family. Some celebrate a great event, but when this is a military victory it is usually a propagandistic method of indirectly crediting some leader with the same. The immense size and mass of these structures is intended to further magnify the powerful figures (and correlatively diminish those not so magnified). Their flamboyance broadcasts dignity and prosperity. Images of esteemed legendary figures (statues, busts, portraits) associate those figures with the one who displays them—boosting credibility, legitimacy, and honor for the latter.

Interior designers who understand non-verbal methods of projecting power are often retained by the government. This is why the furnishings are large and luxurious. Hitler's desk in his office at the Reich Chancellery was fifteen feet long. On its visage were three separate inlaid panels that displayed intimidating mythological characters: Gorgon (any of the three sisters in Greek mythology with whom eye contact turns the beholder to stone), Mars (the Roman war god) bearing a sword, and Minerva (the Roman goddess of wisdom). The message, of course, was that he who sits behind that desk is one of great strength and knowledge. And Hitler himself stated, "When the diplomats who are sitting in front of me at this table see that, they will learn what fear is."

In democracies the message is less direct, but certainly still conveyed. James Clapper describes entering the Oval Office in 2010 to be interviewed for the position of director of national intelligence: "I observed, as I entered, that the office is designed to impress and intimidate. My eyes took in the blue presidential seal, embedded directly in the center of the oval rug. Rays of gold and bronze radiated out from it across the rug and projected onto the vertically-striped walls . . . At one end of the room under three tall windows stood the famous Resolute Desk . . . It both symbolizes and embodies the power and grandeur of the office of the president . . . At the other end of the room a portrait of George Washington hung over the fireplace mantle."

What Clapper describes can be considered the quintessential power scheme. For modern executive offices are devised to portray an intense sense of dignity and authority. One way this is accomplished is to accentuate rich leather upholstery and dark natural woods. Brighter carpet may be included to prevent the effect from becoming too burdensome. (Accordingly, Obama eventually replaced the radiant rug with a solid cream colored one with a white presidential seal.)

The boss sits in a high-back leather chair, usually with a headrest. Visitors chairs are comfortable, yet simpler than those of the office holder, showing they have value, but less than does he.

As aforementioned, luxuriously framed oil paintings of legendary figures (and events) associate the one displaying them with the figures (or events) portrayed. (Obama's message was that he is equal to America's #1 founding father.) Shelves displaying uniform rows of books imply that the office holder is methodical and learned. Thick, sumptuous drapery shows his wealth and good taste.

Elevation connotes power which is why you ascend to its seat. It's also why the judge's bench is always situated highest in the courtroom—the same as the dais for the pastor in a church or imam in a mosque. This arrangement is also exhibited in some legislative halls with the most potent figures seated in a vertical hierarchy exactly as it would be displayed on a chart.

Hitler ordered his architects to attach balconies to the Fuhrer Building, Reich Chancellery, and Nazi party headquarters so he could gaze down at the adoring masses gathered below. Nicholas II, the last czar of Russia, was also known to smile and wave down to admiring Russians from the balconies of his Winter Palace. Former North Korean Chairman Kim Jung Il made rare customary appearance on a platform towering over Kim Il Sung Plaza. In October 2010 his son and successor Kim Jong Un joined him on this structure for an initial public appearance.

Power is often displayed horizontally as well, but the manner in which potency is arranged can vary. Typically, it flows outward and back. Many paintings and photos of historically significant events, such as the signings of treaties, depict the leading figures seated front and center, usually at a large ornate table. Standing in the back and on the far sides are those just influential enough to be included, but not enough so as to be of any real importance. The names of these lesser powers are seldom even noted, and the event could likely have transpired successfully without their attendance.

Games at the Roman Colosseum in the first few centuries A.D. featured politicians seated by rank exactly as just described: Emperor front and center, then senators and knights—flowing outward in order of potency; lesser powers yet seated behind. (The daises at the front of American legislative halls often reverse this order with the *lesser* powers seated in front.)

In military ceremonies Hitler positioned himself three paces ahead of his generals so the troops could observe the hierarchy. He and the generals were, of course, situated on a high point such as a balcony or raised platform at these times.

Power differences are also manifested by the ability to seat oneself in a small political encounter such as a meeting or conference. Historical evidence consistently shows he who must lay, kneel, or stand in the presence of one who picks his own posture (usually sitting) is the politically inferior power. (Convention, however, holds that one addressing a large audience must stand, regardless of power levels.)

Starting in 284 A.D. those who were part of the Roman nobility were required to greet their emperor by lying flat on the floor face down and kissing the border of his robe. The emperor remained comfortably seated on his throne. In modern times a subordinate may sit before a superior, but only with his consent, which is often implied rather than expressed. Nonetheless, by standing until this consent is offered the subordinate acknowledges his inferiority. (Mandating suppliant visitors to stand while he remained seated behind his desk was another tactic employed by Fred Trump to emphasize who, in fact, was the bigger dog.)

One notes this in a courtroom. When the judge enters, a bailiff orders all in attendance to rise in a sort of salute to the judge's superior power. Even though no laws mandate this, people are so accustomed to obeying authorities they do so without even thinking about it. After the judge is seated he gives leave to the attendees to sit. When arguing cases attorneys must stand before the judge and/or jury. And when one who has been convicted of a crime is sentenced, the comfortably-seated judge will not ask, but order, him to stand. Note: I often observe certain power postures in meetings. For example, even when both are seated, the attentive subordinate, eager to please, leans forward, eyes wide open, as the relaxed superior reclines in his chair.

Before you meet with a high-ranking official, you will wait. Sometimes this is just the way events unfold, but often it is the deliberate employment of a tactic. Either way, it is an indication of the power differential. He's a very busy man. His time is more valuable than yours. You, therefore, will wait. Russian president Vladimir Putin is known to employ this tactic on diplomats and even other world leaders in an attempt to psychologically disadvantage them prior to a meeting. Washington attorney Clark Clifford, who was Harry Truman's finest aide and the head of JFK's transition team, employed a specific device. When visitors stepped into his office he shuffled through paperwork on his desk pretending to be so busy he was unaware they had entered. After a minute or so of this, he finally acknowledged them, upon which they felt great relief.

The symbols on display everywhere are representations meant to convey a message. In the case of the monuments, insignia, etc. the message is that the government and its officials are powerful. Uniforms and flags connote both unity and power. (We'll further examine rulers' use of symbols, and their association with deities, later in the chapter.)

A human's desire to influence or control others can be strong. Some believe fulfillment comes by no other method. Career prosecutor Elie Honig, former assistant U.S. attorney with the prestigious Southern District of New York and director of the New Jersey Division of Criminal Justice, "readily admit[s]" he found the "unimaginable power" he held to be "heady . . . dizzying . . . intoxicating." In Hitler, the drive to dominate was so strong he left himself no option but success.

While many people crave and pursue it like a drug, power does not come easily. Involuntary relationships involving dominance and submission are ones of resistance. The essential interests of the two sides can be at odds as the former coerces resources (e.g. taxes, goods, and services) from the latter, who would not otherwise relinquish them. Both sides are constantly probing—testing the limits to see how much the other is willing to give; e.g., a governing official's effort to acquire greater material and symbolic appropriations, a subordinate group's struggle to recover recently lost expropriations and liberties. And once decided, these matters are not self-sustaining, but require constant reinforcement. A great deal of effort, therefore, must be exerted on maintaining the boundaries. To this end, a ruler must justify his position with visible executions of his might and superiority. Each open invocation of power, such as the imposition of punishment, use of a term of inferiority, display of rank, issuance of a commandment, act of beneficence, or parade of grandeur, when accepted by the subordinate, contributes to a pattern of dominance and submission that advertises and affirms the nature of the relationship.

♦ ♦ ♦ ♦ ♦

Historical study reveals certain qualities characterize they who govern, be they autocratic individuals or democratic assemblies. While I do not assert this to be an all inclusive list, the attributes we will examine are some of the most essential. They are so important, in fact, we must dedicate the remainder of the chapter to our evaluation. With this in mind, let's discover what it takes to attain and maintain political power.

Ruthless Ambition

There is no shortage of candidates seeking authority, control, or influence over others. Those who are lazy or indifferent aren't likely to exert the effort or make the sacrifices necessary to achieve this. History has shown that when such a person does find himself so positioned, it is because either an aggressive kingmaker has placed him there as a patsy to carry out the kingmaker's agenda (e.g., Harry Truman early in his political career), or he has inherited the office (e.g., Nicholas II, the last czar of Russia).

Augustus Caesar (63 B.C.-14 A.D., known in his youth as Octavian) overflowed with the natural gifts possessed by leaders: good looks, charisma, intelligence, and an apparently inexhaustible supply of energy. He developed superb communication skills and was endowed with a distinguished vocal tone with which to orate. This great nephew of Julius Caesar certainly also inherited the genes and familial position from which assent was likely. Shortly after Octavian's fourteen birthday, Julius ordered the teen be appointed to a major religious post. When Octavian was seventeen, Julius left Rome to extinguish a rebellion that had erupted in the province of Hispania. Octavian then became sick and was confined to bed, but the instant he recovered he departed to join his great uncle. The fighting had ceased by the time he arrived. Julius, nonetheless, was so impressed by the young man's determination he modified his will, legally adopting his great nephew as his son upon his death.

Octavian resumed his education in the liberal arts when he returned to Rome. After his eighteenth birthday, Julius named Octavian second in command of the army for a military campaign taking place in the Adriatic Sea region. The young man worked his magic at the army's headquarters in Albania—establishing important relationships with other officers. But tragic news soon arrived from Rome—Julius had been assassinated at the senate building. Octavian departed for the capitol as soon as he learned of this. He delivered a magnificent speech at the Forum—honoring Julius and claiming his name and right of inheritance as monarch of the Roman empire. Mark Antony, an army officer who also desired the position, quickly challenged Octavian, but with his Senate and army connections Octavian was able to raise his own militia and defeat Antony. He then demanded the Senate designate him consul: chief magistrate of the republic. Many senators hesitated because tradition necessitated a candidate for this position be at least 40 years old. They also feared he, like Julius, would negatively impact their self-interests by usurping their power. But he retained some powerful supporters in the senate and after an initial period of resistance the rest realized he had become too strong and acquiesced. At age 19 he became Rome's head of state.

Octavian acted quickly to add to his realm those portions of the west under control of rivals. And in 36 B.C. he defeated Sextus Pompey, who ruled the Italian seas. His old frenemy, Mark Antony, had formed an alliance with Cleopatra, Queen of Egypt, and the pair controlled that nation, Armenia, and some of Rome's eastern territories. After a lengthy campaign, he defeated the legendary lovers in 31 B.C. Four years thence, the Senate granted him the title Augustus—Emperor of the Roman Empire.

Because people, like other social animals, constantly pursue higher statuses, there is often tension between individuals who are likely candidates for a promotion. This is also true of they who hold adjacent positions in a hierarchy. The lower has his eye on his superior's position. The superior knows this because he has his eye on his own superior's position. When people are farther apart in rank there tends to be more comfort between them. I directly witnessed this in my corporate days at a telecom giant. The senior manager of the Operations department secretly provoked the vice president of Operations into terminating the regional director who was between them. And in the Prologue, of course, I described how I assisted my ally, Lt. Dean, in eliminating his boss (the Dark One). The latter had, in a similar manner, eliminated his prior boss in order to advance and should have expected as much.

Elite Endorsement

Most rulers come from lofty backgrounds. Some arise from more common milieus, but, whatever their status may have once been, they must retain the approval of those who are presently aristocratic. This includes influential people of every variety: other politicians, men of religious prominence, military and police officials, captains of business, doctors, scientists, and celebrities. Support from leaders of other nations is also helpful. In modern democracies the elite partner with the common in forming broader political parties that propel a prospective ruler to power and help maintain it once he is there.

Augustus, whom we just met, had among his allies a tight group of senators and military officers and we noted how crucial they were to his rise. Constantine (term of office 306-337 A.D.) embraced government officials, high clergy, and kings of barbarian tribes. Both emperors retained cordial relations with the military legions and upper classes of the Roman provinces.

While support from the common is important, especially in democracies, support from the elite is far more so. For history is replete with incidents where a leader's armed forces put down revolts by his ordinary subjects. When the ruler loses support from the nobility, however, the loss of his power inevitably follows.

The English landed class demonstrated its power was at least equal to that of its own sovereign when in 1215 its forces seized London and compelled King John to accept the terms of a document that constricted his authority. The alternative, the nobles threatened, was deposition. Originally titled "Article of the Barons," the document later became known as the Magna Carta. Primarily, it held the king could impose no special taxes without the Barons' consent, but also covered matters pertaining to land ownership, human rights, and the responsibilities of the monarch. Future kings updated and affirmed its conditions, thus leading to a parliamentary government. The document is, in fact, believed to have inspired the constitutions of modern democracies.

In 1876 the people of Turkey were granted a parliament and a constitution. The country was part of the great Ottoman Empire based in Istanbul and the democratic concessions had been allowed to pacify the demands of a younger sect of the Turkish ruling class. (The older faction was reluctant to endorse democracy as they correctly believed the general public too unlearned to decide high matters of state.)

Ottoman sultan Abdulhamid II had just taken the throne and knew better than to resort to any drastic measures so soon. But when he believed his position was secure, he suspended the constitution, thus transferring power from the ruling class back to his regime. In so doing, however, he tore open a rift. Turkey was a key component of his empire and when he offended its elites, they began campaigning for an independent state. With army support, a 1908 revolution restored the constitution. A few years later a consortium of young officers and officials seized power and centralized control of the country in the city of Ankara where it remains to this day. This association, labeled the "young Turks," was the inspiration for the popular conjoined words.

Sultan Abdulhamid's reign drew to an end in 1909 and the Ottoman empire itself collapsed in 1923.

Separation and Protection

Living closely among the common folk is not part of the life of they who govern. Rulers are part of a distinct society. They consort with their own kind. Access to these people is guarded. And the more people and bureaucratic barriers one has around him, the greater his power appears.

The 14th U.S. President, Franklin Pierce (office term: 1853-1857) first established a full-time bodyguard to protect him; a function Congress transferred to the U.S. Treasury department's Secret Service agency in 1902. No U.S. president had been assassinated by the time of Pierce's presidency, however, which suggests the bodyguard may have served more to demonstrate his power than to assure his personal safety. In addition to the massive palace guard, European and Arabian monarchs are known to employ an official called a chamberlain, or bedroom attendant, who controls final access to the ruler. (Entrance into the palace of Hamid Karzai, president of Afghanistan from 2004-2014, required a visitor to pass through seven security checkpoints.)

On a practical level, rulers and other powerful figures must withdraw from the public eye to avoid the hazard that familiarity will lead to contempt. It also avails them of the much-needed opportunity to relax and recharge apart from the formal necessities of their office. In private there is less need to worry they will be caught in the sort of acts that may compromise their meticulously sculpted image.

On a more formal level the separation between a ruler and his subjects is, at least in part, based on a belief he should maintain a distance between himself and the interests he regulates. But because the government cannot function without substantial cooperation between officials and citizens, individuals are often acknowledged as intermediaries of sorts through which both sides can negotiate. These include leaders of unions, churches, and special interest groups.

After the French invaded the North African country of Algeria in 1830, French governors used indigenous officials to mediate between the new government and the native populace. By the 1840s many districts had been subsumed by the new order upon which the mediators were reduced to employment as low level officials.

Power of Coercion

Rulers use numerous methods to obtain their subjects' compliance. Primary among these are persuasion (urging, arguing, reasoning), physical force (imprisonment, violence, torture), and nonphysical force (fines, shame, expulsion). The ruler's strength is best displayed when he relies least on persuasive tactics. That is, he knows his claims to power and the positions he promotes are beyond challenge. Small tribal leaders, whose influence is established by the loyalty and cohesion of the tribe, seldom rely on tactics involving force.

Executives in the three key political levels in the U.S. all have militias to enforce their decisions. The president has the national military and numerous law enforcement agencies (e.g., FBI, DEA, DHS). State governors control the state militia (National Guard) and state police. Municipal mayors command the local police. Leaders of legally questionable private organizations often retain some type of enforcement arm as well. Before he was appointed chancellor, Hitler used the Nazi SA. Mafia bosses employ hit men or enforcers. Some prison gang leaders utilize members, or prospective ones, known as torpedoes. (In other gangs every member is considered an enforcer.) Leaders of legal private organizations coerce with nonphysical force as mentioned above.

Druids, priests who served in the capacity of judges over ancient Celtic societies, could invoke authority by imposing prohibitions on a Celt such as against eating certain foods or attending feasts. When one violated these orders the Druid could impose stronger punishments—social ostracism or banishment.

Prior to the modern day, Roman Catholic officials coerced most severely by issuing interdictions—decrees withdrawing most sacraments and a Christian burial; or excommunication—exclusion from the rights and privileges of church membership.

Secular leaders of ancient Rome also called forth divine jurisdiction in coercing conformity to the law. That is, they claimed it was backed by God and thus if violations went undetected by men, they would still be noticed by God, who would administer punishment.

Some scholars believe the catalog of Mosaic laws was instituted only to serve pragmatic ends. They assert, for example, Moses understood swine carried Trichina worms which is why he banned consumption of the animal. Laws that prevented the Israelites from harming each other were intended to keep the group united and strong in the face of enemy tribes. Instead of proclaiming he was issuing these laws for practical reasons, he claimed God was proclaiming them for spiritual ones because he knew his people were more likely to comprehend and submit to the latter.

Military Support

As we just examined rulers must have arms of protection and enforcement. The amount of control a large societal leader has over his subordinates is directly related to the amount of control he has (or appears to have) over his military. An obedient militia is therefore a crucial component of political power.

In ancient times princes rewarded their legions by methods including: 1) allowing them to keep the plunder of vanquished societies, 2) giving them land, 3) annual salaries, 4) retirement bonuses or other incentives. In modern times obedience is assured by compensation in the forms of salaries, extensive benefits, and bonus pay such as for combat duty and family separation. Leaders also subject their soldiers to an array of mind manipulation tactics to be sure they act in the desired way when ordered to do so. Note: This is a topic I am comprehensively examining, along with others, in a treatise I have tentatively entitled *Advanced Studies in Mind Control*. Unfortunately, for many abstruse reasons, it is questionable whether I will ever publish that work in its entirety.

Rulers usually designate an elite military unit to serve as their personal security force. Hitler created the SS (*Schutzstaffel* i.e., protection echelon) specifically for this purpose. (Its scope was later broadened.) Augustus formed the Praetorian Guard to serve the same function, and Soviet leaders were protected by a secret military organization known as the KGB.

They have been known to mobilize their armies to either demonstrate, or test the limits of, their power. If the military fully obeys, a ruler's control is solid. When he cannot command his troops, his reign is precarious. George H. W. Bush was generally viewed as weak-minded when campaigning for, and beginning, his presidency. A 1988 *Newsweek* article discussing this was titled *Fighting the Wimp Factor*. But when he dispatched the U.S. military into the Persian Gulf in 1990, the public noticed his ability to wield absolute control of this force and united behind him. In doing this, then achieving his stated objective of expelling Iraq's army from Kuwait he, at least temporarily, rehabilitated his image. (Bush's approval rating at this time actually hit 90 percent.)

Russian Czar[1] Nicholas Romanov II (office term 1894-1917) similarly demonstrated his power, uniting the country behind him, when he decided to introduce his army into the conflict that would become World War I. Shortly after his announcement in the summer of 1914, a massive crowd gathered outside the Winter Palace waving flags and cheering the leader. But by 1916 the questionable behavior of Czarina Alexandra's spiritual advisor, Grigori Rasputin, conflated with widespread hunger and heavy Russian losses in the war to erode that support.

The exact turning point came on March 12, 1917, when a sergeant murdered one of the czar's officers, a captain, who had slapped him. Fearing for their own lives, other officers fled and the whole regiment marched into St. Petersburg where the mutiny infected other regiments, all of whom met and coalesced with a mob of revolutionaries. The czar had lost control of his military and his time was at hand when his own general entered the palace, announced that the royal family was under arrest, and installed a captain and detachment of soldiers to enforce the order.

Similarly, in 1958, nationwide division over a proposed union of Arabian states weakened Faysal II, king of Iraq. A confederation of his own army officers saw the opportunity, seized control of the government, and shortly thereafter executed the king and his family. The confederation then

---

[1] History purists prefer the spelling "tsar" for the title of the Russian monarch, but since the word evolved from the Latin "Caesar," surname/title of General Julius and Emperor Augustus, it seems proper to use the spelling denoted. (It further gives me a small measure of satisfaction to defy my old Russian History professor at Coe College in Cedar Rapids, Iowa who strictly adhered to the variant which he pronounced "itsär" instead of "zär.")

declared Iraq to be a republic and set up a three-man sovereignty council. It named the leader of the revolution, General Abdul Karim Qasim, as the new premier.

Underbosses

The issues arising in a large society are as numerous as they are diverse. The head of state cannot possibly address them all. Further, to maintain his power he must apportion it among those who have been, or could be, of assistance. These are key reasons he delegates authority in a hierarchy of subordinate officials.

The parliament of Greece, for example, elects a president. The president appoints a prime minister (PM) as head of government. The PM, in turn, recommends to the president a cabinet of high officials to carry out the president's agenda. If he approves, he appoints them as well. The president himself thus has little official responsibility. He primarily serves ceremonial functions while the PM and his departmental ministers implement and enforce the administration's policies. All of these officials are, of course, members of the party holding the most seats in the parliament. This sort of arrangement exists in many republics throughout the world.

A ruler often relies on a specific official who reports directly to that ruler as a chief advisor and enforcer. Augustus, for instance, depended on the commander of his navy, Agrippa, to act as his right hand. Tiberius retained Sejanus (head of the emperor's Praetorian Guard) in this capacity and JFK appointed his brother Robert as his campaign manager, then after taking office, to the position of attorney general.

Shrewd rulers use intelligence networks to monitor their underbosses. This can help prevent them from becoming too potent and usurping the ruler's power or misusing the authority invoked in his name, thus discrediting him. Less sapient rulers merely trust underbosses unconditionally and all too often find they are more interested in serving the self than the boss.

Ohio Republican Warren G. Harding, the 29th U.S. President (office term 1921-23), was a friendly and honest man with progressive views, but he was also a bit naive and complacent. He failed to supervise his underbosses. Without his observation, a number of his cabinet officials slid into corruption. The most notable of these cases took place as the Secretary of the Interior, Albert Fall, accepted $400,000 in bribes in return for allowing oil companies access to the U.S. Navy's oil reserves in Elk Hills, California and Teapot Dome, Wyoming. (The affair was thus known as the Teapot Dome scandal.) Fall was convicted of a federal offense and spent a year in prison. Attorney General Harry Daugherty also became involved in deals of questionable legality and was pressured into resignation. Harding had no knowledge his officials were involved in these affairs as they took place, but his reputation was poisoned by them nonetheless. When he died in office of a heart attack (1923), public opinion generally regarded him as the worst American president in history.

Underbosses can, on the other hand, serve as convenient scapegoats when scandal befalls a leader.

In June 1972 five members of President Richard Nixon's secret surveillance squad (known as "The Plumbers") were arrested for burglarizing the Democratic National Committee Headquarters at Washington's Watergate office complex. Nixon himself ordered John Mitchell—his former attorney general who was now his campaign director—to conceal the connection to the White House, "I want you to stonewall it, let them (the burglars) plead the Fifth Amendment, cover it up or anything else."

Presidential aide John Dean orchestrated the concealment which succeeded just long enough to ensure Nixon's 1972 reelection. The self-interest of one of the burglars, however, caused the scheme to begin imploding. Sentenced to a lengthy prison term, the "plumber" requested leniency from his judge. In return he disclosed he had been paid by the White House and was even offered a presidential pardon if he maintained his silence. The proverbial cat was now out of the bag.

Nixon demanded Dean accept responsibility for the developing mess, but the aide understandably refused to shoulder the blame for the disaster his boss had created. In the spring of 1973 Nixon fired him.

The Senate initiated an investigation into the affair under a special committee. Like a jilted lover, Dean testified that the commander in chief was directly involved in the operation to cover the burglary up. The committee also learned that since 1970 Nixon had been surreptitiously tape-recording conversations in the Oval Office. The committee's special prosecutor demanded the tapes. Nixon stalled, asserting the privilege of the executive and firing the special prosecutor. But this proved futile. For when a new prosecutor took over the case he continued his predecessor's quest for the tapes—taking the matter all the way to the Supreme Court.

By the summer of 1974 the House Judiciary Committee had voted for three impeachment articles. They accused Nixon of 1) contempt of Congress, 2) abuse of power, and 3) obstruction of justice. In July the Supreme Court unanimously ruled he had to submit the tapes to the special prosecutor of the investigating committee. Nixon knew the evidence was far too damning for his presidency to withstand and resigned the following month. While the fallen leader would escape any punishment beyond this, the same could not be said for his underbosses. Mitchell, Chief of Staff Robert Haldeman, senior domestic aide John Ehrlichman, Chief Counsel Charles Colson, and 22 other regime officials all served sentences in the federal Bureau of Prisons.

Authoritative Age

The age of an individual often factors into authority in both human and animal societies. Grackle flocks tend to disregard signs of distress a young one emits at a harmless situation. But if an older one shows the same reaction, the flock will break into flight. Chimpanzees ignore a younger herd member when he evinces a special skill. When an older member of the herd reveals knowledge of the same skill, however, the herd intently observes, then imitates, him. Chimps will blindly follow their aging leader as they entrust their welfare to his judgment.

Western human societies glamorize youth while nonetheless taking little interest in what young people have to say. A reliable indication of political power is the level of interest others have in knowing one's views and the old adage that young people should be "seen and not heard" aptly captures the mindset behind the age/authority relationship. Although a great deal of scientific evidence shows people reach the pinnacle of intelligence in the early to middle teens, the popular misbelief that one must be old to be wise remains. (For those who are interested, I undertook a comprehensive examination of this subject in Section 2 of *Uncivilized Nation*.)

The age/authority mindset is embodied in the requirements for the U.S. presidency. Article 2, Section 1 of the Constitution actually infuses it into law by establishing a minimum age for the position: "Neither shall any person be eligible to the office who shall not have attained the age of 35 years." It is interesting to note there is no maximum age. If we consider the ages of those who have held the office, we find there is a certain authoritative range. The youngest elected president, Jack Kennedy, was 43 at the time of his inauguration. And even though he had been awarded the Medal of Valor and Purple Heart for heroic actions in World War II and had also served in both the U.S. House and Senate, his supposed youthful inexperience was called into question as a presidential candidate.

Ronald Reagan was elected to a second term at 73 years of age. Many people, even those who supported him, voiced concern over whether his mind was sharp enough to finish it. Dementia had, in fact, already set in when he left office at age 77. The oldest president, Joseph Biden, took the oath in 2021 at age 78.

The most common age of a president at the time of inauguration is 55. Tiberius, emperor of Rome (office term 14-37 AD) ascended to the throne at exactly this age. Bill Clinton defied convention when he was elected governor of Arkansas at the young age of 32. He was, however, only able to hold onto the position for a single term; reacquiring it later in life. And earlier we learned how Octavian (Augustus) took control of Rome at age 19, then of the entire empire by age 31, but we must consider he had to confront some age-related resistance from the Senate as custom required a minimum age of 40. We also must consider that with Julius' name, endorsement, funds, and genes he had the resources most people do not to overcome his society's minimum age of authority.

Appearance of Beneficence

Authorities of all variety show what appears as kindness to their subjects, not because they care but in many instances to establish and maintain a power dynamic. To be able to show mercy upon another, one must have power over him. By offering mercy, the ruler suggests it is he who has the upper hand. By accepting it, the subordinate acknowledges the ruler is correct. Even the most ferocious tyrant must temper his abuse with acts of kindness. The idea is to push as far as possible, then when the limit is reached, relent. Show kindness. It's all part of a plan to obtain as much of the subordinates' resources as possible while keeping them subservient, dependent, and loyal.

When someone accepts a gift he accepts a position of inferiority. Parents who provide for the many wants and needs of their children authenticate their rightful authority and institute a quid pro quo obligation by which the former earn the right to control the latter. America's federal government funds state programs and in turn (unconstitutionally) dictates state law. It provides aid to foreign countries and thus influences their foreign, and sometimes even domestic, policies. It provides assistance to college students on the conditions they maintain at least a 2.0 GPA and progress toward a degree. It rescues struggling companies while demanding they (and perhaps their workers' unions) accept concessions and restructure.

Then-U.S. President Joseph R. Biden sent American citizens a letter on April 20, 2021.

In relevant part, it reads:

> My Fellow Americans,
>
> On March 11, 2021, *I* signed into law the American Rescue Plan, a law that will help vaccinate America and deliver immediate relief to hundreds of millions of Americans, *including you*.
>
> A key part of the American Rescue Plan is direct payments of $1,400 per person for most American households. With the $600 direct payment from December, this brings the total relief payment up to $2,000. *This fulfills a promise I made to you* and will help millions of Americans get through this crisis.
>
> There may be other parts of the American Rescue Plan that *will help you* as well. For example, there is aid for small businesses, an expanded child tax credit for families, and resources to open our schools safely. The American Rescue Plan also extends unemployment insurance and helps *reduce your healthcare premiums* if you have a plan through the Affordable Care Act.
>
> *When I took* office *I promised the American people that help was on the way. The American Rescue Plan makes good on that promise.* The bill was passed to provide emergency relief to millions of Americans. I want to be sure *you receive all the benefits* that you are entitled to.

Biden takes full credit for the blessings bestowed on his subjects when he did nothing more than sign a bill sent to him by Congress. He hadn't even been inaugurated when the $600 payment, for which he implies he deserves credit, was authorized. More importantly, he ignores the fact that all this relief was by and large funded, not by him, but by the very people receiving it (with the possible exception of the Affordable Care Act). The American majority nonetheless credited Biden with his supposed generosity.

The Practice of Expropriation

Energy from the sun enters the troposphere (lowest level of Earth's atmosphere) in the form of sunlight. Via the process of photosynthesis, this energy is first captured by plants. By the time animals (herbivores) consume the plants, only 10 percent of that initial energy remains. And by the time other animals (carnivores) consume the herbivores, only 10 percent of that remains.

Scientists believe that which can roughly be considered farming began after the last ice age concluded, approximately 10,000 to 7,000 B.C. At that time dry periods in middle eastern regions caused a shortage of edible plants growing in the wild. The food supply of people who had settled in those areas depended on these plants and they found it necessary to supplement them. They did so by growing their own crops and storing the overage for use throughout the year. Soon after, they started taming and breeding wild animals native to the region for the same purpose. Agriculture, which supplanted hunting, fishing, and gathering as the primary means of obtaining nutrition, then began spreading to other parts of the world.

Unfortunately, those who provided for their families in this manner were not united and as they produced more than they needed for personal use, were susceptible to predation. Influential elites and other socially dominant figures noticed the opportunity and began using enforcers to obtain excess food supplies by intimidation and force. This continued over thousands of years with strong men becoming rulers and building temples, palaces, bureaucracies, and armies off of the energy from the lowest socioeconomic stratum. In so doing, these men added what is, in essence, a new level to the top of the ancient nutritional pyramid. Therein lies the most powerful and rapacious predators on the planet: those who control nations. That is, rulers, their officials, and aristocrats.[2]

Throughout recorded history a primary duty of the ruler, his officials, and nobles has been to forcefully draw resources from subordinates. These come in two primary forms: 1) economic taxes, e.g., grain, cash, labor, and; 2) symbolic taxes, e.g., acts of submission and respect. And every instance in which these are publicly extracted bonds the two sides in a contract of dominance and submission. As aforementioned, those who receive aid in most cases pay the taxes that indirectly fund what they are receiving back in various forms. Payment of these taxes is, however, so accepted it is merely taken for granted as one of the two certainties in life. And in politics, perception is paramount. Thus, the all-powerful perception that the ruler is blessing the subject, if by no other means than facilitating the aid, remains.

---

[2] Given space constrictions, this is a very concise general history that applies to larger societies. Smaller tribal leaders, as we learned earlier, tend to rely more on the respect, loyalty, and bonds of their people than on coercion. Further, in return for the extorted goods and services, the larger societal ruler was expected to provide grain from the stored supply following poor harvests. He was also obligated to protect the peasants from external threats, such as invading armies, and internal ones, such as rapacious landowners. And it was in his interest to do so because his prosperity depended on theirs.

Superior Resources

Without possession of or access to superb assets, one cannot achieve a position of potency. Control over property inheres upon private individuals an influence over others that is always social and frequently political in its character. Nonetheless, this doesn't necessitate great material wealth per se. While the resources requisite for political power can be found in possessions such as money and property that enable the owner to command the services of others, they can also be found in individual traits such as interpersonal skills, artistic talents, social status, good looks, intelligence, and charisma. Powerful people use resources they have to overcome those they lack. George W. Bush, for example, employed his assets—immense family wealth, a good name, connections, a certain personal charm, and ability to convert potential enemies into allies to rise above his liabilities—primarily low intelligence and questionable integrity. (By his own admission, in younger years, he was a below average high school and college student as well as an alcoholic who had multiple run-ins with the law. His wife evidently keeps him on the straight and narrow and perhaps should be included amongst his assets.)

Adolf Hitler, as we repeatedly note, rose from being a homeless, unemployed artist to master of Europe using little more than innate traits, e.g., courage, conviction, drive, and a razor-sharp insight into human nature. Hitler, however, is an anomaly. The media are fond of portraying certain political leaders as coming from humble or common beginnings but upon closer examination we find, for example, one's father was an army officer and mother was the daughter of a hotelier (Constantine) or his parents were reasonably successful farmers or merchants (Nixon, Truman). What the media are actually referring to is the middle (often upper middle) rather than lower class. There are some, but few, genuine poverty to power stories in world political history.

Those who rule are usually well-educated, often at prestigious universities. America has always been a bit more intellectually and sociopolitically primitive than its first world counterparts and some of its presidents, such as Grover Cleveland and Harry Truman received no higher education. Andrew Johnson had no formal schooling at all. Most, however, were well-educated. The alma maters of some former presidents are as follows:

Harvard: John Adams, John Quincy Adams, Franklin D. Roosevelt, John F. Kennedy
William and Mary: Thomas Jefferson, James Monroe
Princeton: James Madison, Woodrow Wilson
Yale: William Taft, George H. W. Bush, George W. Bush, Bill Clinton
Amherst: Calvin Coolidge
Stanford: Herbert Hoover
Columbia: Barack Obama
West Point: Ulysses Grant, Dwight Eisenhower
Annapolis: Jimmy Carter

Rulers tend to be cultured, using a refined code of manners. They can easily discuss nearly any topic. Many can converse in multiple languages. The highly cultivated Thomas Jefferson fluently spoke French—long considered the international language of diplomacy. Francis I, king of France (office term 1515-1547), enthusiastically studied the broad spectrum of the liberal arts—math, science, geography, history, literature, poetry, and music. He also spoke five languages—Hebrew, Latin, French, Italian, and Spanish. The ruler was both a nimble dancer and skilled hunter. Known for his polished etiquette, he funded spectacular theatrical events for the aristocracy, and there was nothing unusual about this. From approximately the 14th to 20th centuries European rulers often sponsored scientists and artists. The multitalented Leonardo da Vinci was in the employ of

Ludovico Sforza, Duke of Milan; Louis XII, king of France; Giovanni de Medici, aka Leo X, pope of the Roman Catholic church; and Cesare Borgia, Italian Cardinal and military commander. Frederick II (the Great), the cerebral king of Prussia (office term 1740-86), was not only a talented political and military leader, he was also a talented flutist, poet, and composer of baroque music scores.

Unfortunately, refined rulers are rapidly becoming a thing of the past and this is especially true where Americans and those who have arisen from military backgrounds are concerned.

While not a prerequisite to power, having the right surname and lineage certainly doesn't hurt. Brand names function in politics much as they do in manufacturing. The Adams, Roosevelt, Kennedy, and Bush brands are among the best known in the U.S. Safely insulated from politics in his retirement, George W. Bush disclosed the number one secret of his success: "It was a huge advantage to be the son of George and Barbara Bush." In monarchies a ruler usually obtains the throne by inheritance, and this is a topic we will soon further examine.

Exploitation of Human Symbolic Powers

Symbols have proven effective in influencing an audience's values, beliefs, emotions, and behavior. A symbol is, in essence, something that represents or suggests something else; often it is something intangible or simple, which stands for something tangible or more complex. A police officer's uniform is, for example, a symbol which displays an array of related symbols. As such, there is no need for him to say, "I am a threatening authority figure" when approaching a civilian; for the uniform, patches, insignia, radio, and especially sidearm aptly convey that message.

Symbols can be visual, such as lights atop the officer's car, which signal traffic to pull over to the side, or auditory, such as the sirens which announce the same message. They can even be perceived by other senses. For instance, a tap on the shoulder means somebody nearby wants your attention; the smell of smoke means something is burning and may require your attention as well.

As you likely noticed in our earlier discussion—when employed in a sociopolitical context (e.g., flags)—symbols nearly always[3] connote the strength of an in-group unified against opposing out-groups, propagandistic explanations to the contrary notwithstanding.

The use of visual images to represent complex ideas (known as pictograms or hieroglyphs) is believed to have been invented by the Mesopotamians in about 3,200 B.C., marking the beginning of recorded history. In about 3,000 B.C. the Egyptians began borrowing the concept and applying it to their own system of communications. In carved stelae and even in their names, Pharaohs associated themselves with the types of wild animals thought to be dominant. From about 1,000-650 B.C. an uncertain people who lived in the Luristan region (east central Iran) created bronze artwork that symbolized man's sovereignty over nature. Popular among this were standards (objects placed on the top of a staff), which depicted men controlling beasts. Some of the artistic animals were taken from real life, such as lions and eagles; others were the mythological variety, such as sphynxes and griffins. Also about 650 B.C. the Kingdom of Lydia (presently West Turkey) minted the world's first coins of a silver and gold alloy. The issuing authority impressed its insignia onto each to guarantee its value. The practice of minting coins made of precious metals that featured an authoritative emblem quickly spread to Greece, China, India, and Persia (Iran).

---

[3] Those falling outside of the usual category include the red Greek cross on a white background (emblem of the International Red Cross, which provides neutral humanitarian relief) and the plain white flag of surrender. One could, however, argue that these flags are not sociopolitical in nature.

Hittites (Turkey—second millennium BC), Mayans (Central America 300-900 AD), and Aztecs (Mexico 14th-16th century AD) also used pictures to convey ideas. The Mayans, known for mathematical innovations such as the discovery of the zero cypher, used a morse code type of system (dots and dashes) to represent numbers. Images known as glyphs depicted words. Some glyphs stood for sounds, others for ideas.

Western royals and nobles in the ancient world sealed letters and other documents with wax imprinted with a distinguishing image associated with the sender. Augustus chose the sphynx—a symbol of strength and mystery. In the 11th century European nobles such as Godwin, earl of Wessex, popularized emblems representing their families' aristocratic heritage. The same evolved into the coats of arms displayed by knights in the Crusades so allies could recognize them on the battlefield. (One needs only to view a few of these to infer how they inspired the military insignia of the modern day.) By the 13th century the use of symbols to represent leaders, families, churches, and colleges was well-established. England's College of Arms, founded by Richard III in 1484, authorized the use of *arms of achievement* which are governed by the laws of heraldry. (A genuine article is depicted with a photo of the author at the end of this book.)

The seals used by entities of the U.S. state and federal governments, such as the Department of "Justice," can be dismissed as illegitimate *arms of assumption*. Few people are interested in studying the authenticity of these symbols and under U.S. law a person can design any symbol he wishes so long as it isn't protected by copyright or trademark codes. JFK, for example, fashioned a very regal looking emblem for himself which features elements of a legitimate English one. While the creation and use of sociopolitical symbols has exploded in modern times, the message they transmit remains the same—he who bears them is a force with which to be reckoned.

Legitimacy

This is the most important element of authority, which is the reason why we will devote plenty of time to examining the topic.

Subjects must believe their ruler has the rightful power to control them. And in this regard dictatorships are unique entities. In these, legitimacy and authority are interchangeable, inseparable, and self-fulfilling. In other words, the dictator demonstrates that by possessing the strength to rule, it is his right to do so. (This notion is captured in the popular political phrase "might makes right.") His strength can come from a variety of sources including military and economic power, intimidation tactics, inheritance, loyalty of his regime and elites, support from external authorities, personal charisma, and a belief he has special abilities.

Republics, however, are another matter. Legitimacy in these is perceived to arise from laws and rules, and, most saliently, fair elections or appointments by officials fairly elected. In republics, therefore, the integrity of the election process is crucial. And the presidency of John Quincy Adams, son of the legendary second U.S. president, exemplifies this perfectly.

In 1824, Adams won an extremely close, controversial election. Widespread malice, attributable to the questionable victory, pursued Adams throughout his term. Adversaries, for example, relentlessly assailed his positions that the federal government should retain superseding authority over the states and the president held the power to ameliorate social issues. But instead of criticizing the merits of his arguments, they found it convenient to merely assert he could not advance such drastic positions as he had barely won the presidency, and the voters apparently agreed. Andrew Jackson overwhelmed Adams in the following election (1828) and the country could finally rest—satisfied its president at least had been fully elected.

In monarchies, legitimacy is usually established by a doctrine known as *divine right*. Sources older than written history hold that leaders of states are appointed not by men, but by God. Stories from the ancient Chinese colonial empire known as Zhou justified their king's conquests of the more powerful eastern state of Shang on the basis it was carried out by divine mandate. The sources proclaim a deity named Tian commanded the Zhou king, Wen, to overthrow the king of Shang and rule over the territory and its people. By this authority, Wen's son, King Wu, led a coalition of western Chinese forces and seized control of Shang's capitol city late in the 11th century B.C. He and his royal lineage then ruled over the entire empire until the 8th century B.C. The Mandate of Heaven, however, lived on and was invoked by Chinese rulers until China's final royal line, the Qing dynasty, dissolved in 1912.

In a letter to the fledgling Christians of Rome, Paul of Tarsus, a disciple of Jesus, admonishes as follows:

> Let everyone be subject to the governing authorities, for there is no authority except that which God has established. The authorities that exist have been established by God. Consequently, whoever rebels against the authority is rebelling against what God has instituted, and those who do so will bring judgment on themselves. For rulers hold no terror for those who do right, but for those who do wrong. Do you want to be free from fear of the one in authority? Then do what is right and you will be commended. For the one in authority is God's servant for your good. But if you do wrong, be afraid, for rulers do not bear the sword for no reason. They are God's servants, agents of wrath to bring punishment on the wrongdoer. Therefore, it is necessary to submit to the authorities, not only because of possible punishment but also as a matter of conscience.
>
> Romans 13:1-5 NIV

The belief that rulers are chosen by God appears to have arisen as religious and political leaders were, in ancient societies, one and the same. Some, such as the Egyptians, believed their rulers (Pharaohs) actually were gods. Others, including the Caddo Indians (south central U.S. 1200-1850 AD) thought of their leaders as liaisons between the tribe and a supreme being. An Aztec ruler, known as a tlatoani, took on three simultaneous roles: governor, military commander, and chief priest. Califs, rulers of Arabian (Islamic) societies from approximately the middle of the seventh to the middle of the eleventh centuries, claimed their divine right to rule as descendants of the prophet Muhammed was justified in a statement in the Qur'an (4:59): "Believers, obey God, and obey the Messenger, and those in authority over you."

About the same time Jesus' disciples were writing the gospels, the Roman general Vespasian was attempting to ascend to the throne. Emperor Nero had killed himself, and three other military officers, none of whom could claim royal descent, had already forced their way into the top position in successive power struggles. Since he also had no claim of descent from the Julio-Claudian dynasty, Vespasian had to establish legitimacy otherwise. First his soldiers declared their support for him. Then his allies began spreading rumors he was healing the blind and lame. (This was evidently a popular tactic to show divine anointment.) Vespasian then killed Vitellius, the occupant of the imperial office, after which the Senate finally acknowledged him as emperor.

Vespasian was worshipped as a god in the provinces, and upon his death in June 79 A.D. he joined other noteworthy Roman emperors in actually being declared a god by the Senate.

For his part, the storied Macedonian conqueror Alexander the Great asserted he was sired by Jupiter, Chief of the Roman gods, and his family line traced to Hercules—the Greek mythological hero.

Eastern Roman emperor Galerius (term 305-311 AD) proclaimed his actual mother, Romula, had mated with the god of war, Mars, and he, Galerius, was the product of this natural/supernatural union.

In 308, Constantine, emperor of the western portion of the Roman empire witnessed a circle of light surrounding the afternoon sun. This effect, known as a solar halo, is now known to occur when the sun's light rays are distorted by ice crystals high in Earth's atmosphere. Using Christian propaganda that associates Christ with light, bishops convinced the emperor it was a sign from heaven. A dream in which Christ supposedly showed the ruler a protective symbol followed, after which Constantine converted into the first Christian head of state.

Overhead rings of light became symbols of divine anointment and in the following century painters began portraying "holy" figures such as angels, Mary, Jesus, and the disciples with these halos hovering above their heads. Rulers quickly picked up on the idea and demanded a new type of crown—a shimmering, golden and bejeweled one that would resemble a halo. This, of course, was a propagandistic tactic meant to indicate they had been divinely appointed to the throne. To elevate the effect, a high church official such as an archbishop or even the pope himself usually placed the crown upon the ruler's head at his coronation. Valentinian II, Roman emperor from 375-392, is believed to be one of the first monarchs depicted wearing the lustrous divine diadem.

In a monarchy, therefore, legitimacy is usually established by tradition, divine right, and bloodlines. In a republic, it is perceived as being established by laws, rules, and, most importantly, winning a fair election or receiving an appointment by an executive or board who has done so; perhaps with some sort of confirmation by another branch of government. But just as a controversial victory can haunt an elected official (and his appointees), so can a questionable ascension to the throne.

In an attempt to leave nothing to chance Henry VIII set forth that instead of following rules of primogeniture and other conventions, it was he who would decide while alive who succeeded him upon his death. And to assure there were no misunderstandings about this, he commissioned a portrait. It depicted Henry on his deathbed pointing his finger at his chosen one—his son with Jane Seymore—Edward VI. The latter did succeed Henry, but he was a sickly young man and followed Henry to the grave only six years later.

Edward had named as his own successor the teenaged Lady Jane Grey, his first cousin—who was the great granddaughter of Henry VII. England's Privy Council declared Jane queen on July 10, 1553. "Bloody" Mary, Henry VIII's firstborn daughter, was, like her Spanish mother, Catholic. Jane was Protestant. Edward had selected Jane because she would continue in separating the country from Catholicism; promoting instead the protestant Reformed Church of England. But the powerful Catholic block immediately protested Jane's legitimacy. How, they questioned, could she have a stronger claim to the throne than Henry's firstborn child? In reality, of course, these people wanted one of their own in power, but they raised a valid point and the broader English people generally favored Mary for that very reason. The more aggressively they protested, the more Jane's supporters wavered, and on July 19 the Catholics prevailed. The Privy Council reversed itself—deposing Jane and proclaiming Mary to be queen.

Be that as it may, questions of legitimacy in monarchies can be determined by physical force. We already learned how Vespasian, with his superior military, unseated Vitellius to obtain the Roman throne. The same happened about 900 years later in England when Edward the Confessor died, leaving the throne vacant. Anglo-Saxon noble Harold and Norman duke William both believed they had strong claims to the crown. Harold inherited the title earl of Wessex from his father Godwin, who was Edward the Confessor's father-in-law, in 1053. William was the head of the

Normandy duchy in northwestern France. The latter credibly asserted that Edward and even Harold had promised him the throne. Both claimants had blood relations to the royal line.

When the Confessor died childless in January 1066, the Anglo-Saxon nobility selected Harold, who was the most powerful noble on the island. William was unsatisfied with the decision and while Harold was preoccupied with protecting his turf from numerous uprisings and invasions in northern England, William's forces arrived on the coast of East Sussex. After Harold put down the last of the challengers (the Norwegians) his troops marched south. But William's forces were fresh and ready. They defeated the Anglo-Saxons in the day-long Battle of Hastings, killing King Harold himself as he proudly sat under his banners.

William I (the Conqueror) was crowned the first Norman king of England in October 1066.

Even in democracies we have seen questions of a similar nature resolved by the processes of violence rather than those of law.

From the founding of the country until 1865, a debate raged throughout America. Fought primarily by New Englanders on one side and southerners on the other, the issue was the supremacy of the federal government. The northerners pointed to the federal government as the supreme authority, and held that it existed independent of the states. Southerners asserted each state retained jurisdiction over its land and its people. The federal government was, in their view, nothing more than a voluntary union of the states.

The southern faction's argument was more logically and historically sound. But as is often the case, might rather than reason resolved the matter when the northern union conquered the southern confederacy in the Civil War.

While legitimacy is most importantly acknowledged from within the leader's country, its acceptance or rejection by foreign powers can also be a factor. In early 2011 the U.S. and its allies found an opportunity to take down their old enemy Muammar Gaddafi, ruler of Libya, when a civil war broke out in that country. Not only did U.S. and NATO forces assist the resistance militarily, they also assisted in subverting the leader's legitimacy. On March 3 the U.S. president himself addressed the people of Libya, announcing, "The United States is support[ing] the aspirations of the Libyan people." That is, the resistance. He further declared, "Muammar Gaddafi has lost his legitimacy to lead, and he must leave." While the president failed to specify how this had been lost, the very proclamation of such by the leader of the most powerful country on the planet can be considered a factor in that. Taking this lead, the president of France then officially acknowledged the National Transitional Council—the interim government endorsed by the resistance—as the genuine government of Libya. This too can be considered a factor that legitimized the new government and correlatively discredited Gaddafi.

With NATO assistance Gaddafi was captured and killed by the resistance in October. In July 2012 elections were held. The Council passed its authority to the elected General National Congress the following month.

Note: In Chapter Five we will examine a component of legitimacy that can be thought of as honor or prestige encapsulated in its most important form: moral authority.

> We Christian kings have one holy duty imposed on us by Heaven: to uphold the principle of the Divine Right of Kings.
>
> — Kaiser William II of Germany to
> Czar Nicholas II of Russia

Chapter Two

The Official Motivation

The true religion of a prince is his interest and his glory.
— Frederick the Great

First Case In Point

Nationalistic sentiment pervaded Europe's Germanic tribes in late 1871. Prussia had just militarily defeated France (the Franco-Prussian War) and the Germans were also at the pinnacle of their intellectual and cultural achievements. This period yielded some of Europe's greatest geniuses such as architects, artists, poets, and composers of what is now considered classical music. Finding their way of living to be of the highest quality, Germans believed the time was right to unify and begin diffusing their superior culture to inferior societies worldwide. Composer Richard Wagner recognized the auspice of the encompassing atmosphere and proposed establishing a national theatre program. Peculiarly, he envisioned the provincial Bavarian town of Bayreuth as the seat of this.

Wagner presented a proposal to leaders of the community. They understood the theatre would economically boost the town and in January 1872 purchased the land on which it would be constructed. Nonetheless, they left responsibility for procuring the funds necessary for both construction of the theatre, and the promotion of the musical dramas to be held therein, on Wagner himself.

To fulfill his part of the bargain the maestro formulated a plan that required the sale of seasonal subscriptions to his performances. Still, the price of these were such that few individuals could afford them. Associations of patrons thus developed. These groups purchased a single share of the project then distributed tickets to their members. No admission was granted to the general public.

The campaign achieved significant success, but by April 1873 Wagner had only received payment for two hundred of the requisite three hundred subscriptions and had to oblige himself to conduct a series of fundraising concerts. These produced up to $160,000 each, as equated to the present value of U.S. currency. All the same, by August the project was nowhere near fully funded and the composer desperately entreated the assistance of his wealthiest patron, Ludwig II—king of Bavaria.

The monarch was a reclusive and quixotic man who believed Wagner to be sort of an ideological soulmate. He was, however, preoccupied with an agenda of his own—erecting and furnishing one of his fairytale style castles. This one, to be called Neuschwanstein (New Swan

Stone), would be seated on a mountaintop in the Bavarian Alps southwest of Munich. Ludwig would adorn the walls with murals depicting scenes from Wagner's operas. (The Walt Disney Company acknowledges this castle inspired the design of those featured in *Cinderella* and *Sleeping Beauty*.)

As the king's finances and energy were fully committed to Neuschwanstein he denied the request. It appeared Wagner's magnificent musical dream was about to collapse in an inglorious defeat. Fortunately, accepting defeat was not in the maestro's nature.

Through the grand duke of Baden, Wagner appealed to William I who had risen from king of Prussia to emperor of Germany as a result of his triumph over France. But there were no secrets among the aristocracy and the maestro's maneuver was quickly brought to Ludwig's attention. After considering the matter in light of this new development, the romantic, vain ruler rejected the possibility that any prince other than himself should be credited with rescuing the project. Before William could answer, Ludwig dispatched to Wagner a letter apologizing for his earlier denial and promising to loan $2 million (equated to present U.S. dollars) to the program. A contract guaranteeing this was signed on February 26, 1874.

In August 1876, Wagner's Festival of Bayreuth, at which his operas were performed, commenced at the new Festspielhaus National Theatre. Emperor William attended for two days. Before departing he congratulated the tenacious composer and remarked, "I never thought you would bring it off!"

> While the decisions of national leaders are determined by the multiple contexts in which they operate, they are still human beings, subject to the same psychological laws as everyone else.
>
> Jerome D. Frank, M.D., Ph.D.

♦ ♦ ♦ ♦ ♦

Second Case in Point

In the spring of 1540, Thomas Howard, the third duke of Norfolk, sought to reattain the favor of his sovereign, Henry VIII, king of England. The duke had been maneuvered out of power two years prior by the political machinations of Henry's chief secretary, Thomas Cromwell, but had fabricated a plan to show it was he, rather than Cromwell, who could best serve the king.

Henry was a man who was seldom satisfied. And so it was with his fourth wife—the Germanic Anne of Cleves. The fussy king complained that she was "old and ugly" and "neither her bosom nor her belly are those of a virgin." He summarized, "My nature abhors her ... before God she is not my lawful wife."

The crafty Norfolk knew just the cure for Henry's discontent and began inviting the king to his London mansion to become better acquainted with his beautiful sexually-charged nineteen year-old niece, Catherine Howard. Lady Rochford, a peeress of the House of Boleyn, assisted Norfolk by tutoring Catherine as to the manner in which she should behave when in the company of her royal swain. Needless to say, the king's nature did not abhor the firm features of the pretty teen. On July 9, 1540, his marriage to Anne of Cleves was annulled and on July 28 he wed Lady Howard in a small, private ceremony.

Norfolk's political rival, the insidious Cromwell, was put to death shortly after the service.

For the next eighteen months the king was thoroughly satisfied in his matrimony. Norfolk reacquired his master's approval for having cultivated the relationship whence the monarch's bliss arose. Nevertheless, as is often the case with young females so desirable and libidinal, men other than her husband had already taken, and continued to take, an interest in she who was now the queen of England.

Women of this puritanical society were presumed to be virgins on their wedding day, but the unmarried Catherine had already entertained three men in her bed chambers at the Norfolk estate and she continued arranging liaisons with two of these, one of whom was her cousin, even after her marriage. It was an accident waiting to happen.

A female servant in the Norfolk household who felt mistreated came forward with the information and presented it to King Henry. Finding it truthful, he was heartbroken. Catherine was his fifth wife and the one with whom the fastidious and fickle king had fallen most deeply in love. This, the perceptive Norfolk knew, was a recipe for disaster.

The duke was already well aware of his niece's sexual propensity as many of her indiscretions had taken place under his roof during her teen years. Be this as it may, Norfolk, fearing for his own life, pretended to be shocked and outraged at the revelations. He fervently expressed his remorse over both the king's anguish and the dishonor to the Howard family. Norfolk concluded that his niece deserved to be burned alive. Her other relatives, likewise overwhelmed with terror, joined in the condemnation.

The queen's family would be spared the well-known wrath of Henry VIII. Catherine herself would not be as fortunate.

On February 11, 1542, Parliament issued a bill of attainder proclaiming it's treasonous for an impure woman to marry the king. The comely, concupiscent queen was beheaded in the tower of London two days later.

◆ ◆ ◆ ◆ ◆

Abraham Maslow identified several requirements humans must fulfill in order to achieve happiness. He classified these in a graded series (usually depicted in the form of a pyramid) that range from physical needs such as food and shelter at the lowest level to self-actualization (being all that one can be) at the apex.

One of the most difficult tasks facing behavioral scientists as they perform motivational analyses is tracing behavior to an exact motivation. Drives tend to conflate. Consider for example an attractive, young actress who meets a man who is already successful in that industry. Her needs for sex, security, and self-actualization may converge as they seek fulfillment in a single source. (His ability to satisfy multiple needs increases his desirability.) But our duty to carry out the arduous evaluations involved with isolating a drive may be lessened when we understand there is a deeper force propelling every one of them—the most primitive motivation of all—protecting and advancing the interests of the self.

While it may be true that people retain an interest in the welfare of certain other creatures (in addition to causes and beliefs) many fail to recognize these are all predicated in an interest in the self. As is true with needs, this self-interest can be found on multiple levels. We'll designate the concept the Hierarchy of Self-Interest and note its priorities from the top down.

1. Self
2. Children
3. Other family members
4. Tribe
5. Nation, religion, language group
6. Larger spheres of humanity and life

The motivation in the First Case in Point is fairly straightforward. While it may be difficult to comprehend in the context of America's culturally vacuous sociopolitical climate, in Europe from approximately the fourteenth to early twentieth centuries it was considered the hallmark of sophistication to be well-educated and practiced in the fine arts and sciences. And it was proper for royals and nobles to sponsor intellectuals and creative types such as painters, musicians, and scientists.

King Ludwig took particular pride in his image as a monarch who promoted his society's refined culture. He did not want to fund Wagner's project—given his commitment to constructing his own dream castle—but the composer left him no other choice. Whether by careful maneuvering or coincidence, Wagner sent the message that if Ludwig didn't rescue his project, it would instead be William who would be seen as the savior of a grand institution of Germanic culture. Ludwig couldn't bear the thought. By funding it he would 1) avoid experiencing the pains of envy already starting to sprout in his mind, and 2) magnify the image of himself he desired to present to the world. He did not do it for Wagner, nor his people. He did it for himself.

The duke of Norfolk in our Second Case retained an interest in his hypersexual niece. After all, she was his close blood relative who had lived under his very roof. His interest in her (level 3), however, was not as great as his interest in himself (level 1). For this reason, he, along with her other relatives, chose to disown her and save themselves. Under the circumstances had they done otherwise not only would they likely have failed, they would have joined in her fate.[4]

Finally, we note the lowly disaffected servant who brought down the queen for several apparent reasons. Most saliently doing so satisfied her need for vindication. Envy of Catherine and her lovers likely also factored into it, as did the thrill of demolishing someone of such a stature. At the deepest level, of course, she testified because she believed doing so was in her best interests.

In February of 2008 Massachusetts governor Mitt Romney viciously locked horns with his rival for the Republican presidential candidacy—U.S. Senator John McCain. The debates between the two were so fierce they frequently erupted into flagrant animosity. Romney actually alleged his opponent was dishonest and, worse yet, accused him of employing the kind of dirty tricks Ronald Reagan would have found to be reprehensible. McCain, for his part, asserted Romney lacked "the experience and judgment necessary to be president in a time of terrorism."

When Romney failed to win a number of important states in the primary elections, he reluctantly accepted reality and withdrew from the race. For all that, he recognized that if the self (level 1) could not attain the presidency at least one belonging to his own party—with whom he shared values and interests—(level 4) should. Romney thus endorsed his former intra-party rival and began enthusiastically campaigning on his behalf.

So strong is interest in the self, human thinking is affected by an attitude psychologists call the *self-serving bias*. This means they are consciously or otherwise engaged in a perpetual attempt to advance that which they perceive to be in their best interests. And research has shown that when people are instructed to arrive at unbiased judgments, these judgments are still apt to be unknowingly, yet greatly, inclined toward their own interests. As such, even when they promote an argument they believe is based on justice, it is a version of justice that promotes their self-interests. This is true of those considered to be experts in their field, e.g. executives, doctors, and judges, the

---

[4] Some relatives of Henry's second wife, Anne Boleyn, such as her own father, Sir Thomas Boleyn, had taken a similar course years earlier when she was accused of marital infidelity and treason. But in Anne's case there was very little credible evidence of guilt.

same as the average men and women on the street. This bias also leads people to credit their successful endeavors to internal personal qualities, but their failures to external, situational ones. A victorious swimmer may, for example, view her achievement as a consequence of arduous training and self-discipline, while an unsuccessful one ascribes her failure to people who distracted her.

As we work our way down the hierarchy, we find related thought processes occurring on the broader societal levels. Scientists label the relevant mental operations the *in-group* and *group-serving biases*. So-called altruism plays no part in promoting the welfare of those belonging to the same mutual interest group.

Since prehuman times individuals have coalesced into groups that promote their members' image, validate their worldview, and otherwise advance their interests. Because competition pervades most aspects of life, the primary reason for forming groups is to secure an advantage for their members. These individuals thus favor and assume the best in those who are part of their group. Conversely, they disfavor and assume the worst in those they perceive as separate from, and in competition against, themselves. Thus, while people tend to act as peaceful and social beings when they are among their own kind, they can revert to utterly vicious behavior when among those they consider to be outsiders, often viewing the latter as less than human. Archaeologists and zoologists believe such aggression evolved as a result of competition among the belligerent tribes of early man. A typical demonstration of this took place in November 2020 as supporters of U.S. President Donald Trump violently clashed with those of President-elect Joe Biden at a Washington march protesting election fraud.

A group's definition of what one *is* suggests a definition of what he is *not*. And the very act of separating people from the general mass into groups of nearly ever variety can promote the aforesaid preferences and prejudices. For the mere existence of an out-group challenges the validity of the in-group. Some sociologists, in fact, believe the Christian church's persecution of those perceived to be witches from the fourteenth to eighteenth centuries was largely motivated by the church's desire to eradicate competition and monopolize spirituality.

♦ ♦ ♦ ♦ ♦

Similarity among people is conducive to fondness which in turn elicits empathy and aid. People are especially inclined to assist those with whom they share the greatest amount of genetic material. As illustrated in the Hierarchy, generally speaking, the greater the amount of shared material, the greater the self-interest. This a reason why, when superseding factors do not otherwise propel self-interests, people of a common race are more inclined to help each other than those of a different race.

In the early 1500s Spanish conquistadores began invading South America. By 1600 they had subdued nearly all of the indigenous Indian tribes and claimed the continent for the king of Spain. In controlling the land, the Spanish established a social hierarchy exactly following the self-interest hierarchy: Pure Spanish ranked the highest class. Those who were racially mixed, but retained some Spanish blood, such as Mestizos (Spanish/Indian ancestry) and Mulattos (Spanish/black descent) were in the middle class. At the bottom were they who were devoid of any Spanish blood—Indians and blacks.

♦ ♦ ♦ ♦ ♦

If the laws governing the cosmos permitted it, most people would take their material wealth with them into the afterlife. Since they do not, the self-interest hierarchy is often manifested in a document known as the Last Will and Testament. In it one discovers people are predisposed to distribute the greatest allotment of their wealth either to those with whom they share the greatest amount of genetic material, or those who have assisted or will assist in its advancement. This includes those who enrich their lives while they are alive or who promote a cause they hold sacred. It's no accident that wealthy people who discover they have developed a terminal disease, especially if it can be genetically transmitted, "donate" substantial sums to organizations whose purpose is to cure the disease. Let's look at a few instances.

After being diagnosed with Parkinson's disease in 1991, actor Michael J. Fox started a foundation to finance research into curing the disorder.

Rock guitarist Edward Van Halen was diagnosed with skin cancer in January 2000. When part of his tongue later had to be excised at the UCLA Medical Center he became disillusioned with conventional treatment and began investing in a holistic cancer research laboratory.

In the late 1980s New England's prominent Olin family donated millions of dollars to the Connecticut Institute of Living. Children in this family had, in the prior decade, been patients at its facility, which researched and treated neurological disorders.

Michael Milken, the notorious former senior vice president of junk bond giant Drexel Burnham Lambert, was diagnosed with prostate cancer in the mid 1990s. He responded in part by founding an organization called Cap Cure which quickly became the number one funder of prostate cancer research in the U.S.

Income taxes are a good example of the hierarchical nature of self-interest. These assessments fund greater societal entities which redistribute money back to their members in the form of services; which is why some of these entities refer to themselves as commonwealths. Money paid to the U.S. federal government finances a strong military, healthcare, assistance to victims of natural disasters, law enforcement, etc. State taxes fund road maintenance, universities, public schools, law enforcement, etc. Tax revenues received by local governments finance parks, libraries, law enforcement, etc. Most taxpayers are at least somewhat aware that they depend on the services provided by their own taxes. Yet every individual or family (levels 1 to 3) contributes as little as possible to the commonwealth (levels 4 and 5) to ensure operation of these services. There is even a profession comprising tax preparers, accountants, attorneys, et al. devoted entirely to helping the taxpayer contribute as little as possible to the greater societal treasuries on which his survival depends. Americans, in fact, once went so far to reduce their taxable income, they fabricated dependents on their 1040 forms. In 1987 the IRS put a stop to this by mandating the social security number of each dependent be specified. Seven million American "children" suddenly vanished.

When the Corona virus crisis was in its incipient stages in 2020, U.S. public health officials earnestly requested the people wear masks so they didn't project saliva, mucus, and vapor which could infect others. Having less concern for their society at large (levels 4 and 5) than for their own comfort and convenience (level 1) the public mostly ignored the pleas. Months later officials realized their psychological (or sociological as it were) blunder and began asserting masks can also protect the wearer. But it was too late. Already convinced masks only protected people about whom they had less concern, most refused to alter their routines.

One frequently notices a band member who is better looking and/or more talented than her cohort departing for a solo career. Often the elite one (level 1) has been in a close friendship with the bandmates (level 4) for years and has already proclaimed she would never forsake them. She knows the public identifies the group with her, and her looks and talent are essential to its success. Yet, when some industry mogul offers her the opportunity for greater money and celebrity as a solo artist she follows the hierarchy anyway—aggrandizing herself and relegating her bandmates to lives of relative mediocrity. (Hayley Williams, Gwen Stephani, Justin Timberlake and Camilla Cabello all come to mind in this.)

The inverse, however, probably occurs more often—a competent musician who is not a superstar and would like to part from the cohort (or had already parted from it and failed) decides he must stick with it in order to survive. Paul Stanley of KISS showed surprising insight into his own psychological operations when he spoke to reporters in early 2025 concerning his relationship with bandmate Gene Simmons. Stanely admitted a single motivation caused him to stand by Simmons despite personal incompatibility and it was neither love for Gene nor for the band. Said he, "Gene drove me crazy from the beginning . . . but I certainly understood that I was far stronger with him than without him . . . I knew that for my own success and for my own progress, we should be together. So that was purely a decision based upon my wanting to succeed and knowing Gene would be a major ingredient in that happening."

◆ ◆ ◆ ◆ ◆

We opened the chapter with an example showing how the king of Bavaria acted in a manner consistent with what he perceived to be in his best interests. Theresince we've focused on the behavior of people in general and found it no different. Now let's look at a variety of historical situations to affirm officials and civilians alike always place the self first.

When his reign began in 1603, James I, king of England (yes, he who approved the 1611 translation of the Judeo-Christian bible), held an uppity attitude common among royals and aristocrats of the time concerning smoking—it was both immoral and unhealthy. In April 1606 he nonetheless authorized the London Company to establish tobacco plantations in the new world via the first Virginia charter. Duties he collected from tobacco imports quickly began filling his treasure chests and, as his fortune changed, so did his puritanical position on smoking. He now found it to be an acceptable activity.

Leaders of the American Medical Association reorganized their professional society in 1901. As part of this they established minimum educational standards and other basic requirements to practice medicine. And while the public would benefit from this action, it was not done for that reason. For the AMA leaders acted as they did to elevate the prestige of legitimate doctors and exclude quacks against whom they competed for business.

At least seven members of the U.S. Congress personally received thousands of dollars in farm subsidies in 2011. All but two of these sat on the agriculture committees that write farm policies.

In 1990, David Dinkins narrowly defeated Rudolf Giuliani in the contest for New York City's mayoralty. He quickly began hiring police officers to supplement the existing force, not because he had any concern for the safety of his constituents, but because he knew the conservative Giuliani, a former federal prosecutor, was likely to otherwise secure the law-and-order vote. Yet, for all Dinkins' efforts, Giuliani still prevailed in 1994. And ironically it would be he, rather than Dinkins, who would be credited with Dinkins' work in bolstering the police force.

Upton Sinclair's 1906 novel *The Jungle* features a story centered around a man who labors in a Chicago slaughterhouse. While the storyline is entirely fictional, its depiction of the deplorable conditions of American meat processing plants was realistic. As the book became a best seller, the public became incensed. Sinclair thought he would provoke sympathy for the men who worked in these factories. Instead, he provoked anger over the quality of meat. That is to say, the American public did not care about the workers' welfare, they only cared about what was going into their bellies. Meat sales plunged.

The public's reaction reached the ears of President Theodore Roosevelt who ordered an investigation. Congress proposed reform. The meat producers themselves, knowing reform would restore confidence in their product and improve sales, supported it. Later that year Congress passed the Meat Inspection Act which established government oversight on the industry.

New York Governor Hugh Carey purchased a historic Victorian home on the secluded Shelter Island in 1975. The isle, which rests between Long Island's two forked tips, would be his family's summer residence. News that several Long Island residents had died from Rocky Mountain Spotted Fever reached him shortly thereafter and he sprang into action. Using his official power to protect himself, his family, and his investment, Carey ordered Robert Whalen, commissioner of the New York Department of Health, to investigate and control the tick born disease. The inquiry quickly snowballed into a massive investigation involving the public health departments of four states, three universities, and the federal Center for Disease Control and Prevention.

In early 1937 the Roman marble statue Discobulus, carved in the second century, went up for sale. The Berlin State Museum ended up as the winning bidder for the price of $327,000. It promptly paid for the statue with funds from the German government treasury, but still had problems obtaining the Italian government's approval for export. To ease this, Hitler himself visited Italy and along with that country's premier, Benito Mussolini, inspected the statue. Historians believe Hitler personally requested approval for export at that time. Two weeks later Galeazzo Ciano, Italy's foreign minister, informed the pertinent authorities that export was authorized.

Germany finally received the marble figure and unveiled it in the summer of 1937 at the opening of the Great German Art Exhibition.

American authorities confiscated the statue following Germany's military defeat in May 1945. In utter disregard for the fact that it had been legally purchased and imported, the U.S. ordered it returned to Italy in 1948. The new German government protested that it had been lawfully acquired but its plea fell on deaf American ears. For U.S. officials, looking to influence Italy's general election, knew returning the popular antiquity to Italy would reflect positively on the incumbent Christian Democrats—the Italian party those U.S. officials favored.

Fire began consuming Rome on July 18, 64. Nero, emperor of the Roman Empire, was vacationing at his country estate on the Mediterranean coast at the time. When assistants informed him of the conflagration he merely went about his vacation as if nothing were awry. It wasn't until they later told him his newly constructed palace, the House of Passage, had become endangered that he finally returned to the capitol. The Great Fire of Rome destroyed ten of the city's fourteen districts, torching half of the new palace in the process.

The emperor's delay in returning infuriated the people of Rome, and he only added insult to injury by appropriating 250 acres of choice real estate as the site of another new palace—the Golden House. He is famously remembered to have sung and played a stringed instrument while the city burned, but historians are unable to determine whether this actually took place or was the antagonistic maneuver of his enemies. (We'll examine the use of rumors as psychopolitical weapons in Chater Six.)

In 1998 U.S. Senator John McCain (R-AZ) sponsored a bill that would've settled the liability suit brought by over forty states against major cigarette manufacturers. It also included an innovative feature that would've given the Food and Drug Administration (FDA) authority to regulate nicotine as a drug. As the majority of the Senate favored McCain's bill, two dissenting senators arranged a filibuster to indefinitely postpone a vote on it. When a vote was taken to end the filibuster, the bill's supporters lacked three necessary to do so. The 42 senators opposed to the bill had received an average of $17,902 in hard donations from the tobacco industry in the two-year period that preceded their previous elections. The 57 who favored it had only obtained an average of $4,810 in those periods.

A popular Democrat attorney named Peter Sweeny was named chamberlain of New York City in 1866. When he accepted the position, which gave him responsibility for managing the city's bank accounts, he stated he would be the first to reject the custom allowing the holder of that office to keep for personal use interest accrued on city accounts. He proclaimed, "As a taxpayer . . . I am not willing to receive a great or any sum of money against the public's sense of right, however legally justifiable." The money usually amounted to about a quarter million dollars per year and was considered the best perk of the job.

Citizens who suspected Sweeny to be corrupt were astonished. The *New York Herald* newspaper declared his decision to be one of "self-denial and sublime courage never before equaled." Sweeny, New Yorkers generally concluded, was a charitable man of honor.

But modern historians who examined the situation more closely discovered that the supposedly altruistic lawyer paid $60,000 in contributions to party officials in the expectation of such an appointment. Worse yet, they discovered the state legislature was already planning to eliminate the procedure by which the chamberlain could legally retain interest on city accounts.

Sweeny, it turns out, was no righteous moral pillar, rather he considered the matter and arrived at a calculated decision to very openly reject the soon-to-expire access to the interest money because this was of greater political benefit than the remaining funds themselves would be of financial benefit.

♦ ♦ ♦ ♦ ♦

Charitable acts undertaken with no obvious benefits to the giver satisfy him in some less obvious manner. Social norms that require people to act fairly and helpfully motivate most instances of supposed altruism. Helping others is socially rewarded with approval and satisfies one's need to feel socially responsible and morally acceptable. Research has shown that performing charitable deeds reduces negative feelings such as anger or guilt. It can also boost self-esteem.

One gives to an impoverished child in Cambodia because he loves basking in the appreciative letters that arrive from the child. He donates to the local animal shelter because he loves cats and dogs and receives a good feeling knowing he has helped fill their hungry little bellies. In Sweeny's case he sacrificed little, if anything, but received great praise and probably concomitant positive feelings from being perceived as upstanding.

Another reason people help each other should be predictable—quid pro quo.

We look for balance in our relationships. While it often lies below the conscious level, this need is still present. If one partner consistently fails to maintain his side of the equation, the other is likely to find his way out. This applies to every type of relationship. For instance, if you have a friend who dominates conversations—seldom giving you a chance to talk, a neighbor whom you allow to borrow property but who balks when you ask to borrow hers, or a lover who satisfies herself while leaving you unfulfilled, you will likely find yourself avoiding that person. You may even find reasons other than the actual one—an absence of fair exchange—to end the relationship.

If, on the other hand, the chatterbox friend helps you with your college homework, or the neighbor is a cute blonde who struts around her yard in "Daisy Dukes"—conveniently bending over in the direction of your windows, or the lover bakes you a tasty breakfast before departing—you may reconsider. Albeit in different respects, balance is maintained.

Thus, whether they realize it or not, when people perform an act of supposed kindness they do so: 1) to fulfill a social or moral obligation, 2) expecting something good will come back to them, or 3) to return something good that has already been done for them. Chamberlain Sweeny (whom we will meet again in Chapter Fifteen) "donated" $60,000 and received a position of power. He "sacrificed" the interest in city accounts and received praise and good will from his constituency. This *reciprocity norm* especially compels religious and superstitious people to engage in charitable work as they believe spiritual rewards to themselves will result.

Note: Under contract law, something of value given in exchange for something else of value is known as *consideration*. And the quid pro quo arrangement is so important to fundamental fairness that most contracts are unenforceable without consideration to back up the formal promises. (My Business Law II professor forced my class to define a number of possible exceptions to this under various judicial interpretations of the Second Restatement of the Law of Contracts, but I hold these now, as I held them then, to be of little practical significance.)

♦ ♦ ♦ ♦ ♦

Final Case In Point

Hurricane Katrina brought destruction on the Gulf of Mexico's coastal regions in August 2005. Fierce winds and water killed over one thousand people and destroyed hundreds of thousands of homes. The owners of many struggled with their insurance companies to resolve claims. Some hired individual lawyers, most signed up for larger class actions.

By January 2007 Mississippi attorney Dickie Scruggs decided he would have to place his retirement plans on the backburner. He had become the key player in litigating an insurance settlement for houses damaged by Katrina in the Pascagoula area. The lawyer had already raked in billions of dollars in legal fees from mass tort litigation against asbestos, tobacco, and insurance companies. He had gained immense notoriety and drew correlatively immense envy from colleagues in the legal establishment. Perhaps a bit too much. His career, after all, inspired John Grisham's novel *The King of Torts*.

Scruggs' own beach house, along with those of his friends and neighbors, had been laid waste by the hurricane. The State Farm Insurance company was the primary underwriter for homeowners' policies in the area and the company was denying nearly every claim.

While Scruggs was working on the matter, his firm became aware that two former State Farm claims adjusters were in possession of evidence showing company executives had tampered with engineering reports on the cause of the damage. Specifically, they had altered it from wind to water. They did so because a typical homeowner's policy covers the former, but not the latter.

The lawyer legitimized a relationship with the duo by hiring them as consultants with $150,000 annual salaries. As they provided the documentary evidence, Scruggs passed it on to Jim Hood, state attorney general, with the hopes of increasing pressure on the company. The attorney general gladly cooperated in what he believed would be a powerful alliance of self-interests and began an investigation of his own.

Hood held grand jury hearings on the criminal aspect of the matter while Scruggs negotiated a settlement to a civil case representing 640 policyholders. State Farm executives eventually succumbed to the overpowering force by agreeing to terms: $89 million for the homeowners and $26.5 million for the attorneys. The executives, however, were more concerned with their own freedom than their stockholder's money and shrewdly stipulated the settlement enforceable only upon termination of the criminal proceedings.

Scruggs had an enormous financial carrot dangling before him. He now needed to reverse gears and convince Hood not to prosecute the executives.

After his direct requests for dismissal failed, the lawyer offered the politically connected consulting firm of Steve Patterson and Tim Balducci half a million dollars if they could so persuade Hood. But the attorney general had an agenda of his own. An election was forthcoming, and he wanted to appear heroic to the voters. Thus, Scruggs had to resort to a negative inducement.

On January 20, Patterson passed an ultimatum to his friend Danny Cupit, who was Hood's advisor—failure to drop the criminal proceedings would result in Scruggs holding a press conference. At this, many high-ranking officials, including U.S. Senate Majority Leader Trent Lott (R-Miss.)—who is Scruggs' brother-in-law—would proclaim that a settlement had been reached and only Hood's recalcitrance stood between the policyholders and millions of dollars.

Two days thence, Hood drove from Jackson to Memphis, Tennessee for a meeting with top State Farm executives. Hood, aware that Scruggs' press conference would extinguish his chance at reelection, had caved in to the psychopolitical pressure. His individual interest in retaining his position prevailed over his official duty—bringing criminals such as these executives to justice.

To save face, and perhaps his self-respect, the attorney general proposed an agreement whereby he would drop the criminal proceedings only if State Farm agreed to reimburse the state's expenses in the matter and set up a mechanism to process unresolved claims. In the eyes of the executives their own freedom was much more important than other people's money and they cheerfully accepted the terms.

Patterson and Balducci dropped by Scruggs' office in March. Near the conclusion of the resultant meeting, Patterson suggested Scruggs hire his young partner, who was a licensed attorney, on another matter. A lawyer named Johnny Jones had been a partner in Scruggs' Katrina Group venture. Jones had pending against Scruggs a lawsuit to collect what he believed was his share of the State Farm settlement. Patterson asserted that Balducci was like a son to Judge Henry Lackey, who was officiating the matter, and may be able to favorably influence the judge. Scruggs acquiesced to an attempt at this but insisted Balducci do nothing that traverses onto unlawful territory.

Balducci scheduled an appointment to meet with the judge, who, in fact, had been his mentor. After a considerable amount of small talk, the former broached the subject of the Jones lawsuit. He opined that his friends in the Scruggs Katrina Group were being treated unfairly and suggested justice could best be served by dismissing the less viable claims via summary judgement, then directing the stronger ones to binding arbitration. He stated that if the judge granted this personal favor it would place him, Balducci, in good standing with Scruggs. In return, he would employ the judge in his consulting firm upon retirement from the bench. The employment would be in an "of counsel" capacity, meaning Lackey would occasionally represent the firm in litigation.

The judge, all the same, held deeply rooted animosity for Scruggs. The latter was handsome, wealthy, renowned, and had for years been using his talents to manipulate government officials. Balducci was not formally affiliated with Scruggs' firm and had taken it upon himself to initiate the meeting. Thus, Lackey could've merely told his protégé that he was an ethical judge and could not accept the offer. It was his responsibility as a mentor to do so. Yet his personal jealousy of, and disdain for, Scruggs overrode any thoughts of loyalty or decency. This was his chance to take down a much more successful colleague.

Lackey contacted his old friend John Hailman who was chief of the criminal division at the U.S. Attorney's Oxford office. Hailman was receptive to the information but as he was nearing retirement brought his impending successor, Thomas Dawson, into the matter. A discussion with the FBI ensued and an agent fixed Lackey up with state-of-the-art recording equipment.

The judge vigorously pursued his objective—calling Balducci and setting up meetings where he tried to up the ante by asking Balducci to submit a proposed court order written to Scruggs' exact specifications. He also tried to put words indicating Scruggs was directing the meetings into the young attorney's mouth. Balducci, nonetheless, would only reply that Scruggs was generally aware of the meetings rather than their precise nature.

A few more phone calls and meetings followed, but Lackey's initial enthusiasm was waning. Most likely this was because the gravity of his action was finally sinking in. Not only was the judge assisting in the manufacture of a crime, he was also implicating his own protégé in it. He believed he'd done enough work on the matter, at any rate, and wanted to put it behind him.

The judge recused himself from the Jones-Scruggs suit in May. He then went into a state of seclusion, avoiding even his federal handlers. The latter, in spite of this, had their own agenda. They had targeted a high-profile lawyer and Assistant U.S. Attorney Dawson was about to ascend to division chief. He wanted to start his new position with an explosion—an airtight case against the illustrious King of Torts.

These were his thoughts:

> This is a case a prosecutor lives to bring to trial, an arena with spotlights and headlines. I will never again have the opportunity to challenge a defendant so famous and high-powered; to move from the shadows of an assistant prosecutor to the forefront of one of the biggest cases in memory.

Unconcerned with preventing crime and completely concerned with "spotlights and headlines" for himself, the glory-seeking prosecutor and his cohort would have to nudge Lackey. He needed to reconsider his reluctance to fabricate a crime.

The feds tracked the state judge down. In a fervent pep talk they reignited his contempt for Scruggs, prompting him to get back in the game. He revealed, "After talking with [federal officials] and realizing what a monster we were probably dealing with, and the lives he had probably destroyed and the young lawyers whose lives and families he had destroyed, I agreed to get back in it."

Lackey reappointed himself to the Jones-Scruggs case and again aggressively pursued his target. Balducci, in Lackey's words, had been avoiding contact "because he realizes he crossed the line." But crossing a line proved no deterrent for Lackey, who finally reached the young lawyer and repeatedly requested payment for signing the order Scruggs desired. In one meeting the judge tried to finagle Balducci into explicitly admitting Scruggs was aware money was being exchanged for judicial consideration. Balducci finally responded, "He's not even involved at that level, judge. Doesn't want to be. Doesn't need to be."

As it became clear to the vainglorious prosecutor and jealous judge that Scruggs really wasn't aware of what was transpiring between Balducci and his mentor, they decided to try another approach. The feds apprehended the young attorney and coerced him into working against Scruggs.

If he were to receive any leniency for his crimes, the feds asserted, he would have to establish a direct connection between the famous lawyer and payment for a judicial favor.

Scruggs had paid Balducci $40,000, believing the money was for consulting fees to help with jury selection, when it actually went to the judge. For behind the scenes, Lackey had been lying to his protégé, claiming he was in financial trouble and in need of money. The government decided Balducci had to ask Scruggs for an additional $10,000, but this time specify its true purpose.

Balducci, wearing a wire, showed up at Scruggs' office on November 1, 2007, requesting to meet with the firm's principal. The young lawyer showed him a proposed order on the Jones' case and Scruggs suggested only a few grammatical changes. Balducci then stated that Judge Lackey had become "a little bit nervous with that last filing by [opposing counsel] Grady [Tollison] because he thinks they've made a decent argument." He continued, "He's gonna do this, but he thinks he's a little more exposed on the facts and law than he was before, and did I think you would do a little something else, you know, about ten or so more?" With the realization of what Balducci had been up to suddenly dawning on him, Scruggs paused. But his thinking was quickly interrupted by an incoming phone call. When Scruggs hung up, Balducci quickly returned to the matter at hand. "Do you want me to cover that or not?"

His thoughts scattered, Scruggs again hesitated. "Because I've already taken care of everything," Balducci pressed. Scruggs finally groaned in resignation, "I'll take care of it."

By the end of the month the King of Torts was under indictment.

On June 27, 2008, he was sentenced to sixty months in the federal Bureau of Prisons for conspiring to bribe Judge Lackey.

As he had helped government officials further their self-interests by breaking a case he helped create, Balducci was only assessed with twenty-four months. His business partner Steve Patterson received the same.

The Government was well aware all of the defendants had been led into their crimes and in a March 2009 meeting with Scruggs, Assistant U.S. Attorney Bob Norman actually admitted this. Scruggs could only reply, "We tried to tell you that." The fact is it didn't even matter. Only the advancement of self-interests mattered.

Steve Patterson, who had just been released from prison, aptly summed up the situation in a Christmas letter sent to friends in December 2010:

> These prosecutions were, in part, politically motivated and largely media driven ... a senior state court judge was a self-described close friend and mentor to ... an ambitious, young attorney who was a business associate of mine at the time. At the urging of the government, the judge exploited his special relationship by artfully feigning personal and financial distress and then begging for money, all in order to callously ensnare and eventually corrupt his admiring protégé. You see, at its inception, the sole interest of the government's scheme was to use the judge's young friend to bring down its target, a nationally known and politically active trial attorney who was already swamped by controversy.

Patterson, while no saint himself, errs insofar as what he ascribes only "in part" to political motivations are almost entirely personal motivations meant to advance the self-interests of an angry, envious state judge and vain, opportunistic federal law enforcement officials.

Note: Quotes in this Case in Point are found in Curtis Wilkie's book *The Fall of the House of Zeus*—a thorough account of the Scruggs affair.

♦ ♦ ♦ ♦ ♦

The visions of the founding fathers have, over the vast expanses of time, evaporated into the ethereal mists. America no longer embodies any great principles. Its government is nothing more than the sum of the men of whom it is comprised, acting not in the furtherance of some noble purpose, but in the furtherance of their own purpose. Thus, while it may be the role of the government to serve the people, it is the goal of the government official to serve the self.

Instinctive behavioral patterns operate automatically. A significant amount of the mind's social information processing also occurs outside of one's awareness. A person, therefore, seldom fully knows the reasons for his own behavior. In fact, most of the events that transpire in his daily life are the result not of active intentions and deliberate decisions, but of operations put into place by complex processes over which the self has no control. (We'll examine this topic further in Chapter Fourteen). This doesn't stop man from convincing himself the reasons for his behavior and the events taking place in his life are attributable to causes other than their actual ones.

That is, of course, true of government officials. Few could feel any genuine measure of satisfaction if they objectively saw their profession as self-serving and themselves as tyrants who feed their own egos and fatten their own wallets, often harming the very society they are supposed to be serving. Such officials, in reality, spend their entire careers behaving in a way that furthers their self-interests, retire, then eventually die quite satisfied believing they were doing the right thing and making the world a better place.

In the twilight of his life, former U.S. president George H. W. Bush contentedly explained the decision he'd made to expel Iraqi forces from Kuwait in 1991:

> As president, I worried about the loss of innocent life; but I knew in my heart of hearts we could not let a tyrant with the fourth largest army in the world take over his neighbor by force. So, to put it this way: no one wants war against Iraq, but no one wants Iraq to get more terrifying weapons of mass destruction. We must do all we can to work for peace and then, if we have to, fight to protect the lives of the innocents in Iraq.

People need to feel good about themselves; a phenomenon known to psychologists as *ego motivation*. As part of this they must view themselves as virtuous. Thus, they strive to avoid the uncomfortable feelings of anxiety, shame, and guilt that arise following the violation of a personal standard. The anticipation of these feelings, in fact, constrains a great deal of antisocial conduct that would otherwise occur. Further, to avoid incongruence between words and beliefs, they subconsciously adjust their beliefs to cohere with their words. They also heavily engage in *confirmation bias*, searching harder for evidence that confirms, rather than refutes, decisions they have already made.

Bush may have believed in his "heart of hearts" (a popular Christian expression) exactly what he asserted, but the actual reasons he governed as he did are likely found elsewhere. First among these is the ultra-competitive personal nature of an executive who felt it was his duty to protect what he perceived to be his country's interests in the Middle East. If Iraq's invasion of Kuwait was not checked, a force hostile to the U.S. would've controlled 20 percent of the planet's oil reserves. Further, if Saddam's army continued marching into the militarily weak Saudi Arabia, which holds the world's largest oil reserve, this would've increased to 45 percent. And as FDR presciently observed during World War II, "The defense of Saudi Arabia is vital to the defense of the United States."

It is also highly likely Bush himself, a once powerful oil tycoon, and his family, still retained investments that would've been negatively affected were Saddam's action not reversed.

Finally, vanity should never be overlooked as a factor of self-fulfillment. This is especially true in the case of people who seek out positions in the spotlight. They love to perform and, when acting in their public role, want as many adoring eyes on them as possible. Prior to August 1990, Bush was viewed as something of a wishy-washy president. But his confident televised declaration that Iraq's invasion of Kuwait "will not stand" was the exact turning point in this perception. As he followed through, his actions were reinforced by the praise of his military and the American people. (This contributed to another factor—the cascading military-political momentum toward war that can render conflict inevitable.) He savored his newfound glamourous image as an ass kicking commander-in-chief (and certainly also the reelection prospects this appeared to carry).

Bush may have retained some concern about the "loss of innocent life" but as he knocked on heaven's door, he was perfectly at peace with the fact that his decision sent 148 U.S. soldiers and 20,000 Iraqi soldiers to their graves. In fact, after his own son, former President George W. Bush, gave the order that commenced Operation Iraqi Freedom, the elder Bush assured the younger, "It is right to worry about the loss of innocent life, be it Iraqi or American. But you have done that which you had to do."

Looking back on his own presidency from retirement, George W. Bush opined, "when I look in the mirror at home tonight, I will have no regrets about what I see . . . I did what I believed was in the best interests of our country." The junior Bush's decision to carry out a second Gulf war sent an additional 4,530 Americans and 100,000 Iraqis to the boneyard. But like the 41st U.S. president, the 43rd will also die at peace under comforting misperceptions.

A man generally considered to be the most evil human to have lived in modern times, Adolf Hitler, went to his final resting place understanding he had invested his life in an attempt to fulfill "the work Christ had begun but could not finish" and that upon death he would feel "only a liberation from anxieties, sleepless nights, and a severe nervous disease." He clarified, "It is only a fraction of a second; then one is released from all that and has one's rest and eternal peace."

Several of Hitler's former officers were sentenced to death by the Nuremberg courts in 1947 for violating the human rights of their prisoners of war. As these men stood on the scaffolds, nooses tightly fastened around their necks, each defended his career on the basis he was acting not in his own best interests, but in the best interests of his nation. And each perished believing exactly that.

Chapter Three

Fallible Officials

> The present social and political forces that bring leaders
> to power do not necessarily assure a wise selection.
> — Jerome D. Frank, M.D., Ph.D.

First Case in Point

John Dillinger was feeling the heat in the spring of 1934. He and his gang had successfully robbed the First National Bank in Mason City, Iowa, but it had been messy. Both Dillinger and one of his men, John Hamilton, had been injured in an exchange of gunfire with the police and Dillinger found it necessary to use twenty hostages to secure a getaway. The gangsters had committed enough offenses to assure they, if caught, would never see daylight again.

Two weeks later federal agents surrounded Dillinger and his moll (girlfriend) Billie Frechette at a boarding house in St. Paul, Minnesota. While Frechette stalled them at the door, gang member Homer Van Meter coincidentally ascended the stairs on his way to the room. As soon as he noticed the officers, he drew his pistol and fled. The agents pursued Van Meter, which gave Dillinger the opportunity to rush the hallway and open fire. He and Billie then scurried down a rear staircase as the agents returned fire. The gangster was hit in the leg but made it to his car which was parked in the back. Slamming it into reverse he sped backwards through the alley and finally onto a city street where he escaped.

The gang remained at large but needed a quiet out-of-the-way resort where they could unwind and let the heat dissipate. Their leader thus selected the Little Bohemian Lodge located in the pastoral woods of Spider Lake, Wisconsin.

The outlaws and their molls spent the first few days of their vacation in peaceful relaxation. But with this motley crew at the top of the FBI's Most Wanted list, the resort owner and his wife became suspicious that these guests could be the ones sought. They called the authorities.

FBI director J. Edgar Hoover was a shrewd, calculating man. Knowing exactly what makes people tick, he temped Melvin Purvis, special agent in charge (SAIC) of the Chicago office, "Get me Dillinger and the world is yours." To achieve this objective Purvis assembled, under his direction, a multi-agency team of law enforcement officers. They would strike on the night of Sunday, April 22, 1934.

As the "G-men" snuck up to the resort, Purvis' plan immediately went awry. Dogs spotted the posse and erupted into a barking frenzy that alerted the entire compound uninvited visitors had arrived. Three men exited their cabins and crept into the darkness to investigate. Purvis assumed they were gangsters and when the confused men failed to obey his command to halt, issued an order to open fire. All three fell in a barrage of bullets. One later died of his injuries.

Most of the Dillinger gang was staying in a single cabin and fled through a window. They then hiked along a previously determined escape route which ran along the lake shore and into the woods. Purvis' posse vainly fired into the lower floor of the cabin unaware the expected quarry had already departed.

A single important member of the gang had, nevertheless, rented his own cottage as he was enjoying a rare reunion with his wife. He heard the commotion, stormed out, and quickly exchanged fire with Purvis. One of his bullets whizzed by the SAIC's head—missing its target only by inches. The gangster then raced into the woods and attempted to navigate himself to safety. When he came upon a clearing he was pleasantly greeted by an empty parked car whose keys were still in the ignition. Climbing in, he reached for the keys, but before he could even start the engine bright rapidly approaching headlights confronted him.

Purvis had sent Deputy Constable Carl Christensen along with Special Agents J.C. Newman and Carter Braem to call for reinforcements, but they had noticed the suspicious activity and decided to engage it. When they stopped their vehicle in front of the suspect's prospective getaway car, they figured he would merely give himself up. Instead, he jumped out, pointed his pistols at the cops and shouted, "Alright, get out of the car!"

Braem refused, haughtily responding, "We're federal agents."

The bandit was unmoved by this and countered, "I know who you are! I also know you bastards wear bulletproof vests, so I'll give it to you high and low!"

Before they could draw their firearms he unloaded his two .45 automatics into the three cops. He then dragged their bodies out, dropped them on the ground, and sped off in Christensen's car. These unfortunate lawmen, completely unaware of what they were getting themselves into, had no idea that on this very night they would run headfirst into Dillinger's number one gunman, the notorious cop killer Lester "Baby Face" Nelson.

Purvis apprehended zero gangsters that night. His raid had, however, produced one dead officer, one dead civilian, and two seriously wounded of each. For the three men the posse had gunned down at the raid's commencement turned out to be innocent lodge guests. One was a gas station manager, another a cook, and the third a civilian corps camp specialist. Director Hoover himself was publicly condemned for the bungled foray and angry citizens increased the pressure by circulating a petition demanding Purvis' suspension from duty. Comedian Will Rogers aptly summed up public opinion by joking that there was only one way the feds would take down Dillinger—"[He] is going to accidentally get with some innocent bystanders sometime, then he will get shot."

The desperate Purvis needed to save face. And to do so he actually staged Dillinger's death in a dramatic public display outside Chicago's Biograph Theatre on the evening of July 22, 1934. As a man departed the cinema with a beautiful woman on each arm, FBI agents ordered him to raise his hands. He did not comply; opting instead to flee toward an alley while reaching into his pocket. Agents then opened fire—killing him instantly. The dead man turned out to be a small-time street thug who had been set up. His name was James Lawrence. The real Dillinger had already undergone a great deal of plastic surgery and slid comfortably into retirement. He had no incentive to contest his supposed death.

Purvis was eventually fired by Hoover amid questionable circumstances.

On February 29, 1960 the disgruntled former SAIC of the Chicago office sunk his hand into his pocket and drew his automatic a final time. He then rested it against his own head and squeezed the trigger. It was the same pistol he'd used to stalk Dillinger and another infamous bank robber known as Pretty Boy Floyd.

> Many of those who run [for a high office] crave superficial celebrity. They are hollow people who have no principles and simply want to be elected.
> __ Bertram S. Brown, M.D.
> Psychiatrist to Washington's Top
> Bureaucrats

People often believe government officials are so knowledgeable and powerful they can do no wrong and cannot be brought down. In fact, until the modern era, when the English government overburdened the people, it was blamed on the royal advisors as the monarch himself was thought to be beyond reproach. The opinions of authority figures in both the public and private sectors are, in the present day as well, often accepted as credible merely on the basis of their professions or fame. People will even change strongly held opinions when they encounter a contrary position from a source they consider authoritative. Overly confident in their seats of power, these authorities tend to believe themselves to be invulnerable as well.

Officials who work in law enforcement make their money off the flaws and miscalculations of their fellow men. And just as your missteps may have been, or may be, the crowning achievements of their careers, theirs can be yours. Avenging your exploitation provides a feeling of pure exhilaration—a dual rush of power and justice. Many times have I savored the glow of ecstasy as I requite the exact official who wronged me. He cannot mentally process it. It is not in the order of things. The hunted has become the hunter. The tail is wagging the dog.

If you're not yet convinced how common it is for those in positions of authority to make errors, of which you can seize ahold, perhaps you will find the following persuasive. First, we'll examine brief historical anecdotes, then we'll undertake investigations that are more comprehensive.

> The original antibiotic, Penicillin, had, by the early 1960s, proven effective in treating infections of every variety of the staphylococcus virus. Thus, believing the war against microbes was over and man had prevailed, U.S. Surgeon General William Stewart declared, "The time has come to close the book on infectious diseases. We have basically wiped out infections in the United States."

> From 1929 to 1933, Folger Brown, postmaster general under Herbert Hoover, badly abused his authority under the Watres Act: eliminating competitive bidding for airmail contractors and malforming the aviation industry, whose income was reliant on this business. His successor, James Farley, who was appointed by FDR, determined Brown's non-competitive awarding of contracts had cost the taxpayers over $46 million. This finding came in 1934 at the height of the Great Depression and FDR, believing the disclosure to be a huge blow to the already low confidence in both business and government, immediately reacted. The first term president issued an executive order voiding all existing contracts and directing the U.S. Army Air Corps to devise a system to transport airmail using military planes and Army pilots. He allowed only ten days for this to take effect.
> Celebrity aviator Charles Lindbergh immediately foresaw the implications of the president's rash decision and sent a telegram to the White House. The "Lone Eagle" warned FDR that he would be supplanting the world's finest aircraft and pilots with inferior ones and the

latter would be accustomed to neither the routes nor nighttime flying. This, said he, was a prescription for calamity.

The arrogant president dismissed the expert aviator's prediction as a publicity plot by one whose pockets were being stuffed by the airlines that had previously been carrying the mail.

In the first week of operations, five Army pilots were killed in accidents, upon which night flying was cancelled and the use of airplanes to transport mail abbreviated. By the second month of operations, twelve pilots had been killed. The pilots, it turned out, were unfamiliar with the routes and the nuances of flying at night and in adverse weather conditions; exactly as Lindbergh had predicted. The famous aviation figure Eddie Rickenbacker declared via the *New York Times* that FDR's new system was tantamount to "legalized murder."

FDR turned back to the private airlines, giving them three months to prepare contract bids. He never admitted to error or conceded Lindbergh had been right.

Mirabeau Lamar was elected president of the Republic of Texas in 1838. He entered the office with a deep-rooted desire to transform his nation of farmers and ranchers into a great empire of merchants and traders. A key component in this involved expanding south and west to partake of customs desired from the lucrative goods exchange that took place between Santa Fe and Missouri. He thus needed to claim the Mexican territory (now belonging to New Mexico) and integrate it into his nation. To this end he conceived the Santa Fe expedition.

On June 20, 1841, he launched an army of only 320 men to convince the people of Santa Fe to accept a proposal of annexation. He believed they would cheerfully accept this offer to become citizens of his "glorious" land. After a one thousand mile hike the exhausted army arrived in October, only to discover the people of Santa Fe understandably had no interest in becoming Texans. Lamar's men were quickly overtaken by the Mexican army after which they were marched all the way to Mexico City and imprisoned.

Back in Austin, Congress censured Texas' president. Antonio Lopez Santa Anna, president of Mexico, was, however, not so easily placated. The following year he sent troops to San Antonio to subdue and occupy Texas' first city. Texas launched a counter-offensive that drove the Mexican soldiers out. But as they departed, the Mexicans took 60 hostages with them. The Texans then pressed deeply into Mexico where they were overpowered by the Mexican army. The unlucky Texans were tied, blindfolded, and executed by a firing squad. The known cost of President Lamar's mistake was 539 imprisoned Texans, 17 dead ones, and the reprimand of Congress.

In the late 1800s, a top executive of the Standard Oil Company, which owned 90 percent of America's oil supply, stated with absolute certainty that no natural reserves of oil existed west of the Mississippi River.

The rings used to seal sections of the space shuttle Challenger's booster rockets lost elasticity in cold weather. Engineers at NASA and the contractor who manufactured the rings were aware of this and documented it profusely in internal reports and memos to high level officials in the mid-1980s. These officials, however, were not proficient in technology and supposedly failed to comprehend the simple concept. They approved the Challenger's launch on a frigid January day in 1986.

The rings, contracting stiffly in the cold air, failed to seal the adjacent components and shortly after takeoff this set off an explosion which destroyed the shuttle, killing all seven astronauts onboard.

Emails sounding the alarm that foam insulation debris could damage the spacecraft Columbia had been circulated around NASA in late 2002 and early 2003. None supposedly reached the desk of NASA chief Sean O'Keefe. Thus, at a high-level meeting in January 2003 an engineer voiced his concern over the matter. The manager in charge of the meeting, devoid of experience in science and technology, replied that such debris wouldn't be an issue. The other participants fell in line, and she abruptly terminated the discussion. NASA officials, it seems, had learned nothing since 1986.

Days later, Columbia disintegrated as it reentered Earth's atmosphere, killing all the astronauts onboard. The disaster was attributed to damage caused by foam insulation debris.

In a March 2003 Congressional hearing U.S. House Representative Anthony Weiner (D-NY) was among the many who lambasted O'Keefe for incompetence. Weiner charged, "I read this stuff before you did. That's crazy!"

In June 2011 Representative Anthony Weiner resigned his seat in Congress after a woman publicized a picture he'd sent her of his penis via Twitter. In a similar but unrelated matter, he pled guilty to distributing obscene material to minors in May 2017. He was sentenced to 21 months in prison.

U.S. Representative Michele Bachmann (R-MN) launched her campaign for the 2012 presidential election from Waterloo, Iowa. When addressing the people of the small city she declared, "John Wayne was from Waterloo. That's the spirit I have too!" She succeeded only in demonstrating her ignorance and embarrassing her audience as it was not the actor John Wayne who was from that city, but serial murderer John Wayne Gacy.

The U.S. Department of State, ultra-confident in its clairvoyance, proclaimed in its November 27, 1941 special assessment report, "Were it a matter of placing bets, the undersigned would give odds of five-to-one that the United States and Japan will not be at war on or before December 15 . . . [we] would wager even money that the United States and Japan will not be at war on or before March!" Ten days after this bold proclamation, Japan attacked the U.S. Naval Base at Pearl Harbor, Hawaii.

At a January 1989 lunch, King Hussein of Jordan comforted an American general who was concerned about Iraq's intentions following a cease fire in the lengthy Iran-Iraq war. Said the king, "Don't worry about the Iraqis. They are war weary and have no aggressive intentions toward their Arab brothers." The following year Iraq invaded Kuwait and, continuing the faulty predictions, Colin Powell, chairman of the Joint Chiefs of Staff asserted, "I don't see us going to war over Kuwait."

The FBI issued a warning to its allies at the Joint Terrorism Task Force, which includes U.S. Capitol Police, on January 5, 2021. Intelligence agents in the Bureau's Norfolk, Virginia office who had been monitoring electronic communications by "right wing extremists" determined a domestic attack at the capitol was likely the next day during the session in which Congress would certify Joe Biden's electoral college victory. Exact quotes urging violence, that were extracted from the intercepted messages, were included in the warning. On January 6, radical supporters of President Donald Trump stormed the capitol building. Five people, including a Capitol Police officer, were killed. The Capitol Police chief later asserted he had asked the sergeants of arms of both the House and Senate for permission to request the National Guard be placed on standby, but the sergeants replied that they weren't "comfortable with the optics" of this and denied the request.

On April 2, 1917, U.S. President Woodrow Wilson told Congress, "Wonderful and heartening things . . . have been happening within the last few weeks in Russia." Six months later the changes of which Wilson spoke would conclude with communists seizing control of that country and maintaining it for the next 72 years.

> Iran is not in a revolutionary or even a prerevolutionary situation.
> – The. U.S. Central Intelligence Agency six months before the Shah was overthrown (1978).

> FBI investigations confirm domestic and international terrorist groups operating within the U.S. but do not suggest evidence of plans to target domestic aviation.
> – FBI and FAA report to Congress, December 2000.

> I believe al Qaeda is the greatest threat to the country.
> – "Lame duck" president Bill Clinton.
> I have to disagree with you there. The greatest threat is Iraq.
> – President-Elect George W. Bush

> I'm 43 years old . . . I'm not going to die in office.
> – JFK (1960)

♦ ♦ ♦ ♦ ♦

It's one thing to display confidence in your bearing in order to convince others you cannot be unfairly exploited and your system of beliefs is worthwhile. It's quite another to hold to this assurance in an unrealistic manner. In Chapter 13 we will examine the first. Now we examine the last.

A primary cause of mistakes by authority figures is a mentality psychologists have labeled *overconfidence*. This can be simply defined as a falsely inflated faith in one's ability.

In a series of studies that took place from 1993 until 2005 the researcher Philip Tetlock invited academic and government figures who were accepted as masters of political science and world affairs to predict the political futures of three nations—Canada, Russia, and South Africa. The authorities who asserted an 80 percent confidence in their estimates only turned out to be correct half as many times. Yet, when confronted with the fact that the present reality was not what they had foreseen, not one admitted to error. Instead, each defended his prediction with many reasons why, while not exact, it was close enough.

Many criminal justice "experts" (criminologists, political scientists, pundits, etc.) in the late 1980s and early 1990s predicted the rate of violent crime would soon skyrocket to astonishing levels. It had already risen 80 percent since 1975 and this was the number one topic of the national news at the time. When this crime rate instead plummeted toward the middle of the 90s, both the public and the "experts" who had misled them were dumbfounded. Several crime forecasters remained in a state of denial for years, sticking with their predictions and insisting the worst was yet to come. When they could no longer hide from reality, they began issuing a number of excuses. The most prominent of these came from a criminologist named James A. Fox who had authored an essay on the matter for U.S. Attorney General Janet Reno in 1995. Fox defended his prognosis of a violent crime "bloodbath" by saying it was merely an overstatement meant to capture the public's attention. He refused to apologize for using "alarmist terms," but clarified "I never said there would be blood flowing in the streets," as if any significant difference existed between that and the "bloodbath" he did forecast.

While the firmness of one's conviction helps persuade, confidence is no indication of competence. So, if you recognize an assertive official making a number of significant mistakes, he is not as talented as he, or you, may believe.

Nothing can be more intolerable than to admit to yourself your own errors.
— *Ludwig Van Beethoven*

Several factors contribute to overconfidence in these authority figures. The first is an inclination to interpret events in a self-centered and optimistic manner. (Academics refer to the former as *egocentrism* and the latter as *positive illusions* but as they, like many of the other biases, interact and cascade I tend to think of them as a single bias.) It is difficult for leaders to foresee their cherished ideas and endeavors concluding in disaster. Thus they form a mindset in which flaws in their plans either don't exist or aren't serious enough to necessitate corrective action or abortion of the plan.

Secondly, one who is deficient in aptitude or fitness often cannot see the unsuitability of her goals. This *incompetence* feeds overconfidence. Again, one of the key indicators a decision maker is unqualified is a history of executing ineffective schemes. And while the firmness of one's convictions helps persuade, there is no direct relationship between confidence and competence. (This is to say, you should use confidence to convince others, but don't let them use it to convince you or allow your own unwarranted confidence to fool yourself.)

The remaining elements are less intuitive and require analysis in greater detail.

A notion scientifically defined as *groupthink* is often guilty of distorting decision making processes in organizational environments. In other words, it takes place among multiple minds instead of inside just one.

Leaders, like the general population from which they arise, tend to surround themselves with like-minded people. This is best noticed after one is inaugurated into an executive office and replaces the cabinet of his predecessor with those who generally share his world view.

There is an informal American custom obliging cabinet officials to submit their resignation letters upon the inauguration of an executive who did not appoint them, giving the new executive the option of accepting it or keeping them onboard. Most cabinet officials would love to hold onto their positions of power, even under a new boss. And occasionally, as we will see in the next Case, executives retain officials appointed by predecessors if they are of the same political party. However, they rarely retain officials of a different one. Note: Sam Houston, the first president of the Republic of Texas, appointed both political allies and adversaries to his cabinet. But he did not appoint opponents because he had any interest in their advice. He did this so he could monitor and control them. That is, it was purely a self-interested political power tactic. U.S. President George W. Bush kept on his predecessor's CIA director, yet he also did this of an ulterior political motive. He said: "Retaining Bill Clinton's CIA director would send a message of continuity and show that I considered the agency beyond the reach of politics."

The historian Authur M. Schlesinger, Jr. observed "Irreverence irritates leaders, but it is their salvation. Unquestioning submission corrupts leaders and demands followers." By and large, this is correct. Whether they realize it or not, what most leaders *want* is people who will rationalize and carry out what they would like, or have already decided, to do. Nonetheless, what they *need* are devils' advocates to give them honest contrary opinions that will suppress their exaggerated confidence in decisions that will fail.

Irvin Janis, who first formally recognized the mentality, described groupthink as, "The mode of thinking that persons engage in when concurrence seeking becomes so dominant in a cohesive in-group that it tends to override realistic appraisals of alternative courses of action." It is most likely to arise when three key elements are in place: 1) a friendly cohesive group, 2) a distinct separation from groups with competing ideas, and 3) an assertive leader who reveals the decision he favors. According to some insiders groupthink was the impetus behind Operation Iraqi Freedom—America's second war against Iraq which began in 2003. President George W. Bush's advisors, including high-ranking intelligence officials, believed Bush had already decided to depose Saddam Hussein and the war was a foregone conclusion. As they didn't want to be on the bureaucratic bad side of a losing argument, they supplied Bush advice that supported the position they believed he had already taken, thus pushing him into a decision he may not have otherwise made.

In 1926, the German physicist Werner Heisenberg discovered subatomic particles change their behavior when observed. This makes it impossible to know all of a particle's characteristics. For example, a scientist can measure its location or its momentum, but cannot with a high degree of accuracy determine both. This is because the very act of measuring one property unavoidably interferes with the behavior of the other. People, like subatomic particles, change their behavior when they know they are being observed. And this is especially true where those to whom they are accountable, and, with whom they compare themselves, are concerned.

People look to other people for cues on how to behave. A group composed of people against whom an individual evaluates his conduct is known as a *reference group*. A certain mindset overtakes those gathered in such a unit. Nobody wants to be the odd man out. Conformity reigns. Social scientist Gustave Le Bon noted people mentally transform into "primitive beings"—shedding both their character and willpower when they assimilate into a crowd. Correlatively, they attain a feeling of overwhelming group strength. They become receptive to the suggestions of persuasive leaders and bypass their usual inhibitions, adapting their behavior to that of the group.

Another major cause of mistakes within organizations is attributable to the self-interest bias we have already examined.

People tend to act in a manner they perceive to be in accord with their best interests. And when acting within an organization this is likely to follow the *incentives* by which one's leaders motivate him. In our opening Case, J. Edgar Hoover inspired SAIC Purvis to act as he did by offering the SAIC "the world." Hoover added no stipulations demanding Dillinger's rights be observed or innocent civilians' safety assured in making the arrest. And thus a single motivation propelled the agent.

One may reason that when an individual works to advance his own interests the interests of his broader group benefit as well, but we have seen this is not always the case. To the contrary, conflicts often inhere between the interests of the two. To prevent individuals from making these types of mistakes leaders must, therefore, assiduously align individual interests with those of the organization. If subordinates have been incented only to focus on a single goal, leaders cannot expect them to consider greater institutional or societal ones in pursuit of it.

Nobody savors the experience of encountering information that disproves the rectitude of his decisions or cherished beliefs. In fact, it is impossible for normal mentally healthy people to hold beliefs that are truly incompatible. If one attempts to integrate into his belief system an idea that is at odds with an existing one, he will find himself in an unbearable mental conflict psychologists call *cognitive dissonance*. To remedy these unpleasant feelings, the human mind, operating below the level of consciousness, tends to ignore or dismiss information that clashes with that already believed. It further inclines to seek, construe, prefer, and recollect information in a manner that affirms preexisting beliefs. This propensity is known as *confirmation bias,* and it is another key factor contributing to overconfidence.

Scientists have imputed five distinct effects, as defined below, to confirmation bias.

1. *Attitude polarization* occurs as people who are exposed to the same information allow their differing views to become more extreme;

2. *Belief perseverance* takes place when evidence that shows a belief false fails to change it;

3. The *irrational primacy effect* is a preference for evidence initially, rather than recently, encountered;

4. An *illusory correlation* is in operation when factors or circumstances are falsely associated.

5. *Self Verification* occurs as people pursue friendships with those who strengthen their self-image.

These effects are most common when 1) people have a substantial investment in, or commitment to, a belief, 2) emotionally charged issues are involved, and/or 3) they are trying to reach a desired result.

Erroneous decisions made under confirmation bias have been found in many facets of human activity. It is the reason why the "experts" in Tetlock's experiment refused to accept the flaws in their predictions, and it factored into plenty of the mistakes made by authority figures in the incidents we have already examined and will yet examine.

While the aforesaid contribute to decisions, other elements do as well. These include personal feelings and the pressures induced by limited resources such as money, time, energy, and the patience to consider a matter before arriving at a decision. Thus, although I've never come across anything in political science, anthropology, sociology, or psychology textbooks diagnosing it as a specific cause of mistakes, I am convinced based on decades of observing authority figures and acting as one myself, there is another key cause of their many errors: they fail to adequately consider the possible results of their decisions before they reach them. The powerful are busy. They have large duties at hand and cannot get caught up in details. Therefore, they execute quick *intuitive judgements* and deal with the consequences later.

Seventh Federal Court of Appeals Judge Richard Posner conducted a lengthy study into the mental processes used by American judges to arrive at their decisions and in 2010 published his conclusions. Predominant among them: "Judges rely heavily on intuition and also on emotion, both as shaping intuition and as an independent influence on decision making. As a result, judges are not fully conscious of the beliefs that determine their judicial votes." Eighth Federal Court of Appeals Judge Richard Arnold provided evidence for this when he admitted that in one session his three-judge panel decided the outcome of over 50 important cases in a mere 2 hours. This averages less than 3 minutes each. (The court then left it to others, such as interns, to rationalize the decisions.)

In 1971, the chief of General Electric's Human Resources Department wrote of soon-to-be CEO/Chairman Jack Welch: "He . . . tends to over rely on his quick mind and intuition rather than on solid homework and staff assistance in getting into and out of complex situations."

Billionaire entrepreneur Elon Musk is known for his risky, intuitive, impulsive decisions, but nonetheless takes great pride in his way of doing things. "I've shot myself in the foot so often I ought to buy some Kevlar boots," he philosophized.

Legendary WW II General George S. Patton based his military strategies entirely on an intuitive feel for what he should do, rather than on any type of intellectual assessment. In the same vein his peer Douglas MacArthur dismissed the scientifically derived advice of his staff, opting instead for his own intuitive feel, in formulating a strategy for the Battle of Inchon (South Korea 1950).

I was the IT supervisor over the Business Division of a Chicago-based company in the late 1990s. I and the heads of various other departments formed what was called the Platform Committee. We met once per week in a conference room on the top floor of the company's skyscraper. The committee held three basic factions: The Unix people, the Novell people, and the Microsoft people. I was in the latter group. Week after week each sect presented a detailed analysis of the technological, functional, or business justifications for its preferred platform. The lengthy analyses, over the months, failed to change a single position and at the final meeting each faction voted for the platform where its interests were vested. (This is confirmation bias based on self-interest.) I excused myself from the meeting and found the vice president of Operations in his office. I explained that, as expected, we were deadlocked and needed a decision. He replied, "What do you think is the best platform?" I asserted, "Microsoft is the market leader and dictates the direction technology is taking. Unix and Novell both have rapidly diminishing market shares and I see no benefit to investing in obsolescing technologies." We marched over to the conference room. He interrupted the meeting and stated my opinion as if it were his own in declaring his final decision. This man hadn't attended a single Platform Committee meeting and I doubt he'd heard from any of the other factions. As a business executive he probably had some knowledge Microsoft was a leading software company, but I believe he simply made a snap decision based upon my 10 seconds of testimony. He'd promoted me months earlier in the same cursory fashion. (I had stepped into his office to ask who would be replacing my recently departed direct boss and he offered me the position on the spot. It was the first time I'd spoken to him.)

For better or for worse, the powerful almost always arrive at decisions by this sort of intuitive reasoning. And once they've done so they plow forward convinced they've chosen the right path.

One may claim his decision was based on empirical evidence, statistical analyses, expert opinions, etc. and those may, in fact, have influenced it, but you can be sure that he applied his own intuitive interpretation of them in arriving at a conclusion. In my situation above, had the pillar of a competing faction made it to the vice president's office and confidently justified his preference in a way an executive can understand and appreciate, that executive probably would've made a decision that would've led him to the unemployment line.

Second Case in Point

In August 1943 William Bullitt, U.S. ambassador to the U.S.S.R., learned his president, Franklin D. Roosevelt, was planning an alliance with the Soviet Union. The gravely concerned Bullitt cabled the White House from Moscow on the 17th. In his memo he warned the president that Soviet leader Joseph Stalin could not be trusted because the two nations retained inherent conflicts of interests. Inter alia, he cautioned, "Stalin's aim is to spread the power of communists to the end of the earth." Roosevelt, nevertheless, was convinced the obverse nations would arise from World War II as unlikely allies. His thinking muddled by a preconceived dream, FDR replied to the cable, "I just have a hunch that Stalin is not that kind of man. He won't try to annex anything and will work with me for a world of democracy and peace." Firm in his conviction, he concluded, "It's my responsibility and not yours and I'm going to play my hunch."

And play his hunch he did. Roosevelt and his ally, Winston Churchill—Prime Minister of Great Britain, met with Marshal Stalin at the secret Yalta conference in February 1945. There, the three leaders came to multifarious agreements, mostly concerning the territory taken away from Nazi Germany. The brilliant Yale educated Averell Harriman, whom FDR recruited to replace Bullitt as ambassador, quickly learned of the developments and came to the same conclusion as his predecessor. He had already noticed the Soviet government becoming increasingly duplicitous and wasted no time in voicing these concerns to the president.

At Yalta, Stalin had agreed to allow Poland, which it had recently usurped from Germany, to hold free democratic elections in one month's time. This did not happen. To the contrary, he installed a regime designed to do nothing more than carry out his agenda, then barred all U.S. officials from entering Poland. Next, he denied American officials admittance into Hungary when he had promised FDR to allow the U.S. to build military bases there. In Romania, Stalin's men overthrew the king and set up Soviet approved leadership. Finally, Russia's dictator, believing the U.S. was using its air force to assist the anti-communist resistance, grounded U.S. planes in all of the territories he controlled.

The exasperated Roosevelt was resting at his vacation home in Warm Springs, Georgia in early April, when he finally conceded his obvious error to a confidant, "I guess Averell is right. We can't do business with Stalin. He has broken every one of the promises he made at Yalta." The wise ambassador summed up the situation: "We now have ample proof that the Soviet government views all matters from the standpoint of their own selfish interests."

Anticipated by all top U.S. officials but himself, less than two weeks later FDR died of cerebral hemorrhage. And a very oblivious and nervous vice president, Harry Truman, ascended to the top job.

♦ ♦ ♦ ♦ ♦

At the time Roosevelt made the enormous mistake he was serving his fourth term as president. He was, nonetheless, held in such high regard by the American people they selected him in a Gallop poll as the greatest man in world history; surpassing Caesar, Napoleon, Washington, and Jesus

Christ. This sort of adoration (which is evidence of the power of perception) is fuel of the highest octane for overconfidence and the president, declining in physical and mental health, already possessed far too much faith in his abilities. He had formed an intuitive belief, a "hunch" in his own words, that Stalin was trustworthy. Notwithstanding testimony to the contrary by his ambassadors who had actually lived in Russia and interfaced with its leader, the president refused to reconsider his position. (This is confirmation bias.) Stalin was an expert in power politics. He had found FDR's weakness and exploited it to his country's profit.

Roosevelt, to his credit, did finally recognize the inescapable truth: his intuitive judgment that Stalin was trustworthy was erroneous. This is rare, especially among men of such gargantuan egos. Still, he never publicly admitted this and there is no evidence he regretted any of his other blunders. Even as the curtains were drawing on his time in this world he refused to accept the fact that this was so and thus saw no need to include his vice president in his inner circle. FDR expired on April 12, 1945, and Truman entered the presidency knowing no more about the state of world affairs than the average man on the street. Responsibility for the new president's ignorance, of course, rested squarely on the shoulders of the "greatest man in world history." Note: President Eisenhower did learn from FDR's final mistake. When he realized his own health was failing, he faced the reality and began keeping his own vice president, Richard Nixon, well informed; including him in National Security Council meetings and allowing him to represent the U.S. in conferences with world leaders.

Third Case In Point

In mid-1945, Fleet Admiral William Leahy was America's highest ranking military officer. He had graduated from the prestigious U.S. Naval Academy and served as the White House Chief of Staff under FDR. He was now serving in that role under President Truman. In his own mind, with such a stature, he was immune to error.

The admiral was aware of developments in the Manhattan District project where scientists under the direction of Robert Oppenheimer were manufacturing the first atomic weapons. He was also well aware that President Truman was planning to deploy them to conclude the war with Japan, a matter he was inclined to question.

Leahy was on board the U.S.S. Augusta en route to Potsdam, Germany where Truman would confer with Stalin and Winston Churchill when he vented his disbelief in the nuclear project. "This is the biggest fool thing we have ever done. The bomb will never go off and I speak as an expert in explosives." He was so convinced of this that after the conference he repeated his skepticism to none other than King George VI of England. Quoth the admiral, "I do not think it will be as effective as expected. It sounds like a professor's dream to me!"

The U.S. and Great Britain jointly issued the Potsdam Declaration on July 27, 1945. It warned Japan to surrender unconditionally or face "prompt and utter destruction." Japan's prime minister Kantaro Suzuki notified the world the following day that his country was rejecting the terms: "[Japan] does not consider the declaration of great importance. Thus, we must ignore it." The Japanese immediately followed through with action demonstrating their resolve by sending a legion of Kamikaze pilots to destroy U.S. warships. One succeeded in sinking the *USS Callaghan* while 47 sailors were onboard.

On August 5, a U.S. Army B-29 bomber plummeted the atomic bomb named "Little Boy" onto Hiroshima, Japan, instantly obliterating the city. Another B-29 leveled Nagasaki on the 8th when it dispatched the 10,800 lb. A-bomb "Fatman." Two days thence Japan announced it was now "ready to accept the terms enumerated in the joint declaration, which was issued at Potsdam . . ."

♦ ♦ ♦ ♦ ♦

In an amazing, yet typical, demonstration of confirmation bias, Leahy refused to admit he had been wrong even after the war: "It is my opinion that the use of this barbarous weapon at Hiroshima and Nagasaki was of no material assistance in our war against Japan. The Japanese were already defeated and ready to surrender because of the effective blockade and successful bombing with conventional weapons." This, of course, completely disregards the reality of Japan's position prior to America's deployment of the nuclear weapons. The admiral further ignored the fact that the "conventional weapons" of which he spoke (including incendiary bombs) had burned alive men, women, and children in Tokyo's residential area in adding a moral argument he hadn't previously raised: "My own feeling is that, in being the first to use it, we had adopted an ethical standard common to the barbarians of the Dark Ages. I was taught not to make war in that fashion and that wars cannot be won by destroying women and children."

Fourth Case in Point

A promising, young lieutenant commander in the Japanese Navy was appointed to the post of naval attaché for his country's Washington embassy in 1918. His name was Isoroku Yamamoto. Japan had little direct involvement in the first world war but was allied with Great Britain, which was allied with the U.S. Japan, thus, was a friend of a friend and U.S. Department of State officials welcomed the bright, sociable officer to live and work in the nation's capitol. Arriving that summer, Yamamoto quickly fell in love with the America of the early twentieth century. He immersed himself in a study of its business practices, culture, and customs. The administration at Harvard University also adored the young officer and admitted him as a student the following year. He would be accompanied by about seventy other Japanese students on the campus.

Yamamoto enjoyed unwinding from his busy work and study schedule by playing all types of table games. He particularly enjoyed Bridge and often pitted his own wits against those of U.S. naval officers in contests that lasted late into the night. As he built up his skills in competitive strategizing, he became unbeatable. But no matter, these were only games. America's officials and citizens loved Yamamoto and he loved them back. Or so it seemed.

During his time in the land of the once free, Yamamoto discovered advances it was making in industrial technology; especially in regard to aviation. And it was at this time he came to believe the most important ship of the future would be the one that carries airplanes.

Yamamoto briefly returned to his homeland in 1921 where he attended the Navy Command School, and, upon completion of the curriculum, continued visiting western nations, mostly the U.S. In a 1924 sojourn he toured America's Naval War College and was so inspired by what he discovered he changed his specialty from gunnery to naval aviation. From 1925 until 1927 Yamamoto was stationed in Washington, which gave him the opportunity to continue closely observing and learning about America's political and military systems. He did so by attending diplomatic affairs, studying the operational methods of Navy planes and ships, and becoming intimately acquainted with naval officers, all the way up to the secretary himself.

The Japanese officer returned to his homeland on a steadier basis in the late 1920s upon which he began using the knowledge he acquired to design the world's most advanced air force. With his Harvard education and familiarity with the U.S. Navy he was quickly escalated in station, rank, and honor. In 1928, he started a hands-on exploration of naval aviation when he was given the captaincy of a moderately gunned warship, then an aircraft carrier. He was appointed chief of the Navy aeronautical department's technical section two years later and began working closely with the heavy equipment manufacturer Mitsubishi to develop faster, more versatile combat planes. After this, he implemented refinements to carriers, modified pilots' training programs, and formed a land-based air force to work in conjunction with the sea-based group.

Yamamoto was promoted to commander of the 1st Air Division in 1933. He quickly broke with the Navy's tradition of deploying single independent aircraft carriers, reasoning instead that pooling them together and coordinating their operations would produce a more powerful assault. The following year he was elevated to vice admiral, then dispatched to a disarmament conference where he would represent his nation.

The Japanese people despised the 5-5-3 shipbuilding treaty which held that Japan could only build 3 warships for every 5 constructed in Great Britain and the U.S. At the conference Yamamoto emphatically rejected it and for doing so was given a hero's welcome upon returning home. This culminated in an escort to the imperial palace where he was congratulated by Emperor Hirohito himself. While his decision sparked a new ambiance of self-assurance in Japan, it also dramatically intensified tensions with the U.S. and Great Britain.

The admiral still retained a secret affinity for America, and he was skeptical of Japan's ability to defeat the behemoth if the two engaged on opposite sides, but he was beginning to be swept up in the patriotic euphoria which accompanied his nation's hatred of the U.S. He was also starting to acquiesce to the fact that war appeared unavoidable.

Yamamoto took a position at the prestigious Navy ministry where he increased the production of aircraft carriers and in 1936 the emperor advanced him to the position of vice minister of the Navy. He was given complete command over the combined fleet three years later and was promoted to full admiral in 1940.

Admiral Yamamoto's attack armada which consisted of 28 ships, 3 submarines, and hundreds of bombers, fighters, and torpedo planes arrived at a predetermined oceanic location 200 miles north of Hawaii on December 7, 1941. At 8:00 a.m. sharp the Japanese force began raining bullets, bombs, and planes on the U.S. fleet at the Pearl Harbor Navy base. After only two hours of unilateral bombardment, Yamamoto's force wrecked or sunk 8 battleships and 3 destroyers. Over 300 U.S. planes were demolished, and 5 airfields laid waste. 1,178 American men were wounded and 2,403 killed.

♦ ♦ ♦ ♦ ♦

The U.S. paid a heavy price for its officials' aberrant judgment in befriending and educating the Japanese naval officer. And it was only the beginning.

In April 1943 U.S. Navy cryptanalysts and translators read a message which contained the schedule for a flight he would be taking from an airbase in Rabaul to an airfield on the island of Bougainville. Shortly thereafter, Yamamoto directly paid the price for his own mistake in directly challenging a more powerful country: a U.S. Army Air Force crew shot down his plane en route.

The Japanese officer had long retained well-founded reservations about the prudency of engaging the U.S. in combat and would've been wise not to waiver. Instead, he succumbed to the pressures of groupthink and, caught in a swell of national patriotism, relented to making the strongest possible effort to win an unwinnable war. Yet, killing the admiral as a pure act of revenge rather than a strategic maneuver also proved to be a misjudgment on the part of they who ordered it: Navy secretary Frank Knox and Admiral Chester Nimitz. For unbeknownst to them, by the time they decided to assassinate Yamamoto, his reservations had transformed into a full conviction that Japan could never win the war. And he was the only leader with both the power and credibility to convince his nation of this. Historians believe he was about to take the position that Japan should negotiate a peaceful settlement that would've ended the war about two years earlier and saved countless U.S. lives. The ambush was also a mistake as it revealed the Americans were monitoring Japanese military transmissions and had deciphered the communications code.

Lost in the intoxicating effects of groupthink, influential Japanese, specifically Emperor Hirohito, Prime Minister Hideki Tojo, and the Japanese nationalists who supported them, erred most catastrophically in starting an unnecessary war against a nation that was larger, more technologically advanced and possessed greater natural resources. (It was intended to be a short and limited war to undermine America's opposition to Japan's expansion in Asia.) U.S. Major General Curtis LeMay wiped out enormous sections of Tokyo, slaughtering over 100,000 citizens in his merciless fire-bombing campaign of March 1945. An estimated 230,000 citizens were extinguished by the atomic bombs delivered in Hiroshima and Nagasaki the following month. Over 1.4 million Japanese lost their lives as a result of the war against America.

♦ ♦ ♦ ♦ ♦

Ever failing to learn from the mistakes of their predecessors, U.S. officials in the 1980s provided funds, intelligence information, and military training to Arab Afghans resisting the December 1979 Soviet invasion of Afghanistan. One of the leaders of the resistance was a promising young fighter named Osama bin Laden.

♦ ♦ ♦ ♦ ♦

The question is no longer whether government officials err, but when and how significant the errors will be. It appears some are barely capable of making effective decisions and we find it astonishing they even rose to power in the first place. Certainly, we've seen they are just as fallible as the rest of us and there is no reason to hold them in awe. For we can exploit their human frailties just as they would like to exploit, or perhaps already have exploited, ours.

> *Many great empires of the past have collapsed because their leaders did not have the good judgment to use their powers wisely.*
> *— Francis Wilcox, Dean of the Johns Hopkins School of Advanced International Studies*

SECTION II: STRATEGIES

Chapter Four

The Realm of Psychopolitical Warfare

> The only people who will no longer
> see war are the dead.
> — Plato

One takes a casual stroll through the countryside on a glorious summer day and savors the wonder of it all: birds chirping, frogs croaking, shimmery blue-green dragonflies lightly hovering above a glistening stream. Somewhere off in the distance lonely wolves howl. The spectator takes in a deep breath, believing he is beholding a system of perfect harmony. What he actually observes, however, is something much more pernicious. Not all of the birds are of the social variety. Some are issuing warnings that they are strong, and peers would do well to stay out of their particular piece of the biotope. Others are social and are rebuking those inferior in rank for improper conduct. Solitary frogs, like solitary birds, are advising peers not to enter their domain. A few of the bolder dragonflies who are too close to the surface of the water are about to be devoured by hungry fish lurking below. And the wolves, out stalking rabbits and squirrels, caution competing packs to stay out of their hunting grounds.

The world does not sing in perfect harmony. To the contrary, it reverberates with brash dissonance—the struggle for survival. As you read these words it is taking place all around us. It is real. It is frightening. And it is often very destructive.

The physical and mental components that have evolved to survive and succeed in this incessant state of belligerence have become so advanced there should no longer be any question as to whether they have been produced by the species preserving function of Natural Selection. Geological evidence reveals an astonishing developmental contest between offensive and defensive implements of war: one species evolves a superior assaultive mechanism, and its adversary derives an equally adroit method of countering it.

An unavoidable aspect of life, conflict arises when the essential interests of organisms collide. This discord can be *intra*specific, which is usually motivated by the aggression drive (e.g., the solitary birds and frogs contending with peers for space), or *inter*specific which is usually offensively motivated by the hunger drive and defensively by the flight/fear drive (e.g., the wolves stalking rabbits and squirrels).

Regardless of the species, victory in an *intra*specific dispute can be recognized by several methods. They include the decision of a neutral party, a party's admission of inferiority, or a party's realization he has neutralized his opponent. The most potent way of imposing one's will on an adversary is to make him suffer until he relents, or if he persists in his resistance, simply destroy him.

FORCING THE GOVERNMENT'S HAND

Conflicts within the most advanced species are frequent. Many of these arise among peers—a woman likes to hold boisterous, disorderly parties, but her next-door neighbor savors the solace of the night; a man develops an infatuation with a young married woman whose husband is not interested in sharing her affections; an intoxicated motorist on her way home from the tavern sideswipes a bicyclist on his way home from college classes.

Conflicts also arise between people and their superiors—a manager fails to show appreciation for his hard laboring worker, a landlord fails to address his tenant's maintenance issues. Perhaps the most intractable problems of all arise when our interests collide with those who have the greatest power over us. Yet, their thoughts seem so elevated, their lives so perfect, their authority so supreme, how could we ever hope to prevail?

The historian Robert K. Massie once observed, "The cat does not negotiate with the mouse" and this has some relevance to the dynamics of power and predation even among the highest species. It is possible to move potent officials to carry out our wishes, but it is unlikely to come easily. To convince them to do what you want at least one of two relevant conditions must be met:

(1) They perceive you are able to help them.
(2) They perceive you are able to hurt them.

Those who can do one have some power. Those who can do both have great power. Those who can do neither, like the mouse caught between the cat's paws, may as well say goodbye.

People throughout the history of organized societies have employed a variety of methods to achieve their desired political ends. Some failed. Some prevailed. Most transformed to fit the social conditions of ever evolving or devolving societies. It is difficult to classify these because there is so much crossover involved. There are nonetheless distinctions as well. We thus categorize them as follows:

I. Elective Avenues

Voting is one of the most common procedures employed by those who live in democratic societies to influence the direction their government takes. As a typical citizen is busy with his family and career, he lacks the time and energy required to personally throw down with the system. Therefore, every so often he simply drives to his local precinct and casts his ballot for the candidate he believes will best advance his interests. In some cases, an elector then votes for the favored regional candidate. In others, a majority of individual votes directly determines the outcome. The former method, known as the electoral college, is, for example, used in selecting a U.S. president. The latter, known as the popular vote, can be used to propose a new law (initiative), approve or reject a proposed law (referendum), remove elected officials (recall), or elect local officials.

Once sworn into office the elected official appoints subordinates, such as underbosses, to carry out his will and that of they who placed him in office.

Examples in action:

a. The people of Great Britain stunned the world in 1945 by choosing Labor Party candidate Clement Atlee over the illustrious incumbent Winston Churchill to serve as their prime minister.

Atlee literally replaced Churchill in the middle of the Potsdam Conference in which the leaders of Britain, the USSR, and the U.S. were determining the future of post war Europe. The world was less astonished when, in 1951, Churchill reattained the office.

b. Elected legislators in the American Federalist party, aware their group was about to lose power in the executive and legislative branches as a result of the 1800 election, voted to pass the *Judiciary Act of 1801* to protect their interests and the interests of those who had voted them into office. The act conceived the federal circuit courts of appeals, and, with them, sixteen new judgeships. Lame duck President John Adams consequently attempted to fill these slots with Federalist judges who would carry out the will of the party and its supporters. Eminent among the nominees were William Marbury and John Marshall.

II. Legal Remedies

Lawsuits wherein the plaintiff seeks an order compelling officials to perform or abstain from performing a specified act are common in republics. *Injunctions* and *writs of mandamus* are the primary mechanisms by which this may be accomplished. A procedure known as *declaratory judgment*, which can be considered an authoritative definition of the party's legal rights and responsibilities, may also be used. This, however, does not directly mandate any specific acts.

Examples in action:

a. In the 1800 election, the majority passed the power in the U.S. Government from the Federalist party to the Republican party. Naturally, the Republicans opposed the aforesaid *Judiciary Act of 1801* and the Federalist nominees it produced.

When he was denied his commission by the administration of newly inaugurated president Thomas Jefferson, William Marbury petitioned the Supreme Court for relief. In the landmark case *Marbury v. Madison*, the judicial nominee sought a court order compelling Jefferson's secretary of state, James Madison, to deliver to Marbury the commission papers. Chief Justice John Marshall answered by upbraiding Madison for interfering with the process of law but held that the Court lacked the jurisdiction to grant the relief sought.

b. In 2006 sex offenders in a New Jersey prison petitioned a U.S. District Court to order state officials to protect them from assaults at the hands of other inmates. The officials protested that their type of case necessitates class certification and the relief sought was beyond the breadth of that required to resolve the issue. The court ruled the evidence demonstrated that all plaintiffs were at risk by the nature of their convictions, the case did not necessitate class certification, and further, the relief sought was "not overly broad because it applies to a particular group of inmates who are likely to be targeted by other state inmates and it does not apply to any inmates [who] are unlikely to be targeted." The court issued the requested injunction. (See *Riley v. Brown*, 2006 U.S. Dist Lexis 41273.)

III. Collective Actions, Social Movements, and Civil Disobedience

These usually begin as people of common interests cohere to rectify a perceived injustice. The initial idea typically involves a peaceful protest conducted in a highly visible manner to show the "powers that be" a strong, unified block opposes the oppression. Among the forms found in this class are sit-downs, strikes, marches, and riots.

Examples in action:

a. A revolt arose in 1794 when the U.S. Congress passed an excise tax on whiskey. Farmers in western Pennsylvania, whose grain was distilled into that liquor, believed the tax would make the end product more expensive, thus, reducing its sales and their income. They organized and objected by yelling, displaying signs, and even dumping tar and feathers on federal officials, whom they subsequently paraded through the streets. President Washington suppressed the uprising with a force of 15,000 U.S. soldiers.

b. Occupy Wall Street began in New York City in September 2011 as a collective action to protest financial inequities and the influence of money in politics. But it quickly gained momentum and transformed into the larger Occupy social movement which held general anti-establishment protests in major cities throughout the U.S., and eventually in other countries. It reached its apex in 2014, then slowly fizzled out.

IV. Militant Actions

When people threaten violence or actually employ it as a means to achieve political ends, such an activity takes place. This is the most drastic method of provoking change and is therefore mostly used by radical individuals and groups. Forms include the *coup de' etat*, assassination, domestic terrorism, and various other paramilitary assaults.

Examples in action:

a. In the previous chapter we learned that in 1958, a regime of Iraqi army officers led by General Abdul Karim Qasim assassinated King Faysal II and took control of the country's government. As so often happens, however, the events of history have a way of repeating themselves. For only five years later another group of army officers, with support of the Baath party, assassinated Qasim and seized power. The group then named two of its own to the top offices. Abdul Salam Arif became president and Ahmad Hasan al-Bakr prime minister. Both were army officers. Later the same year, Arif actually used the military to remove supportive Baath party illuminati from power so he could fully control the government. When he died in 1966, his brother assumed the presidency. Two years thence al-Bakr overthrew the second Arif and returned control to the elite Baath party. Al-Bakr became president, and, under his regime, a party leader and government official named Saddam Hussein attained great influence.

b. Following General Robert E. Lee's 1865 surrender of the Confederacy, Union General Philip Sheridan, commander of the subdistrict of Texas, used the threat of military force to replace the state's conservative governor, James Throckmorton, with the moderate Elisha Pease. Sheridan did so because he found the incumbent governor hostile to the federal government's Reconstruction policies, while Pease was amenable to them. This act of questionable legality literally reversed the result of the previous year's election in which Throckmorton defeated Pease.

V. Psychopolitcal Manipulation

This occurs when an individual or group influences government officials to act in a way they would otherwise not. It is primarily achieved through the use of positive and/or negative inducements. But the form of engagement is often misunderstood. Lobbyists, special interest groups, business executives, and government officials themselves may practice it on a daily basis, while a typical member of the general public seldom does. It can take place before our eyes, but we may fail to recognize it because its methods tend to be insidious. It is, nonetheless, often carried out quietly behind the scenes and all we hear about is a surprising resignation, early "retirement," or abrupt policy change.

Examples in action:

a. A series of unusual farm animal deaths occurred in western U.S. states over the 1970s. It appeared the critters had been carefully killed with surgical instruments. Farmers and ranchers thus believed Satanic cults were responsible. Veterinarians were unable to determine the causes of the deaths, so local leaders quietly used political influence to compel federal agencies to assist. Both the FBI and ATF launched inquiries which were collectively named "Operation Animal Mutilation." After consulting scientists and forensic investigators, officials concluded the deaths were ascribable to natural causes and the postmortem condition to natural decomposition.

b. In February of 2021 the Texas Inmates Family Association (TIFA) succeeded in politically pressuring officials of the Texas Department of Criminal "Justice" to amend a policy enacted a year prior that banned inmates from receiving greeting cards. The supposed purpose of the ban was to prevent free people from sending in cards soaked with intoxicating "K2" chemicals. (In reality, nearly all K2 is transported into the prison system by crooked officers.) The amendment TIFA coerced allows inmates to receive plain single ply cards on predetermined dates, such as the weeks preceding a major holiday.[5]

c. When Peter Mayhew, the actor who played Chewbacca in the first film of the Star Wars series, attempted to carry a "light saber" aboard a 2012 Dallas flight, officials of the Transportation Safety Administration stopped him from doing so. This act may seem reasonable enough at first glance, but in considering that the saber is not an actual weapon and, further, that it doubles as a cane without which the large, crippled man cannot walk, it is not reasonable at all. As he sat in his wheelchair at the gate the frustrated actor decided moving quietly behind the scenes was not the best approach for his issue. Instead, he determined shedding plenty of light on the issue—by sending Twitter "Tweets" broadcasting news of the oppression to the world—would be more effective. What went around quickly came back around. Mayhew's fans took up his cause—humiliating the officials for their exaggerated security reaction. They were left with no choice but to reluctantly return the saber/cane. The actor summed up the situation, "The magic words to the TSA is (sic) not 'please' or 'thank you,' it's 'Twitter.'" More accurately stated, the magic method is psychopolitical coercion.

Having considered some of the more popular methods of influencing a desired political outcome, let's consider the viability and practicality of putting them to use.

Elections rally the loyalty of subjects in democratic societies by allowing them to participate in the functioning of their government. By and large they satisfy the citizenry. But this statement is qualified for good reasons. First, the voters are not always pleased with the candidates selected by the political parties and merely vote for the one they believe to be the lesser evil. Second, elections are zero-sum. Thus, while the majority of voters may be delighted after they propel their candidate to power, social and political opinions can be so polarized and elections so close that a very large minority can be left bitter after one. Third, the bizarre manner in which the electoral college translates the popular vote, conflated with the aforesaid close margin of victory in recent U.S.

---

[5] On August 6, 2023 the TDC "J" administration suddenly locked down the entire state prison system and banned all paper mail in favor of digitally scanned mail. This action, motivated by politics rather than pragmatism, was attributable to 18 drug related deaths earlier that summer. When all mail ceased, I, and an array of allies, used negative publicity, written notifications specifying the supposed rights and laws being violated, etc. to press the classification director and state executive director into carving an exception for business mail. While this did little to resolve the issue with personal mail, it fulfilled my main objective as completion of this book necessitated the receipt of paper mail from businesses. The policy was amended, effective November 6, 2023.

presidential elections (e.g. Bush v. Gore, Trump v. Biden), has called into question the very legitimacy of the process, leaving both sides unsatisfied. (Trump's surprising 2016 triumph over Hillary Clinton was such that even the victor had to encourage his supporters, telling them they would achieve a more complete conquest in the next election.) Further, even when the party succeeds in the installation of its preferred candidate, this is unlikely to automatically produce solutions to specific problems. For that, more action is needed.

The Greek philosopher Aristotle recognized the many flaws of the system and announced, "Democracy is corrupt rule by the majority, a dangerous form of mob rule." Famed American aviator Charles Lindburgh similarly concluded, "Democracy is an error of the brain." These two may have been correct.

The playing field is far from level in any legal action in which a governmental entity of any variety is a litigant. With a higher standard (beyond reasonable doubt) for a government agency to defeat individuals in criminal cases, but a lower standard (preponderance of the evidence) for individuals to defeat the government in civil cases, the government still wins 97-99.9 percent of all cases litigated against individuals. This is made possible by 1) broad judicial "discretion" to make judgments by personal choice rather than by rules, and 2) "deference" to these decisions by those ostensibly charged with reviewing such matters.

The lack of legal constraints and accountability on government officials in general, and judges in particular, has reached a point so extreme American law can no longer be said to exist. That which is often referred to as "the law" has become so broad, vague, elastic, and arbitrarily dependent on the people, rather than the conduct, involved, it no longer even fits the definition of law. For actual law requires a uniform set of substantive and procedural codes applicable to all similarly situated persons.

U.S. Supreme Court Justice Antonin Scalia (dec.) and federal Seventh Circuit Court of Appeals Judge Richard Posner (ret.) concede they who sit on the bench make decisions obversely to the prescribed order. Seldom applying conscious reasoning, they first make whatever decision personally satisfies them as subjective men rather than objective officials. According to Scalia they then, "scour the law for some authority to support that decision." Posner admits judges make decisions in a manner designed to "advance one's political goals," and to accomplish this, "judges have a tendency to report the facts in their opinions in such a way as to make them fit the legal conclusions smoothly." He later acknowledges some judges go so far to reach the desired conclusion they engage in "conscious falsification of facts."

The self-interest hierarchy applies to judges (to the extent they are even worthy of the title) the same as it does to everyone else. And judges tend to sympathize with government officials, whom they see as their own kind—members of the fraternity. Further, public officials constitute an enormous influential block of voting citizenry. The same cannot be said of an individual who sues them. Thus, if a citizen, like William Marbury, sues an official, like James Madison, with the expectation of a favorable ruling, that citizen will likely waste his time, energy, and finances. Elie Honig, former assistant U.S. attorney (SDNY) and director of New Jersey's Division of Criminal Justice, reports "The law . . . generally protects public officials from liability when acting in their official capacities. These cases almost always result in quick dismissals." (It took plenty of research for me to find a somewhat recent case where inmates prevailed over officials to use as an example for legal remedies, *Riley v. Brown*, ibid, but we also note the court assessed the officials with no financial damages.)

Even though an individual is nearly certain to obtain an unfavorable ruling, lawsuits can provide highly effective forums for citizens to air grievances and obliquely, rather than directly, resolve them. They can serve as ultrabright spotlights on corrupt officials who prefer to creep in the shadows.

Collective actions and social movements are good examples of those to which game theory refers as *non-zero sum* contests, as conflict is conflated with mutual dependence. These can be massive undertakings and while not inherently violent[6] when likeminded people gather, they incline to extremes. Further, because crowding elevates the proclivity toward aggressive behavior, when these likeminded types are packed together, they are even more apt to turn violent. Add an outgroup, such as counter protesters or police officers, and it is a recipe for disaster.

Occupy Wall Street well demonstrates the problems encountered with these methods. As we've already learned, it began as a collective action whose purpose was to protest economic inequalities and the influence of money in politics. When it transformed into the broader Occupy social movement, participants had to travel to the protest site only to discover their peers were grieving issues not in accord with their own. Nearly every cause of which one can conceive (e.g. a communistic society, higher minimum wages, better student aid packages, prison reform) was on the agenda of the participants.

A lack of consistent ideas, goals, and convictions helped propel the movement to its doom. As is typical, bloodshed, arrests, and collateral damage (mostly to property) coalesced into what the broader public perceived as moral inferiority. And this sealed the movement's fate.

To the contrary Mohandas Gandhi, a leader in the Indian National Congress, succeeded in obtaining greater political power and eventually complete independence from Great Britain through extensive use of nonviolent civil disobedience. Acts of protest included the boycott of British goods and the unlawful production of salt. This, however, was a revolt by a unified people of a common Hindu ethnic religious society (Muslims worked for independence separately) against an unpopular foreign government which could assert no claims to legitimate authority.

It is difficult to transform anger at an injustice into an effective collective action or social movement. Doing so necessitates a cohesive membership and the availability of scarce funds. Access to secretive communications networks may also be necessary lest opposing interests, such as political groups or law enforcement agencies, thwart the campaign in its inception. (In the early 1770s America's founders spoke the language of treason via underground networks, one of which became the U.S. Postal Service.) Again, the activists must also be perceived as adhering to the higher moral ground. This important element is often overlooked and when a group turns violent, its purpose can be undermined—especially when those who are uninvolved with the conflict are injured. Finally, to succeed, the opposed institution must already have been weakened (preferably by internal ideological division). Note: Rumors and gossip (Chapter Six) and propaganda (Chapter Seven) can be powerful tools to sew and exploit discord in enemy ranks.

When militant actions fail to provoke change, it is often attributable to the same reasons collective actions and social movements fail to do so. Additionally, the intentional use of unlawful violence can cause numerous issues, not the least of which is the undermining of the militant group's moral authority. Unless the plotters are high elites or military officers with loyal legions, there is

---

[6] A petition drive where signatures are gathered from a large number of people on a one-by-one basis is a good example of a collective action with little chance of turning violent.

little chance of success, especially against a strong government, and those who take the risk and fail are likely to end up imprisoned or dead.

Timothy McVeigh's 1995 destruction of the Murrah federal building illustrates the failure of a militant action. He may have succeeded in eliminating a number of tyrants and drawing some attention to the oppressive nature of the U.S. Government, but the collateral damage, including that to the very citizens (e.g., women and children) he sought to protect from government oppression, was so high it excoriated any moral authority he could've enjoyed. In the end he feigned acceptance of his death penalty, hoping to be viewed as a martyr. In the eyes of most he is only viewed as a domestic terrorist.

The goal of the Irish Republican Army (IRA) is to see North Ireland liberated from British rule and reunited with Ireland. The Palestine Liberation Organization (PLO) seeks a Palestinian state, independent of Israel, for non-Jewish Arabs. Both of these groups spent decades using paramilitant and terroristic methods to achieve these ends. And both failed. After considering the reasons for this, they found unlawful violence negatively affected their causes and have, accordingly, abandoned it. They now work to fulfill their goals through the exclusive use of political strategies. Note: The PLO should not be confused with Hamas, Hezbollah, or other groups that do employ violence.

Psychopolitical manipulation, which relies on the use of cunning rather than physical force, can be carried out legally or otherwise. It can produce adverse side effects, as described in the Prologue and Chapters Nine, Fourteen, and Fifteen, but this is true of any form of engagement. The likelihood of eventual success for the shrewd, experienced practitioner is high and the cost/benefit ratio tends to be favorable. This form of engagement is inherently nonviolent and can operate within existing social and political structures. The latter, in fact, is one of its most powerful features.

Using an enemy's own strength against him is part of the essential nature of the Japanese martial art called Aikido. And the same is true in our realm. Instead of using what little power we possess, we tap into overwhelming governmental power and redirect it against its own officials for our benefit. In doing this we often find creative approaches to dealing with stubborn officials to be much more fruitful than conventional ones. Paul Wright is now the director of the Human Rights Defense Center. But when he was incarcerated in the Washington state prison system, officials erected electric fences to prevent prisoner escapes. Wright knew this was dangerous and unnecessary and decided to do something about it. He researched the matter and instead of investing a large amount of time, money, and energy in an exasperating legal action, found a cheaper, easier solution that proved effective. Using the power of the federal government against the state, he wrote the U.S. Fish and Wildlife Service and explained how the fences violated the Migratory Bird Treaty Act of 1918. After investigating the matter, officials of the federal agency agreed. They ordered the state to remove the fences.

> If conventional thinking makes your mission impossible, then unconventional thinking is necessary.
>
> — Elon Musk

♦ ♦ ♦ ♦ ♦

Man has never created a type of weapon he has not used. He has also never created a weapon from which he has not developed some form of protection. Nuclear weapons have now existed for eighty years, however, and the primary shield against these is psychological. Yet, it has proven effective because it takes place on the most fundamental level.

Any nation that deploys small tactical nuclear weapons knows doing so could open a Pandora's box of uncontrollable escalation. And any superpower that launches more powerful nuclear missiles at another knows it will receive missiles back. This tenet, which Secretary of Defense Robert McNamara (term 1961-68) implied as *mutually assured destruction*, operates entirely on self-interests. And the fact that you are reading these words today testifies to its validity. Had Soviet leaders such as Leonid Brezhnev and Nikita Khrushchev not cared about their society, their families, and, most importantly, themselves, they would've already destroyed the United States.

> To be a successful soldier, you must know history. Read it objectively; dates, even minute details of tactics are useless. What you must know is how man reacts. Weapons change but the men who use them change not at all. To win battles you do not beat weapons, you beat the soul of every man.
>
> — General George S. Patton

The mind is the final battlefield. All disputes are ultimately resolved in this arena. Those who believe the fist is stronger than the psyche or the sword mightier than the pen misapprehend the true source of power. The brain constitutes only 2 percent of a human's body mass yet consumes 16 to 20 percent of the body's available energy. It uses up to 20 times as much energy as an equivalent mass of muscle tissue.

In prehistoric times man introduced the Dingo, a wild subspecies of the domestic dog, to Australia. Dingoes quickly recognized they were contending for prey against aboriginal carnivores such as the marsupial wolf and Tasmanian devil and a rare instance of violent interspecific competition for resources broke out. The native marsupials were both larger and physically stronger, but the dingoes were more intelligent and better organized. They also used fighting techniques of greater sophistication. Sharing no interests with their intellectually inferior competitors of differing species, the dingoes eradicated them. (When one has no interests in common with a rival, game theory defines the two as existing in a state of *total conflict*.)

Man, similarly, has not arisen to dominate all other species because he is physically the most powerful. Indeed, he controls beasts many times larger, stronger, and faster. He is, instead, master of the planet because he has the advantage of hands with which he can create (i.e., finger-thumb opposition) and a superior mind with which he can reason and strategize.

In 1732 Marshal de Saxe, who would command the French army during the War of Austrian Succession, opined that maneuvering is the essence of war, with combat to be undertaken as a last resort and even then only when prospects for victory appeared certain. The ancient Chinese military strategist Sun Tzu (ca 300 B.C.) held that one who can subdue his enemy without having to physically fight him has reached the pinnacle of the art. That being the case, the psychopolitical method captures the essence of war in its highest form of engagement.

PERSPECTIVES OF POWER

In the 1850s, Egypt began building a 100-mile-long artificial waterway in the northeastern corner of the country. It traversed the Isthmus of Suez—the narrow strip of land connecting Africa to Asia and would, accordingly, be named the Suez Canal. While Egyptian capitol and labor contributed to the project, a heavy infusion of French finances were also required.

The canal opened for business in 1869 and was heavily utilized in the ensuing years. But the Egyptian government had difficulty meeting the even heavier financial obligations involved and was forced to sell its shares in the canal to Great Britain. It could no longer even afford to operate the canal by 1876 and, a few years later, the French and British governments took over financial control.

Jamal al Abd al-Nasr, the leader of a military unit, seized control over the government of Egypt in the late 1940s. When the U.S. withdrew its offer to extend financial aid for an extensive irrigation project in 1956, al-Nasr nationalized the Suez Canal company and assumed control of its operations. Britain and France viewed this as an act of hostility because 1) it aggrandized al-Nasr who was attempting to form a coalition of Arab states to compete against non-Arab foreign powers and 2) they still retained substantial monetary investments in the canal.

Israel, a neighboring non-Arab country, believed al-Nasr's canal seizure provided the opportunity it needed to diminish the strength of a hostile neighbor who had been tampering with its frontier. The three countries—Britain, France, and Israel—thus reached a secret agreement to coalesce, invade Egypt, and overthrow al-Nasr.

In October 1956 Israel entered Egypt and advanced toward the Suez Canal. Britain and France assisted by dispatching ultimatums demanding Egypt withdraw from the canal zone. Al-Nasr refused, giving the two European countries the grounds necessary to enter and occupy part of that zone. Other nations, however, had interests of their own in the area. The Soviet Union sold arms to Egypt and the U.S. retained investments in Saudi oil fields. They recognized their own interests were threatened by the action of the Britain, France, Israel coalition and began exerting political pressure on it. The coalition, recognizing the reality, had no choice but to withdraw. While this was an embarrassment to the leaders of the three coalition countries, it was a tremendous political boost to al-Nasr throughout the Arab world.

We're generally raised to believe good and evil are absolute concepts. Those who think as we think and act as we act are the good guys. Those who think and act differently are part of an outgroup. They are the bad guys. In some people who never fully emerge from their cocoons, these beliefs solidify and remain until death. Other people broaden their perspectives, travel the world, and learn to see life through the eyes of other cultures. These people see reality much more clearly and come to understand good and evil are, in fact, relative. It's all a matter of perspective.

Think about the last meat you consumed. After devouring it you probably considered it a satisfactory meal. But have you ever paused to consider the perspective of the animal whose flesh satiated your hunger? If so, you safely presumed it preferred to live freely as long as possible rather than to be caged and killed so its corpse could serve as your nourishment. Thus, what was bad for it was good for you. Yet, had the balance of power been different and its life spared while your belly growled, this would've been good for it and bad for you.

Government officials and you may be on the same side. Perhaps you are one of them who is interested in learning more about how to increase or protect your power.[7] If not, you may be situated on the other side of the field and an official's perspective is not yours. For example, you may see yourself as a righteous freedom fighter and the official as a lying tyrant while she sees herself as an honorable public servant and you as an annoying scoundrel. You may see your cause as a noble mission to advance those who are oppressed while she sees it as the frivolous angst of a people whose plight is ascribable to their own irresponsible living.

We've already learned self-interest is the primary concern of man. But people have different ideas about what advances this. And this is true even at the workplace. Nonetheless, we know officials generally want what workers of other varieties want: career advancement, praise, respect, money, leisure time, the belief they perform their jobs well and, of course, power. Yet, as to the

---

[7] This book is not written with the intent of advancing the interests of tyrants. In fact, there are many types of people I would prefer not to purchase it. But it is a reality of the publishing industry that I cannot control this.

order in which the official values these, it varies on an individual basis. It has been my experience that law enforcement officials crave power and praise above all else. Many prison officials simply want to earn as much money as possible while doing as little work as possible. And while I consider sex to be more of a personal rather than professional motivation, plenty of male officials correctly believe greater success leads to more and better sex. (I can speak from experience, however, when I assert that following a heavy work, travel, and study schedule to achieve and sustain success can negatively impact and even eliminate the opportunities for such encounters.)

People are constantly evaluating information presented to them. You can say "this" all day long, but your listener is subconsciously processing it through a mental filter that interprets it according to her individual characteristics such as family background, life experiences, culture, ethnicity, sex, and unconscious preconceptions. Her filter may, therefore, translate your "this" into "that."

What you perceive to be in your best interests is unlikely to be what the official perceives to be in hers. This challenges you not to *tell*, but to *show*, her doing what you want somehow advances hers. In so doing you should keep in mind that high level officials possess neither the time nor the inclination to analyze voluminous or detailed information. With short attention spans and heavy demands on their time and energy, they are more receptive to general statements: concepts and comparisons summarizing that which is bulky or specific.

The crisis surrounding the Suez Canal is particularly interesting because it illustrates two fundamental elements of power politics. The first is that which we've just been discussing. Let's briefly review the relevant facts.

- British officials sought to protect Britain's investment in the canal and prevent an adversarial Arab coalition from forming.

- French officials sought to protect France's investment in the canal and prevent an adversarial Arab coalition from forming.

- Israeli officials wanted the opportunity to reduce the power of a hostile neighbor.

- Egypt's ruler desired to elevate his power and form an Arab coalition to compete against foreign powers (especially Israel).

- U.S. officials desired to protect American oil investments in the region.

- Soviet officials needed to secure their country's sale of weapons to Egypt.

We thus have six different nations with six different interests. Yet, Britain, France, and Israel had a common enemy and their interests intersected. It best served them to remove al-Nasr and their perspective was in accordance. The U.S. and USSR were not on friendly terms during this period, but they needed no alliance. Egypt was allied with neither, other than as a business partner with the Russians. While these latter three nations' individual interests were different, they also intersected. They were best served by al-Nasr remaining undisturbed by the coalition, and their perspective was in accordance. Now let's look at the second element. The Suez Canal conflict began at a regional level within Egypt and between that nation and Israel. But it quickly escalated, as such disputes often do, and caught the attention of European powers (Britain and France) which were looking to protect their interests in the region. When they allied with Israel and began acting as they perceived necessary, (a mistake caused, at least in part, by the egocentric reasoning we discussed in Chapter 3) this, in turn, attracted the attention of the two global superpowers. The U.S. and USSR believed the actions of the coalesced lesser powers would negatively impact their own interests, so they shut the coalition's operations down completely.

As in global theatres of operations, so in individual ones.

Rules of courtesy, and often procedure, require us to resolve problems by starting at the bottom of the command chain. If this is unsuccessful we may then work our way up. Rules of power, however, require the opposite. This is one facet of life where an old adage actually rings true: sh-t flows downhill.

The skilled psychopolitical warrior should constantly be looking to exploit discord in enemy ranks: finding its sources and maximizing the stress. To this end, if you're having trouble with a certain official it may be that his boss is as well. We've already learned tension frequently strains relationships adjacent in a hierarchy. The boss may welcome the opportunity for an alliance with you when it serves his interests. You should nonetheless be aware those employed in law enforcement agencies tend to already have in place protective in-group alliances. (I believe this is attributable to many coming from a military background where that culture prevails.) But most law enforcement agencies also have some sort of branch that, at least in theory, polices the police. It is often known as Internal Affairs or the Office of the Inspector General.

This isn't to say you can't exert pressure high in a law enforcement agency to obtain results. It is to say a police officer's peers are likely to protect him and his supervisors are less likely to discipline him. They may nonetheless proclaim he did not err and refuse to formally punish him while quietly implementing corrective action that shows the opposite. (I've seen this more times than I can count.)

My experience is that I usually have to go several levels higher than the targeted official to get the desired results. But sometimes, as we saw in the Prologue, one can go a level below the target and help a scheming subordinate bump off a boss so he can take his place. Whichever strategy you find appropriate, any disciplinary action will, in the end, flow down from above.

Those who sit high on the pyramid are high in the light. Their moral authority is crucial. And perception is paramount. They have the ability, and often the desire, to remove anyone who impedes their progress. Your job is to discover the targeted subordinate's misdeeds, pull them out of the shadows, portray them as hypocritical and evil, associate the target with the spotlight official, and then flaunt it all before the spotlight official, other spotlight officials, and the public.

In the Prologue we saw how I slowly fulfilled my goals by doing exactly that and in Chapter Nine we will see similar instances.

> We must face the truth that people have not yet been
> horrified by war to a sufficient extent to force them to
> go to any extent rather than to have another war.
> — JFK

Chapter Five

Mind Games

> Without a doubt psychological warfare has proved its
> right to a place of dignity in our military arsenal.
> — Dwight Eisenhower
> Five Star General

In the early twentieth century the Italian general Giulio Douhet published the seminal work *Il Commando del Aereo* (The Command of the Air). Therein he issued what is considered to be a primary principle of combat: "The form of any war . . . depends on the technical means of war available."

Every strategy of human warfare has as a central element an intent to maximize the strategist's strength while exploiting his enemy's weakness. One type does this directly by attempting to eliminate as many targets as is necessary (attrition); another indirectly by creating and exploiting points of vulnerability (maneuver). Conventional wars are nonetheless fought to a much greater extent in the realm of the physical—land, sea, and air. Our form can be carried out in any forum but is always resolved in that which lies between the ears. Here we need not concern ourselves in the same way with formations, lines of operation, armament, terrain, procurement, logistics, navigation, weather conditions, disease, and numerous other factors that are so crucial in conventional combat. It thus goes without saying that the "technical means" of which Douhet wrote are the least of our concerns.

In this chapter we will focus on understanding strategies that can be used to either compel the adversary to do as we wish, or, as is so often the case with degenerate American officials, prevent them from doing as they wish to us.

FORCING OBEDIENCE

It has been said that every man has his breaking point. Agents of power are, of course, aware of this and employ a number of methods to mentally debilitate their victims and ease the process of compliance. They have been utilized by some of the most infamous cult leaders in history, but those who have been criminally processed within U.S. territorial or maritime jurisdictions will likely recognize these as their own government employs them upon any perceived enemy—foreign or domestic. In the military context they fall under strategies known as *exhaustion*.

Torture

Inflicting physical and mental pain upon a recalcitrant victim to compel cooperation is an approach as old as time. Sadly, this remains in use in the modern day, even by nations fraudulently claiming to be leaders in human rights.

In 2005, U.S. officials kidnapped, drugged, then conveyed foreign terrorism suspects to American "safe houses" in third world countries where they were viciously tormented. Using what they euphemized as "enhanced interrogation techniques" American officials subjected their detainees to acts including: 1) anal probing, 2) confinement in small wooden boxes that contained insects, 3) threats their children would be murdered, 4) mock executions, 5) being hanged upside down, 6) electrical shocking and burning, 7) stabbings and mutilation, and 8) freezing. The methods employed in the witch hunts (14th-18th centuries) and Inquisition (13th-19th centuries) produced inauthentic confessions and this was no different in the terrorism torture of 2005.

Energy Depletion

The inducement of fatigue such as by overwork or sleep deprivation is a popular method of denying basic physical needs. In the first Gulf War (Desert Storm, 1991) the U.S. led coalition opened with relentless air bombing. While some of this constituted maneuvers designed by the brilliant but controversial Air Force colonel John Warden (*The Air Campaign: Planning for Combat*, 2000) to take out the power grid, communications infrastructure, supply lines, and possible WMD bunkers, many assaults were simply undertaken to tire the enemy. Commanding general H. Norman Schwarzkopf elucidated, "For the first 48 hours our objective was to give the Iraqis no rest. We wanted to maximize the shock that relentless bombing can produce . . . as our war planes shifted to the fiercest stage of the air campaign, I knew Saddam's soldiers were no longer getting much sleep in their bunkers or foxholes. Day and night our B52s, fighter bombers, and attack jets were pounding their positions along the front."

Exhausting Iraqi troops to break their will was so important it was a key factor in Schwarzkopf's decision as to when the ground war would be launched. "Assuming that our bombing has worn down the enemy to the extent we need," he explained, "the optimum time has always been the middle of February [1991]."

Removal From Home Base

Extracting a man from his residence and inserting him into a new environment is a "thought reform" technique known as *milieu control*. It is known to diminish vitality and incite depression. Totally isolating him reduces his ability to adapt to the new environment and can provoke psychosis.

As the distance he is transported from his home base increases his willingness to fight, and ability to do so effectively, decreases. For this reason, it is in the best interest of the predacious official to get his prey out of his comfort zone; especially in criminal proceedings (in which the suspect is theoretically presumed innocent). Bernard Kerik, former New York City police commissioner, affirms, "Any good investigator will tell you that you have about a 10 times greater chance for a resolution in your case if your target is in jail."

Cult leaders mandate new members leave their homes and join the group on its compound. Friends and family from one's old life are only allowed if they join the group and do the same. Cult members, like inmates, are given new associates and most contact with the outside world is severed.

Removal of Personal Property

Possessions are a major source of psychological security and, therefore, even the most extreme communistic countries have been unable to completely banish them. One of the initial acts performed on a new inmate is revealing in its intent—he is ordered to strip naked upon which all of his clothes and personal effects are removed. In so doing, the government strips him of an essential element of his identity—the apparel of his choice, which is reflective of his personal tastes and social standing. Next, of course, the government clothes him in its own garments which usually have the name of the captor emblazoned upon them. This shows the inmate he is, like the salves of yore, mere property; in this case the government's. Chuck Colson, special counsel to President Richard Nixon identified this as a "first step in the deindividualization process" and explained, "men stripped of dignity and self-worth are easier to control."

A classic mental manipulation tactic, some cult leaders practice this as well. New members are given new clothes identical to other members while the leader is clad in a manner that indicates 1) a relationship to the group, 2) that is superior. (This is the same in prison, where inmates are all dressed in a uniform of a distinct color and the officers are dressed in better uniforms of a different color.)

Anxiety

This can be induced by physical or psychological pressure. It is usually employed by an amalgam of the two. Government attorneys commonly agitate their targets, be they civilians or fellow officials who are political opponents, by charging criminal misconduct. (Female citizens have recently been doing similar by accusing all variety of men of sexual misconduct.)

Once an accusation is made it festers in the minds of the public. "Did he really do something so reprehensible?" It rambles in the mind of the accused. "What will those whose opinions I value believe? What will the powers that be do to me?" Some emphatically deny it, then when new evidence surfaces their credibility becomes more questionable. Allies abandon the accused, fearing for their own reputation. And this lack of support, especially for one whose power depends on it, induces tremendous distress.

To break the will of U.S. soldiers in the Vietnam war, the Vietcong successfully used a variety of strategically placed booby traps and mines which synthesized psychological sanctions of surprise, uncertainty, and frustration with the obvious physical ones. A group of soldiers would be walking about and one was maimed or killed in an instant. His peers then panicked and as they darted about in confusion more were hit. Needing instant revenge, they searched for enemy soldiers but found none, only more mines. Eventually patrols sent on night missions merely ventured out a few hundred yards from camp upon which they rested for the night. The next morning, they returned to camp, reporting that they'd fulfilled their mission, but found no Vietcong.

Predicaments

The master magician Gustav Kuhn aptly stated, "If you are given a choice, you will believe you have acted freely," when, in fact, nothing could be further from the truth. And some in the field believe this to be one of the darkest secrets of psychological warfare.

Working memory is the dimension of remembrance in which information is held for the duration of the time in which a problem is being resolved. But unfortunately, it is very limited. Further, we can only truly focus our attention on one object or matter at a time. For these reasons, we struggle to fully comprehend complex matters and often make flawed decisions. One of the ways law enforcement officials exploit these weaknesses is by forcing suspects in a common case into a conundrum known as *prisoner's dilemma*. Codefendants are booked into a jail, then separated. The interrogators trick them into believing the other has betrayed trust and testified. Neither suspect can be sure if this is true as they are unable to communicate, but the interrogators assure each that if he does testify he will be shown lenience. If not, they'll throw the book at him. (Only government attorneys can legally make sentencing agreements, but the interrogators don't mention this.)

Confessions are the number one means by which convictions are secured. Thus if each co-defendant refuses to testify, both will either go home free, or, in the worst case, be lightly punished in a plea bargain. But if one talks and the other doesn't, the talkative one will be lightly punished (or maybe even set free) while the quiet one is heavily sentenced. If both talk, they are likely to receive light to moderate punishment, but not as light as it would've been had both stayed silent. So, it appears to each he will be better off talking, yet if both do, they are both worse off than had neither done so. This is a ruthless approach (often combined with others) designed to exploit self-interest and overwhelm the suspects' ability to think clearly and arrive at rational decisions. (Due to space considerations, this is a concise description of prisoner's dilemma.)

Despair

When the mark has abandoned all confidence in himself or his cause, compliance is assured. In World War I, the allies used a propaganda campaign in which they dropped into German trenches pamphlets indicating Germany was losing the war. Some contained info that was correct. The remainder, such as notices of surrender purporting to issue from German authorities, was counterfeit. (As we will examine further in Chapters 6 and 7 conflation of an easily established fact with fiction is potent because the former serves as a credibility anchor for the latter.) The strategy was successful. Dispirited German troops, believing all was lost, fought less effectively and as they did so the fiction became reality. The nation was eventually compelled to agree to terms of surrender so oppressive they sparked the second world war.

While American law enforcement officials oppress their targets using the methods we've already examined, it only gets worse. As the case "progresses" they increase the pressure. (This is a military tactic we will see used *against* crooked officials in Chapter 15.) In so doing they employ an array of sinister devices such as: imposition of unreasonable bonds that cannot be met; placement of liens on houses and vehicles (e.g. *lis pendens*); the filing of motions to impose consecutive sentences on each count; threatening maximum sentences; public shaming, such as by the issuance of press releases revealing damning new evidence that, of course, blends truth with lies; the addition of new charges via superseding indictments; the addition of charges in other jurisdictions; and denial of recreation and access to a law library. The pressure is intensified to the point many inmates attempt to kill themselves. (Suicide is the #1 cause of death in U.S. jails.) Others take psychotropic medications so powerful they can barely comprehend what is taking place. Nearly all come to accept that resistance is futile and sign anything the government puts before them.

The Mind Scrub

Some of the aforementioned are conflated with other techniques to produce a form of conditioning known as *brainwashing* (or in the academic idiom as *coercive persuasion*). Invented in the twentieth century, it was successfully used by Korean communists to convert American prisoners of war into supporters of their cause. Consequently, these soldiers stayed among their former enemies after the conflict concluded. The process can produce an effect known as *Helsinki syndrome* where a prisoner comes to identify with his captors. (Another notable instance is found in the 1974-75 kidnapping case of Patti Hearst, daughter of newspaper publisher W.R. Hearst.)

Three basic phases are involved in this.

1. *Separation.* The victim must be removed from his societal reference groups: those against whom he compares his beliefs and behavior (e.g., family and friends). This is often facilitated via arrest, kidnapping, or psychological manipulation. Separation is crucial as it enables the authorities to deprive their victim of competing sources of information and other distracting sensory stimuli. (Censorship, therefore, is often practiced in jails, prisons, cults, and dictatorial countries.) It is also important as it gives the captors the exclusive ability to provide for their victim's wants and needs, rendering him totally dependent.

2. *Softening.* Resistance to the authorities' new ideas must be reduced. According to 1958 congressional testimony this is accomplished by techniques that include the imposition of "hunger, fatigue, tension, threats, and violence," (all of which are listed above).[8] In extreme situations this is assisted by the administration of hypnosis and drugs.

3. *Indoctrination.* The authorities use the methods of propaganda and persuasion (Chapter 7) to convince their victim his former society has betrayed him and cannot be trusted. They market themselves as his new family and, to this end, engage him in relationships (emotional, romantic, or sexual) to tether him to the group. They convince him they are his true friends—his protectors, the only ones he can trust.

INSUBORDINATION

Dominant individuals and groups must take seriously any condition that can threaten their hold on power. A ruler requires the support of the elite and individual elites must have the support of their peers. In autocracies it is helpful to have the support of the majority of the governed, but it isn't always necessary. Saddam Hussein, for example, ruled Iraq from 1979-2003 even though his ethnic/religious group of Sunni Arabs was outnumbered 3 to 1 by opposing Shiite Arabs. By contrast, we recall from Chapter One that in 1553 the English governed found Mary's legitimacy greater than Jane's and replaced the latter with the former.

People do not act according to facts; they act according to their *perception* of facts. For this reason, they who dominate must also strive to maintain the appearance of unanimity among themselves and an appearance of consent by the governed. Because unity means strength, those in power are well served to keep disputes among themselves private. For if underlings detect division, they may seek to exploit it. In the previous chapter we learned one of the keys to a successful social movement is found when the institution opposed is already weakened, especially by internal ideological division. The U.S. Government is aware of this and trains DOJ employees to avoid engaging in disputes among themselves when in the presence of subordinates such as citizens or inmates.

America's founders recognized consent of the governed to be so important they implied it to be the central component by which republics are legitimized: "... to secure these rights governments are instituted among men deriving their just powers from the consent of the

---

[8] I should note there is great division among academics over whether, by definition, coercive persuasion must be accompanied by physical restraint or abuse or is "applicable to all instances of persuasion or influence in which the person is constrained by physical, social, or psychological forces from leaving the influencing situation." (Schein, 1961) I lean toward the latter view.

governed." (See Declaration of Independence, para. 2.) We should note, however, that actual consent is not to be confused with the perception of it.

Just as the dominant usually prefer to keep disputes among themselves private, they prefer to keep dissent from below quiet. But when it is well noticed or the ruler is powerful enough, he may choose the exact opposite extreme to set a vivid example by which further rebellion is preempted. Factions of the Pennsylvania Line, one of the Colonial Army's largest regiments, rebelled in the spring of 1781. The entire regiment had already abandoned their posts to protest nonpayment of wages earlier that year and those in the Army's high command knew, if not checked, this mutinous attitude would spread. And if the revolution failed, their own treasonous necks would be stretched by George III, king of England. Forsaking due process General George Washington ordered two of the deserters summarily executed. Loyal soldiers located the rebellious ringleader and shot him and another deserter point blank in the heads. The remaining striking soldiers then reluctantly returned to their base.

In 1814, U.S. Major General Andrew Jackson punished a new recruit for the ostensibly minor offenses of talking back to an officer and abandoning his post with the most severe of all penalties. The soldier, clad in white, was forced to kneel on his soon-to-be coffin in front of his own platoon which then obliterated him with enormous 70 caliber rifles. (We recall from Chapter One that the Russian Revolution was kicked off by a single act of rebellion—a sergeant killing a captain who had slapped him.)

Likely taking a cue from the history books, Kim Jong Un, chairman of North Korea, executed his uncle (Kim's 2nd in command) and two deputies in 2013 for a litany of (likely exaggerated) offenses. These included exploiting the country's natural resources (e.g., coal, metal, fishing grounds) for personal profit. In Kim's view the acts constituted disloyal and insubordinate behavior and an example needed to be set. Kim gave great publicity to the accusations, trials, and especially the punishments. The three were taken to a military training area outside of Pyongyang where they were blasted into pieces by anti-aircraft cannons and their remains incinerated with a flame thrower.

Acts of insubordination can be highly contagious. The chain can begin with a tiny fracture of respect such as the refusal to applaud, bow, salute, address by formal titles, or apologize for a minor transgression.[9]

A refusal to conform to any protocol raises the question of why any of the others should be observed. Thus, when done in the presence of other subordinates, this can set off an escalating wildfire of disobedience. Even a dirty look or defiant bearing can be considered insolent and can constitute a challenge. If the dominant party does not defend his honor, the essential nature of the relationship is likely to be changed.

By the close of the 1980s, the popularity of Nicolae Ceausescu, the second communist president of Romania, had plunged to an all time low. The once popular leader had become increasingly repressive during the 1970s as his secret police began controlling the media, surveilling the people, and violating their human rights. His approval rating continued eroding throughout that decade and into the next as his mismanagement of the economy escalated foreign debts. Ceausescu's decision to export large amount of industrial and agricultural products in an attempt to repay these

---

[9] In the federal Bureau of Prisons an act of insolence toward a staff member falls under the lowest category of misconduct—300 series. (400 series offenses are no longer enforced.) But it has been my experience that when an officer determines an inmate has committed this offense, the inmate is immediately locked up in segregation. (This is true of no other 300 series violations.) I have, however, literally seen inmates realize they crossed a line, apologize, acknowledge they are the inferior in the relationship, and walk away unscathed.

loans substantially lowered the quality of life in the early 1980s as Romanians found themselves on burdensome rations of food, water, oil, heat, electricity and medicine.

In December 1989 massive protests against his leadership had erupted in the city of Timisoara. He responded by commanding his military to fire on protesters at a December 17 demonstration. When the people discovered their own leader had ordered this, riots spread throughout the land. Ceausescu then decided to make a public display of his power. He would hold a televised rally in the capitol, Bucharest; reasoning that as he showed his people he was still in charge and they acknowledged it (consent of the governed), his reign would be secure. And had the first two conditions been met, the third probably would've as well. But the event did not transpire as the president anticipated.

When Ceausescu commenced his fiery denunciation of those opposed to communism on that fateful morning, audience members began objecting—booing and scoffing. When this reaction radiated and increased in volume, the millions watching on television could hear it. And it infected them. Studio techs scrambled to introduce canned applause to cover up the remonstrance, but the damage had been done. The whole country knew he was weak and scores joined the insurrection.

The rebellious momentum continued with an afternoon of anticommunist demonstrations, then a night of violence in the capitol. The president could see he was losing control. He and his wife fled Bucharest in a helicopter, but the military had already defected (we know from Chapter One what this means) and the pair was quickly captured by their own soldiers. They were summarily tried and convicted of subverting the economy and killing people for political ends. President and First Lady Ceausescu were executed by a firing squad on Christmas Day 1989.

UNPLUGGING THE POWER SOURCE

In the first chapter we studied qualities associated with they who govern. These are all crucial components of authority and interfering with any of them, or perceptions of them, can spell serious trouble for he who bears the scepter. Instances showing ways this has been or could be accomplished are listed throughout this text. For example, earlier in this chapter we explored methods used to weaken the will (ambition) and the Third Case of Chapter Thirteen demonstrates this on a level much more political in nature. In Chapter Fifteen we will find two men undercutting the elite's support of an alliance of officials who monopolized power over America's largest city. We'll investigate methods to counter any image (symbol), position, or perception the enemy is promoting in Chapter Seven. Insolence, which we just examined, can rapidly erode a ruler's powers of coercion.

You can often identify the importance of an element in an opponent's system by detecting how well protected it is. If it is open and exposed, it is likely to be insignificant. If it is concealed and nested in layers of security, it is of great consequence (or at least he perceives it to be). Thus, its status as an essential component does not automatically render it the weakest link (what military strategists refer to as the *critical point*). For example, in the 1980s the U.S. Army came to believe the Soviet Union may try to strike the Alaskan pipeline to interrupt the oil supply to the continental U.S. and began planning to position soldiers along its length (between Alaska and the mainland). But oil company experts informed Army officers they held plenty of extra sections of the pipe in storage and could easily replace any damaged portion. The most important elements, as it actually stood, were the pumping stations along the route. Once aware of this, the Army instead posted troops at these stations—revealing their importance yet also rendering them harder to disable absent some sort of remote tactical strike.

When an opponent invokes a deterrence strategy, he also acknowledges a point of vulnerability in his system, and we will examine this shortly.

The most important quality a ruler or government must possess is legitimacy—the right to rule. Opponents of John Quincy Adams, as we observed in Chapter One, exploited this in the context of a close controversial election to thwart Adams' political agenda and limit his presidency to a single term. England's Catholics, as we further noted, took advantage of it in the context of biological descent to supplant the Protestant queen with one of their own denomination. There has evolved, however, an element to legitimacy that is called into question much more easily than the above. While those who do so may not comprehend the underlying principles by which their actions are so effective, subverting this is now the most popular method used to bring low those who are high.

Honor and Moral Authority

Citizens look to their leaders for guidance on how they should behave. We expect them to act better than we do, and we have every right to expect this. Our taxes fund their salaries. They're in special highly sought positions of power. And they're the very ones who create, interpret, and enforce our laws. They must lead by example.

America's 2nd president, John Adams (father of the aforesaid less successful 6th president), correctly observed, "Because power corrupts, society's demand for moral authority and character increases as the importance of the position increases." Moral authority, as the founding father termed it, can be roughly defined as the superior psychological position enjoyed by one who adheres to behavior accepted as righteous and just.

In considering the potential for political instability in a foreign country, a key quality monitored by the CIA is the legitimacy of the ruling regime. Honor is so important to this the CIA evaluates a foreign regime's "*perceived* level of corruption" and "record on human rights violations" as predominant determining factors.

In a nation where morality has been legislated, this component of legitimacy has proven to be the softest spot in the armor of they who dominate. The U.S. Government, of course, knows this and its Code of Federal Regulations (internal administrative law) is filled with rules designed to render it impervious to accusations by which its moral authority can be undermined. The code, for example, allows it to disqualify applicants from federal employment when they are perceived as having engaged in "criminal, infamous, dishonest, immoral, or notoriously disgraceful conduct" or the "habitual use of intoxicating beverages to excess." (See 5 CFR § 302.203). The CFRs also obligate employees to "endeavor to avoid any actions creating the *appearance* they are violating the law or the ethical standards . . ." (See 5 CFR § 2635.101).

The powerful usually have a great deal to hide. Historically, most have had the ability to keep their skeletons in the closet. But as the ease at which information is recorded and disseminated increases, the ease at which skeletons are kept closeted decreases.

John Edgar Hoover, legendary director of the Federal Bureau of Investigation (term 1924-1972), serves as the embodiment of the arrogant "do as I say, not as I do" philosophy embraced by Christians and officials of Christian societies. On Hoover's orders, FBI agents expended 23 years infiltrating homosexual rights groups to collect their members' names, record their speeches, and photograph their demonstrations.

Hoover also undertook a mission to locate "all sex deviates in government service" so the government could be cleansed of people so objectionable. In this quest, however, he overlooked the biggest offender of all . . . himself.

It is now well-known Hoover was a closeted homosexual. And not only did he persecute his own kind, but he also pursued pornographers, whom he declared to be "peddlers of filth, those parasites of the deadliest variety." In 1960, he upbraided one of his agents in the presence of his colleagues for possessing a mere Playboy magazine. An FBI official at the time explained the incident: "The director looks upon those who read such magazines as moral degenerates."

Hoover, nonetheless, enjoyed viewing newly collected obscene films in a Bureau screening facility known as "The Blue Room." Assistant FBI Director William Sullivan (dec.) also conceded that Hoover's desk drawers were filled with "lurid literature of the filthiest kind . . . lewd magazines that deal with all sorts of unusual sexual activities."

Dr. John Money, Professor of Medical Psychology at Johns Hopkins University School of Medicine (dec.), opined that Hoover's sexual dichotomy conforms to archetypes frequently observed among law enforcement officials: "They may look like knights in shining armor, but they're undercover agents psychologically as much as by profession."

He specifically notes of the former FBI director:

> Hoover's life was one of haunting and hounding people over their sexuality, brutalizing them one way or another because of it. He took on the role of being the paragon, keeping the country morally clean, yet he hid his own sexual side. His terrible thing was that he needed constantly to destroy other people in order to maintain himself. Many people like that break down and end up needing medical help. Hoover managed to live with his conflict by making *others* pay the price.

Similar is true of Earl Warren (dec.) Chief Justice of the U.S. Supreme Court from 1953 until 1968. To take one of many examples from his life, Warren, as district attorney of Alameda County, California, and attorney general of California, relentlessly tormented the operators of liquor stills and speakeasies during the Prohibition era. He stood out as one of the most effective prosecutors in the nation for reducing the manufacture, distribution, and sale of intoxicating beverages. Be this as it may, the rabid enforcer of sobriety saw no need to obey the law to which he so diligently burdened those under his authority.

After a long, arduous day of locking up moonshiners and closing down distilleries, the presumed pillar of virtue enjoyed relaxing with a few shots of straight Bourbon whiskey or Scotch that had been confiscated by agents in his charge. Warren made a sorry attempt to rationalize his hypocrisy to lying to his impressionable young children—in whose presence he openly drank. He told his little ones the substance he was consuming nightly was in fact lawfully obtained "medicine."

J. Edgar Hoover can accurately be described as a man who invested the greater part of his professional life not in exploring violations of law by ordinary people, but in probing trespasses of social mores by those he suspected could pose a threat to his hold on power. These included the various presidents and attorneys general who came and went during his tenure.

Earl Warren similarly consumed a great deal of time as California's attorney general wrangling with his political adversaries, such as the governor and a liberal law professor at his alma mater—U C Berkeley.

These two meretricious law enforcement officials were committing the same offenses as those upon whom they preyed. Yet, none of the latter responded by discovering and exploiting that vulnerability. With the hypocrisy that would've sent them plunging into the dungeons of disgrace remaining unexposed until after their deaths, the scoundrels soared to the dizzying heights of power and remained there until only the natural effects of aging finally intervened.

Former New York State Attorney General Elliot Spitzer, a law-and-order zealot of the new millennium, earned a sterling reputation for his crusade against Wall Street corruption. The results he delivered in 2000 so pleased a state rocked by financial misconduct, its voters elected him governor in 2006. But the financial security staff at Spitzer's bank, likely less appreciative of the way he profited from the errors of their peers, kept a close eye on his accounts. When they discovered suspicious fund transfers, they believed their governor to be laundering money. Backed by the Patriot Act and Bank Secrecy Act that law and order conservatives like Spitzer had endorsed, the bank reported the info to federal law enforcement officers. The latter set up a wire tap.

Spitzer hadn't been involved in the suspected financial crimes, but the G-men discovered the married governor's questionable transfers were for something just as illegal, but a tad more lurid: payments for sexual services he'd received from a high-end prostitution service. The feds estimate he paid up to $80,000 for extra-marital gratification while serving as attorney general and governor. The scandal made local, state, and national news.

With his moral authority eviscerated, the governor resigned in 2008 amidst great ridicule.

Note: In 2013, the ever-ambitious Spitzer ran for the office of New York State Comptroller, but, unable to rehabilitate his image, failed. Three years later he was investigated for abusing a woman, again not his wife, in a Manhattan hotel room.

While it is profitable to show an official violates society's general standards, it is often more effective to show he has violated, or better yet, is presently violating, the specific standards on which he was propelled to power: a representative praised for promoting a law increasing penalties for theoretical sex offenses and thought crimes who lasciviously queries his own underage male assistants on their sexual fetishes; a president elected on the catchy slogan "Read my lips, no new taxes!" who signs a bill raising gasoline and incomes taxes; a senator endorsed by veterans and law enforcement associations because of his hawkish votes who took questionable steps to avoid the draft. The best possible situation is found when he transgresses both sets of standards: a "sensitive crimes" detective promoted to chief of his division because of his merciless persecution of sex offenders who criminally penetrates a vulnerable inmate under his custodial, supervisory, and disciplinary authority.

TOURNAMENTS OF RISK

Strong-willed men throughout history have challenged rivals to contests that jeopardized the safety of both. The dual, which became popular in the 15th century, featured two armed combatants who would walk in opposite directions, then take shots at each other when they had reached a predetermined number of paces. Duals often arose to settle matters of personal honor, and the most famous example took place as the hard grudging American statesmen Aaron Burr and Alexander Hamilton faced off in 1804. With neither of the prideful men willing to back down, the conflict was resolved by shooting skill alone and ended with Hamilton dead on the field.

A similar contest that developed in the early 1900s was known as Chicken. A dispute over superiority or honor arose. A challenge was issued on one side and accepted on the other. The headstrong contestants drove to a secluded road, usually late at night, and positioned their cars about a half mile apart. On the signal of a neutral party, who stood at a halfway point, the opponents drove down the center line toward each other. Whichever swerved first to avoid the collision lost the contest and prestige. In some cases, he also lost to the winner the title to his car.

It's seldom easy to impose your interests above those of rival peers. And it becomes no easier when you're in conflict with rapacious and powerful officials. The characteristics of human nature and power politics are such that you will probably suffer to achieve the end you seek. But in so doing you must always strive to minimize the negative impact on yourself while maximizing it upon your adversary.

The art of driving a situation to an intolerable head in order to force a desired result is known as *brinksmanship*. In this there are both conflict and common interest among the combatants. One of the most prominent examples took place during the "cold war" between the USA and USSR as each side stockpiled nuclear weapons to keep the other in check. The tension reached a head in the Cuban Missile Crisis of 1962. Let's examine the key events:

1. In March 1961, newly inaugurated U.S. president John F. Kennedy executes the "Bay of Pigs" military operation which immediately fails. (The mission, which the CIA had already been planning under the Eisenhower administration, involved U.S. trained Cuban exiles who attempted to invade their native country and overthrow communist leader Fidel Castro.)

2. The Soviet Union responds by engaging in an enormous arms buildup in Cuba. It claims this is necessary to protect its communist ally from the U.S. As part of this, Soviet Premier Nikita Khrushchev secretly installs sites for 24 medium range (1,000 mile) and 18 intermediate range (2,000 mile) nuclear missiles. (He believed this would compensate for his country's nuclear weapons deficit and also meet its stated goal of protecting Cuba from the U.S.)

3. An American U2 spy plane discovers and photographs the Cuban missile sites.

4. After careful consideration JFK announces the discovery. He indicates the U.S. must not allow the Soviet Union to deliver any more missiles to Cuba and, to this end, the Navy will prevent Russian ships from reaching the island. He also threatens a nuclear confrontation and promises America's own military will invade Cuba and dismantle the missiles already in place if Khrushchev does not remove them on his own.

5. Khrushchev defiantly replies that Kennedy is driving civilization to "the abyss of world nuclear missile war."

6. JFK dispatches the Navy to intercept Russian ships headed to Cuba and also amasses a force of a quarter-million US soldiers in Florida to prepare for an invasion.

7. Sixteen Soviet ships carrying missiles come within sight of U.S. Navy ships and cease their advance.

8. Khrushchev sends Kennedy a telegram obliquely offering to remove his military forces from Cuba if Kennedy recalls the Navy and promises not to invade Cuba. Khrushchev then broadcasts a second message adding a new demand—Kennedy must remove U.S. missiles from Russia's neighbor, Turkey, in return for Khrushchev's removal of the Cuban missiles.

9. JFK cables a reply formally accepting the first condition but ignoring the second. Behind the scenes JFK sends Attorney General Robert F. Kennedy to meet with Soviet Ambassador Anatoly Dobrynin. RFK threatens that if Khrushchev will not remove the Cuban missiles, the U.S. will remove them and there would be "not only dead Americans, but dead Russians as well." (RFK tempered this by verbally acquiescing to Khrushchev's second condition—the removal of U.S. missiles from Turkey.)

10. The next day both Krushchev and JFK endorse RFK's deal, formally ending the crisis.

Krushchev believed Kennedy to be young and weak, and Kennedy had given him little reason to believe otherwise. The Soviet leader had analyzed the Bay of Pigs operation and concluded that a president who ordered such a feeble offensive would passively acquiesce to the stationing of Soviet military forces, including nuclear missiles, near his homeland. While Kennedy evidently preferred the risks inherent in delay and dormancy to those of action, when the rubber met the road, Krushchev was the first to actually demonstrate an unwillingness to wage war. He halted the advance of his ships and, in so doing, placed his nation at a political and psychological disadvantage. Secretly, however, Kennedy was just as unwilling. He had planned all along to remove U.S. missiles from Turkey, but only as a last resort to avoid war. Transcripts of his cabinet meetings show he conceded: "We can't very well invade Cuba with all its toil, and long as its going to be, when we could have gotten (sic) them out by making a deal on the same missiles in Turkey." Kennedy didn't want to remove his missiles from Turkey any more than Khrushchev wanted to remove his from Cuba, but each side pushed the other to the point both had to relent to avoid disaster. With the disadvantage, Russia did so first; the burden then shifted to America. They had conflict: each side wishing to keep its missiles in place, but not wanting the other to do so. They also had common interest: primarily, avoiding war.

The peaceful conclusion of the crisis was a feather in JFK's hat, notwithstanding the fact that he ordered the bungled invasion of Cuba which instigated it. This, once again, is the power of perception.

Ronald Reagan showed himself to be an expert brinksman in the spring of 1981 as he, also a newly inaugurated president, faced down the unruly Professional Air Traffic Controller's Association (PATCO).

These are the main events:

1. With union contracts set to expire, federal air traffic controllers demand an increase in wages. They believe themselves to be highly skilled officials with stressful jobs and thus set the desired gain at a full 100 percent.

2. Reagan agrees they hold high pressure jobs that deserve an increase, but not at such a lofty amount. He decides instead on a much more reasonable figure: 11 percent. His Secretary of Transportation, Drew Lewis, extends the offer while informing union leaders their members are public safety employees who are prohibited from striking. If they strike, Lewis cautions, the president will no longer negotiate at all.

3. The sides find themselves too far apart and negotiations deteriorate. 70 percent of America's 17,000 controllers vacate their posts.

4. Reagan refuses to resume negotiations and issues a press release giving striking controllers 48 hours to return to work. Failure to do so, he threatens, will result in permanent termination of employment.

5. Union members discuss the matter and decide firing the strikers would disrupt the travel of hundreds of thousands of voters and damage the economy. They also conclude that with the cold war still on, employment termination would ground Airborne Warning and Control System (AWACS) planes and jeopardize national security. Certain they hold the upper hand and believing Regan to be bluffing, the strikers decide not to return to work.

6. Reagan's administration meets with the Federal Aviation Administration, Department of

Defense, and a group of private air traffic controllers. They put together a coalition of competent controllers from the public and private sectors to replace the strikers if they do not return.

7. Flight Controllers in Canada and France begin closing down airports in a show of solidarity with their US peers. The Reagan administration, in turn, announces it will permanently ban flights to those nations if they do not reopen their airports. Knowing the economic impact of this sanction, Canadian and French leaders order their own controllers back to work.

8. Secretary of Transportation Lewis privately consults with economics professors, American Federation of Labor/Congress of Industrial Organization (AFL-CIO) leader Lane Kirkland, and even with Democratic pro-union political leaders such as Ted Kennedy. All opine PATCO is asking too much.

9. The two-day deadline passes, and the strikers fail to return. Reagan fires them all.

10. The new coalition combines with the 30 percent who did not strike and together they quickly restore a safe, fully functional air control system.

The air traffic controllers skillfully pushed the number one official to offer an 11 percent increase, but they should've known when to fall back. They failed to recognize the slightness of their actual support, the excessiveness of their demands, and how easily replaceable they really were. They also committed an error we will examine in Chapters Six and Twelve: misperception of that which is taking place in the mind of the opponent. Further, they had signed contracts promising not to strike and were walking a legally thin line. Reagan would've been within his rights to arrest their leaders, but he took the high road, opting to merely replace the strikers.

Winning the high stakes showdown tremendously boosted the new president's prestige. He'd saved the taxpayers $700 million per year in what otherwise would've been salary increases. His decision helped control inflation and set the standard for government wage negotiations. For example, employees of the US Postal Service, half of whom were preparing to strike, cancelled their insurrection the instant they learned the fate of the PATCO strikers. His victory in the crisis also ended up as an important influence on foreign affairs as other nations, including the Soviet Union, recognized he was a confident risk taker who backed up tough talk with tough action.

A year after the contest the defeated flight controller's union, PATCO, dissolved.

In the Prologue I described how hard I pushed U.S. officials to eradicate the smoking and drug problem at a federal correctional complex. With every means at my disposal, I pulled the problem out of the darkness and flaunted it. I kept escalating the tension. Something had to give. The officials I challenged wanted it to be me. But I held moral authority and called it forth to humiliate them at every opportunity. When they and their bosses came to accept that not only was I right, but would back down at nothing short of death, they were left with no choice but to do so themselves.

As a man serving an unjustly imposed life sentence on a first offense for consensual sex with my teen girlfriend, I really had little left to lose. They were free men. They had excellent jobs, nice cars, houses, and families. Perhaps more importantly, they also had prestige. Society viewed them as upstanding, honorable men. They had far more to lose, and my work threatened it all. They knew it and so did I. Ironically, this disjuncture—if correctly exploited—empowers the otherwise politically weakest person of all: the prisoner.

When it came to the issue with the "gangsta rap," the black supremacist officials, like the flight controllers, failed to recognize the danger and refused to back down at all. And some, like the controllers, forfeited their premium federal jobs for it.

INDICATIONS OF INTENT

If your circumstances allow for it, you will be well served to take some time to consider the matter and reach a level-headed decision as to whether or not you will pursue an oppressive official. (Research has shown people tend to have a greater degree of satisfaction with decisions when they have done so.) If you decide to engage him, it is important to maintain a peaceful appearance and avoid revealing any weakness that could be used against you.

Displaying a peaceful demeanor can help lower your target's suspicion and aggression. If he becomes aware you are trying to harm him it can provoke a primal defense mechanism and cause him to try to harm you.[10] Revealing vulnerabilities gives him more to use against you if (or when) he does become aware. In the Prologue we saw how the Dark One's search through my medical records uncovered a weakness of mine he was able to exploit. (In hindsight I'm not sure there was much I could've done to better conceal that weakness. Perhaps limiting my grievances to verbal ones could've avoided a paper trail, but the medical staff documents verbal discussions and his status as an internal investigator afforded him access to my medical records without my consent.)

Federal case law prohibits government officials from punishing one who takes a constitutionally protected action against them. (E.g., Crawford-El v. Britton 523 U.S. 1574 (1998)). A great deal of administrative law and policy holds the same. (E.g., 28 CFR 115.67 (a)). And, where this prohibition is concerned, there is no legal difference between actually taking the constitutionally protected action and declaring an intent to do so. (E.g., Ripp v. Foster 2010 US Dist. LEXIS 145811.) There are, however, plenty of exceptions to this general rule and as I've indicated judges tend to protect those whom they see as their own kind.

Officials already know the consequences of retaliation and are unlikely to do so in an obvious manner. (In Chapter 9 we will see how I laid waste a BOP lieutenant who did so.) Instead, they are likely to sit back and wait for you to slip or bait you into it. Further, rather than directly delivering retaliatory actions, the official will almost certainly have a trusted colleague or subordinate carry them out. (This was a favorite scheme of the BOP officers with whom I was allied. I was so trusted, in fact, they often made such plans in my presence.)

The retaliatory accusation is likely to be a blend of fact and fiction—a potent alchemy we will examine further in the next two chapters.

Toward the end of my time in the federal BOP my reputation among officials all the way to the national director was well known. Yet, I saw few indications most held any great fear of me. Many would go "by the book" in my presence. Some officers (not my protected allies of course) refused to work the A-North unit in which I was housed, but this is typically as far as it went. I was laying political enemies on the chopping block like Robespierre during the French Revolution, but there were still plenty more, inmates and officials alike, willing to stick their necks out and take their chances with me.

People often fail to appreciate a danger until it directly impacts them or someone close to them (a matter we will discuss in Chapter 7). Further, there is a psychological quirk that leads people with

---

[10] Depending on the nature of the situation his awareness may be inevitable; for example, if you file a complaint against him with a professional board or sue him. Even then you should strive for a peaceful appearance outside the forum of resolution. Your manner should show it is not personal, even if it is.

a certain attitude to challenge the most formidable player in a field in the hope they can pridefully assert they conquered the great one. It is not in your best interest to incite this. Your resources are better invested in battles of your own choice. For all of these reasons I have found it best to keep a hostile intent concealed as long as possible.

PREEMPTIVE STRIKES

Chinese military and political leader Mao Tse-Tung (1893-1976) famously stated "The best defense is a good offense" and this is usually correct. History shows the side that begins an engagement has the best chance of winning it. Taking the strategic initiative inheres an advantage in nearly every form of warfare. For he who initiates the action defines the character of the conflict and therefore enters into it with a greater amount of control. Where he acts, his opponent can only react without choice, whether he is prepared or not.

In 1962 Chicago's now legendary mayor Richard J. Daley was preparing for a reelection campaign. His opponent would be the Republican Ben Adamowski, who had been the state's attorney until Daley and his corrupt Democratic political organization, informally known as "The Machine," unseated him in the election of 1960.

Several high profile scandals had taken place on Daley's watch. These include: municipal court employees fixing traffic tickets, that court's chief judge ordering bail money to be returned to bondsmen whose clients failed to show up for hearings, sewage department officials profiting by inflating contracts and, worst of all, a police gang that burglarized businesses.

When in office Adamowski had humiliated the mayor by fervently indicting Machine members for their parts in these. Daley, however, insulated himself by claiming he had no part in the unlawful activities. He correctly asserted two of the top officials involved—the chief of court staff and the chief judge—were elected by the people rather than appointed by the executive. But the same could not be said about the superintendent of police—whom it was politically necessary to replace. (For this, Daley selected a by-the-book criminology professor who would turn the department upside down.)

The mayor himself was generally clean and maintained a certain honor by his ascetic lifestyle. He frequently attended church services, was faithful to his wife, and abstained from alcohol and night life. Even his children were well behaved. (Aside from church, the same is believed true of Kim Jong Un.) Nonetheless, he'd spent his life working in Illinois politics and was certainly aware of how corrupt the organization that propelled him to power was. Adamowski believed he could associate Daley with the corruption and undermine his moral authority.

Daley knew Adamowski was going to attack with these issues and decided to launch a preemptive strike designed to interfere with his opponent's offensive. (In military theory this is known as a *spoiler attack*.) The new state's attorney, whom Daley and The Machine had placed in power in the previous election, quietly dug for dirt and found records Adamowski left behind indicating he may have used money from his department's contingency fund for his 1960 campaign. As the old school mayor had a policy that prevented him from personally attacking opponents, his Machine leaked the evidence to press allies and let them do it for him.

The blindside sent Adamowski reeling. Instead of opening with a massive assault against Daley, the disoriented mayoral prospect was forced to defend himself from Daley's offensive. The press softly questioned Daley on his own contingency fund, but he was shielded by a city ordinance exempting the mayor from any obligation to account for it.

When, at long last, Adamowski regained his footing and floated his own accusations he was unable to prove Daley had any responsibility for the mistakes of his subordinates. The mayor appeared as a righteous reformer even though he had initiated no reforms until his underlings were caught and exposed.

Daley was reelected by a margin of 138,000 votes.

If your intel indicates 1) an opponent or predator of any variety is planning to attack and 2) either you or he will lack the ability to sufficiently retaliate (we'll soon examine this) it may serve your interests to unexpectedly strike first—both to obstruct his injurious plot and to place him on a defensive stance where he is much weaker.

DETERRANCE

One forms a deterrence strategy to preserve the status quo. That is, he applies it with the intent to dissuade one who has the potential to inflict harm from doing so by directly appealing to his self-interests. In this business we tend to use negative inducements. In fact, there are those who consider this approach to be inherently negative. But the truth remains that positive inducements or combinations of both can also be employed very effectively to the same end. These may be invoked along the lines of the following:

> **Negative:** D.A. Smith, if you file fraudulent charges against me, my family will release evidence you embezzled money.
>
> **Positive:** D.A. Smith, if you don't file fraudulent charges, my family will endorse you in your next campaign and issue a $10,000 donation to your reelection fund.
>
> **Both:** D.A. Smith, if you file fraudulent charges against me, my family will release evidence you embezzled money, but if you don't, they will endorse you in your next campaign and issue a $10,000 donation to your reelection fund.[11]

Again, if the powerful are to do your bidding you must be able to help them or hurt them. The combination, if the circumstances render it available and appropriate, is, therefore, the most potent formula.

We just examined the brinksmanship strategies employed in the Cuban Missile Crisis. Deterrence strategies were infused into these as well. For the use of nuclear missiles by one side would provoke the same by the other and would likely escalate into mutually assured destruction. Each side's need to deter the other from using these weapons formed the psychological skeleton around which the nuclear arms race and cold war evolved. Most military strategists now accept nuclear weapons of any variety can only be tools of deterrence. And since the world first witnessed their destructive force when the U.S. employed them upon Japanese civilians in 1945, they have only served this purpose.

By the end of the Korean conflict, in which the U.S. (via the U.N.) attempted to prevent the spread of communism, USAF bombers had destroyed nearly every structure in North Korea. They had literally run out of targets. But just like neighboring Japan, North Korea rebuilt and is stronger than ever. (These, along with perhaps the Black Plague of 14th Century Europe, strike me as instances of that which is known in economics as *Creative Destruction*—the incessant cataclysmic replacement of the old with the new, which eventually results in a superior creation.) Present ruler

---

[11] The communication in this example is very direct because it is necessary to clarify and distinguish the inducements. If the common man were attempting to so induce an actual official he would have to be much more oblique, likely employing an intermediary, soft statements, and disguise. For all his power, even J. Edgar Hoover refrained from directly blackmailing other officials. Academics should also be aware the words "negative" and "positive" are used here in their everyday meaning (bad and good) rather than in the specialized meaning applied in operant conditioning.

Kim Jong Un's testing of nuclear missiles, especially Intercontinental Ballistic Missiles (ICBMs) capable of reaching the mainland U.S. (2017), has successfully deterred America from seriously considering any kind of new military offensive against that country. It even brought U.S. President Donald Trump to three consecutive "summits" (always on neutral territory for reasons discussed in Chapter One) to preserve the peace. Kim revealed:

> When one is firmly equipped with the capability to make precision strikes with nuclear weapons against aggressors and strongholds of aggression, no matter where they are on the face of the earth, no aggressor can dare to attack recklessly, and the greater and more powerful the nuclear strike capability, the greater the power of deterring aggression will be. Especially in the case of our country, whose opponent is the United States . . . it is necessary to firmly bolster the nuclear armed forces both quantitatively and qualitatively.

Kim has also repeatedly acknowledged the depositions and brutal killings of Saddam Hussein (Iraq) and Muammar al-Qaddafi (Libya) as sufficient evidence of what the U.S. does to rulers who have relinquished their WMDs. Leaders of Ukraine made the same mistake in 1994: they voluntarily dismantled nuclear weapons the former USSR had stationed in that territory in return for a vague assurance the nations of the world would not threaten or use force against Ukraine's territorial integrity or political independence. No sooner had the country destroyed its WMDs than Russia seized its territory of Crimea. With no sufficient deterrent, Russia pulled out all the stops in early 2022, invading Ukraine in an attempt to reintegrate it.

Deterrence strategies are employed when there is both conflict and common interest among the parties. He who employs one implicitly acknowledges his opponent has located his critical point, but proposes that (in the case of a negative inducement) if the opponent does not strike it, neither will he strike the opponent's critical point.

The number 1 factor that inhibits desired aggression is its cost. Therefore the method this world's most powerful leaders believe best to prevent a potential aggressor from striking is to convince him in advance that if he does attack he will receive punishment so severe the costs of his aggression will exceed their benefits.

As they directly appeal to the opponent's interests, deterrence strategies are most effectively employed by one perceived to be:
1. capable of using destructive force,
2. in dire straits,
3. reckless,
4. willing to use said force (we'll soon examine the legitimacy of threats);

against an opponent who:
1. has plenty to lose,
2. is of a sound mind, and
3. cautiously computes the costs, benefits, and dangers of a possible confrontation.

One who does not think reasonably, such as a religious extremist, an insane person, or one who is in an irrational state of militant enthusiasm, is likely to misperceive what is in his best interests and may not be deterrable. If your target is rational and calculating, but nonetheless believes he is deprived of choices other than confrontation (or otherwise feels he has more to gain than lose) he may also not be deterred. Further, the self-serving bias we discussed in Chapters 2 and 3 inclines one toward immediate incentives more than away from distant oblique disincentives. So, if your opponent has a strong motivation to quickly carry out an action you wish to prevent you must be sure the credible threat of direct, immediate, heavy reprisal is on the front of his mind.

Successful deterrence can only be achieved by the potency that will remain after receiving an initial attack. In other words, if A wishes to dissuade B from attacking, A must demonstrate that even after B attacks, it will still have force sufficient to harm B. Otherwise, instead of dissuading B, its prestrike force may inadvertently provoke B to strike first. This principle is known in military studies as *second-strike capability*. One of the ways the USSR accomplished it in the cold war was by implementation of its "Dead Hand" system. This can be thought of as a computerized command network that monitored communications on military frequencies, temporary seismic disturbances, and atmospheric conditions such as heat, radiation levels, and air pressure. If its measurements indicated the Soviet Union had been attacked by nuclear weapons, it commenced a series of actions which would culminate in launching ICBMs at the United States. The USSR thus deterred a U.S. first strike by assuring it had the means to obliterate that opponent even while its own heads of state lay dead.

The U.S. (and Canada) in turn, psychologically preempted a Soviet first strike with the North Warning System. This included short range radar, long range radar, and Distant Early Warning environmental re-radiation equipment deployed across five zones in Alaska and the Canadian Arctic. If a Soviet bomber or missile was detected, the system reported the location, track direction, and time of detection to the North American Air Defense Command (NORAD). The system led Russian leaders into accepting the U.S. could detect a Soviet first strike and launch a massive retaliatory strike before the Russian first strike even hit the U.S.

THREATS

We tend to think of a threat as an indication of both the ability and willingness to inflict harm on an opponent if he doesn't accede to demands. But it is more accurately characterized as a rite undertaken by the threatener to save himself from incurring the costs that could be involved with imposing a sanction. These costs can be tangible resources (e.g., bodily integrity, property) or intangible ones (e.g., time, energy, finances, prestige).

Threats may be issued directly, such as JFK's and RFK's words and actions in the Cuban Missile Crisis, or indirectly, as when U.S. leaders placed their Continental Air Defense Command and global military forces on an elevated Defense Condition of three (DEFCON 3) in response to the USSR's indication that it may intervene on Egypt's behalf during the incipience of the Arab-Israeli War (1973).

Scientists note that when many mammals threaten an adversary, their facial muscles display a mixture of the fight (aggression) and flight (fear) drives. When the mind of a dog is filled with equal parts of rage and fear in the presence of a menacing opponent, it threatens by wrinkling the snout, raising the upper lip, baring teeth, laying back the ears, and growling. But, in an attempt to avoid injury to the self, it will only strike as a last resort—when the opponent has entered a vital safety zone. If its inclination to attack is not inhibited by fear, it issues no threat; with a face that is mostly serene it merely strikes without warning.

Snakes warn adversaries (which should not be confused with prey), by coiling into a position where the head is retracted and ready to strike. Some hiss, inflate a hood, or shake a rattle at the end of the tail. The ones that do so prefer to warn because if they must strike they risk incurring costs such as breaking a fragile tooth. Where vipers are concerned there is also a high energy cost involved with replenishing venom. And in natural settings where food is scarce, survival necessitates the conservation of energy.

One issuing a threat either does not want to deliver the promised sanction or is incapable of doing so. This is exactly what causes a threat to arise in the first place. If he perceives there is no potential cost to himself, the aggressor merely attacks without warning (e.g., the dog aforesaid). He has no incentive to do otherwise. Again, the primary inhibition against combat is simply its cost. And the recipient of a threat usually has at least some understanding that it is the product of reluctance. General experience teaches that when a threat is issued and the demand not met, the promised sanction seldom follows. This is well known among top military strategists and in 2004 Pentagon spokesman Lawrence Di Rita acknowledged as much: "If you're going to threaten the use of force, at some point you're going to have to demonstrate your willingness to actually use force." To be effective, therefore, the threat must be credible.

There are several methods to legitimize threats and promises. First, you can show the target the cost of *not* making good on your commitment exceeds the cost of doing so. For example, in the negative inducement aspect of the foregoing scenario, it would be easy to show the corrupt DA it will cost you less to release evidence of his embezzlement than to hire a defense attorney. You can also do this by showing your sanction will be carried out automatically (e.g., the aforementioned Dead Hand system). Another way is to demonstrate a high risk-taking propensity; perhaps you will make no rational calculation of costs and benefits in the decision to execute the sanction. (E.g., In 2012 Kim Jong Un implicitly threatened a preemptive nuclear strike upon the "U.S. Mainland." U.S. leaders took this very seriously, in part, because Kim had continued building and testing his nuclear arsenal with zero concern for the severe financial impact of the correlative UN sanctions and reduction in tourism.)

One of the most effective methods of legitimizing a threat involves dissecting it into a sequential series of smaller threats, preferably with sanctions that increase in severity, so one can impose a sanction upon the first offense (or series of them) to demonstrate, at a relatively low cost to the threatener, the promised sanctions will be fulfilled on the rest.

Let's say a certain official, Major, has been oppressing you for some time. You've suffered long enough and just delivered without warning psychopolitical action A which caused serious political damage to some other officials. You then indirectly suggest to Major, "Now you've seen what I can do and that I am desperate and resolute. You must stop violating my rights or I will deliver actions B, C, D, and E—a series of politically punishing acts, escalating in severity." He condescendingly laughs and commits a new transgression to show his lack of fear. You deliver B on his subordinates. It was more damaging than A but didn't directly affect him and he's not sure you can. He's no longer laughing when your paths cross and while he commits no new offenses he's still oppressing you under an ongoing original offense. You deploy C on one of his equals. This hits harder yet and a little closer to home. Only now is he finally willing to back down so you don't need to carry out D and E, which would've directly inflicted severe damage on him, but at a much higher cost to you.

Finally, as shown in the example just presented, an appropriate motive must be incorporated within an effective threat. The threatening scheme, therefore, must be such that its target believes: 1) the promised injury is probable, 2) the damage he sustains will not be mild, and 3) if he acts in the desired manner a better outcome is possible. (We'll examine these criteria again as they apply to the fear techniques of propaganda and persuasion in Chapter 7.)

The common man's attempt to intimidate government officials is seldom effective. And when I have the means to deliver a severe sanction, I have found speed, secrecy, deception, and their ultimate product—surprise—are far more profitable than warning. This is especially important when you're dealing with a stubborn and powerful adversary. For the whole purpose of surprise is to avoid his strength. That is, if he is so weak his reaction is inconsequential, surprise serves no purpose. But if there is any doubt you should never underestimate an opponent's abilities. Even the so-called lower animals who hunt as individuals, rather than in packs, only succeed when they take their prey unexpectedly. (You should note that if your adversary has become accustomed to you fighting in an irregular, unconventional manner, he will expect this, in which case he may actually be surprised by a direct, frontal approach.)

Maintaining friendly appearances or otherwise giving no indications of ill-intent helps to lower your opponent's defenses and aggression level—exponentially amplifying the intensity of the attack he failed to anticipate.

A survivor of the 9-11-2001 assault on the Pentagon vividly recollects the experience:

> From the back of the room there was a [moving] heatwave-like haze . . . before I could register or complete that thought, this force hit the room, instantly turning the office into an infernal hell. Everything was falling, flying, and on fire and there was no escaping it . . . I felt the heat and I heard [myself] sizzling . . . oxygen disappeared; my lungs felt like they were burning or collapsing. My mind was like sludge and thoughts took forever to form and longer to reach the brain and even longer to make use of . . . Everyone lost his or her sense of direction.

This is the power of a surprise attack.

> *Suaviter in modo, fortiter in re*
> (Gently in manner, strongly in deed.)
> — Latin political mantra

Chapter Six

The Faces of Deception

First Case in Point

DISTRACTION/CONFUSION

In October 2001 al-Qaeda lieutenants and their allies began transmitting a heavy amount of "chatter," communications via radio, telephone, and computer, that suggested the terroristic organization was going to deploy radiological or nuclear weapons to strike the U.S. Intercepted Signal Intelligence (SIGINT) indicated Pakistani nuclear physicists were developing warheads, some of which were being transferred to al-Qaeda, and plots were also afoot to use conventional explosives to detonate nuclear devices already inside the U.S. One report mentioned an aircraft would be hijacked and plowed into a nuclear facility such as an energy plant or military base where nuclear weapons are stored.

At a National Security Council meeting on October 29, George Tenet, Director of Central Intelligence, briefed President George W. Bush on the Threat Matrix, an index of dangers to the American homeland. Most of the information on which it was based emanated from highly credible sources. Some described exact targets which included landmarks, military facilities, colleges, and shopping malls. Tenet advised the President to lock down U.S. embassies and overseas military bases. He also recommended executing emergency procedures designed to ensure the government continues to function in the event its leaders are eliminated. The CIA director promised he would soon meet with the Director of Homeland Security and the Secretary of Transportation to plan the restructuring of security at American airports in the hope that, by altering the procedures terrorists encounter, their scheme would collapse.

With vivid visions of 9/11 still fresh in their minds, the threat of a nuclear version of the same sent the president's war cabinet into a frenzy. FBI Director Robert Mueller III and Attorney General John Ashcroft prepared to issue a second global alert to an already spooked public. Stock prices plummeted. People stayed home from work. Swamped by Secret Service agents, Vice President Dick Cheney retreated into an underground bunker in a secret location outside Washington. Security at public transportation facilities, government buildings, military bases, and embassies was increased, and their internal routines altered. Principle officials were separated from their deputies. Ten teams of technicians operating vehicles equipped to detect radioactive materials were secretly dispatched to major American cities. Defense Secretary Donald Rumsfeld scrambled nine combat air patrols—ordering them to protect nuclear reactors, missile sites, and other possible targets such as the White House, tall buildings in New York and Chicago, and major amusement parks. Bush ordered General

Tommy Franks, chief of U.S. Central Command, to prepare military response options to a second al-Qaeda attack on the U.S. mainland.

The President had initially dismissed advice from the Secret Service that he also leave Washington, but to soothe his frayed nerves, and those of the American people, he temporarily acquiesced—flying to New York City where he attended a Yankees game and, wearing a bulletproof vest, threw the ceremonial opening pitch. Nonetheless, he quickly returned to the White House. Fully braced for Armageddon, the President and all his men anxiously awaited the end.

◆ ◆ ◆ ◆ ◆

Deception is one of many techniques in our evolutionary repertoire. Every organism capable of doing so deceives to advance its self-interests and assure its survival. The Venus Fly Trap of the Carolina coast offensively evolved a leaf meridian to lure and capture insects. The Malaysian Swallowtail caterpillar defensively developed on its dorsal end the shape and markings of a snake's head, which deters predators such as birds. The Gaboon viper offensively evolved a color pattern that makes it indistinguishable from leaves on African forest floors. The White Angled Sulphur butterfly of Argentina defensively developed wings whose shape, pattern, and colorings render the insect indiscernible from the leaves on which it rests.

These concepts are, of course, not lost on man. The male may wear high-heeled boots and puff his chest to enlarge his appearance in the hope of luring women and intimidating competitors. The female may cake on makeup and clothe herself in garments to make her hips appear slimmer or chest larger in the hope this will lure men and intimidate competing women.

Man will also employ verbal deception. A male who offended his girlfriend offers an insincere apology to ease the tension so she will satisfy his sexual appetite. A couple tells their kids the boogey man will get them if they stay up late, because they don't want the hassle involved with them oversleeping the next morning.

Man even deceives nature. To repair or enhance his body he will incorporate into it foreign parts made of materials the body won't recognize as such and reject. She injects into her blood steam preparations of weakened or dead microorganisms (or their RNA) to trick her immune system into a response that artificially increases resistance to living versions of these microbes.

Man is indeed the master deceiver. By and large, people will do whatever it takes to get their way.

The great nuclear version of 9/11 never materialized; yet by sending misleading communications that amplified and exploited its enemy's expectations, al-Qaeda confused America's top officials and sent the government into disarray. The terrorist organization had already pulled off an epic attack and FBI Director Muller had just warned President Bush that 331 possible al-Qaeda operatives remained on U.S. soil. The officials had every reason to believe this organization could pull off another assault on a much larger scale. Years later, Bush revealed, "For months after 9/11 I would wake up in the middle of the night worried about what I had read . . . The overall image was unmistakable: the prospect of a second wave of terrorist attacks against America was very real."

Al-Qaeda's operation can be understood as the type to which military strategists refer as a *Type-A deception*. It uses techniques to evade, blur, or confuse the actual plan and thus render it indecipherable to the target. The idea is to make the plan appear as ambiguous as possible so the enemy spreads his suspicions (and defenses) far and wide—not knowing where or how to protect himself. (A more typical example is Plan Bodyguard of WWII, in which the Allies misled Germany into believing they may invade Scandinavia, Western France, Italy, and Eastern Mediterranean areas in order to keep German forces spread throughout those areas instead of concentrated in the actual invasion site—Normandy.)

Taking the strategic initiative and regulating the velocity of combat (decreasing the speed of the activity when the strategist's forces are vulnerable, increasing it when the same is true of the enemy's) are important elements of a successful campaign of irregular warfare. By acting as it did, al-Qaeda controlled the conflict while America could only react. The latter could've been investing enormous resources in an offensive operation against al-Qaeda following 9/11, but instead it wasted plenty of them defending against an imaginary threat. And the terrorists thereby won precious time, prestige, and satisfaction.

The gargantuan and conventional U.S. was unaccustomed to fighting guerilla warfare. Its many officials required time to confer, discuss the myriad options, and arrive at strategic, operational, tactical, and technical decisions. Ideas needed formulation. Plans needed authorization. It could not quickly respond to 9/11.

The terrorist organization, by contrast, was trim, efficient, and technologically savvy. It struck at America's critical point—a big, clumsy bureaucracy. Like a bat whizzing in, striking the dragon, then flying away to safety while waiting for its prey to die, al-Qaeda inflicted immense damage on a behemoth completely unprepared for it.

Perception is paramount in politics. And as in politics, so in war. Still, nowhere is this more the case than where the peculiar variety of warfare known as terrorism is concerned. The aggregate fear of the general public, especially in politically and economically stable countries, is maximized by unlawful acts that are random and violent. To this end the targets selected are nearly always symbolic. In addition to the World Trade Towers and Pentagon, al-Qaeda had on its hot list CIA Headquarters (Langley, VA), the Sears Tower (Chicago), the TransAmerica Tower (San Francisco), and the White House. All are symbols of American power and as we learned in Chapter One symbols are important components of power. The foregoing are, therefore, essential elements of successful terroristic assaults. Losses of tangible resources are insignificant. Victories are achieved not by maximizing physical damage, but by maximizing psychological injury: mass confusion, panic, tension, despair. And this, as such, is the less obvious motivation for Al-Qaeda's "Nuclear 9/11" campaign.

Deception can be especially effective when employed against the U.S. Government because its analysts frequently reject it as a possibility when they see no evidence of it. But seeing no indications should be considered at least somewhat axiomatic. For as Jack Davis, who worked with the Directorate of Intelligence and National Intelligence Council, informs us:

> If deception is well planned and properly executed, we should not expect to see evidence of it readily at hand. Rejecting a plausible, but unproven, hypothesis (assumption concerning an event) too early tends to bias the subsequent analysis because the analyst does not look for evidence that might support it. The possibility of deception should not be rejected until it is disproved, or at [a minimum] until a systematic search for evidence has been made and none been found.

◆ ◆ ◆ ◆ ◆

Complex arrangements are more likely to succeed when they are executed by the side that has the luxury of the initiative. And strategic deceptions are often complex operations whose success necessitates a significant amount of time. Further, the one who initiates deception knows what the actual plan is while his target can only guess and expend time in an effort to figure it out; time by which the deceiver benefits. For these reasons, elaborate deceptions tend to be offensive operations.

Defensive deceptions, at least in the military context, are less advantageous as they are constrained by time, range, and perhaps are also lacking in resources that are prioritized in favor of combat operations. They are usually passively employed in the form of camouflage or feigned exercises designed to draw the opponent's weapons away from the deceiver's potential targets. Note: I have, however, employed defensive deception numerous times in the psychopolitical context to protect myself from retaliatory actions; using it to confuse powerful officials or dangerous inmate gangs as to who exactly is working against their interests. I've demanded, via proxies, the FBI investigate crooked officials and had the cells of neighboring inmates hit (to expunge contraband that negatively affects me) while also targeting the cells of non-neighboring inmates to draw attention away from myself as a possible source of the strike.

History invariably demonstrates that the advantage in any correctly executed plan belongs to the side that initiates the engagement while employing deception.

Those who work in investigations or intelligence operate under the assumption that as a subject advances toward his goal, he must prepare. And the preparation, in turn, signals his intent.

In all contexts of warfare absolute secrecy is rare, and, when the inevitable leaks of the actual plan result, the best antidote is deception: the dilution of signals created by the real preparation by an infusion of artificial interference. Because most of those who can be considered targets actively seek out indications of what their adversaries are planning, properly transmitted relevant deceptive signals are usually received intact and interpreted as desired. Deception, nonetheless, does not always succeed. Five distinct possibilities are involved here:

1. The target receives and interprets the information as the deceiver intends.

2. The information is intentionally or unintentionally altered after it is sent. E.g., the signal is electronically distorted, or an intermediary modifies it to suit his purpose.

3. It is received intact, but misperceived. E.g., the hint at A is misunderstood as a hint at B.

4. It is received intact but disregarded. E.g., the analyst receives contrary information from a different source that he finds more credible.

5. It is sent but not received. E.g. the deceiver fails to transmit it correctly or the target isn't monitoring.

ELEMENTS OF A SUCCESSFUL DECEPTION

In the previous chapter we examined the characteristics necessary for a threat to succeed. Because offensive deception is basically an attempt to manipulate the target to take a desired defensive posture, the qualities necessary for a successful threat are analogous to those of a successful offensive deception. But because a threat is not inherently dishonest, and deception is, some new characteristics are added.

1. **Secrecy**. The target must be unaware deception is being employed against him. Again, complete security even in well organized and orderly operations has historically proven unobtainable, so the deceiver must expect some leakage of either the deception plan or the actual operational plan. If the leaks are such that the deceiver confirms his target is sure of

his plans, he must reconsider them accordingly. If, however, the target suspects but isn't sure of the plans, the leakage may not jeopardize success. In fact, leaks often enhance his confusion, leaving him to guess which of the scenarios is the actual one. And better yet for the deceiver with slightly flawed security, targets often find the false information more credible than the actual. An investigation on this found that when ten pieces of information (5 pertaining to the actual plan and 5 pertaining to the false one) reached a target, he believed all of the false ones but rejected four of the five genuine ones as too obvious to be anything but deception. Dick Cheney, Secretary of Defense from 1989-1993 and Vice President from 2001-2009, aptly opined on this very matter, "It's not always bad to send the enemy mixed signals."

2. **Plausibility**. The false plan must be worthy of belief. Several conditions contribute to fulfillment of this.

   a. The target perceives the deceiver has the ability, and is willing to do, that to which the lie commits him. (Since we already examined the plausibility of threats in the previous chapter we will not repeat that discussion.)

   b. Confirmation.

      i. People see fragments of reality emerge from many points—some contrary, some concealed, some apparent. Thus, from the complexity of existence they develop a need for verification. Intel analysts, who are the primary front-line targets for deception, emphasize this by insisting claims be confirmed and evidence scrutinized and rated in accord with its reliability.

      A lie can appear plausible when it is confirmed by diverse sources. A top-secret 1944 report on covert and deception procedures issued by the Supreme Headquarters Allied Expeditionary Forces (SHAEF) to the Allied high command went so far as to conclude: "[The] enemy will not react to information from a single source. He will react only on information from one source confirmed by at least one other." Therefore, with the expectation that a variety of cohesive tips is likely to be accurate, the greater the number of channels the deceiver can manipulate to transmit signals that strengthen each other, the more believable is his deceit.

      ii. Confirmation can also be achieved by weaving lies into reality. By infusing several of the less significant points of the false scenario into the opening stages of the actual plan, the target can confirm the items as they transpire and thus start to accept he has obtained the actual plan. Then as more components in the developing illustration are verified he is likely to dismiss the ones that don't conform, but these will be the more important inconsistencies between the true plan and the false one. The deceptive scenario portrayed for the target should be as close to the actual plan as possible—preferably eighty to ninety percent accurate.

   c. Credible Sources. As we've already noted, intel analysts often rate the reliability of evidence. Credibility can be both subjective and relative. While analysts may credit a few sources known to be reliable over many of dubious credibility, if reliable sources are scant, the latter often rate better than an impartial analysis would otherwise justify. Further, as we will discuss in Chapter Twelve (Tactical Intel), little can be more common than for two people exposed to the same information to form different opinions on it. Therefore, what may seem credible to the potential deceiver may not to his target.

MANIPULATING EXPECTATIONS

The mind instinctively craves consistence (which is another topic we will explore in Chapter 12). To this end, it naturally inclines to perceive what it expects, and once these perceptions have taken root (which happens quickly), they are highly resistant to change. Thus, when a target receives information contrary to his predispositions, he is likely to make it conform to his existing way of thinking, ignore it, or dismiss it altogether.

The first task in managing this matter is to discover his predispositions by collecting information. You may study his preoccupations and thought routines to determine this. E.g., The allies in World War II learned Hitler nursed a fear they would invade the Baltic states and thus repeatedly tricked him into believing they would do so. You can also infer what he may expect by examining what the strategic nature of the situation requires. E.g., The fact that the allies would have to launch an attack on the European mainland via the English Channel was mutually accepted. Therefore, instead of attempting to discount this, the allies broadcast signals via many channels (SIGINT, spies, etc.) truthfully affirming they would do so. They were not truthful, however, as to the exact location and method of attack. Thus, they rolled the truth and lie together into a single deception package that Hitler completely accepted.

Once you have acquired some knowledge of what is going on between his ears and in his conference rooms, you can select one of the following approaches:

1. **Amplifying and Exploiting His Predispositions**. In so doing you formulate a deceptive plan catering to that which he already expects and an actual operational plan that is slightly different from it. (We just noted an effective way to incorporate the deception plan into the actual plan.) He is likely to believe the false plan because it's what he already expects. And when some of the unavoidable leaks on the actual plan reach his ears, he will probably dismiss them because they aren't in conformity with his expectations. He thus does much of the work for you—building his forces to counter the false plan and leaving himself vulnerable for you to blindside him with execution of the true plan. (He will, of course, inevitably notice the execution of the actual operation. For maximum impact you lead him to believe it is only a feint meant to distract him and the real attack will still take place as he expected.) The aforesaid examples of the World War II allies playing upon Hitler's expectations in their deception plan then executing something slightly different in their actual ones illustrate this.

2. **Creating Expectations**. While the most popular method of managing a target's expectations is to amplify and exploit them, the nature of the situation may show it profitable to instead create them. You accomplish this by conditioning your opponent to anticipate something he hadn't previously regarded, thus conditioning him for a future surprise. Historically, military deceivers tended to do this by creating a fantasy that the deceiver conforms to a certain practice or routine that the target comes to expect and therefore ignore. Then when the real operation is executed, the target misunderstands it and fails to rapidly or pertinently respond. An example of this took place in early 1942. The Germans had steadily increased their jamming of British coastal radar. After this jamming had become so intense it rendered the radar useless, two German warships sprinted through the English Channel undetected. The Brits had become so accustomed to the jamming, they failed to comprehend it had been intensified to the point their

radars were ineffective.

3. **Overturning Expectations**. A third approach to managing expectations is to reverse them. Changing anyone's mind, much less that of a hard-headed policymaker, is extremely difficult and should only be attempted when no other approach is viable. To do so you must deliver a significant concentrated jolt upon the target's complacent assumptions. The new information you feed him must be received at a single occasion, or at least within a short timespan, and meet the other requirements already specified. It is best delivered when the target is in a moderate state of tension and vigilance. That is, he knows he must make a decision but is not pressed to do so, because he has sufficient time and options to arrive at one. As he has this luxury, he is open to both confirming and disconfirming evidence with respect to his expectations and is likely to search for, evaluate, and perhaps even accept information he would otherwise ignore or dismiss. After evaluating the information, he may reject it anyway, but when he is under greater or lesser pressure for a decision, he is unlikely to consider it in the first place. For example, after their North African victories in 1942 the allies knew their next target had to be the Italian peninsula; specifically, the small island to its south—Sicily. Hitler knew this as well. Therefore, it was the allies rather than Hitler who were under the greatest pressure. They had little choice but to change his expectations and they did this by planting the corpse of an imaginary courier who carried false operational plans pointing to an invasion at nearby Sardinia. This was supplemented by rumors and signals to several other areas. The deception succeeded in confusing Hitler as to where and when the invasion would take place and he reduced his Sicilian forces, spreading them to areas he falsely believed could be invasion targets.

MONITORING AND MANAGING

Once the deception plan has been finalized and its execution commenced, the prospective deceiver must not relax and assume it will function as desired. Increasing the chances of its success and maximizing its impact require ongoing activities. We now examine them.

1. **Feedback**. After you have begun transmitting signals, you should monitor the opposing camp to determine which of the five possibilities we earlier noted have resulted. As you do so you must consider that deception can be a double-edged sword: just as you attempt to deceive your opponent, the opponent may attempt to deceive you. Therefore, you must guard against counter deception. Government intelligence agencies do this in part by using secretive methods such as espionage and analyzing encrypted communications, but the same factors that determine the plausibility of deception determine the plausibility of counter deception.

2. **Adaptation**. The purpose of feedback is to ascertain whether the plans are able to continue or need to be modified. If, for example, the target misperceived the deceptive information, it may be necessary to alter the actual plan or send new signals to direct his attention to the desired false plan. Unexpected events also may have arisen on his end, and these may require modification of either plan.

As we will comprehensively examine in Chapter Fourteen, *Tales of the Unexpected*, nothing in war is static. So, as real events change, the deception must as well.

Second Case in Point

TRAP/SURPRISE

In the first Persian Gulf war (Desert Storm: 1991) the U.S. coalition's success was such that swarms of Iraqi soldiers quickly began waving white flags and falling at the feet of coalition troops—by all appearances grateful for the opportunity to cave in without a fight. Thus, when U.S. and U.K. intelligence in the second Gulf war (Iraqi Freedom: 2003) received a substantial amount of information from credible sources indicating Iraq's Fifth Division had lost the will to fight and was ready to surrender, they found it plausible. America's military command believed it as well and dispatched a squadron of only sixty soldiers in minimally armored Land Rovers to the Tigris River to accept the surrender. When they arrived, however, the coalition troops found neither white flags nor Iraqis falling at their feet. Instead, machine guns, artillery and even anti-aircraft cannons from a thousand enemy soldiers let loose on the sixty.

Outnumbered, outgunned, and outsmarted, the coalition squad—some of whom were special forces troops trained for exactly these types of ambush scenarios—made no stand. While attempting to flee eight of their eleven utility vehicles became stuck in the sand. They set charges on these so the explosions would create a distraction which gave them a chance to regroup and escape in the three mobile vehicles. To save face, the retreating soldiers, draped over the sides of their overcrowded Rovers, fired at the Iraqis until they reached the safety of a dry riverbed where Chinook helicopters would evacuate them.

♦ ♦ ♦ ♦ ♦

Military strategists retain in their arsenal of tricks the method known as an *M type deception*. Unlike the A type we analyzed previously, this seeks to reduce ambiguity. It does so by indicating precisely the details of an action, but falsely so; thus, leading the target to the wrong time, location, method, intent, etc. It is usually employed offensively in situations where one side wishes to concentrate its enemy's forces in areas it doesn't wish to attack so the areas it does wish to assault are left less defended. E.g. Operation Fortitude, WW II: Allies misleading Germany into believing their main invasion would take place at Pas de Calais instead of Normandy.

While the A type and M type strategies exist separate conceptually, they are often executed simultaneously (e.g. Operation Bodyguard) or blended together. The latter action typically occurs because the target doesn't respond to the misleading direction in the desired manner and the deceiver must resort to merely confusing the target on its intent. (If you have trouble remembering the distinctions between the two types, think of A as ambiguous and M as misleading.)

One would think America's civilian and military intelligence, and the high-ranking officials to whom they report, would've learned to be a little more judicious by 2003. The history books are filled with one account after another of both political and military ambushes set up by deception. From the Greeks depositing a giant wooden horse filled with soldiers at the city gate of Troy to Hitler sealing an alliance with Stalin only to invade the U.S.S.R. even as Russian trains brought supplies into Germany, there is plenty to convince us to be wary.

Some officials are of course brighter than others.

In previous chapters we saw JFK mislead the Soviet Union in a game of brinksmanship. He threatened a nuclear confrontation and amassed troops in Florida for a supposed invasion of Cuba in order to convince Soviet Premier Nikita Khrushchev to remove his missiles from Cuba. In reality, Kennedy had no intention of carrying out the threatened sanctions. And while Ronald Reagan may have done exactly what he promised in the case we examined; he still retained a knack for deceit. It is a little-known fact that the man, of Irish ancestry, was cursed with a short neck. As a former actor who knew the importance of physical appearances in politics, the "great communicator" wore custom made shirts with collars designed to make his stubby neck appear proportionate to his head and body. (Kaiser William II of Germany, who had a miniature left arm as a result of an accident of birth, similarly had his clothes designed with special pockets so he could conceal his defective limb.)

Third Case in Point

BAIT AND SWITCH

In 1989 Intuit's money management software named Quicken came to the attention of Microsoft CEO Bill Gates. Quicken was rapidly setting the industry standard for financial applications—outselling its nearest competitor six to one. This product threatened Microsoft's supremacy and required closer inspection.

Gates instructed an executive in his applications marketing division to meet with Scott Cook, head of Intuit, to propose a buyout. Cook saw a massive increase in his net worth and was receptive to the idea. The two companies began preliminary negotiations.

A predominant stipulation in the pending deal required Intuit to turn its source code over to Microsoft. Cook was amenable to this, given the two companies were about to become one. Intuit sent Microsoft the code and Gates' programmers analyzed it and figured out how the program functioned.

Shortly after the technical study was completed, however, Gates dispatched a Microsoft executive to meet with Cook and deliver grim news: Microsoft was calling off the deal.

In 1990 Gates and company released Microsoft Money, a blatant appropriation of Quicken.

Had Cook done his homework he could've avoided this mistake; for years earlier, Gates had done the same. Apple Computer partnered with Microsoft in 1982 so the latter could develop application software for the Mac. This included the Excel spreadsheet and a word processing program simply named Word. Of course, the creation of these required Apple to supply Microsoft prototypes of the Mac hardware and copies of its operating system code so Microsoft programmers could understand the platform on which their programs would run.

It should've come as no surprise that some of the Mac's core concepts ended up being incorporated in Microsoft's popular Windows program. Salient among these were operating system functionality and the graphical user interface (GUI) which eased interaction between the user and applications software. The GUI, however, was not even an original Apple idea. Steve Jobs, the company's CEO, had taken inspiration for it from displays on Xerox photocopiers. Rather than investing countless hours of labor developing the GUI, Gates borrowed Apple's source code. He also hired five of the programmers who had originally developed the interface at Xerox.

The Federal Trade Commission (FTC) began investigating Microsoft for engaging in anticompetitive practices in October 1990. In his testimony to federal officials, Intuit's Scott Cook, who had just been tricked by Gates, nonetheless defended the Microsoft chief. Cook opined that Gates' actions were those of a talented and intelligent leader. Apple, on the other hand, had already shown itself to be a sore loser. It sued Microsoft for plagiarizing its product in 1988. The FTC closed its investigation on August 20, 1993. Only four days later, a federal court dismissed Apple's suit.

The victorious Bill Gates married a Microsoft project manager named Melinda French on New Year's Day in 1994. Fortune magazine had just listed Gates as the world's wealthiest man.

♦ ♦ ♦ ♦ ♦

Organisms require a mutual understanding of the environment in which they operate in order to competently and sanely do so. For this reason, they subconsciously presume they all experience the same general totality of real things and events. If I am, for example, walking to the store and see plenty of sidewalk ahead, I don't expect it to suddenly drop out beneath my feet. I assume the planet on which I live won't stop spinning and leave me in a permanent state of day or night. When I live a productive, honorable life, but make a harmless slip of human nature, I trust my government's officials to deal justly with me. After all, my taxes, in part, put the food on their tables. But more importantly, this is America, where I have been told my whole life that my country has a constitution along with numerous checks, balances, and other safeguards to protect the citizens from arbitrary self-serving tyranny. Not only do I presume all of this, but I presume everyone else does too. And everyone else presumes the same of everyone else here. This is the mutual understanding of a shared reality. And it is difficult to believe our basic presumptions could be wrong.

Humans have developed a number of flaws in the processing of information. Scientists label these *cognitive biases*. These vulnerabilities allow others, such as rapacious government officials, to prey on us by violating our shared understandings of reality. That is to say, they can only misrepresent if there is already an anticipation of fairness. They can only mislead if there is a mutually accepted set of facts to circumvent.

We've already examined how confirmation bias inclines people to seek evidence that strengthens, rather than weakens, a position already held. Let's look at more of the key flaws that allow us to be deceived.

Honesty Bias

In the absence of information to the contrary, people tend to accept the accuracy of the information brought before them. This is an automatic cognitive inclination psychologists call the *Honesty Bias*. It has evolved via the process of collective learning.

On the whole, collective learning has proven a tremendous benefit to mankind, because we don't have to scrutinize every piece of information we encounter, we just presume it is accurate. And more often than not this is the case. Let's say, for example, CNN shows a man in a suit standing behind a podium with flags and the Department of State seal in the background. If he declares an accord with a foreign country has been reached you won't doubt it. The news network is at least semi-respectable and is presenting what appears to be an important official in a press conference. You take the info at its face value.

Authority Bias

When he was the U.S. Attorney for the Southern District of New York, James Comey joined his newly hired prosecutors as they took their oath of office. After they did so he "told them something remarkable was going to happen when they said they represented the United States of America—total strangers were going to believe what they said next."

Social animals tend to trust those in positions of authority over them. A significant amount of their behavior is compelled by the need to obey authorities. You make an effort to keep the speed of your vehicle near the set limit because the government mandates it. You submit reports by the deadline because your boss mandates it. We must obey authorities, and this implies a certain trust. It inclines you to believe the words of the official on CNN. It also means that when the FBI agent promises to show you mercy if you "cooperate," you believe him.

Not only are we apt to trust the authorities, absent conflicting information, we presume them to be more enlightened than we are. (It is necessary, therefore, to devote an entire chapter, #3—*Fallible Officials*, to showing this is not always the case.)

The deference we show the powers that be is an evolutionary device that holds together the hierarchical societies necessary for survival. But it is not without its flaws.

The three key secrets to disappearing acts in magic performances are: 1) stimulating expectations so the audience members' minds become accustomed to seeing a certain object or movement, then 2) directing or distracting the singularly focusable attention of each member, and 3) relying on a 1/10 second delay that occurs between the time the eye (retina) detects and the brain (visual cortex, et al.) processes and interprets something. That is, physical actions take place faster than neuronal ones which causes the mind to see what it expects rather than what is actually happening. The result is the audience "seeing" something that isn't there. This effect, known as the *persistence of vision*, is the explanation behind the phrase "The hand is quicker than the eye." Thus, after one sees an object or event, what she believes she has seen is an admixture of memory, expectation, prejudices, and unawareness.

Where traps and related Bait and Switch approaches are concerned, three conditions are necessary for success:

1. The presentation of actual evidence,

2. which must be superficial—concealing an underlying scam,

3. and accepted by the mark as genuine. (This causes him to believe the incorporated assertion must be also. In other words, the aura of authenticity covers everything, and everyone, involved.)

Using a portion of something to make determinations about the whole is known as *extrapolation*. Doing this is inherent in human (and animal) nature. This is another evolutionary trait that usually works to one's advantage, but when keenly exploited by an opportunist can be a point of vulnerability. In the usual consumer version of the bait and switch, a company advertises goods or services at a low price, but when a prospective customer attempts to accept the offer, a salesman leads him to higher priced (i.e. more profitable) goods or services. The versions that take place in inter-business, political, legal, and military environs are, as we saw above, higher stakes variants in which the victim is lured in with the promise of something favorable, then delivered something of lesser or no value. He may be harmed, even severely.

All magic acts are illusions. And the audience is, all too often, complicit in the effect. By allowing the magician to lead them in the direction he desires, and refusing to look at the situation with a skeptical eye, it conspires in its own deception.

People who are deceived tend to be in a needy or hopeful state of mind. Often they are desperate. But even then if the prospective deceiver cannot establish an exact claim, especially a fraudulent one, he must provide at least a vague basis for belief. One way to do this is by telling the mark what he wants to hear. When he wants to believe it, he will consciously or otherwise search for evidence it is true.

Scott Cook (Intuit) saw dollar signs flashing in his mind. He badly wanted to believe Gates would add him to the billionaires' club. Blinded by wishful thinking, he never bothered to investigate Microsoft's past to discover how it had scammed Apple in a similar manner only seven years prior. He was ripe to be deceived.

♦ ♦ ♦ ♦ ♦

HOAX

A hoax is a scheme orchestrated with an intent to deceive people, usually a great number of them, via the diffusion of false emotionally stimulating information. It is often the product of a desire to exploit. Plenty have, nonetheless, arisen out of a mere quest for attention or entertainment. It is always accomplished by veiling the truth or manipulating public opinion. An audience is selected, a false story that will specifically interest it, and perhaps supporting evidence, is fabricated. The story is released and spreads, sometimes with prodding by the original perpetrators, but often on its own. As the number of people who believe it increases, the effect cascades until its target audience generally accepts it, at least for a time, as factual.

We will soon examine the potency of other political weapons in provoking insurrections, but first we'll examine how the hoax has been a contributing factor in a major uprising.

In 1899, four drunken Denver newspaper reporters concocted a scheme. They would announce they had met a team of American engineers who had been contracted by the Chinese government to destroy that country's Great Wall. This, they would claim, was being done as an expression of good faith to foreign countries and a solicitation for commerce with them.

The reporters all worked for separate newspapers. Each wrote slightly different versions of the story, and with the four "independently" reporting the same general account, it had credibility. When the story was printed it spread like wildfire. Other U.S. newspapers, including a major New York one, picked it up, adding their own details. It then reached Europe, Asia, and, ultimately, China.

A society of Chinese known to Westerners as the Boxers, due to their practice of gymnastics, calisthenics, and martial arts, caught wind of this. The Boxers were already opposed to the colonialism of Chinese territory and the influence of Western nations, so news the wall was to be destroyed to further assimilate their nation into the Western world pushed them over the edge.

The Boxer Rebellion (China 1900)

Strategy: Uncertain, likely self-promotion and entertainment.

Hoax: The Great Wall of China would be destroyed by an American crew so China could improve relations and trade with foreign countries.

Effect: Boxers rampaged China destroying anything they considered alien. They killed Chinese Christians and those who promoted Western culture, while also burning the houses, churches, and schools used by those people. Military regiments from eight different countries finally put down the insurrection later that year. To settle the matter, China reached an agreement with eleven countries. It would: 1) execute or otherwise punish culpable officials, 2) destroy military fortresses, and 3) pay approximately $330 million in damages. The rebellion accelerated the deterioration of China's Qing dynasty (which had ruled since 1644 and would be overthrown in 1912) and permanently affected the nation's foreign relations.

These days what has always been considered a hoax has been reclassified as "fake news," or, if it is part of a political strategy, as a "disinformation" tactic. And while the hoax of old and fake news of today may be diffused through different media platforms, they operate in exactly the same socio-political manner and with the same potency.

Researchers at Ohio State University believe three fake news stories determined the outcome of the 2016 U.S. presidential election.

1. Hillary Clinton was suffering from a serious illness;

2. Pope Francis had endorsed Donald Trump;

3. Clinton, while serving as Secretary of State, had approved the sale of weapons to ISIS.

After conducting a thorough survey, filtered with multiple regression analysis for other influential factors (e.g. age, sex, race, income, education, political inclination, and illogical feelings), the researchers concluded 11 percent of those who had voted Democratic in 2012 voted Republican in 2016 because they believed one or more of those stories. This should come as no surprise as Massachusetts Institute of Technology (MIT) scientists found stories featuring fake news collected from Twitter from 2006-2018 circulated with six times the speed of a truthful story. The results, which were screened for the impact of "bots" (computer programs that repeat tasks), also showed false news spreads over a substantially greater distance. Lead scientist on the study, Soroush Vosoughi, Ph.D., concludes: "false news travels farther, faster, deeper, and more broadly than the truth in every category of information—many times by an order of magnitude." Twitter sources that release truthful stories have more followers, but it is the wild stories that are more likely to become popular.

Deception is facilitated by some sort of platform, known in the intelligence business as a channel. In political and military intel these channels tend to be the enemy's reconnaissance satellites, electronic intercept systems, foreign media (e.g. news broadcasts, websites, blogs), diplomats, and operatives such as spies. Note: In 2010 a BOP officer ally tipped me off that I was on a special communications monitoring list due to my political and legal activities. I then began using the telephone, snail mail, and eventually email to strategically mislead BOP officials on various topics.

Using the aforesaid platforms, the one intending to deceive transmits information—which is known in the business as signals. These are hints (fragments of evidence) he desires the target to assemble into a full picture the target falsely believes is accurate. For example, in military intelligence a signal may be an increase in the amount of army radio traffic, a news story describing a troop buildup in a country bordering the target's, or a phone call made via an insecure line between an ambassador in the bordering country and a state department official in the deceiver's vaguely discussing an agreement.

Taken in context these pieces may present a larger picture suggesting the deceiver has reached a deal to militarily assist the neighboring country against the target's country; (when in actuality, perhaps, the deceiving country just wants to dissuade the target from invading his neighbor's land and wishes to do so without a heavy troop commitment as the deceiver's forces are already engaged in conflict elsewhere.) Note: In early 2011 inmates employed at Unicor (federal prison industries) went on strike to protest the administration's forthcoming removal of washing and drying machines from housing areas. The administration hadn't expected this strike and it sent them into a frenzy. They locked up, charged, and transferred all inmate ringleaders. Seeing the opportunity, I quickly began dropping hints in letters and calls to free world friends that inmates were organizing a second strike. It didn't take long before I was summoned to the office where the Dark One's underlings interrogated me. I "reluctantly" gave them the big picture: I'd heard but could not confirm that two specific inmates were coordinating the second strike. In reality, these inmates were threatening my safety and I came up with a creative way to remove them without harm to anyone. Since I was very clear this was only a rumor, they were locked up and transferred, but charged with no offenses.

We've already unmasked some of deception's deadly faces. Now let's look at some more you can use to subvert the authority of opportunistic officials and protect yourself from their predation.

PROVOCATION

A year after a U.S. led coalition invaded Iraq in the 2nd Gulf War (Iraqi Freedom: 2003-09) hostile forces—some loyal to Saddam, all opposed to Western control—remained strong. Sunni Muslims exactly shared Saddam's faith and the focus of their resistance was Al-Fallujah, a city of 350,000 situated on the Euphrates River in central Iraq. Fallujans defied the U.S. and its Iraqi puppet government by organizing their own local administration complete with a city council, manager, and mayor.

The tension came to a head on March 31, 2004, when Fallujan resistance fighters ambushed a convoy of jeeps escorting trucks that would be used to transport food service equipment to American camps. Four employees of the private security firm Blackwater USA were shot and their corpses publicly desecrated. After being torn apart and dragged through the city, the remains of two bodies were hung from the main bridge over the Euphrates for half a day. Jubilant Iraqis filmed the carnage.

The insurgents considered this to be a victory of sorts and became all the more inspired to resist foreign authority. Al-Fallujah quickly came to be seen as the embodiment of American vulnerability as its people showed the world the U.S. and its Iraqi pawns weren't really in charge. But this, American leaders knew, could not stand.

On April 5 U.S. forces composed mainly of 2,500 Marines besieged the city. Fierce gun battles erupted over the following week. Tanks, Cobra AH-64 attack helicopters, and F-16 fighter jets pounded targets such as a power plant and the mosque compound where the rebellion was believed to be headquartered. Even though the city was mostly without electricity, resistance was fierce. An internal Marine Corps memo read, "Insurgents surprise U.S. with coordination of their attacks: coordinated, combined, volley-fire RPGs, and effective use of indirect fire. Enemy maneuvered effectively and stood and fought." Seeing the strength of the resistance, yet more Iraqis were encouraged and joined it.

Lt. Col. Brennan Byrne, commander of the Marines, was the first to solicit help from the U.S. Army's Psychological Operations Department. PsyOps and Marines came up with an idea to offend the Fallujans. First, they concocted a variety of insults. U.S. friendly Iraqis translated them into Arabic and yelled them over a public address system. When enemy Iraqis had all they could take they stormed out of remaining mosque structures wildly firing AK-47s only to be immediately gunned down by Marine sharpshooters who lay in wait. Second, PsyOps pumped the austere Muslims into fits of militant rage by calling the city Lala Fallujah (a pun on the Western music festival Lollapalooza) and by blasting loud music by heathenish Western rock bands such as AC/DC and Guns and Roses. And again, when enraged insurgents emerged firing indiscriminately, they were shot on sight.

The U.S. declared a ceasefire after a weeklong battle. Approximately 150 U.S. soldiers and 800 Iraqis, hundreds of whom were women and children, lay dead. Half of the city's buildings were destroyed. Marines renamed the bridge where the corpses had been defiled Blackwater Bridge and scrawled upon it in black magic marker: "This is for the Americans of Blackwater who were murdered here in 2004, Semper Fidelis..."

♦ ♦ ♦ ♦ ♦

Provocation can be a form of deception used in a variety of contexts. It is often used as the bait in a trap. The idea is to trick your opponent into doing what you want by arousing his emotions until he becomes mentally unstable and snaps—speaking or acting in the manner you desire. Attorneys employ it in an attempt to incite hostile witnesses into conceding what the attorney wants, but this isn't always effective as these witnesses are usually well rehearsed by their own attorneys to handle intense cross-examination. The types of government officials who regularly testify in legal proceedings are trained on this early in their careers and are unlikely to lose their cool in court. For example, I managed to provoke an FBI agent to get hot under the collar as I cross-examined him in a 2006 federal civil proceeding; yet for his beet red face, eye squinting, hateful sneers, and other manifestations of anger toward me, he never misspoke. In Chapter Fifteen we'll see how a crafty reporter was able to corner an experienced politician at exactly the right moment and trick him into engaging in discourse that led to a damning temper tantrum.

The variety of provocation deception employed in the military context cited above is known as *Scatalogical Warfare*. Scat in Greek is excrement. Thus, in practicing this, one insults his mark (metaphorically smearing him with excrement) until he can take no more and throws caution to the wind. It worked well on the devout Muslims, especially as it came from morally inferior Americans they already despised. Tapping into the mental arena, PsyOps was able to flush out insurgents the Marines had been unable to safely access by any other method.

♦ ♦ ♦ ♦ ♦

BLUFFING

After quickly accomplishing the military objectives of the first Gulf War (1991) U.S. leaders decided it was time to wrap up their offensive. From Washington, Chairman of the Joint Chiefs of Staff Colin Powell called commander of allied forces General H. Norman Schwarzkopf at his command bunker in Riyadh, Saudi Arabia suggesting as much. In their February 27 conversation Schwarzkopf agreed this was feasible, asserting he was in a position to cease fire at midnight on February 28, the fifth day of the ground campaign. He proposed labeling it the "Five Day War." Powell liked this and discussed it with the White House. Washington countered that it would be more politically profitable to terminate it at 8:00 a.m. so they could package it as the "100 Hour War."

Ending hostilities meant terms and conditions had to be reached and a conference between Iraqi and American commanders was necessary. General Schwarzkopf searched for the right location. His first choice was the battleship USS Missouri, because General Douglas MacArthur had received Japan's surrender on the deck of that very ship in 1945. Not only would history be somewhat repeated, but the symbolism—this was the place where defeated nations surrender— would also psychologically disadvantage the Iraqi delegation.[12] One problem, however, remained. President George H.W. Bush had allotted only 48 hours for the conference to commence. While the ship was present in the theatre, it was stationed in the middle of the Arabian Sea. The logistics of transporting the Iraqi delegation, along with representatives of coalition nations and the press, within that time limit, rendered its use impossible.

The general's second choice was Jalibah, a large Iraq airbase captured by U.S. forces on day three of the ground war. It would be easy for the Iraqis to reach as it was 95 miles inside the Iraq/Kuwait border. There was a representational element in this choice as well—the general

---

[12] Choosing a surrender site that will particularly humiliate the vanquished nation is an old political/military tactic. In June 1919 the allies myopically forced Germany's official surrender of World War I in the Hall of Mirrors at the Palace of Versailles (France) because this was the very place where 48 years earlier the Germans declared the commencement of their German Empire after defeating the French. In 1940 Hitler reciprocated by forcing France to surrender in the same location (forest of Compiegne, France) and even the very rail car in which Germany had been forced to sign the initial armistice that ended hostilities in World War I (November 1918).

believed that if the Iraqis personally witnessed the U.S. military in control of an airbase deep in their own territory, they would understand just how powerless they were. But this too turned out to be impractical, for live ordnance surrounded the area. Schwarzkopf settled on the Safwan Airfield—an Iraqi military airstrip only a few miles north of the border. He would nonetheless soon discover there was also a problem with this choice. The general had issued orders for his troops to capture the sector the previous day and he had received confirmation that his 1st Infantry Division now held it. But this information was incorrect. His order had not been carried out and the field was not under U.S. control.

The sector was reconnoitered, and Schwarzkopf's deputy commander reported it was, in fact, occupied by an Iraqi Unit consisting of a brigade commander and sixteen Republican Guard tanks. Out of any alternate sites for the conference, Schwarzkopf ordered the commander of his Army forces to order the Iraqi Unit to withdraw. But the Iraqi commander refused, and the American general was now in a bind. A plan was formulated.

That afternoon fifty U.S. tanks encircled the Iraqi Unit. Three companies of American troops waited nearby and Apache attack helicopters filled the skies. When the overwhelming display of military force reached its peak, the U.S. brigade commander approached the Iraqi commander and announced that his men were looking for a fight. The Iraqi immediately ordered his unit to withdraw.

The Iraq/Allied forces conference took place at the airstrip two days later.

Washington had proposed, and General Schwarzkopf had approved, a temporary ceasefire. The President had announced on TV that the war was over. It was not in Schwarzkopf's best political interest to reignite it. But he had to get the Iraqi Unit out of the prospective conference site.

A bluff is somewhat similar to a hoax but involves a quick show of strength to intimidate an opponent. A hoax is a more elaborate, lengthy scheme the premise of which is often absurd. The strategy to take the Safwan airfield was one of both brinksmanship and bluffing, a popular combination. If the Iraqis had opened fire, U.S. forces would've had to fight back. But Schwarzkopf wasn't about to initiate combat. As we learned in the previous chapter, when someone issues a threat it means he either doesn't want to make good on it or can't. Had the Iraqi commander simply stood his ground—refusing to withdraw without opening fire—the U.S. forces would've withdrawn without opening fire. Schwarzkopf bluffed and the Iraqis blinked.

PRETEXTS

In 1907 the Germanic Austro-Hungarian empire unexpectedly annexed the small Slavic state of Bosnia, a move unwelcome by citizens of the latter state. Nearby in the province of Serbia, some of these Bosnians worked with Serbs in plotting a rebellion. A terrorist organization of Slav nationalists based in the capitol city of Belgrade was the most talented of these groups. It propagandistically named itself National Defense but was equally propagandistically labeled by opponents as the Black Hand. Led by the Serbian army's intelligence chief, the group concocted various violent schemes to dissolve the already weak government of their overlords and blend likeminded Slavs into a unified southern kingdom.

Archduke Franz (Francis) Ferdinand, crown prince of the Austro-Hungarian empire, visited Sarajevo—the capitol of Bosnia—on June 28, 1914. Members of the Black Hand waited in the crowds that lined the streets to see the prince as his entourage drove toward City Hall. One hurled a bomb at Ferdinand's car as it approached, but the driver was able to dodge it. The Austrians convened with the Governor of Bosnia at City Hall where they discussed safety. They collectively decided the distinguished visitors would depart the city via an alternate route. Nonetheless, on the way out the driver of the lead car forgot to adhere to the new path and turned onto the old. The archduke's driver followed, then realized his mistake and stopped. A young Black Hand member instantly reacted—drawing his pistol and assassinating Ferdinand and his wife.

Back in Vienna, Austrians and their government seethed. Their crown prince had been viciously killed and, worse yet, by a Slav of Serbian descent. Austria's ally, Germany, was pressing it to take swift, severe action and in this tragedy it found opportunity—a chance to redeem its honor and beat the rebellious Serbians into submission.

The Austrian government issued an ultimatum on July 23. It proclaimed Ferdinand's murder had been orchestrated in Serbia, officials of that province had provided weapons to the assassins, and its border guards had arranged their passage into Bosnia. If Serbia was to avoid war, it further declared, ten strict demands must be met. The most important required: 1) admittance into the province for Austrian officials who would conduct an investigation into the murder, 2) the abolition of Slav nationalist propaganda against Austria, 3) dissolution of Slav nationalist groups, and 4) removal of all Serbian officials opposed to Austrian rule. Serbia was given 48 hours to reply.

Leaders of other nations recognized the demands were unreasonable and a mere formality for a decision already made. With this in mind, Austria was astonished when, on the 26th, Serbia very apologetically agreed to all of the demands. They did, however, temper the first. This gave Austria's foreign minister, Count Leopold von Berchtold, grounds to claim Serbia had not accepted the ultimatum. He rejected the response and on the 28th Austria declared war. The next day its army began an artillery bombardment on Belgrade. It was the opening of the conflict that quickly escalated into World War I.[13]

In the previous chapter we studied threats. We discovered they are actually rites undertaken to prevent costs to the one issuing them. In some situations, however, one either wants, or has already decided, to take a drastic action but sociological, political, or legal constraints prevent him from doing so unless: 1) the target strikes him first or 2) he first warns his target and provides some sort of option by which disaster can be avoided. We've already examined provocation deception. In that case it was used to flush out hidden enemies, but it certainly can be, and often is, used to draw a target's offensive action so the deceiver can attack while claiming self-defense. Now we also see a counterfeit threat—the warning issued in the hopes the target will not or cannot meet the demands. If he does meet them, the threatener usually asserts some dubious grounds for a claim the target has not complied and delivers his desired sanction anyway.

Counterfeit threats that are issued to conceal the actual intention or plan are common in politics, warfare, and even business.

The issuance of a threat in this manner is part of a strategy that deceptively intends to justify a negative forthcoming action. It cannot be considered an actual threat and the characteristics associated with real threats, therefore, do not apply to one.

♦ ♦ ♦ ♦ ♦

---

[13] As is the case with most, if not all, of world history, there are many interpretations of these events. I am describing the account I find most credible. We will examine methods used to determine the accuracy of historical, and current, accounts in Chapter 8.

DISGUISE

The powerful often enjoy direct confrontation with the weak. The reason for this should be obvious—they retain the advantage. For example, the American detective knows he can bully, badger, insult, and lie to the suspect because nothing he says will come back to haunt him. But anything the suspect says can and will be used against him.

While insubordination that directly challenges the authority of the official can be highly contagious, it can also be highly dangerous. The inherent weakness of the subordinate seldom allows him this privilege. Thus, he usually must invoke methods that are subtle, indirect, and open to interpretation—outwardly showing his powerful superior the highest respect all the while.

The weak have devised a number of schemes involving the propagation of messages to surreptitiously attack the strong. The information spread via these methods can be false, but is frequently factual. That being the case, they are not intrinsically deceptive. The identities and motives of their authors along with the channels through which they are conveyed are, however, another matter. Let's now examine two of the more popular and successful forms.

Rumor

Reports without any apparent source that become widely disseminated have proven to be potent psychopolitical information weapons. Most of us have been negatively impacted by these at some point in our lives and once they've had the chance to sink in and putrefy, they're difficult to extinguish. For even the rumor about rumors is generally accepted: "You know what they say about rumors—they're usually true."

This particular devise flourishes in conditions where:

1. The essential interests of the population are at play,
2. Credible specific information is scarce.

In these situations, such as the early phases of war, natural disasters, epidemics, and political and economic turmoil, people crave information. Most commonly they desire to know the "five Ws": who, what, where, when, and why. Some of this inquisitiveness may arise from natural human curiosity, but most has a more personal meaning—the impact to the self. They consider the possibilities: Did it affect me? Could it? Is there anything I can do to profit from this or at least avoid being harmed by it?

In modern western societies we have a rabid news media, but the same have earned a healthy degree of skepticism. The conservative sources portray one perspective and the liberal sources another. This only encourages rumors. Further, some societies are relatively closed (e.g. companies, government agencies, colleges, military bases, prisons) and have no real news source. Such environments are ripe for rumors.

Once a rumor is launched it cannot be controlled. And those who propagate such a message are likely to alter it to conform to their views. Thus, it will take on a life of its own and may well have an unintended effect. Circulating it orally nonetheless permits it to be distorted via a network in which so many actors and words are involved it becomes impossible to discern from whom it originated. This is often the case even when circulated electronically if the author hides behind protective pseudonyms.

Dominant classes understand the potency of rumors. Emperors of the Roman Empire employed teams of officials to monitor, gather, and report them. Historians believe they are responsible for provoking several insurrections, two of which are most noteworthy.

1. **The French Revolution (1789)**
    Strategy[14]: Inducement of wishful thinking.

    Rumors: 1) The people would be able to elect representatives; 2) The king would start acting in good faith to resolve grievances; 3) Abolition of tithes, feudal dues, and hunting restrictions.

    Effect: Peasants began behaving as if the rumors were true, leading to a conflict that culminated in the overthrow of the monarchy.

2. **St. Dominique Revolution of Haiti (1816)**
    Strategy: Inducement of wishful thinking.

    Rumors: The king had granted slaves: 1) Three days of liberty per week, 2) Freedom from corporal punishment.

    Effect: Slaves took the three days off believing their masters were disobeying the king's order and the resultant conflict escalated into a revolution by which the country obtained independence.

The above rumors were false.

Note: The Great India Rebellion (aka Sepoy Mutiny) of 1857-58 is generally believed to have been induced by rumor. Nonetheless, because every account I've studied on it differs in some important respect, I removed it as an example.

GOSSIP

This information weapon is very similar to rumoring. The chief distinctions are that it is directed at a specific entity (e.g. person, company, government) and is malicious by design, intending to ruin a reputation. As a veiled form of social aggression, it almost intrinsically retains no identifiable source, but plenty of enthusiastic messengers. Thus, it has the same advantage of anonymity as does the rumor. If someone is caught spreading either gossip or a rumor she can merely assert it was what she was told and in so doing is absolved of the more serious offense of having originated the tale: "It's just what I heard. I never said it was true."[15]

Gossip is typically used as a form of social control among peers—to pressure them into conformity with group values, shame them when a personal conflict arises, or drive them out of the group altogether. Nonetheless, it has been successfully used by subordinates to impugn the character of superiors. Superiors, in turn, can certainly employ it to force subordinates to heel, but resources in this arena tend to favor the little guy.

For gossip to be effective, three conditions must exist:

---

[14] I am inferring a strategic intent behind these rumors based upon the available information. I've been able to find little on their genesis which comes as no surprise, because, when properly executed, such should have no identifiable author.

[15] In some circumstances it is easy for the target to identify the source. For example, if nobody but you had original knowledge of his offense, or if you are one of a few and the target knows you are the friend of a gossiper, it isn't hard to discern. Further, if you are dealing with a small group of people and wish to remain anonymous, you are advised to secure, in advance to revealing anything, a promise to keep your name confidential. People love to stir up trouble to amuse themselves and some will go straight to the target, especially if he's a peer, and confront him. E.g. "Hey, Stanley just told me you did this! What the hell is wrong with you?" When this happens it is highly effective in humiliating your target, but is highly ineffective in protecting you from your humiliated target's recrimination.

1. The target is a member of a society. Most people are part of several societies and thus can be targeted in any or all. You, for instance, are probably the citizen of a nation and state as well as a resident of a community. You are probably also part of other societies such as a college, company, or social club. The society can be any type—from a face-to-face group to an online clique. People who may technically be part of a society but have, as a practical matter, dropped out of it (e.g. hermits, pariahs, undesirables, the one scummy family in the neighborhood nobody talks to anyway) are not suitable targets.

2. Societally accepted behavioral standards. Without agreed upon norms of right and wrong there is no benchmark against which grades of departure can be measured and found offensive. Some underworld standards are so contrary to those of their broader aboveboard counterparts it can be difficult to find violations. For example, in prison, gossip that an inmate is a career criminal, sadistic sociopath, or dope fiend just means he's a typical inmate and may even elevate his status. Gossip that he is a snitch or thief, however, places him in a precarious position. Such a person is held in contempt in prison society as he is a threat to the self-interests of the population.

3. The target has a reputation that is of some worth. Anyone who holds power inherently has a standing of value in some form. Most powerful people have it in multiple forms. While this gives one of them great strength, it also gives his enemies more fronts on which his reputation can be assailed. For instance, if your target is a church deacon, that status is of value. Credible community gossip that he is cheating on his wife is likely to have an impact. But when the man admits to a number of affairs and renounces his faith, his social standing changes. If he is then caught in another affair, gossip about it is unlikely to further impact his social standing. If, on the other hand, he holds power in another aspect, say as a shrewd business executive, his status in that position still has value. Thus, credible community gossip that his mismanagement of company funds is leading to his company's financial implosion may harm his professional standing. (If the company is publicly held it is likely to also affect the price at which the stock trades. Rumor and gossip can cause major fluctuations in this.)

Malignant gossip, probably originated by revolutionaries, conflated with less malicious rumor to become a factor in one of the most significant insurrections in world history.

The Russian Revolution (1917)

Strategy: Political sabotage—undermining the moral authority of the sovereign.

Gossip: 1) Empress Alexandra and her spiritual advisor Grigory Rasputin were in a sexual relationship (her young daughters were later added to his supposed conquests); 2) The empress' best friend Anna Vyrubova, conspiring with Rasputin, lured both the empress and her husband, Czar Nicholas II, into wild orgies; 3) Rasputin and Vyrubova were influencing official appointments and policy decisions; 4) Alexandra and Rasputin were spying for Germany during World War I (The credibility of the latter was found in the fact that she was a German princess of the Hesse line who had married into the Russian royal family.)

Effect: Russian Prime Minister and Minister of War Alexander Kerensky notoriously opined "If there had been no Rasputin there would have been no Lenin." While this may be true, other factors were involved in causing the revolution. They include enormous Russian casualties in the war, fierce hunger among the people, and

Nicholas' general incompetence. Even when Nicholas abdicated to his younger brother, a massive protest erupted that a republic, rather than another czar, was desired. Gossip, nonetheless, certainly aggravated discontent among the public, the soldiers, and the elite.

The gossipers spread their messages via word of mouth, newspaper stories, lewd drawings, and even dirty limericks. Most Russians accepted the allegation that Rasputin was Alexandra's lover and many found the rest possible. In reality, the empress was heavily influenced by the advice of her spiritual advisor while the czar was away directing the war. In fact, she often convinced Nicholas to order exactly what Rasputin suggested. All of the remaining stories were, however, false. The royal couple never formally renounced the gossip or explained that Rasputin was in their life because he had a mysterious ability to temporarily heal their son, Tsarevich Alexi. They took this strategy because they did not want Russians to know the future czar had an incurable disease (which ran in the empress' line). But as we will shortly see again, the failure to deny an accusation can—in and of itself—lead people to believe it is truthful.

COMBINATIONS
Hoax, Entrapment/Provocation, and Distraction/Confusion

Lyndon Johnson was in over his head in 1948 . . . or so it seemed. He had lost the 1941 Senate race to Texas Governor W. Lee "Pappy" O'Daniel and now he was in another Senate race against the immensely popular Coke Stevenson who had replaced O'Daniel as governor in 1941. Stevenson had just retired after nearly eight years in Austin's executive seat, but decided he wasn't ready to fully relinquish a career in politics. There was every reason to believe he could defeat Johnson who had been unable to rise above the position he'd held since 1937 as a U.S. House representative. Johnson had already known a great deal about political maneuvering when he arrived in Washington, but in his eleven years as a congressman he had learned plenty. This senate race, therefore, would be different.

Johnson conflated several distinct aspects of deception together to turn the tables on his stronger opponent. Let's examine them.

The Hoax

1. After years of promising state labor leaders he was in their corner, Johnson's congressional record began demonstrating the opposite. The congressman strongly opposed President Harry Truman's civil rights oriented package known as the Fair Deal. He'd also voted in favor of the Taft-Hartley Act of 1947 which banned certain union activities, such as secondary boycotts and closed shops (companies that only hire union members). The Act further empowered the President with the ability to delay for 80 days strikes that could endanger the public's health and safety.

2. Because Johnson's actions were such, the Texas chapter of the American Federation of Labor (AFL) endorsed his opponent, Stevenson, in early 1948. The latter accepted it hoping he could acquire some liberal votes in addition to those of his massive conservative base.

3. The great majority of Texans were strongly opposed to organized labor, which they associated with corruption, ethnic minorities, and, worst of all, the dreaded red beast—communism. Johnson understood what seemed to elude his opponent and seized the opportunity by accusing Stevenson, via the media, of making a secret deal with labor leaders.

4. Six hundred angry AFL delegates quickly assembled and voted to condemn Johnson's accusation. The June 25 Dallas Morning News reported this under the headline "Infuriated AFL Delegates Vote to 'Get' Johnson."

5. Johnson recognized condemnation by labor unions made him more popular with the vast majority of the voters and upped the ante by specifying the nature of the imaginary deal: If the union would get Stevenson elected to the Senate, Stevenson would vote to repeal Taft-Hartley. Johnson challenged his adversary to come clean about the deal.

6. Stevenson had a lifelong policy to not dignify personal attacks by engaging them. The voters, he repeatedly asserted, knew his record and there was no need for him to answer such an accusation. The closest he came to addressing it was to issue a vague statement in a July 3 interview with a reporter from the small town of Abilene: "My policy is to let everyone alone unless he needs regulating. But when any segment of society becomes a monopoly, it needs to be regulated. I think the Taft-Hartley Act is all right as far as it is needed to keep down a monopoly." This was hardly the sort of fierce anti-union rhetoric Texans wanted to hear. His strategists recommended he clarify the comment, but he refused to offer anything more.

7. The forgoing statement was ambiguous and received little publicity. Most newspapers, therefore, asserted the former governor was actually remaining silent as to his position on Taft-Hartley. Johnson ran with this, relentlessly assaulting his opponent in any media available—radio, newspapers, mail, word of mouth, etc. He repeatedly demanded Stevenson reveal his position on Taft-Hartley and disclose the terms of his "secret deal" with the unions. But no answer was forthcoming.

8. With the accusations unanswered, many Texans came to believe they were true. Big business leaders thought Stevenson may be working against their interests and substantially reduced donations to his campaign. Conservatives switched their allegiance from Stevenson to Johnson.

Entrapment/Provocation

1. On July 26, 1948, both Johnson and Stevenson left Texas for business in Washington, D.C.: Johnson to attend a special session of the Eightieth Congress; Stevenson to hobnob with confederates, such as Senator Tom Connolly, in order to establish he was politically connected and could make things happen in the nation's capitol.

2. Johnson maintained Washington connections far superior to those of the former governor and wasted no time in putting them to use. He asked a reporter ally to invite Stevenson to hold a press conference. Likely seeing no harm in free publicity for his trip, Stevenson agreed.

3. Johnson primed several of his reporter allies to loathe Stevenson—telling them he was just another corrupt Texas governor who, like his predecessor (O'Daniel), sold pardons. He was an ignorant redneck "cave man" and had struck a secret deal with labor bosses in which he would try to repeal Taft-Hartley if they assisted in his election. Johnson was fully aware Stevenson would not defend himself from any insulting personal attacks, so he instructed his reporters to question the candidate aggressively, especially as to his stance on Taft-Hartley.

4. Leslie Carpenter, who worked as a Washington correspondent for several Texas

newspapers, one of which was the Johnson favoring *Dallas Times-Herald*, opened the assault: "Is the large number of pardons granted in your governorship an issue in this campaign?" This, of course, implied he had sold pardons. Offended, Stevenson tensed up and curtly replied, "I wouldn't know." The other reporters joined the onslaught in a fast, furious interrogation. At one point, Stevenson awkwardly attempted to explain that his critics were erroneously including three or five day clemency leaves, due to a prisoner's family emergency, with the total number of pardons. The reporters, however, couldn't comprehend the difference. Carpenter then fired the exact question suggested by Johnson: "Do you think the Taft-Hartley law is a good law or a bad law?" The target answered that the matter was too complex to be dissected into a simple diagnosis of good or bad, but as he attempted to elucidate, Carpenter interrupted him by repeating the question. Finally, Stevenson just answered, "That's a loaded question" and referred the reporter to a statement he had already made on the matter (apparently the one in Abilene on July 3) that they could reference. That segment of the conference then concluded.

5. The conference resumed that evening. Carpenter stated he could find no previous statement on Taft-Hartley and again insisted Stevenson reveal whether he thought it was a good or bad law. The interviewee lost his composure and angrily replied, "I'm not going to let the *Times-Herald* shape up my campaign." An assertive young reporter named Jack Anderson then joined in the interrogation. The colloquy follows:

Anderson:	What did you say about the Taft-Hartley law?
Stevenson:	I couldn't repeat it from memory.
Anderson:	Could you give us the gist of it?
Stevenson:	I might be able to, but I don't see any value in it.
Anderson:	All I want is a yes or no.

Stevenson refused to provide this upon which Anderson asked why he was dodging the question.

Stevenson:	Because you all catch me here away from my notes and put me under cross-examination.
Anderson:	It seems like a simple thing to remember how you stand.
Stevenson:	The people of Texas know.

Other reporters were offended by this assault and intervened to stop it, but Anderson summed up: "It appears to me you are trying to carry water on both sides, Governor."

Indeed, it appeared that way to many.

Texas newspapers presented the conference exactly as it took place. The *Ft. Worth Star Telegram* stated Stevenson "dodged a direct question, asked five times, as to whether he considered Taft-Hartley to be a good law or a bad law." The *Austin-American Statesman* reported, "A dozen newsmen . . . tried for twenty minutes to get an answer from him on the question."

Distraction/Confusion

1. By late August, Stevenson, on the advice of his campaign strategists, had reluctantly decided to fight fire with fire—launching charges of unpopular conduct against his opponent. But mysteriously, Johnson was always perfectly prepared for these and issued identical charges on the same or following day.

2. Stevenson, for example, gave a speech in Austin on August 19. He asserted Johnson was "waging what is probably the most expensive political campaign in the history of Texas," and added that Johnson's supporters funds were being "spent like water" to obtain victory. In Fort Worth that very day Johnson declared over the radio that it was Stevenson, instead, who was "spending money like water" to prevail.

3. Stevenson also accused Johnson of falsely portraying himself as a conservative. To support this, he revealed that former Secretary of Agriculture and Vice President Henry Wallace—who was now chief of the liberal Progressive Party—had endorsed Johnson and even provided an aide to raise funds for Johnson's failed 1941 Senate campaign. Stevenson questioned of the two: "Are they still together to the extent that the money they are spending is coming from the same source?"[16] The following day Johnson countered that Wallace was actually Stevenson's secret ally. Over the radio he asked: "What promises of support did he (Stevenson) extract from Henry Wallace when Wallace cooled coffee with him in the governor's mansion back in 1944?" (Johnson's staff had done their homework and discovered Stevenson accepted a visit from Wallace while serving as governor.) Johnson appended: "I see . . . that the black bag of the labor bosses has finally arrived from the North to swell the shush fund being spent to defeat Lyndon Johnson."

4. As to that very topic, the August 20 issue of the Corpus Christi *Caller-Times* observed: "The question by Johnson pushed the political merry go round full circle and left each candidate implying the other was—or had been—associated with the head of the Progressive Party." Confused voters thus simply inclined to the candidate who could spend the most money to amplify his accusation. And that candidate was Lyndon Johnson.

♦ ♦ ♦ ♦ ♦

In truth, Stevenson was far more conservative than Johnson. Further, it was Johnson, not Stevenson, who had actually made a "secret deal" with labor, but Texans weren't aware of this because it was mostly labor bosses in the Congress of Industrial Organization (CIO) and United Mine Workers (UMW) out of Washington and New York City who were quietly providing funds for his 1948 campaign. Johnson was so skilled in the art and science of political deception he was able to not only mislead scores of voters, but actually convince them reality was its polar opposite. He also possessed an intuitive insight into locating and exploiting weaknesses, both in his opponent personally and in his agenda politically. He had thoroughly studied Stevenson and was aware his tremendous self-respect and sense of dignity prohibited him from even acknowledging attacks. The more personal and insulting they were, the more he resisted what he saw as legitimizing them with an answer. So, Johnson put together a simple formula: Deliver a degrading personal charge and when Stevenson ignores it accuse him of dodging the issue.

In military strategy this is known as a *relational maneuver*—the direct application of force upon an opponent's precisely diagnosed weakness (critical point). The strategy aims not to destroy the enemy himself, but to disable him by disrupting the system through which he functions, be it a network of allies, a technological apparatus, or in this case, the popular political ideology. The idea is to avoid his well exposed strength, focusing instead on his hidden vulnerabilities.

---

[16] This is a deceptive tactic frequently employed by influential figures—suggesting, rather than actually stating, something is true. You can be sure that if a shrewd accuser had the evidence to support an allegation he would flaunt it. We'll see this again in Chapter 15.

The results of this depend upon:

1. accuracy of the diagnosis of the critical point,
2. the level of surprise effected,
3. the rapidity and precision of the strike.

In Johnson's case it was a direct hit on all of the criteria.

Stevenson failed to quickly adapt to the circumstances, stubbornly standing by a formula of his own that had previously worked: his deeds spoke for themselves; the people of the state knew him, and his reputation was impeccable—honest, trustworthy, conservative.

Some self-proclaimed "expert power strategists" assert it is a fundamental law of power to "always say less than necessary," but doing exactly that cost Coke Stevenson his power fifty years before the "experts" proclaimed it a law. (In fact, Henry Ford had already erred in a similar manner in a bid for the U.S. Senate during World War I by failing to quickly and emphatically deny a false accusation that he employed German sympathizers in his auto plants.) I tend to agree with a historian who observed "brevity can be a weakness when too much is left unsaid." That is, in reality, you should only say as much as necessary, a matter we will examine in Chapter Eight. The "experts" further opine a reputation is one's most precious asset, but the crafty LBJ also proved that "law" false before it was declared. The underdog used his skills in psychopolitcal manipulation and information warfare to systematically excoriate his opponent's well-earned honor, establishing once and for all where the true power lies.

But not all of the deception came directly from Johnson's mouth. For he employed what are known as "walking delegates" to deceive on his behalf. To be sure their audiences were receptive to the ideas and would not suspect they were associated with Johnson, these people were always local and part of whatever group they would talk to—e.g. an area Catholic for the area Catholics, a neighborhood black for the neighborhood blacks. They wandered around to houses, churches, taverns, etc. and engaged people in conversation. Then, when the opportunity was right, they diffused a little sinister gossip about Stevenson. Note: In 1955, the campaign strategists of Chicago politician Richard Daley put an interesting spin on this idea by issuing counterfeit advertisements supporting Daley's opponent Alderman Robert Merriam. These asserted Merriam held a certain position and urged the recipient to vote for him for this reason, but they were distributed only to people who would naturally be opposed to that position. For example, his staff printed brochures that requested a vote for Merriam because he favored a ban on overnight street parking and placed them under the windshields of cars parked in crowded neighborhoods at night. Similarly, they mailed into white suburbs letters from the imaginary American Negro Civic Association that requested a vote for Merriam as he would assure blacks were able to live in every part of the city.

Johnson also invoked a number of propaganda tactics, referring to his adversary as "Calculating Coke," "Mr. Do-nothinger," "Mr. Fence-straddler," and "neanderthal." He drilled these into the voters' heads until they associated his opponent with those qualities. "Labor leaders made a deal with Calculating Coke, they couldn't get out of me," he announced at a speech. Johnson went so far in early August as to suggest Stevenson was the leader of a communist conspiracy. In one radio broadcast he proclaimed: "[Communist] birds of a feather ... have flocked together in a united effort to defeat Lyndon Johnson, who refused to wear their red feathers in his hat, and they are using Coke Stevenson as their silent man Friday." He continued, "My opponent has refused to promise that ... he will not ... return control of labor unions to racketeering Communist leaders who take orders only from Moscow." The next day he added: "Does it mean he would amend the law so that labor bosses could have secret Communist connections?" His four-page propaganda newsletter *Johnson Journal*, which was formatted to give the appearance of an actual news publication, went further yet. The headlines that month blared: "COMMUNISTS FAVOR COKE."

When Johnson began instantaneously returning Stevenson's accusations, Stevenson's campaign managers suspected something even more devious was afoot. Their candidate's strategies, even his schedules were known by the adversary only minutes after they were decided. And their suspicions were correct. Johnson's assistant John Connolly, who would go on to govern the state from 1963-69, later conceded, "Occasionally we would have a telephone operator" monitoring Stevenson's calls. He also offered, "We may have had someone in his headquarters reporting to us." Thus, when Stevenson was making a charge against Johnson, Johnson was simultaneously issuing the same charge against Stevenson. The barrage of identical charges distracted and confused the public, successfully deflating Stevenson's accusations.

Near the final primary, Stevenson did, at long last, follow his advisors' wishes and clarify his position on Taft-Hartley, but by this time 1) his funds were nearly depleted so he couldn't get it publicized and 2) the primary was already upon him.

On August 28, 1948, Johnson defeated Stevenson by 87 questionable votes. He trounced Jack Porter (GOP) in the November election and was sworn in as a senator in 1949. Two years later (1951) he became the party's "whip" or assistant floor leader. Another two years thence (1953) he rose to Minority Leader; within another two (1955), he was the most potent Majority Leader in the history of the Senate. He was elected vice president in November 1960 and ascended to the presidency upon JFK's 1963 assassination. In 1964 the American people elected him to be their president.

> I do understand power, whatever else may be said about me.
> I know where to look for it and how to use it.
> — LBJ

Chapter Seven

Propaganda and Persuasion

Upon the unexpected death of Governor Beauford Jester in 1949, Lieutenant Governor Allan Shiver ascended to Texas' executive seat. The relatively young politician, age 41, had already learned a great deal about political machinations and become exceptionally adroit in the art. He had started his career as a state senator then served two terms as the state's number two executive. He was the first in that position and its concurrent role, Chairman of the Budget Board, to mold the Senate into conformity with his ideas by influencing its agenda and controlling its committee appointees.

The new governor quickly began meeting with lobbyists—requesting they influence lawmakers into raising taxes to fund much needed improvements in state services and, to that end, he convened a special session of the legislature the following year. In addressing it he praised businessmen for propelling their state to the top in the production of oil, cotton, and goats. He then juxtaposed this achievement with the failure of state officials who let Texas plunge to last in medical and mental health services.

The lawmakers who sat before him knew exactly what he wanted and responded accordingly. They modestly increased taxes and correlative appropriations for state hospitals and universities that very session.

In his 1954 reelection campaign, Governor Shivers found himself in a tight contest against the liberal one-time judge Ralph Yarborough for the Democratic nomination. The former had shown some sympathy for workers, but the latter was more extreme in his support for organized labor, a position unpopular with the conservative majority. Believing reform to the state's hospitals and educational institutions would be an issue in the election, Yarborough challenged Shiver's record on the matter. The prescient governor was, however, able to show his efforts years prior were already beginning to resolve the issue. Yarborough thus switched his accusation to a scandal that had taken place on the governor's watch: insurance company lobbyists had succeeded in relaxing insurance regulations, but this resulted in one insurance company declaring bankruptcy each of the seventeen months preceding the campaign. The slick governor had nonetheless carefully insulated himself and Yarborough could point to no evidence directly linking his adversary to corrupting influences. Neither could he produce evidence showing the governor was even aware of such influences.

Shiver countered by charging Yarborough was supported by Communist labor racketeers. The confluence of perception and fortuitous timing served this position well when retail employees who were members of a Port Aurthur CIO (Congress of Industrial Organization) chapter declared a strike that closed twenty stores in the area. Shiver seized the opportunity by asserting the strike was inspired by communists and appointing a committee to investigate the matter. His panel, quickly reaching the conclusion its creator desired, affirmed this was possible as communist threats existed in that part of the state. The governor then convened a special legislative session wherein he requested lawmakers pass a bill making membership in the communist party a criminal offense. They responded by declaring such to be a Class Two felony, punishable by two to twenty years of imprisonment. Finally, Shiver hired a video production company to produce a short haunting movie showing the idle businesses and deserted streets of Port Authur while a narrator cautioned that this was what awaited Texas if unions took over the labor force with a Yarborough victory.

When the U.S. Supreme Court ordered the desegregation of the public school system (Brown v. Board of Education) the governor saw another opportunity arise. He sprang into action disseminating information intended to deepen whites' mistrust of blacks (e.g. describing how blacks heavily engaged in crime and refused to bathe or work) while charging Yarborough with supporting a fully integrated society. In reality, Yarborough hadn't even committed himself to a stance on the issue.

Shiver defeated his challenger in the Democratic primaries by 80,000 votes. He retained the governorship in the general election as well, then retired in 1956 after serving as the state's executive for 7-1/2 years—at the time the longest tenure for the office.

♦ ♦ ♦ ♦ ♦

In its advice for military public affairs, NATO (North Atlantic Treaty Organization) defines propaganda as "Information, ideas, doctrines, or special appeals disseminated to influence the opinions, emotions, attitudes or behavior of any specified group in order to benefit the sponsor either directly or indirectly." The U.S. Department of Defense similarly characterizes it as "Any form of communication in support of national objectives designed to influence the opinions, emotions, attitudes, or behavior of any group in order to benefit the sponsor either directly or indirectly." However one may choose to define it, there is no question propaganda involves the deliberate spreading of messages as a means to influence beliefs and thus behavior. It is a method by which public opinion is created rather than merely controlled. Considered a special type of communication, it uses artful, unfair, and insidious means to manage representations and can take forms that include the written and spoken word, images, and music. Signs, signals, and language that call to mind graphic illustrations are key elements. Propaganda creates the greatest impact in the visual dimension, but any medium can be used to convey its messages.

At one end of the propagandistic spectrum Edward Bernays recognized *state propaganda* as that utilized by government officials to influence public opinion. On the other end, Jacques Ellul proposed that people retain a subconscious desire to be manipulated, which leads them to manipulate themselves, via *sociological propaganda*, to conform to socially expected beliefs and conduct.

At the highest level of the craft propagandists employ a strategic communication model involving a multi-step process designed to fully indoctrinate their target. It operates as follows:

1. An individual passively receives information;
2. He takes an interest in it and actively solicits more;
3. He further studies the matter and accepts the message;
4. The message is reinforced and integrated into his system of beliefs;
5. He becomes an opinion leader who indoctrinates others.

A propagandistic message is most effective when it: 1) seamlessly transitions between distorted and undistorted information, 2) presents true pieces intentionally selected out of a larger whole to elicit an inaccurate perception, 3) is received by those who are undecided on the matter and are 4) unaware of its manipulative intent.

Propaganda can be a component of psychological warfare and those who promote it do not advertise it as such. For this reason, it can be difficult to identify. One of the best ways to do so is to determine the one sponsoring it has an interest in the outcome. Because this is at least somewhat intuitive, the actual source of the message is often (but certainly not always) concealed and the message itself imbedded in what appear to be unbiased sources such as reports issued by news, government, historical, or scientific authorities. It can also be diagnosed by the use of sly language, garbled images, and the fact that it is usually directed more to the interests of specific groups rather than those of the general public.

In an age before it was heavily practiced in the state's political contests Allan Shiver integrated techniques of propaganda and persuasion into his political strategies and used these to tighten his control over Texas.

In praising the success of the businessmen, then immediately denouncing the failure of the officials he drew attention to the contrast between the two extremes, shaming the legislators into making the changes he desired lest he subject them to further embarrassment. By using lobbyists to pass the message that he wanted a tax increase, he avoided the necessity to directly request it, an act that may have been viewed in a negative light by his conservative constituency. Publicly he only implied drastic improvements were needed and left it to the lawmakers to decide how best to effect them. They could take the heat for choosing a tax increase as the method while he took the credit for the result. He pulled it off flawlessly and the press portrayed him as a hero.

Four years later he brilliantly displayed his political prowess in securing his party's gubernatorial nomination. The contest took place at the height of the cold war, with its concomitant McCarthyism, and Shiver was well aware of the common man's fear of real or imaginary communistic threats. If they selected his opponent, went the message, communists would take control of labor and their unreasonable demands would bring businesses to their knees. This, of course, would demolish the economy. He selected people he knew would support his position to form an investigating committee and they reached the conclusion necessary to frighten the voters into doing as he wished.

Years later the power of his manipulation was revealed when committee members confessed they had actually found no evidence whatsoever of communist influences in the state's labor unions. They had just carried out his bidding. As for the chilling video showing the deserted streets of Port Aurthur, it was, in fact, shot at 5:00 a.m., long before any of the local businesses had opened for the day.

The shrewd governor was well aware the voting majority was white, and their culture was incompatible with that of blacks. The whites had no desire to be forcibly blended. With racial tensions already high, he amplified them even more, showing why whites should dislike and fear blacks while also promoting the belief that electing his opponent would lead to exactly the sort of racial and moral pollution the majority dreaded.

◆ ◆ ◆ ◆ ◆

In 1888 Thomas Edison found himself embroiled in a vicious public relations campaign against his chief competitor—George Westinghouse. As part of his effort to establish that his direct current (DC) was safer than his competitor's alternating current (AC), Edison teamed up with H.P. Brown, an electrical engineer from New York City. Brown had become aggrieved over the many deaths of colleagues, which he ascribed to AC, as marketed by Westinghouse and generated by Nikola Tesla's AC Polyphase System.

Edison invited Brown to his famous Menlo Park laboratory to perform cruel experiments demonstrating the dangers of AC. Reporters from the *New York Times* were invited to the event and they watched as Brown "Westinghoused" 1 horse, 2 calves, and 24 dogs with deadly AC current. The *Times* published explicit details of the gruesome electrocutions along with the repeated implication of Westinghouse in their deaths.

When the latter published a response claiming AC was no more dangerous than DC, Brown upped the ante—challenging the opponent to put his money where his mouth is by taking AC current through his body while Brown takes DC through his. Westinghouse knew how this would turn out and could not accept. Thus, with actual demonstrable results speaking louder than words, Westinghouse continued losing the PR battle.

As Brown developed an AC powered chair to kill humans, Edison furthered the cause, providing to Brown some of his most talented staff, including the Irish mathematician A.E. Kennelly, who would go on to a Harvard professorship.

The first execution on the electric chair took place in August 1890. Witnesses were mortified by the barbarisms and to Edison's and Brown's delight spoke accordingly to the press. One reported, "To the horror of all present, the chest began to heave, foam issued from the mouth and the man gave every indication of reviving." A doctor who was present opined: "I would rather see ten hangings than one such execution as this." The *Times* concluded that the event was "worthy of the darkest chambers of the Inquisition of the 16th century."

The public outcry nearly terminated implementation of Tesla's brilliant AC Polyphase System. Later that year work on its induction motor was aborted. Two years would pass before effort to make it more practicable resumed.

♦ ♦ ♦ ♦ ♦

Propaganda should be thought of as one-sided self-serving communications. It always employs one or more platforms to reach an audience. These include media, (internet, newspapers, magazines, radio, TV, etc.), public speeches, administrative remedies, letters, and lawsuits. Even those who spread rumors and gossip, as we noted in Chapter Six, can be effective platforms.

Edison had a congenial relationship with reporters at the *New York Times*. The *Times* management also knew anything the "Wizard of Menlo Park" had to say was newsworthy. He and Brown thus used the newspaper as the primary platform to spread their message to an audience.

Generally speaking, alternating current has always been a more productive form of electricity than direct current. But it was, and still is, far more dangerous. Edison and Brown knew this and milked it for all it was worth. In so doing, they employed two specific techniques: 1) vivid demonstrations, which imperceptibly impress the mind far more than any other form of evidence, 2) persistent associations of their adversary with something negative: electrical deaths.

The demonstrations featuring live animals and even a live person being horrifically killed by AC electricity left spectators aghast. And those spectators graphically described their observations to the general public which was just as appalled. Edison and Brown found the most effective way to associate these deaths with their opponent was to replace the word for this type of death with his very name. The creatures were not "electrocuted," they were "Westinghoused." Edison and Brown, therefore, showed themselves to be the good guys, here to protect the public with safe electricity, while Westinghouse and Tesla were the bad guys, looking to harm the people.

A street thug who murdered his mistress paid for his crime in the worst way possible. William Kemmler, a helpless pawn caught in a gargantuan struggle to manipulate public opinion, became the first human to be executed by electricity. He suffered an atrocious death to advance the self-interests of powerful manipulative men he'd never even met.

◆ ◆ ◆ ◆ ◆

Throughout any campaign of political warfare, you will be communicating to audiences you wish to persuade. When doing so you will be composing and delivering specific messages. Sometimes you will have the opportunity to prepare your message before you deliver it. Sometimes you will not. But your audience will have little concern about the peculiarities of your circumstances. In order to reach them you must communicate effectively.

The persuasiveness of a message is maximized when five conditions are met:

1. **Attention Catching.** People can truly focus their attention on only one object or matter at a time and to make your point you must have their attention. Further, if your audience considers your message in a deep, focused manner, rather than a light superficial one, you are more likely to effect lasting changes in both attitudes and behaviors.

    Addressing your audience by name or a pronoun, such as *you*, can draw its attention, as such words awaken each individual's mind: the info pertains to him. (This, however, is not especially helpful when the audience is already seeking the information.) For example, in Chapter One we considered part of a letter then- President Joe Biden sent to the American people. In the full letter, which is only a single page, he (or his crafty communications wizards as the case may be) wrote *you* (or *your*) 12 times. He also referred to "*our* schools . . . *our* nation . . . *our* economy . . . and *our* children;" and concluded with encouraging statements that led to the confident unifying declaration, "I truly believe there is nothing *we* can't do as a nation, as long as *we* do it together." See Appendix Two.

    Information that is clear, impressive, and directly received makes a stronger impression than that which is vague, dull, or received secondhand. Stories and analogies tend to be more interesting than statistics. The latter can, however, be potent when presented alone in a simple format. When grouped together or when too much clarification on the meaning is needed, they become confusing. Graphic visual images make the strongest impressions. We recall the result of Shiver's spooky video and Edison's and Brown's hideous live electrocutions. An example we're familiar with in modern times is the spectacular video of the 9/11 attacks. It so deeply struck Americans that their leaders needed little additional propaganda to justify the desired military response. (The same could not be said for the subsequent military operation, Iraqi Freedom.)

2. **Understandable.** People have trouble processing information that does not cohere with what they already know or believe. For this reason, it is usually best to present as little new information as possible when you're attempting to persuade them. And when presenting new information, you should blend it well with what they already know or accept.

    Avoid using language that confuses your audience. This includes technical terms, ethnic slang, and excessively elevated words and phrases with which they may be unfamiliar. Speak as they speak and write as they write. Government officials have at least a high school diploma (or the supposed equivalent). High-ranking ones are likely to be college educated. If you're litigating before a court you may wish to study the language and style used by attorneys before presenting oral and written arguments. (I have long used Supreme Court opinions as a benchmark for this.) Jurors best understand evidence when it is presented to them in the form of a story they can easily translate into a simple theme. E.g. The defendant is a nice guy who fell in love, thought romantically instead of practically, and committed a crime of passion. Jurors, of course, are merely somewhat randomly selected members of the public at large. So, there is no reason to believe what a juror understands is any different than the public from which he has been selected. (A good defense attorney, however, should expel government officials from the jury panel in a criminal case as these tend to sympathize with their own kind.)

3. **Convincing.** The most important condition, this mandates you prove your argument to the recipient. I often say, "Don't tell me, show me," and this is crucial in persuasion. Humans have a tendency to trust information presented to them. (This is the Honesty Bias we discussed in Chapter Six). But human thought processes also interpret input in accord with personal experiences, beliefs, culture, sex, etc. Because of this, little can be more common than for people exposed to the same information to form different opinions on it. Let's consider this. In so doing, we will examine a movement that reached its pinnacle in about 2019: Black Lives Matter.

This organization's message is not directed at blacks. Rather it is directed at those of different races. Thus, if non-black A encounters the message and his positive experiences with blacks outweigh negative ones he's likely to agree. If non-black B's experiences were equal or he is devoid of experiences altogether, he could go either way. (These "men in the middle" are the best propaganda targets.) If non-black C's negative experiences with blacks weigh more strongly in his mind than the positive ones he's likely to reject the message.

The mostly liberal media, evidently unaware of the implications of their editing, often juxtapose the BLM slogan with pictures or video footage of blacks and their supporters blocking traffic, destroying property belonging to others, assaulting people of other races, and generally engaging in anti-social behavior. Non-black A takes in the message and either sympathizes with those blacks or finds they are an exception—the few bad blacks. Non-black B, who is in the crucial category, takes in the graphic images and is repulsed. A negative association forms and he starts to believe black lives may matter, but only in a negative way. And this is not easily reversed. Non-black C sees the message and it only reinforces what he already believed. And as he already believed an association exists between blacks and anti-social behavior, he is more likely to notice and recall affirming instances.

The message presented in this format fails to persuade. Worse yet, it takes on the form of a new message that is counter-productive to its intended purpose. (We'll soon examine messages intentionally crafted to counteract other messages.)

Instead of just saying, "black lives matter," those sending the message must also show they do. They could do this by pointing to blacks who have overcome great obstacles to achieve success; adducing, for example, blacks who composed impressive symphonic pieces, invented devices that improved the quality of life, or discovered cures for diseases.

The movement has a catchy slogan and for reasons we are about to examine, repetition can make a point more believable, but one must always provide credible support for one's arguments.

4. **Memorable.** This condition is related to the first. To meet it, however, you must go further, not only catching the attention, but also forming a lasting impression. Short-term memory and working memory are very limited in the amount of information they can retain. This is

why your message must be transferred into its recipients' long-term memory, which is virtually unlimited. You can do this by instilling in their minds themes that key in on their self-interests while evoking emotional responses; using, for example, striking images, vivid anecdotes, or disturbing accusations.

Repeating the message also helps lock it into long-term memory. The very exposure to an idea subconsciously creates a bias favoring what is frequent and familiar. Thus, the more one is exposed to it, the better he remembers it and the more believable it becomes. Political strategists are aware of this and employ the tactic in every campaign. Paul Bolton, LBJ's wily speech writer, once stated of an accusation against an opponent, "You knew it was a damned lie, but you just repeated it and repeated it and repeated it. Repetition—that was the thing."

5. **Compelling.** To fulfill the final condition, you must present the message in a way that drives it home, stirring the recipient who accepts your idea to act upon it. This is best achieved by keying in on his self-interests. What motivates him? Is he looking to fatten his wallet or increase internal satisfaction? Perhaps he wants to advance a special interest and you can help in this. He may be vain and looking for someone to swell his pride or elevate his status. As we already learned, to compel cooperation from a government official you must either be able to help or hurt him. Therefore, you may wish to present a case, such as by composing a short vivid story, demonstrating that if he doesn't act in the desired manner he will be adversely affected. This is exactly what Allen Shiver accomplished with his messages on racial integration and communism. (We will examine the invocation of fear as a compelling device at the conclusion of the chapter.)

♦ ♦ ♦ ♦ ♦

Adolf Hitler thoroughly understood the importance of propaganda and persuasion in attaining power. The master revealed:

> Effective propaganda must concentrate on a few plausible points and hammer away at these in the form of slogans. It must . . . avoid any attempt at objectivity. Not even the shadow of a doubt in the rightness of one's cause is permissible. Propaganda must present love or hate, right or wrong, truth or lies—never half this way and half that way.

Repetition has an effect. And it is the reason why the ideas he promoted could be and usually were translated into simple, credible mottoes which he drove into the minds of his audience where they became entrenched and eventually germinated and blossomed.

The importance of symbolism was also not lost on the führer. When he discovered a member of the Nazi party, the dentist Friedrich Krohn, had created an emblem for use at the initial meeting of Krohn's local party unit, Hitler examined it and instantly recognized its psychological value. Nonetheless, he knew it could be improved and modified it by affixing the black swastika to a white disk which he then laid on a brilliant crimson field—the precise aggression provoking hue by which Russia's Bolshevik party represented itself. This would become the image emblazoned upon the armbands and flags brandished by party members.

Hitler later invested a great amount of time and energy studying heraldry and art at the Munich State Library. As a result, he designed the eagle that would be perched atop the swastika for military insignia. He also instituted the elevated straight arm salute (which is a variation on Mussolini's Roman version) and the mandatory greeting of "hiel" as a self-esteem boosting act of respect among party members. Noting the psychological power of the black shirts worn by Italy's Fascists, he transformed them into the brown shirts donned by the S.A. He would later clothe his elite SS soldiers in black uniforms (designed by none other than Hugo Boss) embellished with mystical Nordic runes and the famous Death's Head emblem. Shiny black boots finished off the ensemble. He found this outfit affected both his soldiers and those who beheld them. It was unifying and beautiful, yet also intimidating.

What can arguably be considered the most successful propaganda campaign in American history began as rich merchants, prominent planters, and influential clergymen in the colonies came to despise their British king, George III, and his parliament for their efforts to tax them unfairly and otherwise diminish their rights. (We learned in Chapter One what it means when a ruler loses the support of his elites.) Through newspapers, pamphlets, and sermons this group protested what they perceived as oppression. They stirred up latent resentment among colonists of every variety; so much, in fact, it cascaded out of control.

British officials dispatched 4,000 soldiers to Boston in October 1768. The tension was already high but when those underpaid soldiers arrived, they quickly began competing with locals for scarce jobs. And this did nothing to improve relations.

On the evening of March 5, 1770, a mob of Boston's street ruffians assembled outside the British customs office. They began cursing and heaving snowballs and rocks at a small detachment of British soldiers who were peacefully standing guard outside the office. As the mob of Bostonians grew and became rowdier, the injured soldiers started fearing for their lives and opened fire, killing five Boston thugs.

Colonial propagandists twisted the incident into one that featured unarmed colonists rightly protesting unjust treatment when they were needlessly gunned down in cold blood. Paul Revere crafted a painting graphically depicting this perspective. Other propagandists such as the minister Joseph Warren, dramatically eulogized the dead as martyrs whose grieving widows and children deserved the utmost pity. The dead men, in reality, had been neither husbands nor fathers.

To crank the tension even higher, Samuel Adams organized public anniversaries commemorating the shooting. Colonial propagandists styled it "The Boston Massacre."

◆ ◆ ◆ ◆ ◆

A little-known propaganda tactic is one we'll call *emotional transfer*. One may come across a rare reference to it in older texts such as those analyzing implements of psychological warfare deployed in the two world wars, but it appears the Government has successfully concealed most of its information on the matter. To invoke it one arouses in his audience an emotion pertaining to one target which he then stealthily redirects to another target having some common ground with the first, but that would otherwise be unable to elicit the intense feeling. Let's look at a hypothetical example.

A Southern Baptist pastor does not want long-haired men in his church building. He believes all men should wear short hair because the bible states that while long hair glorifies a woman, it shames a man. To accomplish his goal, he draws the attention of his congregation to John Doe, a man who drugged and raped a woman. Discussing the crime in an incendiary manner he infuriates his congregation. He then displays a picture of Doe who is clearly wearing long hair. Next, he points out the biblical prohibition on rape, along with its opinion that long hair disgraces a man. He adds that long-haired men are nonconformists who are prone to antisocial behavior and should, for all of the foregoing reasons, be banned from the church.

The congregation is moved by this and agrees. Some recall personally experienced negative encounters with long-haired men they had previously forgotten. After the service the Parish Council meets and unanimously approves a measure prohibiting from church grounds men with hair that extends beyond the collar. All members start looking askance at such men, avoiding them like the plague.

This effect occurs because awakening an emotional state causes it to attach to other objects insinuated at that time. And this can be exploited for positive emotions as well.

We'll say the same pastor desires to elevate his prestige in the eyes of his congregation. He is well aware the role of the warrior is highly esteemed in his society, but as he chose the seminary instead of the military, he cannot claim it. Thus, when delivering a Veterans Day sermon he waxes eloquent on the honor due those who have served, mentioning along with it that his father and several uncles are veterans and some of his cousins are active. He adds that a few of his relatives served in foreign wars. Furthering the effect, he wears a red, white, and blue tie and an Army lapel pin he purchased on eBay.

After the service a couple who have a son at the Air Force Academy tell the pastor how much they appreciate his military heritage and homage to servicemen. A woman compliments him on his tie and pin, stating it is a nice form of tribute. A few VFW members in his congregation inform him they consider him "one of us."

In the first instance, he incites the hatred people feel toward the rapist, then surreptitiously attaches it to innocent long-haired men by using long hair as a common denominator. In the second he awakens the respect society feels for one who has protected it, and furtively claims it for himself by a note of his relatives who have served and are serving, a display of patriotic and militant symbols, and a devotion to those who serve.

◆ ◆ ◆ ◆ ◆

An instrument I've found successful in subverting a position an opponent is promoting is known as the *poison parasite*. To deploy it you first find a message sent by your adversary. It can take any form: images, slogans, gestures; no form of communication is off limits. You then corrupt it and redistribute it as a weapon that will damage his interests. He does the hard part by creating and advancing the message. You merely come up with a clever counterpoint, infuse it—like a virus—into the message, and send it on its way. Let's look at a hypothetical that is based on some actual situations.

We'll say my opponents are hermits. They live in the woods and have started to attract negative attention by breaking into cabins and stealing food while the owners are away, especially during the winter months. I own a cabin and have been repeatedly victimized by them. I'm not so concerned with the food, which is easily replaceable; the invasion of my privacy, on the other hand, is deeply offensive.

Hermits prefer solitude but believe they must band together and clean up their image in order to let the adverse attention subside. They have, to this end, put together a PR (public relations) campaign based on little more than the catchy slogan "Hermit Lives Matter." Their families publish the slogan in newspapers and online. The general public notices it and considers whether it may have merit. Most have had no encounters with actual hermits and are undecided. But my fellow cabin owners and I have also united and put together a campaign of our own. Since we have parasites of the poison variety on the mind already, we decide on an even catchier rhyming counter-slogan, "Hermitites Are Parasites." The hermits say their lives matter, but they fail to present evidence supporting this. My neighbors and I support our counter-slogan with a few bullet points describing how our opponents are destroying our woodsy neighborhood and to this we attach some striking images: an actual photo of the mess they left behind in a burglarized cabin and a staged photo of a vicious derelict with a crazy facial expression prying open a door, not to a cabin, but to a typical looking suburban house. We distribute our anti-advertisement via newspapers and on the internet. The counter-slogan causes an association between hermits and parasites to form in the minds of our audience while the bullet points, and especially photos, alarm them. That house in the second picture looks a little like their own. They wonder if that madman will be prying their own doors open.

The hermits continue asserting, "Hermit Lives Matter," but every time they do, our audience thinks, "Hermitites Are Parasites," and recollects the evidence we presented. Crowds wander the woods looking for these pesky parasites. Some film them. Others question them. Plenty harass them. The hermits, despising the negative attention, pack up and relocate to woods much farther away.

In real life I concocted a poison parasite which an artist ally illustrated in 2019. It is depicted in Appendix Three. If you look at it regularly what will you think of when you see the U.S. flag?

♦ ♦ ♦ ♦ ♦

In orchestrating his rise to power, the Nazi party portrayed Hitler as a sort of modern-day messiah who was immersed in a global conflict against the forces of evil. He would, in their words, "finish the work Christ had begun, but could not finish." Hitler referred to himself in this way as well, depicting his number one enemies, the Jews, as a group who sought to invade heaven and overthrow God. But fortunately, as Hitler himself proclaimed, all was not lost; for he would be the one who "in a mighty struggle hurls the heaven stormer back to Lucifer." He was, the Nazis declared, the good guy and all who opposed him the bad ones.

There is nothing new or unique about this. It has been going on as long as conflict itself. In our own generation we witnessed the same in the verbal exchange between the U.S. and its Middle Eastern enemies. Each side portrayed itself as endorsed by God. It was the embodiment of all that is righteous and honorable and, by contrast, its enemy the embodiment of all that is evil and wrong.

On the morning of September 11, 2001, U.S. President George W. Bush began his address to the nation: "Freedom itself[17] was attacked this morning by a faceless coward and freedom will be defended." The following year Bush referred to his country as a Christian one whose goal was to "extend the peace by encouraging free and open societies on every continent." He asserted America was merely "exercising our right of self-defense" in its military operations against Mid Eastern adversaries. Bush labeled Saddam a "tyrant" and later maligned Iraq's government: "This is a regime that has already used poison gas to murder thousands of its citizens, leaving the bodies of mothers huddled over their dead children. This is a regime that has agreed to international inspections, then kicked out the inspectors. This is a regime that has something to hide from the civilized world." Bush designated the three countries who were most at odds with the U.S. (Iran, Iraq, and North Korea) an "axis of evil" and was quoted in the October 7, 2005, issue of *The Independent*: "God told me to invade Iraq."

---

[17] Of all nations worldwide the U.S. has imprisoned the greatest percentage of its own people. It holds only 5 percent of the world's total population, yet retains 25 percent of its prison population. It incarcerates more of its citizens than much larger China and Russia as well as the so-called police states of Iran and North Korea. Some powerful mass psychological manipulation is at work when the president of the least free land on Earth can get away with dishonestly referring to his prison nation as "freedom itself."

The U.S. Government named the military campaign against al-Qaeda, which commenced with air strikes in Afghanistan on October 7, 2001, Operation Enduring Freedom. It designated the segment of the Iraq War in which combat missions regularly took place (March 2003 until August 2010) Operation Iraqi Freedom. From that point until December 2011 the mission in Iraq was entitled Operation New Dawn.

Bush's successor, Barack Obama, professed America was a land "of freedom" whose people were "call[ed by] God" to act in accordance with divine principles. Later, he opined an Islamic militia known as ISIS promotes "extremism" and inflicts "cruelty."

On the other side of the world Iraqi officials criticized American "infidels" who were pointlessly "harassing the peaceful people of Iraq." Saddam himself branded America, "The Great Satan" (a clever catchphrase he borrowed from Ayatollah Khomeini) which was ruled by the "criminal gang in the White House." After the U.S. led coalition assumed control of the country in 2003, Saddam labeled the coalition, "The infidel, criminal, cowardly occupier."

Osama bin Laden proclaimed in late September 2001, "I have only a few words for America and its people: I swear by God Almighty who raised the heavens without effort that neither America nor anyone who lives there will enjoy safety until safety becomes a reality for us living in Palestine and before all the infidel armies leave the land of Muhammad." The following month he added, "God has struck America in its Achilles' heel and destroyed its greatest buildings. What America is tasting today is but a fraction of what we [Arabs] have tasted for decades . . . so when God Almighty granted success to one of the vanguard groups of Islam, he opened the way . . ."

In a 2004 speech addressed to The Great Satan, bin Laden asserted that "Allah knows" striking the U.S. had never entered his mind. But unfortunately, the "oppression and tyranny of the American/Israeli coalition against our people" provoked this. He artfully claimed America's and Israel's demolition of the towers in Lebanon (1982) inspired his demolition of New York's World Trade Towers, stating it was just to "punish the oppressor in kind" and doing so would deter the U.S. from "killing our women and children" in the future.

On another occasion, he summed: "Our terrorism against America is praiseworthy terrorism in defense against the oppressor, in order that America will stop supporting Israel who killed our sons . . . [I am] perform[ing] my duty in imposing what is right and forbidding what is wrong."

All this rhetoric is, of course, biased propaganda. Both sides portray themselves as instruments of God's will; fighting not against a temporal adversary as such, but justifiably engaged in a titanic heavenly battle against the great forces of evil.

To understand just how polarized this is, let's recap just the language involved.

U.S. Words to Describe Itself and Its Actions	U.S. Words to Describe Mid East Enemies and Their Actions
• Freedom itself	• Faceless coward
• Extending the peace	• Tyrant
• Encouraging free and open societies	• Murder[s] thousands of its own citizens
• Exercising our right of self-defense	• Leav[es] the bodies of mothers huddled over their dead children.
• Civilized	• Has something to hide.
• God told me to invade	• Axis of evil
• Enduring freedom	• Extremism
• Iraqi freedom	• Cruelty
• New Dawn	

Psychopolitical Warfare... / Eric Wise

- Land of freedom
- Called by God

Mid East Words to Describe Itself and Its Actions	Mid East Words to Describe U.S. and Its Actions
• Peaceful people	• Infidels
• [Testifies] by God Almighty	• The Great Satan
• [Motivated by] safety . . . for us living in Palestine.	• Criminal gang
• Allah knows [my intent]	• Infidel, criminal, cowardly occupier
• God Almighty granted success . . . [and] opened the way.	• Infidel armies
• Praiseworthy . . . defense	• Struck [by] God
• Perform[ing] my duty	• Oppression and tyranny
• Right	• The oppressor (used twice)
	• Kill[s] our women and children
	• Killed our sons
	• Wrong

We recall Hitler's earlier description of propaganda. We also recall how we just learned he and his party portrayed him as ordained by heaven and his enemies as the forces of hell.

Most of the propaganda we encounter attempts to manipulate the opinion of the public or specific groups within it. Nonetheless, it is heavily employed in military contexts as part of a larger campaign of psychological or information warfare.

From an offensive perspective this variety of propaganda should serve the following purposes:

1. Implant confusion, doubt, apprehension, and despair in the enemy's ranks;
2. Encourage in the propagandist's ranks bravery, trust, and an expectation of success;
3. Maintain good relations with neutral parties.

Defensively, the military propagandist must:

1. Refute his enemies' accusations, lest they be believed (as we saw in a political context in Chapter 6 when Coke Stevenson refused to deny LBJ's);
2. Resist his enemy's efforts to divide his people;
3. Show his allies are meritorious and their side will prevail so long as they do not slacken their efforts;
4. Demonstrate his side's leaders are acting for the greater good and the sacrifices their subordinates are making are worthwhile.

As part of its psychological warfare strategy the Allies in World War II distributed propaganda directly to German soldiers. In addition to the well-known radio broadcasts,[18] planes dropped

---

[18] Great Britain used the BBC to transmit its perspective under the guise of news. At one point in 1944 it was sending out 230 stories per day in 48 different languages.

pamphlets over enemy lines. These presented a comparison of rations between allied countries and Germany showing, for example, British leaders fed the British better than Germany's leaders fed the Germans. The steady increase of U.S. troops in Europe and the dramatic increase of living costs in Germany were also flaunted. This, of course, was propaganda, keying in on offensive goal #1 by demoralizing German soldiers. Some pamphlets also featured photos of smiling German POWs in allied camps eating large meals, playing games, or relaxing in the warm sun. The message sent by these can be thought of as the flip side of #1—give up and life will be better. To this end a slogan was eventually added: "Better free than a prisoner of war. Better a prisoner of war than dead."

The tactics were so successful the U.S. military deployed them again nearly 50 years later in Operation Desert Storm. Between raids U.S. aircraft dispersed millions of propaganda pamphlets to Iraqi positions below. A popular edition featured featuring a smiling Saudi (ally of U.S.) sitting before a fire, serving coffee to his guest. The reverse side depicted Saddam ferociously attacking a guest with a knife. It was accompanied by the caption, "See what Saddam has done? You are occupying your neighbor's land [Kuwait]. If you come to us we will treat you as an Arab brother." As with the World War II pamphlets the idea was to demoralize the troops and drive a wedge between them and their leaders. In this case by showing Saddam to be the bad guy as he violates the Arabian cultural standard mandating cooperation and hospitality among all Arab nations and peoples. It also appealed to self-interests by tempting them to give up the fight, sit by the fire, and enjoy a tasty cup of coffee with the good guys—their Arab brothers in Saudi Arabia.

◆ ◆ ◆ ◆ ◆

It is common for those involved in psychological and political warfare to find themselves in wars of accusations, such as those that took place between LBJ and Stevenson. If this happens to you there are several techniques you can employ to protect yourself and possibly even gain an advantage.

If your opponent fails to engage your accusation, always point out "He does not deny the truthfulness of this." (When Stevenson refused to answer their charges, LBJ and his allies accused him of dodging the issue, which is similar but less direct.) If he admits to anything you should not only cite it as true but preface it with "By his own admission." As we will see in Chapter Eight, little evidence better inculpates than a person's own testimony against himself.

If you can disprove even one of your opponent's accusations against you, you will call into question his entire account, shifting the negative attention from you to him. (The best defense, after all, is a good offense.) By the same token, if you can prove true one of your own accusations against him, the audience is likely to believe the rest of them. Chicago mayor Richard Daley, whom we met in Chapter Five, fell victim to this by initially defending, rather than reforming, his police department as accusations against it grew. When in 1957 the popular *LIFE* magazine asserted Chicago's police department was the nation's most corrupt one, Daley dismissed this as an "unwarranted slur" and declared that his squad was, to the contrary, one of the nation's finest. Then when it came to light his police officers had actually been stealing from those they were supposed to be protecting, he was physically and emotionally devasted. The public understandably assumed every other accusation against the police must also be true and Daley could no longer defend them. He had no choice but to bring in a new chief to make major changes. Note: Some of these details were not presented in Chapter Five as they are immaterial to that discussion.

When the evidence supporting an opponent's accusation is so strong the facts can't be denied you may still be able to argue pertinence. Daley successfully did so in the scandals involving traffic ticket fixing and bail bond fraud by pointing out the officials at the heads of the departments involved—the chief of court staff and chief justice—had been elected by the people, not appointed by the mayor.

THE FEAR FACTOR

It can be difficult to change deeply held opinions by using strong emotional pleas. Techniques that frighten can, however, assist when you are trying to provoke your audience into taking an action necessary to prevent an unfavorable result. To succeed in this, three conditions must be met:

1. Your audience must believe in the probability of the threatened outcome. Fears are compelled less by calculation and reason than by primal emotional states and reactions. And if occurrences of something readily come to mind, or can easily be imagined, your listener will assume it is likely. E.g., many promiscuous non-drug using heterosexual males failed to take seriously the threat of HIV in the 1980s. But when basketball star "Magic" Johnson claimed he'd obtained it from a woman, these men suddenly believed themselves more vulnerable than they actually were.

2. They must fear the intensity of the menacing outcome. If they believe their self-interests will be negatively impacted, but only slightly, they are unlikely to act in the manner you desire. E.g., when inmates in the Texas prison system who believed they'd been infected by the Corona virus reported the only effects were a loss of taste and smell, many of their peers stopped wearing protective masks they considered annoying.

3. As a corollary to the aforesaid conditions, they must believe that, with action, a better outcome is possible. Even if your audience accepts that something very bad is probable, they must also trust that by acting they can avoid it. If they feel there is no hope, they'll do nothing different. E.g., during the height of the "cold war" (late 1950s, early 1960s) some U.S. families took the drastic and expensive measure of installing fallout shelters in their yards so they could survive a nuclear strike by the USSR. Most couldn't afford it, but plenty of others who could simply felt that while a nuclear attack was likely, survival would be impossible and they just went about their lives as usual.

Coming Soon to a Neighborhood Near You—The Drug Crazed Killers of FCC Petersburg

A scream ripped through the frigid January night. Prisoners Ernest "Stalker" Stevens and Christopher "Bloodbath" Barnes, blasted out of their minds on drugs and desperate for postage stamps to purchase more, hoisted their victim, Gregory Phillips, high into the air. His pleas for help ignored by lazy, irresponsible prison officials, Stalker and Bloodbath piledrove Phillips headfirst onto the concrete below, shattering his head like a melon. Then they took his stamps and raced off to buy their next fix.

"His mother screamed and cried," Officer Hotchkiss revealed. "I was in the office when the unit manager gave her the news over the phone. It broke my heart. That never should've happened." While I fully agree with Hotchkiss that it "never should've happened" I think we can all agree the refusal of officers like him to take seriously their responsibilities is exactly the reason it did.

Stalker and Bloodbath were not charged because U.S. Government officials do not want to draw attention to the fact that other U.S. Government officials provided the drugs that propelled this hideous crime. The murderers, unreformed and unrepentant, will be released to the District of Columbia very soon. Their cravings for drugs have been festering and we have already seen they will do anything to satisfy them. Anything.

Stalker Stevens.
Bloodbath Barnes.
Will they be visiting your neighborhood?

From the start of my anti-drug/smoking lawsuit I carefully crafted my litigation to portray the targeted DOJ officials as the powers of darkness who violated their oaths of office, defrauded the taxpayers, and corrupted the vulnerable inmates in their charge in order to fatten their wallets. During the course of the exhausting litigation, which went on for over three years, intoxicated inmates committed some notorious offenses, including two gruesome murders.

I knew this was important and seized the opportunity by tying the targeted officials to the murders. By the drugs some supplied, and refusal of others to do the work they were being paid to do, they were just as culpable as the actual killers. I, on the other hand, was the reformed knight in shining armor paying for the corrective lawsuit out of my own pocket, laboring diligently to eradicate the filth and transform the prison into a healthy facility where inmates could rehabilitate, and then return to society ready to contribute positive attitudes and skills. It was I who was, in reality, working to protect the public; not the officials.

The short story above is an accurate account. I inserted it into a 2012 legal brief. This was not done for the benefit of the so-called judge, for I was by this point aware of her reputation: a typical American politician who dons a black robe and defrauds unsuspecting litigants of honest adjudication. But I had noticed my documents were reaching high-ranking federal officials and was using the case as a forum to advance my agenda. Because it is easier to influence opinions and actions if a message is dramatic, vivid, and personal to its recipient, I heavily colored it with attention grabbing, and fear enhancing, creative writing techniques. (Those wishing to learn more about such are encouraged to study Creative Writing, which is beyond the scope of this text.) Further, as this variety of propaganda is most effective when based on reality, I tailored it to officials who themselves lived in the D.C. area, where the inmate murderers were from, and to which they would return. The idea, of course, was to influence them to clean up my house, the prison, lest they personally suffer the consequences in their own houses. There was no need for me to recommend an exact method by which to do so. Federal law enforcement officials know how to enforce the law. My task was compelling them to do it. And in that I succeeded far beyond my expectations.

Chapter Eight

Anything You Say . . .

> He has a dignity and power which startles every now and then . . . I watched him sitting in his chair, listening, with eyes almost closed. When he speaks, it is tersely. Every sentence is a naked idea, stated in as few words as possible.
>
> — Joseph Davies, U.S. Dept. of State speaking on Joseph Stalin's demeanor at the Potsdam Conference

One aspiring to become an electrician must devote an immense amount of time to learning the craft. Starting as an entry level apprentice, he spends the first 8,000 (yes, eight thousand) hours studying and working under the charge of a master. During this period he learns skills such as how to install and maintain conduit, electrical circuits, protection devices, generators, and industrial batteries. Upon completion of the apprenticeship, he is deemed a journeyman, which means he is considered an experienced practical electrician. He must nonetheless continue laboring for another 2,000 hours under a master before he can take the test to become a master himself. In passing, he can finally work independently, but must still complete another 800 hours of service and receive a license from a state regulatory board if he wishes to work as a contractor.

Just as a prospective electrician must dedicate assiduous study to understanding the unwieldy and dangerous characteristics of electricity so he can protect himself while channeling it to serve his purpose, those who wish to execute or challenge the incomprehensible political power of a first world government must invest a tremendous amount of time and effort into learning its nature. Most government officials have been trained in its ways and have at least some understanding of them.

Bureaucrats, such as judges, congressmen, the president, and their various spokespeople, often announce to the public decisions they have made or intend to make as well as the alleged reasons for doing so. They have to speak. Support of the people, especially the elites, is important in maintaining the power of elected or appointed officials. Yet, when we analyze the meaning of what these people say, we often conclude they have said little of substance; the true impetus for their actions fully concealed.

Career officials employ myriad tactics to communicate while conveying little of substance. They obfuscate, deflect, dissemble, and employ terms so broad, vague, and elastic they can be interpreted in many ways. In 1972 federal judge Marvin Frankel asserted "an absence of explanations is the hallmark of injustice." While it certainly is a mechanism meant to protect the one withholding the explanation, even when an official offers one, it is unlikely to be the true reason he acted as he did.

Actual explanations are accidents waiting to happen. It may be in the best interests of the public to know why the government acted as it did, but it is seldom in the best interests of the officials to reveal this. Above all else, therefore, those officials who are most prescient serve themselves by religiously adhering to what is, in most circumstances, a cardinal precept of power: silence is golden.

SAYING AS LITTLE AS POSSIBLE—THE OFFICIALS

Cases In Point
First Case

In the weeks leading up to the 1952 presidential election Dwight D. Eisenhower (Ike) needed to increase his lead in the polls. A matter about which he'd spoken little was the involvement of U.S. soldiers in the United Nations force that was fighting to prevent the spread of communism in Korea. This was the primary political concern of most Americans, but the great general had been reluctant to commit to a position until he could travel to Korea to personally assess the situation. He had already determined he needed to fly a reconnaissance mission over the front lines, talk with the soldiers and commanders, and study the terrain in so doing. To win the election, however, he first needed to speak on the matter.

In a Detroit press conference on October 24, he announced that upon inauguration he would "forego the diversions of politics and concentrate on the job of ending the Korean war." He added, "That job requires a personal trip to Korea. I shall make that trip. Only in that way could I learn how best to serve the American people in the cause of peace. I shall go to Korea."

Ike's proclamation showed this key issue had his attention. It also catered to what most Americans desired—an end to the Korean conflict. Nonetheless, it left his options open. For he gave no indication of how precisely he would end it. Those who wanted him to keep driving until a U.N. victory was achieved knew he was the leader best suited for this. Those who preferred an armistice and a major withdrawal of U.S. troops also knew of no candidate better qualified to reach such a conclusion. The ambiguity of his statement thus provided a conspicuous and convincing method to secure votes while maintaining honesty and elasticity.

Second Case

In the first news conference of his presidency, a reporter asked Eisenhower if he knew "many members of Congress feel that the agreements [reached at the Yalta Conference] were never binding . . . because they were not presented to the Senate" for ratification. He was, of course, well aware of this, but not wishing to open a Pandora's box of political and legal issues, he obfuscated: "Well, I think that there are, in our practice, certain things that are binding when the people are acting as proper representatives of the United States—say, in war, or in establishing staffs and that sort of thing. That extends out into some fields that are almost politico-military in nature."

Later, when a reporter queried him on whether he would advocate a plan to maintain the excess profit tax bill, he responded: "I would say this—I can't answer that in exact terms—I shall never agree to the elimination of any tax where reduction in revenue goes with it." After rendering the vague statement, he smiled, waved, and quickly departed; leaving it to the people to determine what he meant, while nonetheless leaving with them the perception that he had the situation well at hand.

The strong do not answer to the weak. When they do it is evidence of either a shifting power dynamic or momentary lapse of reason. But often the perception of the situation is merely mistaken.

Perhaps the one who appears strong is not. Perhaps the "weak" one is strong. More often than not, however, that which is perceived as an answer is really something less.

As we discussed in Chapter One the ancient belief in the divine right of kings is predicated on the idea rulers are appointed by God and answer to no earthly beings. An English theorist on royal authority in the 1500s elucidated the concept: "A King is, in this world, without law and may at his lust do right or wrong and shall give account but to God only."

Many American officials continue applying this self-serving theory to themselves—believing any action taken by the government, and by extension its officials, is inherently correct. Thus, like their royal counterparts, they feel no obligation to account for themselves. Then-President George W. Bush clarified, "The interesting thing about being the president [is that] maybe somebody needs to explain to me why they say something, but I don't feel like I owe anybody an explanation."

Unlike their royal counterparts, elected officials often find they must provide some sort of justification for their actions if they wish to maintain their power. These explanations, however, need not be accurate or even intelligible. Rulers know what the subjects don't, the less said the better.

In 2008 Alex Acosta prosecuted the politically connected Jeffrey Epstein for his alleged role in pimping underage prostitutes to the rich and powerful. When Epstein received a sentence of eighteen months in prison the hysterical American people, most of whom had also participated in unlawful underage sex at some point in their lives, demanded answers. Their media representatives grilled Acosta.

The Florida prosecutor, who had formerly served as a U.S. Secretary of Labor, was well-versed in the art of speaking without substance. First he merely stated the deal was the best he could obtain. When pressed that Epstein had been lightly punished because he was an undercover intelligence operative, Acosta craftily replied: "This is a case that was brought by our office, it was based on the facts, and I look at the reporting and others [sic]. I can't address it directly because of our guidelines, but I can tell you that a lot of reporting is going down rabbit holes." (When an official responds to an accusation in this manner, the strongest counter is to charge that he does not deny it.)

The aristocratic FDR was an expert in strategic speaking. The tactics involved in this were so ingrained in his mind that even on his last day of life when his maid asked him if he believed in the afterlife, he answered with a question of his own: "Well, tell me, do you believe in reincarnation?" The maid replied, "I don't know if I do or not, but in case there is such a thing, when I come back I want to be a canary bird." The president merely laughed, considering her hefty build.

When Harry S. Truman took over the presidency, he began training his daughter Margaret in the art. Following his death she revealed, "I had to learn to say as little as possible when reporters were around."

Asking very appropriate questions, instead of providing answers to President George W. Bush's questions, was a method repeatedly employed by Defense Secretary Donald Rumsfeld in war cabinet meetings following September 11, 2001. Secretary of State Colin Powell was a bit more perceptive than Bush and found Rumsfeld's questions to be a shrewd way of contributing to the discussions while avoiding a position that could come back to haunt him later.

In post 9-11 National Security Council meetings, the purpose of which were to determine the U.S. response to al-Qaeda's attacks, Cofer Black, Director of the CIA's Counterterrorism Center, similarly noticed the tendency of his high-ranking peers to speak in general terms. They did so, he revealed, because they were aware American lives would be lost in the necessary military course of action and had little self-interest in attaching their names to a plan that would yield such an outcome. It was thus left to Black to personally warn the president there would be a significant loss of

American lives. By doing this, however, Black placed responsibility for the loss directly on the commander in chief.

SAYING TOO MUCH—THE SUSPECTS

Third Case

On December 25, 2001, the Food and Drug Administration (FDA) notified Sam Waksal, CEO of the pharmaceutical company ImClone, that his company's application to commercially market the anti-cancer drug Erbitux had been denied. Waksal's daughters and his accountant placed several phone calls on the 27th to Douglas Faneuil, a client associate at Merrill Lynch, requesting liquidation of the Waksal family's ImClone holdings. When Faneuil's boss, stockbroker Peter Bacanovic, telephoned the office later that morning, Faneuil informed him of the developments. The shocked Bacanovic directed the assistant to transfer him to the office of one of their best clients: celebrity homemaker Martha Stewart. The latter was, however, unavailable at that moment so the broker left a message with her assistant requesting she call Faneuil as soon as possible. Bacanovic placed a follow-up call to Faneuil and told him that when Stewart calls, he should apprise her of the ImClone developments. When she later did so, Faneuil acted as instructed. Stewart responded by ordering Faneuil to discharge her investment in the precarious company. The transaction was completed that afternoon with ImClone publicly announcing the FDA's denial of its Erbitux application the following day.

Investigators in the Compliance Department at Merrill Lynch noticed the large volume of trading preceding the announcement among those they suspected to have inside information on the matter and launched an inquiry into possible violations of both company policy and the Security and Exchange Act of 1934. Company officials referred the matter to the Security and Exchange Commission (SEC) when the probe was complete.

Bacanovic was questioned via telephone by attorneys with the SEC's Enforcement Division on January 7, 2002. On February 13 he testified under oath in a face-to-face hearing before the SEC. A Merrill Lynch attorney was present.

Martha Stewart was twice interviewed by government officials such as FBI agents and SEC attorneys. The first of these sessions was held at the office of the U.S. Attorney for the Southern District of New York on February 4, 2002; the second was conducted via telephone on April 10, 2002.

Bacanovic and Stewart were subsequently indicted, tried, and convicted, but not for insider trading—the charge for which they were originally investigated. The evidence for such an offense had, in fact, always been weak.

At the conclusion of a five-week trial for both defendants, the jury found Bacanovic guilty of falsely stating, during his January 7 questioning, that Stewart had instructed him to sell her shares for the sole reason that the price had dropped. He was also convicted of rendering perjured testimony at his February 13 SEC hearing. There, he stated that on December 27 he had left Stewart a message informing her only of the price at which ImClone was trading (to support the defense the stock was not sold because of inside information on the FDA decision, but because they had already agreed on a stop loss order at $60).

The jury convicted Stewart of lying to investigators during her February 4 and April 10 interviews by reporting the following: 1) she did not remember if she and Bacanovic had spoken about Waksal on December 27; 2) she did not recall being informed that any of the Waksals were selling their ImClone stock; 3) in her December 27 conversation with Bacanovic she instructed him to liquidate her ImClone holdings because the stock was trading below $60 per share; 4) she decided to sell her stock at that time because she didn't want to be disturbed with business matters while on her forthcoming vacation to Mexico; 5) she did not know if any record of a December 27 message from Bacanovic existed in her assistant's computerized message log; 6) she had only spoken with Bacanovic about ImClone one time since the December 28 Erbitux announcement and indicated this had not concerned confidential matters; 7) Bacanovic had not indicated, after the 28th, he had been questioned by the SEC or asked about her ImClone transactions.

The two were also convicted of conspiracy and obstructing an official proceeding. The jury determined they had corroborated to effect all three elements of the conspiracy: issuing false reports, perjury, and obstructing the proceeding of a federal agency.

Peter Bacanovic was sentenced to five months in the federal Bureau of Prisons, two years of supervised release, and a $4,000 fine. Martha Stewart was given five months of imprisonment, two years of supervised release, and a $30,000 fine.

It is seldom in the best interest of a criminal suspect to speak to government officials at all. Those who believe they can talk their way out of trouble usually find they are only talking their way into it.

Law enforcement officials question suspects for two predominant purposes: 1) to use their own words against them, 2) to use their words against others. As exemplified above, without the testimony of the accused, the government often lacks evidence sufficient to obtain a conviction. Confessions are far and above the predominant means by which convictions are secured. And for those who don't confess, but nonetheless testify, the government can, at a minimum, usually secure the type of process related convictions just described.

A suspect can delay speaking to law enforcement in demanding an attorney be present during questioning. When the attorney is present, however, the suspect may be obliged to speak. Nonetheless, he can still invoke the Fifth Amendment by refusing to testify against himself. It appears neither Peter Bacanovic nor Martha Stewart would've been convicted of anything had they done so. (Those who are interested in some legal minutiae of this may wish to examine the authorities cited in Appendix Four.)

A nearly identical mistake was made in 1974 by Chuck Colson, Chief Counsel to President Richard Nixon. As a seasoned attorney he should've known better, but his thinking was clouded by anxiety as he decided to testify at his grand jury hearing. Colson, who had been under investigation for involvement in covering up the burglary of the Democratic National Committee headquarters at Washington's Watergate Hotel, told his lawyer, the illustrious Dave Shapiro, "Get me a chance to testify and there won't be any trial. You'll see." Shapiro advised against it, but Colson wouldn't listen. Two days after Colson testified, the Assistant U.S. Attorney told Shapiro, "We're going to indict your client." Colson, like so many suspects, talked his way into prison.

In 2016, General James Cartwright showed even he could not learn from the mistakes of history. The powerful Vice Chairman of the Joint Chiefs of Staff had fallen under investigation for leaking classified information pertaining to America's "Cyber weapons." The general naively believed he and the FBI were part of the same team and agreed to an interview without legal representation. Similar to Martha Stewart, he was indicted and convicted, not for the acts for which he was investigated, but for lying to investigators. But dissimilar to America's homemaker, he had an ace in the hole. Ideologically corrupt lame duck president Barack Obama pardoned his offense and restored his security clearances before leaving office the following year.

Absent thousands of years of evolutionary adaptations, human nature does not change. And there is nothing new to the foregoing. Anne Hutchison and her family arrived in the "new world" in 1634. A woman of peculiar religious beliefs, she quickly took to criticizing the heads of church and state in Massachusetts Bay. When various authority figures questioned her to explain by what means she came to her opinions, she implied, but did not specify, she was blessed with divine revelation apart from the clergy or bible. Because her beliefs could neither be proven nor disproven by scripture, they were open to interpretation. So far so good. But in the view of the puritanical governor of Massachusetts Bay, her views threatened the foundation of his colony, and he kept the pressure high.

In 1637, magistrates and ministers put the woman on trial. During the proceeding an intense doctrinal debate took place. She fared well at first by demonstrating her knowledge of scripture to be just as thorough as that of her inquisitors. And when she challenged them to clarify her offense they were unable to do so. But just when she had nearly outsmarted them she proclaimed her knowledge of God was acquired directly "by an immediate revelation . . . by the voice of his own spirit to my soul." She had at long last said too much. The woman indirectly admitted before her accusers that *biblical* moral law is irrelevant to the spirit. The colony's rulers exiled Hutchison and her followers to Providence, a city conducive to non-conformists.

You can likely recall numerous instances in which you have been in hot water for acting questionably in the eyes of various authorities—parents, teachers, bosses, etc. In each of these you probably felt a nagging compulsion to offer some sort of reason for acting as you did. Perhaps in some of those situations the explanation lessened the severity of the sanction. More likely, it made no difference, or, as in the examples above, aggravated it. Jesus said, "The truth shall set you free," and many people find this simple slogan axiomatic. Jesus, however, did not live in the Uncivilized Nation and as we are about to see knew better than to follow his own prescription for others.

Obedience to authorities perceived as legitimate constitutes a large part of social animals' behavior. People seldom realize how much of their daily activities involve doing what the powers that be have commanded, because doing so is infused into their routines. When these serious and powerful people direct, we follow. And when they ask, we feel obligated to answer. This is the conditioned response. Even when someone who is not an authority figure questions us we feel obligated to provide some sort of answer, because this is what we have been conditioned to do. It takes plenty of reprogramming to defensively alter this tendency. Surprise and nerves certainly work their evil magic as well. We seldom know exactly what accusatory questions will be asked until they are and when confusion and anxiety are added to the mix we cannot reason clearly.

Law enforcement officials are exceptionally adroit in the administration of systematic questioning. Many have studied it and most have spent their careers perfecting the art. An interview with these officers is not an impromptu haphazard event and seldom is it an attempt to ascertain the truth. Rather, it is a meticulously sculpted process designed to extract the desired answers by psychologically manipulative strategies and tactics. Let's turn our attention in this direction to discover some of the ones employed in what can be considered a typical example of an interrogation.

Hypothetical Interrogation

The investigators in the case are very talented, such as those in the employ of the FBI, so they have waited as long as possible to speak to the suspect. During this time, they have gathered as much evidence as they can to use against him. By the time they interview him they already have a fairly good grasp of the case and just need to give him enough rope to hang himself.

We'll say the subject of the inquiry is not already incarcerated. Therefore, the officers "invite" him into their lair under the guise they just need to clear up a little issue and would appreciate hearing his side of the story.

Upon arrival at the designated precinct the target is escorted to a small, fully enclosed room devoid of anything that could distract his attention from the matter at hand. For reasons already discussed, taking him out of his turf and into the officers' weakens him and empowers the officers. Isolating him also deprives him of any possible sources of help and assures the interrogators' perspective is the only one influencing him during the critical process.

Officers open the encounter on their best behavior, establishing the rapport necessary to make the vulnerable suspect comfortable and talkative. They offer some soda and candy, then engage in pleasant small talk which includes insincere compliments and expressions of sympathy for his predicament. Once a harmonious relationship is established, the conversation rapidly takes a nefarious turn. In what one psychologist labeled an "ingenious aspect of American interrogation," the officers stun their subject by suddenly declaring they are absolutely certain of his guilt. This presumption shifts the supposedly mandated burden of proof, forcing the suspect to prove his innocence. He attempts to do so and says something they don't want to hear. They interrupt him, asserting their disbelief in his account, then badgering him with versions of what they "believe" happened. As part of this they point to a supposed inconsistency between elements of his explanation which are actually perfectly consistent. In one instance they accost the subject for first stating the purpose of a trip was business, then changing his story by saying it was pleasure—when he actually said the weekday portion was for business and the weekend portion for pleasure. They also point out physiological and psychological signs he is being deceptive. (We will examine these shortly.)

Investigators bombard the target with questions likely to induce embarrassment, anger, and confusion in the hopes he will blurt out something incriminating. And sadly he, like so many, takes the bait. (This is deceptive provocation as we studied in Chapter 6.)

As shocking as it may be, American cops are allowed to lie in questioning suspects and one of the more insidious aspects of this phase involves the introduction of fabricated evidence. They falsely assert a witness has issued a statement incriminating the target and claim they have secured other inculpatory evidence such as correspondence, photos, and videos. They even produce some counterfeit versions of the same to substantiate that. This accusative phase takes place over the course of several hours and its purpose is to overwhelm the subject's will by confusing him, eroding his confidence, and exhausting his physical and mental capacities. Resistance, goes the message, is futile. (We detailed this early in Chapter 5.)

In concluding the process, investigators appeal to the suspect's self-interest, persuading him that by cooperating, and thus confessing, he will obtain the most favorable outcome. In so doing, they mislead him into believing they will punish him lightly and will put in a good word to the judge to assure this. They imply only a confession stands between him and a release to freedom when in actuality only a persistent *refusal* to confess guilt stands between him and release. As we've already learned, a confession is the essential element by which most convictions are anchored.[19] He is finally read his rights and signs a document waiving them. They then walk him through a confession,

---

[19] As we also learned earlier, there are two ways to get government officials to do what you want and some people who confess to the authorities do get out of trouble. But these are people who can provide a significant amount of assistance. That is, they have enough information on the crimes of others that they can help government officials advance their self-interests. For instance, Sammy "The Bull" Gravano, number two in the Gambino crime family, escaped a life sentence by cooperating with the government, but he also had information sufficient to convict his boss, John Gotti, in return. (This was a rare instance where a suspect, Gotti, did not confess.) If, after consulting with an attorney of your own, you decide to "cooperate," you should be aware that only government attorneys, not detectives or other law enforcement officials, can extend binding agreements.

directing it and typing it, as he says what they want to hear. He signs it and is escorted to the jail's Booking Department.

These strategies and tactics—which conflate the impact of an interrogator's coercion with a subject's vulnerability—are so effective most suspects reveal information contrary to their self-interests. They are, in fact, so effective they frequently extract confessions of guilt from the innocent. Many scientists have thus recognized their crafty, manipulative nature renders them even more treacherous than overt physical torture. (For an illustration and analysis of the diabolic techniques used by forensic psychologists, i.e. suggestive questioning and the implantation of false memories, see Appendix Five—an abridgement taken from my treatise *Advanced Studies in Mind Control*.)

As a device to evade the net of incrimination, powerful people of the past often asserted a failure of memory. For example, in hearings held in the late 1950s before the Senate Rackets Committee, Jimmy Hoffa—the notorious vice president of the Teamster's Union, avoided divulging inculpating information by repeatedly claiming he couldn't recall the particulars of the events in question. Finally throwing in the towel on behalf of the Government, committee chairman Senator John McClellan dismissed Hoffa by declaring the hearing had "proceeded to the point where the witness has no memory" and the committee's investigation had become "useless and a waste of time."

What worked for Hoffa in the 1950's, however, did not work for Martha Stewart in the 2000s. The celebrity homemaker discovered the hard way the Government has become so aggressive and refined in its prosecutorial methods it no longer surrenders upon the pronouncement of forgetfulness. For the assertion of an inability to remember is an absolute statement. And an absolute statement is subject to being proven false. But it is a more arduous task to disprove a statement that either cannot be understood or can only be understood in many ways. As we saw in the cases of the wily Dwight Eisenhower, et al., powerful officials know this well.

♦ ♦ ♦ ♦ ♦

Conversations can contain many elements, such as subtle verbal and visual cues, innuendo, sarcasm, body language, and vocal tones. Investigators look for lies in these. As Leon Alberti, one of Leonardo da Vinci's major influences noted, "Movements of the soul are made known by movements of the body."

When speaking to investigators and other officials you should act calmly and normally. As you are likely to be anxious, the appearance of this can be lessened by inhaling for a count of 4, then exhaling for a count of 4 (to lower respiration), relaxing your eyebrows (which furrow when you're upset), and relaxing your shoulders. If seated, sit erect, but not overly stiff. If standing, the same type of bearing applies. Law enforcement officers have been trained to notice things most people do not and constantly monitor the position of a possible adversary's hands as they are the primary source of danger, usually from weapons. If you are in an adversarial encounter with them you should not form fists or conceal your hands (e.g., in pockets). If seated before such, you may place your hands nearly flat on your legs slightly above the knee. If the type of meeting is not such that the official sees you as a potential threat to his physical welfare, you may wish to lay your hands on top of each other or clasp them together in front to give an impression of sincerity. Appear relaxed, speak politely, and look the official in the eyes when answering questions.

It is believed recollection causes the eyes to take distinct patterns. Most behaviorists assert they stay straight ahead or veer to the upper left for visual memories and turn to the middle or slightly lower left for auditory ones. The FBI, nonetheless, teaches its agents that if a right-handed person glances to his left or a left-handed person to his right when answering a question it indicates he may be trying to retrieve an actual memory for an honest answer. Conversely, if the right-handed person looks to his right or the left-handed person left, he may be attempting to fabricate information. That is, a dishonest answer. With this in mind, if you need a break from the constant eye contact you can let your eyes wander a bit in the "honest" directions as you "remember" something. Don't close or cover your eyes or turn your head to look away when answering questions.

A failure to maintain eye contact, speaking irregularly ("Um...well...I...uh..."), and symptoms of nervousness (clearing the throat, twitching, fidgeting, and sweating) are believed to indicate untruthfulness. High levels of stress in the voice are also believed indicative of this. Note: Every system of lie detection, from ancient to modern times, operates under the premise that some kind of uncontrollable physical response accompanies a lie. While scientific studies have yet to confirm this, the assumption remains. The polygraph, invented by a University of California student in 1921 looks for elevations in one's pulse, blood pressure, perspiration, and breathing rate. Most law enforcement agencies now use the Psychological Stress Evaluation and its digital cousin the Computerized Voice Stress Analysis (CVSA) to determine whether a suspect is rendering accurate testimony. The latter, which electronically detects the amount of tension in the voice, is believed to be more accurate than the polygraph.

Elie Honig, the lifelong federal and state prosecutor we met earlier, opines that liars can be intuitively spotted by "the stammering, the pausing, the pretending not to hear, the feigning of ignorance about basic words." (Bill Clinton's response to his congressional inquisitor to "define sex" comes to mind in the latter category.) Some social scientists also believe if an innocent person is directly confronted with an accusation he will expressly deny it; e.g. "I did not have sex with that woman" instead of "Why would I have sex with that woman when she's not my type?" In 2021 Prince Andrew of Great Britain avoided exactly stating he was innocent of having sex with a minor and some sociologists see this as suspicious, but Bill Clinton did exactly state, "I did not have sex with that woman" even though he did. I do not see exact denial as a sign that one is innocent of an accusation, especially among those skilled in communication techniques, but you should be aware some influential people hold the view that it is.

In addition to the above types of signals, investigators also measure the plausibility of the account itself and often elicit an explanation more than once, in a different manner, to see if it matches the ones already given.

Consistency is, in fact, the key to two of the primary methods historians use to determine the accuracy of accounts on historical events.

1) Historians compare the accounts of the author in question with those of other authors of the time to determine whether they cohere. If, for example, writer A says this, but writers B and C say that, mathematics already favor the latter two.

2) The scholars note the writer's accounts of astronomical events (e.g. comets, eclipses) and compare them with the findings of modern scientists, who are able to calculate exactly when such took place in the past. If the ancient writer told the truth about the celestial fireball passing overhead, goes the reasoning, he likely tendered truthful testimony about other events.

Thus, your story is most believable when it: 1) forms a logical and harmonious sum, 2) matches the accounts of others, 3) matches itself when you retell it, 4) matches some external verifiable fact, and 5) is submitted in a calm, confident manner.

♦ ♦ ♦ ♦ ♦

To speak while skirting the issuance of harmful information and false statements, you may wish to utilize a soft or subjective manner that characterizes a perception of reality rather than absolute hard reality, independent of individual thought.

To understand the difference let's look at some imaginary examples of statements to government officials formulated in these two modes:

Hard: I don't remember if we spoke on the matter.

Soft: In a hectic life such as mine, it can be a challenge to recall the details of day-to-day conversations.

Hard: Officer Kenosha performed the pat search to gratify his sexual desire.

Soft: The manner in which Officer Kenosha performed the pat search impressed me as being done to gratify his sexual desire.

Hard: I saw a photo of D.A. Lubbock in women's clothing. He is a tranny!

Soft: I saw a photo of what I understood to be D.A. Lubbock in women's clothing. Therefore, it is my opinion he is a tranny.

Hard: We are allowed to walk in that area.

Soft: It has been my experience that we are allowed to walk in that area.

Hard: The assistant U.S. attorney uses drugs and is an egomaniacal fop.

Soft: It has been my observation that the assistant U.S. attorney displays symptoms suggestive of substance dependence with borderline narcissistic traits.

Hard: Nicotine is not addictive, senator.

Soft: I do not believe nicotine is addictive, senator.

Hard: I do not stay up all night.

Soft: People have different ideas about what it means to stay up all night.

Hard: The FBI agents violated the law.

Soft: There's been some talk that the FBI agents behaved in a law violative manner, and I find those perspectives credible.

Hard: Sheriff John Brown always hated me. Why? I don't know.

Soft: By his words and deeds over the course of many years, I inferred that Sheriff John Brown hated me. I can't be certain of the reasons for this hatred.

Those officials who operate at the pinnacle of the art also employ terminology that appears to be absolute, yet actually connotes something less than absolute certainty. In their repertoire one finds statements such as:

- That cannot be ruled out.
- We may seek a military solution.
- We're reviewing that alternative.
- All options are on the table.
- It is possible we will respond in kind.
- The evidence is consistent with that conclusion.

Speaking in this manner indicates a probability of 1 to 99 percent. (In the case of the last statement 51 to 100 percent.) Doing so, thus leaves the audience to infer some arbitrary degree while protecting the speaker from specifying it.

Note: When, in my day-to-day interactions, I am asked a question I am not inclined to answer, I use replies such as, "I'll have to think about that," "I'm not sure," "That's a good question," or my favorite, "That's an interesting question although perhaps not susceptible to the precise sort of answer for which you may be searching." Occasionally, I answer in a foreign language, with a question of my own, or quote the punch line of a cartoon, e.g. The Neighborhood, Garfield. Often I just stand there silent and expressionless, leaving the questioner to guess the significance of this. Some of these represent my own modifications on tactics I picked up observing federal officials. For example, DOJ officials love to answer "I'll get back to you" which means the request is denied. I prefer, "I'll have to think about it" because it carries less of an obligation, but the same general meaning. You should be aware that those who avoid answering a direct question may avoid divulging inculpatory information while also avoiding the issuance of false statements, but as we discovered earlier (in the discussion on Prince Andrew) they can arouse suspicion.

SPEAKING DEFENSIVELY: THE INTERROGATION AND NONRESPONSIVE ANSWERS OF JESUS CHRIST

Background

Judea was under the jurisdiction of the Roman Empire in the time of Christ. Pontius Pilate served Emperor Tiberius as the Roman procurator of the province during the years of Christ's ministry.

Although the Jews remained under the ultimate authority of Rome, a number of Jewish ecclesiastical societies also exerted powerful political and religious influences over their countrymen. The *chief priests* were in charge of worship services at the temple in Jerusalem. *Scribes* were scholars well versed in the administration of Old Testament law. Jews known as *elders* held authority mostly by virtue of age and experience and included lay members of the Sanhedrin, the high Jewish court. *Pharisees* were members of an exclusive legalistic group who diligently strove for conformity with the written Mosaic law as well as the unwritten customs of the elders.

Jesus' ministry was marked by his attacks on the insincerity and hypocrisy of the aforesaid groups.

In his opening challenge to the Jewish authorities, Jesus stormed the temple courts, overturned the tables of the merchants and money changers, then drove them all out. In so doing he declared "Is it not written 'my house will be called a house of prayer for all nations?' But you have made it into a den of thieves!" This contravened the self-interests of powerful Jews as it both defied their authority and hurt their commerce. Thus, they began looking for a way to arrest him.

Technique: Shifting the Inquiry

The disciple John informs us that an early attempt to ensnare Jesus occurred at the very temple courts in which he had so aggressively protested. Now using them for their intended purpose, he was teaching the masses when antagonists interrupted his sermon. John describes the encounter:

> Then the scribes and Pharasees brought to him a woman caught in adultery. And when they had set her in their midst, they said to him, "Teacher, this woman was caught in adultery, in the very act. Now Moses, in the law, commanded us that such should be stoned. But what do you say?" This they said testing him, that they might have something of which to accuse him.
>
> But Jesus stooped down and wrote the sins of each of them on the ground with his finger. So when they continued asking him, he raised himself up and said to them, "He who is without sin among you, let him throw a stone at her first." And he stooped down and wrote on the ground. At this, those who heard went away one by one beginning with the oldest, even to the last.

The Roman rulers of Judea retained the exclusive right to order the death penalty. Had Jesus opined the adulteress should be stoned pursuant to the Mosaic law he would've been in conflict with the Roman government. Had he opined she should not be stoned he could've been accused of opposing the laws laid down by Moses. So, instead of doing either, he placed the burden back on his opponents, implying one who executes judgment upon her for her sins must be without any of his own. (This notion captures the essence of moral authority.) Since he had revealed he was aware of their sins, this left nobody qualified to do so.

Jesus rendered the scribes and Pharisees no basis on which to accuse him. He surely also embarrassed them by evading their trap and revealing the fraudulence of their virtue. With their plot thwarted and their moral authority undermined, they could only silently depart.

Second Example

The disciple Luke provides the following description of another confrontation between Jewish authorities and Jesus in his account of Christ's ministry:

> Now it happened on one of those days, as he taught people in the temple and preached the gospel, that the chief priests and the scribes, together with the elders, confronted him and spoke to him saying, "Tell us, by what authority are you doing these things? Or who is he who gave you this authority?"
>
> But he answered and said to them, "I will also ask you a question and answer me: The baptism of John—was it from heaven or from men?"
>
> And they reasoned among themselves saying, "If we say, 'from heaven,' he will say 'why then did you not believe him (John)?' But if we say, 'from men,' all the people will stone us, for they are persuaded that John was a prophet."
>
> So, they answered, "We do not know where it was from."
>
> And Jesus said to them, "Neither will I tell you by what authority I do these things."

By responding to a loaded question with a loaded question of his own, Jesus deftly transferred the obligation from himself to his persecutors. His particular question was so clever it forced them into a position where they were damned by either of the possible answers. They perceived this and were left with no choice but to reluctantly reply that they did not know. This surely damaged their credibility in the eyes of the people as they appeared unknowledgeable and thus unauthoritative.

Technique: Evasive Answer

Herod Antipas was the son of Herod the Great who had been the Roman king of Judea from 37 to 4 B.C. At the time in question, he was the Roman governor of the Galilee and Perea provinces. The influential Jews who supported the rule of his family were known as *Herodians*.

While the Pharisees were vehemently opposed to Roman rule, they nonetheless found common ground with the Herodians in the quest to eliminate one they believed to be threatening their self-interests. Appearing sincere and employing flattery in an attempt to lower his defenses, representatives of the two groups interviewed their target. Disciples Matthew and Luke inform us of the incident:

> Then the Pharisees went and plotted how they might entangle him in his talk. And they sent to him their adherents, with the Herodians, saying, "Teacher, we know that you are true and teach the way of God in truth; nor do you care about anyone, for you do not regard the person of men. Tell us then, what is your opinion? Is it lawful to pay taxes to Caesar or not?"
>
> But he perceived their craftiness and said to them, "Why do you test me? Show me a denarius. Whose image and inscription does it have?"
>
> "Caesar's," they replied.
>
> And he said to them, "Render therefore to Caesar the things that are Caesar's and to God the things that are God's."
>
> But they could not catch him in his words in the presence of the people. And they marveled at his answer and kept silent.

Yet again, Jesus masterfully handled his well-educated adversaries. The matter was delicate. Had Jesus directly acknowledged Jews should remit taxes to Caesar he would've alienated his followers, as they refused to recognize the legitimacy of their Roman overlords. On the other hand, had he advised the withholding of tax payments, he would've advised behavior contrary to Roman law.

Note 1: The qualifications for electricians described at the opening of the chapter vary from state to state.

Note 2: I am among the many who are doubtful biblical events occurred exactly as described (especially prior to the time of Solomon). In some cases, however, this is irrelevant to their ability to demonstrate psychological and political lessons. We know, for example, the detective Sherlock Holmes is the product of Arthur C. Doyle's imagination. Yet, many of the fictitious sleuth's principles and tactics are gainfully employed by real law enforcement officers (and he who writes these words) to this day. Thus, whether Jesus Christ was a real person, the product of the Gospel authors' imagination, or some synthesis of truth and fiction (my diagnosis) has no bearing on the value of the illustrations.

On a similar note, I find the Judeo-Christian bible to be the quintessence of propaganda. It is by far the most successful tool of manipulation employed in world history. I've read it from cover to cover many times and can hardly turn a page without feeling it tug at my emotions. And when I feel this, it is because they who authored it are subtly, yet imperiously, affecting me.

Chapter Nine

The Brazen Rule

Shortly before his 1996 death, the great scientist Carl Sagan described a number of rules traditionally applied in exchanges. The best known among these is *Golden Rule*. The latter, which is derived from the teachings of Jesus Christ as codified in Matthew 7:12 and Luke 6:31, advises one to treat others as he wishes others to treat him. According to Sagan, however, if one is doing evil unto you and you return it with good, you positively reinforce negative behavior. He wrote more favorably of what is known as the *Brazen Rule*: Doing unto others as they do unto you. That is, good for good, evil for evil.

At first glance the Brazen Rule seems reasonable enough, but there are two problems with it. The first is how to begin an engagement. To solve this he modifies the rule into one he calls "tit-for-tat." That is, the practitioner first cooperates with the others involved after which he does unto them as they do unto him. Tit-for-tat, said he, is more likely to compel proper treatment for oneself. A certain "expert power strategist," who fails to show any real-world experience in his craft, simply advises returning aggression with the same to show persecutors one is not an easy target. Albeit perhaps for reasons more philosophical, Anton LaVey, author of the *Satanic Bible*, promulgates a similar idea: "Kindness to those who deserve it instead of love wasted on ingrates."

I've spent decades putting the philosophies to the test. What I have found is returning good for good under either rule is an excellent method of fulfilling the quid pro quo demand of interpersonal relationships. It satisfies the other person's self-interest and, in fair exchange, mine. The good for evil necessitated by the Golden Rule, on the other hand, can promote exactly what Sagan describes—more evil treatment for me. Nonetheless, I have also found it can deflate the aggression of an adversary who views this as a sort of submission, thus taking me off his radar so I can focus on matters more important than entertaining his boredom and insecurity. The Brazen Rule's requirement of evil for evil can pack a wallop but can also backfire. Successfully applying it requires a great deal of skill, knowledge of the target, and often a favorable juncture of circumstances.

You can likely recollect a situation in your life where someone acted in a manner that offended you. In turn, you did something he found offensive. And this open exchange rapidly escalated into a messy full-scale feud in which you now wish you'd never been involved. And this is the second problem with the Brazel Rule; that which Sagan labels "unending vendetta." While these situations are quite common, they can easily be avoided. A superb historical example comes to us from the Roman Empire in the first century of the common era. To better understand what's involved here, let's examine the key events:

1. After replacing Titus Flavius Vespasianus (Titus) as emperor of the Roman Empire in 81 AD, Titus Flavius Domitianus (Domitian) quickly began acting inappropriately. He offended the Senate by his arrogance—taking little interest in its activities and carrying on his imperial affairs from his secluded estate outside the capitol. He also executed fourteen adversarial senators and exiled many stoics—members of an austere philosophical group with whom senators identified.

2. In September 96, conspirators burst into Domitian's bedroom and stabbed him to death.

3. The Senate condemned Domitian's memory and installed as a replacement former consul (chief magistrate) Marcus Cocceius Nerva, who arose from an illustrious family.

4. Just as the Senate had not identified with Domitian but now approved of Nerva, the vast array of legions which had identified with Domitian now failed to approve of Nerva.

5. The elite military unit charged with protecting the emperor, known as the Praetorian Guard, mutinied in 97. They stormed the palace and pressured Nerva to reveal the names of Domitian's assassins. He did and the Guard rounded them up, then tortured and murdered them. Afterwards, they forced the emperor to publicly show them gratitude for their service—a grave humiliation.

6. Nerva knew he was weak without the support of his military. (Recall the lesson on this from Chapter One.) Therefore, he took strategic action, adopting as a son Marcus Ulpius Traianus (Trajan)—a general from the Roman province of Hispania who retained many loyal legions. Nerva bestowed upon Trajan the titles imperator and caesar, thus designating him as the successor. In return Nerva obliquely asked Trajan to avenge the dishonorable treatment to which the Guard subjected him.

7. Nerva expired in January 98. Trajan ascended to the throne and immediately executed the Guard leaders who had organized the rebellion which embarrassed his adoptive father.

8. Trajan wrote a letter to the Senate promising the senators he would not deal with them as had Domitian. Cautious not to offend either his legislators or his soldiers, the new emperor deftly maneuvered behind the scenes to increase his strength. Trajan proved personable, generous, and productive. He is still considered to be one of the Roman Empire's finest rulers.

Domitian evidently initiated the poisonous relationship with the Senate by his disrespectful treatment. The resulting exchange, however, was not profitable for him, the specific fourteen senators who openly opposed him, the conspirators who assassinated him, or the Guard leaders who assassinated the assassins. All forfeited their lives for their fruitless part in the conflict. The one who most benefited from it was Trajan. The tit-for-tat, in which he previously had no part, elevated him to the imperial office. To restore the honor of the one who had promoted him he had to administer one collective blow, but he assured it would be the final one. After doing so he worked hard to put an end to the conflict.

Behaviorists believe people who are highly anxious about their level of security, virtuousness, social acceptability, and standing are ones who display the highest levels of aggression. And a simple reason an open exchange of evil for evil can fail is embedded deep in our evolutionary instincts: aggression tends to provoke aggression. Thus, before reaching a decision on whether to apply the evil for evil component of the rule, you should evaluate the following factors:

1. The targets aggressivity;

2. Whether his political power is equal to or greater than yours;

3. His ability to retaliate after he becomes aware you are trying to harm him or have already done so;

4. Whether he thinks rationally. E.g., he may not be of a sound mind or may retaliate impulsively without considering the costs and benefits of his action.

If you openly return evil for evil and these factors are not in your favor, you may find yourself either being destroyed or hopelessly locked in an unwinnable feud.

Long ago, when I followed the misbegotten advice of self-proclaimed "experts," who preach without having practiced, I found myself entangled in a feud I could not win. I retaliated against an impulsive, extremely aggressive individual whose political power and ability to retaliate were about equal to mine. This conflict quickly escalated with factions forming behind each side. After a few years of heavy political and quasi-legal casualties on both sides, my second in command, "Mike," abruptly relocated. I quickly considered the matter and spoke to my chief enemy the next day. First, I laid blame on Mike for extending the campaign beyond what was necessary without my approval. (Mike was gone forever, so this did not prejudice him.) Second, I offered a truce. My enemy knew this was in his best interest. He said he suspected Mike was the cause of the recent actions (I doubt he fully believed this, but he, like I, needed some justification) and gladly agreed to a cessation of hostilities. To save face neither he nor I apologized. This was a cease-fire, not a surrender.

As peace does not keep itself, the agreement required monitoring. For a few years afterward, if something was said or done that could be interpreted as a hostile action by either faction, I quickly conferred with him to be sure there were no misunderstandings that might reignite the conflict.

Hard feelings eventually subsided, and I ended up becoming friendly acquaintances with his second in command.

Note: If you wish to retaliate but without your enemy's knowledge you are the source of the action you may: 1) pretend to not feel offended by his transgression; 2) allow some time between his offense and your response (the human mind naturally inclines to associate events that occur closely together or in a sequence); 3) have your action carried out anonymously or by someone he doesn't suspect to be your ally; 4) deliver the action in such a way he believes others are negatively affected by it so he doesn't suppose he was targeted. (This defensive deception, while not foolproof, has allowed me to safely lay some serious smack down on some very dangerous people since the old days when I was too bold for my own good.)

If the factors are in your favor this is an entirely different situation. Not responding can hold consequences of its own. In accord with what is known in war studies as the *Offense-Defense Theory*, potential aggressors become tempted to attack as their offensive forces grow strong and their military and political objectives appear more easily obtained. Let's look at an example.

Terrorists had struck the U.S. a number of times before 9/11/2001 with the American response surprisingly weak. These are some of the key incidents:

1. Attack: Hezbollah assaulted U.S. military barracks and embassy in Lebanon (1983).
   Response: Pentagon ordered airstrikes against Syria which caused little damage and made the U.S. appear ineffective. President Reagan removed his military.

2. Attack: In Somalia, terroristic warlords and their followers shot down U.S. helicopters and publicly murdered soldiers (1993).
   Response: President Clinton withdrew his military.
3. Attack: al-Qaeda bombed two American embassies in eastern Africa (1998).
   Response: President Clinton launched cruise missiles at mostly vacant al-Qaeda training camps. (Osama bin Laden supposedly left one of the camps only hours before the missile strike.)
4. Attack: al-Qaeda boat bombed U.S. Navy ship *USS Cole* near Aden, Yemen, killing 17 sailors (2000).
   Response: Navy improved its training program.

Terrorists thus had little incentive to stop. Former President George W. Bush reveals:

> . . . it was clear the terrorists had interpreted our lack of a serious response as a sign of weakness and an invitation to more brazen attacks. Al-Qaeda messages frequently cited our withdrawals as evidence that Americans were, in the words of bin Laden, "paper tigers" who would be forced to "run in less than twenty-four hours."

Having considered situations in which the Brazen Rule shouldn't have been followed but was and should have been followed but wasn't, let's turn our attention to some instances in which I personally applied it to great success.

♦ ♦ ♦ ♦ ♦

Ambition must be made to counteract ambition.
— *James Madison*

In the summer of 2018 federal Bureau of Prisons (BOP) Psychologist Rick Paulson called me to his office for a meeting to discuss the offenses for which I am incarcerated. I harbored no desire to meet with him but had no choice in the matter. After waiting an hour in the Psychology Department hallway, I was summoned into his office. I stood before the seated official.

Paulson briefly reviewed the nature of my convictions, then repeatedly castigated me for committing my federal offenses, which primarily involved trading nude pictures with my underage girlfriend in 2002 and 2003. When at long last he finished, we silently stared at each other. He breached the silence, "Well, what do you have to say for yourself?"

Having worked as a communications engineer, I was well aware that most men keep porn, legal and otherwise, on their computer. I had no interest in entertaining his delusion of superiority and decided to shift the locus of the inquiry. "You're pretty quick to find fault with my behavior, but what about yours? What contraband would I find if I searched your computers? What items pertaining to your own forbidden sexual propensities might I embarrass you with if I searched your house as the police searched mine?"

He squirmed nervously in his chair while gazing down at his desktop. Did I know something about him, or did I just know something about human nature which applies to him just as it does every other man on the planet? After about a half-minute of silence he finally glared up at me and, while nervously blinking, issued the only reply he could, "We're not here to talk about me." He then abruptly concluded the meeting and allowed me to depart. This man would give me no more problems. When I saw him out and about on the compound he avoided even making eye contact.

Little is more common than to encounter a news story featuring some government official plummeting from the heights of glory due to a scandal. The laws these officials create and enforce have become so contrary to human nature they are nearly impossible to obey. And many of the same end up caught in a web of their own creation. (We noted some examples of this in Chapter 3.)

We have, therefore, an amalgamation of officials administering laws they cannot themselves obey upon a citizenry who also cannot obey them. And just as they will take advantage of your human frailties to further their self-interests, you are perfectly justified in using theirs to protect and avenge yourself from their abuse.

♦ ♦ ♦ ♦ ♦

> The power drive of men and nations has traditionally been checked by the power drive of other men and other nations. On every level of human activity, from the family to the nation, there operates a *principle of countervailing force* which, more often than not, makes for a rough equity by preventing any one person, group, or nation from gaining domination over all others.
>
> — J. William Fulbright
> Chairman of the Senate
> Foreign Relations Committee (dec.)

The Portly "Protector"

Sunday, July 10, 2016, was a beautiful day in Hopewell, Virginia. A few puffy clouds bespeckled the azure heavens as I darted across the prison's courtyard walkway to the recreation area during the 2:00 p.m. activity move. I could hardly wait to walk the track and absorb the sunlight.

As I passed the C-South housing unit, Officer Wendy Henderson called words I've come to despise, "Hey you! Come here!" Rolling my eyes, I stopped.

"Yes?"

"Give me your bag!" she commanded.

I sighed and handed her my mesh recreation satchel, certain it contained no contraband. She began picking through each sheet of paper in my legal folder, which was still in the bag from my visit to the law library the previous day. I wondered if this overweight officer was going to even allow me to make it to Recreation before the ten-minute activity move closed. And as she continued her meticulous examination of each document the move closed with me standing idle. This was legal work. What was the problem?

The whale of an officer had settled on page one of my printout of the case *Brown v. U.S.*, 576 A.2d 731 D.C. App 1990—an important case discussing double jeopardy as it pertains to sex offenses. I printed it off in preparation for a double jeopardy claim I would file the following year: *Ex Parte Eric R. Wise* WR-72 1220-05 Texas CCA 2017.

The woman of great heft exclaimed, "This is a child porn story!" I sighed and pointed at the stamp at the bottom of the page which read: "© 2016 Matthew Bender and Company, Inc. LEXIS NEXUS" to indicate it was not as she said. But as I should've expected of a woman so large, she was unmoved.

"I have children of my own and I have to protect the children of America from creeps like you!" she exclaimed, failing to indicate how violating a prisoner's supposed rights protected America's children.

Henderson returned my bag and the contents, except for the *Brown* page. My afternoon sunlight denied, I glumly plodded back to the unit where I laid on my bed staring at the ceiling. At least I had been spared the loud rap "music," I rationalized. Still, I would be given no peace. The unit officer whipped open my cell door and announced "Ehdic, I need you gather up all child porn stories and give to me!" Henderson had called him and requested he check my cell for more of what she erroneously considered "child porn stories."

In the Prologue I discussed how I temporarily formed a mutual alliance of self-interest with a Mexican gang. During that period those who were bilingual taught me many Spanish words and phrases. I had already learned a moderate amount of French in my pre-incarceration life, because I often traveled to Montreal and Paris on business. Thus, speaking two foreign languages, I occasionally employ them in avoiding unwanted discourse with inquisitive officers. This only works, of course, if my interlocutor doesn't already know I speak English. For example, if it's an officer who already knows me or I am summoned to the Lieutenants' Office to discuss a grievance I wrote in English, I cannot pretend not to speak it.

In other circumstances, I quickly assess the racial composition of my inquisitor. If he's white, a black American, or Latino, I answer in French. This is because many of the same can speak enough Spanish to form some idea of what I'm saying and how to respond.[20] If he's African, I speak Spanish because some of the African countries from which these officers are imported were once colonized by France and their people remain fluent in that language.

I made an instant assessment of this officer's racial identity and determined by his ultra dark skin, accent, and use of my first name as if it were my last, that he was one of the African nationals imported by the U.S. to labor in the prison system. Thus, I answered in Spanish. Sure enough, he countered in French. Spanish, French, and Italian retain similarities as they all descend from Latin.

He may have picked up on a few words; nonetheless, I continued only in Spanish, so we could not establish the colloquy he desired but I did not. This dissonant exchange continued for a few minutes, then he gave up and left.

I had no "child porn stories," whatever those may be, and thus nothing to relinquish, but I didn't need him looking around, misconstruing my legal papers to be such and taking them. I needed them for my forthcoming habeas corpus.

After the evening count, I finally left my cell. The other inmates had heard what was going on and were laughing at and taunting me. The rumor that I was caught with a "child porn story" had devolved into one that I was writing such stories as well.

This type of problem was nothing new: some fanatical female official confiscates my legal work, misinterprets it to suit her agenda, and deprives me of the ability to effectively litigate—frustrating and humiliating me in the process. I'd had it with the abuse these women inflicted on me in their misguided mission to "protect" the so-called "children."

Most women are irrational creatures driven by emotion. They seldom practice what they preach and easily fall into forbidden relationships themselves. Male inmates are always on the lookout for female staff members to do their bidding. That is, they seduce gullible women into romantic relationships so they can get the women to transport contraband into the prison. I learned early in my incarceration that this is the predominant method by which it enters the system. I've never had any interest in that. Whatever they may say about the forbidden relationship for which I am incarcerated, at least my motive was pure—I only wanted a girlfriend.

I'd barely noticed the obese officer prior to July 10, but she was certainly "on my radar" now.

---

[20] A white officer I knew well confided in me that he was articulate in Spanish, but conversed in it as little as possible, "so I can hear what the Mexicans are discussing without them knowing it."

Government officers should know better than to get into situations where they are vulnerable. They've been trained on this. Like all humans, however, they err. Believing themselves omnipotent, they slip, stumble, and fall. My job is to help that process along.

Anytime I was walking the compound courtyard, I would look for Henderson to see what she was up to. Given her immense girth and loud mouth, she wasn't hard to locate.

It didn't take long for me to discover that, for the reason described above, even she had attracted an inmate suitor. On every activity move during her shift an inmate who was half her size could be found in her company. He was easily recognized by tattoos of devil horns on his head. When I initially began surveilling the two, I did so from a distance. I soon perceived she was paying me no notice. This made my job much easier.

One evening in September the portly woman worked as a substitute recreation officer. Knowing she was oblivious to my investigation I positioned myself as close to her as possible. Her inmate friend soon appeared. The pair cozied up as they conversed. I was close enough to hear portions of the discussion. Henderson spoke to him like he was her boyfriend, describing her workday and personal life.

She pulled out a cigarette and smoked it in an area where smoking is prohibited, and the two began strolling about as if they were on a date. I now kept a notebook in my rec bag, so I jotted down notes of the occasion. That evening I transcribed them along with some previous ones into an email addressed to Special Investigative Agent (SIA) Dean, chief of the Special Investigative Section (SIS).

A few days later I walked out to the recreation yard and noticed Henderson exiting the F-South unit. Her inmate consort waited about 30 yards away. She was so excited to see him she actually made a beeline directly across the grass instead of following the indirect route across the connecting sidewalks. When they met he lifted his shirt bottom out of his pants as if he were preparing to put something down there. (Inmates often sew pockets into the crotch area of their pants or boxers to hide drugs in a place officers aren't allowed to easily check.) Due to the distance and the fact that I was in motion, I couldn't tell what this may have been. I logged the incident in my notebook, then described it in an email sent to SIA Dean that night.

As summer transformed into fall, the couple continued meeting nearly every day without anything otherwise significant taking place. I noted each occurrence.

One morning early in October I took the 10:00 a.m. activity move and noticed Henderson's bloated backside as she tried to hide behind the F-South stairwell. When I approached the recreation yard I also glimpsed a devil-horn tattooed head. The couple appeared to be clothed, but I couldn't tell what they were doing. I could see smoke drifting from the vicinity, and he was clearly in an unauthorized area with a member of the opposite sex. I noted the particulars and emailed the SIA that evening. It was the last time I saw Officer Henderson.

A few days later I observed her inmate friend on the recreation yard. He paced nervously about—devil-horned head bowed as if he perceived the hammer was about to fall on it. This was the last time I saw him.

On the 29th of October I was summoned to the Lieutenants' Office. Wondering if I was in trouble I trudged up the middle sidewalk, knocked on the door, and entered. Standing in the lobby, Lt. Robertson tilted his head in the direction of the first office on the left.

I opened the door and entered. SIA Dean, a tall, thin black man, was seated behind a large desk talking on the phone. He pointed to a chair, and I sat down in it. After talking another minute or so he hung up, tapped a few things on his computer's keyboard, then looked directly at me. "Wise, I guess you know why you're here."

"I'm not sure," I answered.

"You haven't sent me any emails lately?"

"I send a lot of emails. You'll have to refresh my memory."

A subtle grin formed as he perceived that I was well-versed in the art of speaking defensively. He continued with nearly as much ambiguity, "You haven't noticed any changes on the compound lately?"

"Change is the norm, Mr. Dean, you'll have to be more specific."

His grin widened. "You haven't noticed the disappearance of a female officer you've been emailing me about lately?"

"If you could just indulge my curiosity by specifying exactly who this may be, perhaps I could be of better assistance."

He chuckled aloud, then handed me a document: a proposed affidavit summarizing my emails. It awaited my signature. I suspected the meeting was friendly by the fact that he'd directed me to sit, and he was already an ally, but still, he was one of "them" so my caution had been necessary.

I relaxed a bit and read the document. Dean had put his own self-serving spin on my emails. While I had no love for this woman who had wronged me, I wanted her taken down by honest testimony and demanded he alter the document to comply with reality. He corrected the electronic version, printed it, and handed it to me. I read it, made the final change, which I initialed, then signed and dated it. He signed it also, then asked me if I wanted a copy. I did. He advised against this, but I insisted. He photocopied the original and handed me the copy. (See Appendix Six.) He then placed the original in a folder containing other materials that appeared to be legal in nature. I could see a CD Rom and queried him as to its contents.

"It's the footage of the incidents you emailed me about as captured by the new video surveillance system."

"Has she been fired?"

"Not yet. She's sitting out there on administrative leave waiting for me to confront her with the evidence."

"When will you do that?"

"Whenever I feel like it."

Less than four months after the incident in which she caught my attention, Officer Henderson's employment was terminated on charges of 1) engaging in an improper relationship with an inmate, 2) aiding and abetting inmate rule violations, and 3) notoriously disgraceful conduct. It was my fastest takedown yet.

Like so many law enforcement officers, Henderson thought she could violate my rights and in so doing somehow "protect the children of America." Now with no marketable skills and an employment termination for which she cannot account, the unemployed woman who couldn't control her own feelings for a forbidden lover probably has trouble providing for her own children.

All I had wanted was to get to the recreation yard and enjoy a sunny afternoon.

The New Sheriff

August of 2015 saw a new correctional counselor arrive at my housing unit. One in this position determines housing assignments, answers initial grievances, and supervises and disciplines inmates. The new individual was named Noble. I knew his brother, who worked as an officer for several years. While I'd gotten on fine with the brother, the same was not to be destined for the other

Noble. For reasons unbeknownst to me, the latter carried a peculiar grudge against sex offenders (S.O.s) of every variety.

I made a good faith effort to get along with my new counselor, going so far as to introduce myself and mention the fact that I was cordial with his brother. He immediately responded with hostility, casting doubt upon my assurance that the other Noble even was his brother. But I was a sex offender, he knew it, and I already knew he hated S.O.s. He and I were, in the words of Adrian Vandenburg, headed for a storm.

About the same time another hothead began working at the prison—a racially mixed lieutenant in his 50s who fancied himself a *dramatis persona*. This lieutenant named Flair was often spotted about the compound whipping up big scenes. Inmates who'd been caught in the minor offense of sneaking food from the cafeteria back to their housing units were gathered up and marched across the courtyard in a formation with their hands behind their heads—Flair at the rear barking out orders. This served no purpose other than to attract the attention Flair craved. Once when doing this I heard him shout, "There's a new sheriff in town!"

In the summer of 2016, a huge D.C. black who went by the apt alias "Psycho" raped a small, white S.O. in my unit. When staff caught wind of this, they were both placed in the SHU (segregation). A week later, the victim, "Little Dave," returned to the unit. After another week had passed, Psycho also returned.

While I was surprised both had been released back to the same unit, the bigger shock was that they had both been returned to the same cell—A-North #57. This is a 4-man cell and it now housed Psycho and three young white S.O.s.

The whites immediately informed Counselor Noble that this was not a safe arrangement. After one of the meetings in which this happened, I noticed my friend "Bird," an occupant of the cell, walking out of Noble's office shaking his head in exasperation. I was sitting in my customary out-of-cell spot, on the balcony's corner between cells 54 and 57, when Bird stopped and described how he had told Noble that Pyscho was victimizing the young whites. Noble, he stated, refused to move anybody. I was livid at the news.

I'd had a run-in with the deranged D.C. inmate myself about a month earlier. He'd stormed out of his cell and demanded I move because my customary spot was beneath the pipes from which he liked to do pull-ups. I replied, "I'll be here until noon. You may do your pull-ups at that time." Psycho whooped and hollered, flexing his impressive muscles, but I just sat there, eyes affixed to the TV screen as Kristen Luhers, the super cute channel 5 weather/traffic girl, updated me on Richmond's extended forecast. Psycho finally stomped off in a rage. The younger whites, however, weren't psychologically equipped to handle these ultra-aggressive black bullies. I knew this and so did Noble. He hated S.O.s and had taken it upon himself to add to their punishment.

The situation came to a head in October, when Psycho pinned Little Dave to the wall while choking him. But for the intercession of another inmate, Little Dave would probably have been killed.

Other inmates were at risk as well. Noble had placed a nice looking young white man in the same cell with an older Puerto Rican inmate nicknamed, "The Claw," who'd just been convicted of raping a mentally challenged young white inmate less than two years earlier. He also housed a young white transgender in the same cell as an older D.C. pimp and that situation was turning out predictably—the young white being manipulated into prostitution.

I considered the matter and decided to file a complaint against the unit management under the Prison Rape Elimination Act (PREA). I declined to specify Noble as the exact agent responsible, leaving investigators to infer this. As he was the one who orchestrated cell placements, it wouldn't be hard for them to do so. I filed the complaint with the Psychology department, which sometimes becomes involved in PREA cases, then forwarded it to the Office of the Inspector General (OIG) in Washington. I chose this method because emails sent directly to the OIG are not saved on the file server. I wanted a record of the complaint. (A redacted copy of this email I obtained under the Freedom of Information Act is depicted in Appendix Seven.)

A few days later I was in my cell drying off after a shower when the unit officer opened my door. "Wise, let's go. The Lt. needs to see you."

I replied, "I just got out of the shower. Can I get fully dressed first?"

"I have instructions not to let you out of my sight."

This did not bode well. I dressed while he watched my every move. He then escorted me out of the cell and unit, radioing the Lt. that I was en route. As I made the long walk up the center of the courtyard I glanced back. He watched to be sure I didn't deviate from my destination. This did not bode well at all.

Flair waited at the office. The Psychology Department had forwarded my email to Correctional Services, the security department of the BOP (formerly known as Custody). The email had fallen into Flair's hands, and he declared he would be conducting his own investigation into the matter. As usual, I hadn't committed any actual offense, so he had to sidestep policy. Flair placed me in the hole to "investigate" the matter. Neither the victims nor the perpetrators of the sexual abuse described in the email were also segregated as part of his "investigation."

The staffs of prisons are, by and large, fraternal. And nowhere is this fraternity tighter than in the federal Bureau of Prisons. I had alleged Flair's peer was intentionally placing hated inmates in harm's way. Flair was retaliating on his behalf.

When I was released back into the general population, I was pleased to see signs posted announcing an audit to determine the prison's compliance with the PREA would soon be taking place. There was a name and address posted. Those who had information pertaining to this were invited to write.

After composing several drafts, I arrived at the final copy of a letter for the woman conducting the audit. The letter explained: 1) unit management was intentionally housing vulnerable inmates with predacious ones; 2) the latter were abusing the former; 3) I'd reported all of this to administration; 4) Flair retaliated against me for doing so; and 5) policy prohibits retaliation against one who reports such.

Along with the letter, I enclosed copies of policy from a BOP program statement (PS) and the Code of Federal Regulations (CFR). They are as follows:

> Bureau inmates are encouraged to report allegations to staff at all levels, including the local, regional, and Central Office. PS 5324.12 § 115.51(a)

> The agency shall establish a policy to protect all inmates and staff who report sexual abuse or sexual harassment... from retaliation by other inmates or staff and shall designate which staff member or departments are charged with monitoring retaliation. 28 CFR § 115.67(a)

> For at least ninety days following a report of sexual abuse, the agency shall monitor the conduct and treatment of inmates or staff who reported the sexual abuse to see if there are changes that may suggest possible retaliation by inmates or staff and shall act promptly to remedy any such retaliation. Items the agency should monitor include any inmate disciplinary reports, housing, or program changes. 28 CFR § 115.67 (c)

SIA Dean had secretly provided me with a copy of Flair's detention order and I included it as well.

About a month later I was in my cell painting some new shelves I was about to install in my locker when the unit officer ordered me to go to the Lieutenants' Office. I wondered if more retaliation was afoot, but I washed the paint off my hands and headed that way with no escort—a good sign.

At the office I was met by three men in dark suits. Their serious and forbidding faces glowered at me as one pointed to a back office. I'd never seen any of these men before and would not see them again. I could only presume they were from either the regional office or Washington.

A nice black woman named Maria Clinton, who worked as an independent auditor, interviewed me for about 30 minutes alone in the office. She complimented me on presenting the evidence in a format that was logical and easy to understand. I could tell by her demeanor and the fact that she had allowed me to sit, that this was not a hostile interview. Nonetheless, I stuck to the facts exactly as I had written them. At the conclusion she sighed and stated, "My job is to make sure these types of things do not happen again. Mr. Wise, it was a pleasure meeting you and I thank you for your time today."

I reciprocated, "It was my pleasure meeting you as well, Ms. Clinton, although I wish it had been under different circumstances." I then departed.

The three suits were crowded outside the door as I emerged. "Excuse me, gentlemen," I said as I walked between them.

"Hold it, Wise!" one announced as I reached the door. I turned around and faced them. They stared me down hard.

One called to Robertson, the Operations Lieutenant, "Do you need Wise for anything else, Lt. Robertson?"

He strolled out from a side office, "Um . . . no . . . he can go."

In order to pass the audit it was necessary for the BOP to take corrective action on the retaliation. The "New Sheriff" vanished as quickly as he had arrived.

Noble, it appeared, escaped unscathed. But such is the nature of warfare. It doesn't always turn out exactly as we hope or expect.

These represent only two the many instances in which I've successfully repaid evil with evil. For reasons mostly legal in nature I had to fully redact the accounts of two of my proudest: the takedown of a DOJ psychologist (not the one mentioned in this chapter), and my part in pressuring a district attorney not only to terminate his reelection aspirations, but to abruptly resign from office months before the election.

SECTION III: TACTICS

Chapter Ten

Powerful Alliances of Self-Interest

In 1406, Robert Stewart, the 1st Duke of Albany, was appointed to govern Scotland as his sovereign, James I, had been imprisoned in the Tower of London. Albany had long perceived the power of the Scotch nobility was rising to a level where it could successfully challenge the supremacy of the crown. Archibald Douglas, the 4th Earl of Douglas, for example, possessed funds nearly equal to those of the king. The tribal chieftain Donald, who already held the entire Western Isles, had just conquered the Earldom of Ross and was nearing the status of a prince in his own right.

Three orders dominated Scotch society: the crown, the nobility, and the (Roman Catholic) church. To combat the threat to the former, Duke/Governor Albany formed a partnership with the church and acquired significant muscle in a relationship that would last for over 150 years. Even though Albany himself was a member of the nobility he believed he had a greater responsibility as governor to defend the monarch than he did as an aristocrat to defend the welfare of his peers. From these circumstances, in 1411 his army, with full church support, entered Donald's territories and confronted him. If Donald was to live, Albany declared, he must relinquish Ross, submit to the sovereign, and further, remit hostages as a guarantee on his future behavior. The territorial chief knew he was faced with a challenge beyond his ability to defend and capitulated. The conquest of Ross thus became the opening maneuver in a succession of offensives which concluded in the crown acquiring all of the titles and estates held by Donald and his descendants.

King James I, who finally took control of the government in 1424, expanded on Albany's idea by restoring to himself and the church properties which had fallen into the hands of the nobility. As part of this plan, he arrested over fifty of the country's aristocrats and seized their estates. This left the nobles steaming and they coalesced for a mission of revenge.

In 1436 a group led by Walter, earl of Altholl, captured and quickly assassinated James. With the king dead and each earl in charge of a small army of his own soldiers, the power of the united nobility was nearly absolute. And for the rest of the decade, they remained unchallenged.

James II, however, had a few tricks up his sleeve and in 1440 he employed one. The king of the Scots invited the fifteen year-old 7th earl of Douglas and his younger brother to his castle for a friendly "visit." The two accepted, but when they arrived were arrested, subjected to a sham trial, pronounced guilty, and beheaded. Under the influence of James Kennedy, the archbishop of St. Andrews, James II repeated this ploy in 1452. This time he invited William Douglas, the 8th earl of Douglas and cousin of the 7th, to confer with him at Stirling castle. Douglas understandably hesitated. But James II followed by assuring Douglas' safety in writing and further issued this assurance under the royal seal. With the king's honor thus at stake, Douglas finally accepted.

The earl rushed to the court enthusiastically hoping to ameliorate tensions. And he was graciously welcomed. After supper that night James II sprung his trap—he demanded the dissolution of a confederation into which Douglas had entered with Alexander Lindsay, the 4th earl of Crawford. When Douglas refused, the king and several of his courtiers stabbed Douglas until he lay dead on the floor.

This tit-for-tat continued over the century. On the part of the lords, for instance, the earl of Crawford plundered Archbishop Kennedy's lands and the Douglases imprisoned both James III and James V. The church and crown, in turn, contributed to the feud by imprisoning, or driving into England the Protestant nobility, confiscating their property, passing a litany of laws contrary to their interests, and implementing a judicial system in which all suits they initiated would be decided by a tribunal; the president and majority of which would be clergymen.

James V died in December 1542, thus passing the throne to his infant daughter Mary, during whose reign the great dispute between the allied aristocracy and allied church/monarchy would ultimately be decided.

The nobles who had been exiled to England, the most notable among whom were the earls of Angus and Douglas, returned to Scotland in January 1543. In his last will James V had appointed a cardinal named David Beaton to be the nation's regent and guardian of the minor queen. But the nobles alleged the will had been forged. They imprisoned Beaton and replaced him with one of their own—James Hamilton—the 2nd earl of Arran. Lord Arran expeditiously reversed the attainders which had deprived his peer allies of their rights and estates.

Arran presented to parliament a petition requesting the people of Scotland be allowed to read the bible in a Scotch or English (i.e. protestant) translation. The Catholic church objected to this with every fiber of its might, but without the backing of the government, it had much less of that. The proposition passed.

Cardinal Beaton was quickly set free and remained the predominant thorn in the side of the nobility. In March 1546, he burned at the stake Scotch Reformation leader George Wishart. Leading nobles had already been conspiring to assassinate the dishonorable, yet powerful, cleric and in May a detachment of them stormed St. Andrews Castle and did so. One of the conspirators chopped open Beaton's skull, then used his sword to spill the dead cardinal's brains onto the castle floor. He then concluded, "That fellow won't be getting up again."

The group of nobles seized control of the castle and transformed it into a stronghold for their Scotch Protestant Reformation movement. An illustrious aristocrat named John Knox carried the seal of approval of French theologian John Calvin himself. And with a group of students he arrived at the castle to join the movement in April 1547. All went well until June when military assistance from the Catholic nation of France came upon the scene. French soldiers deluged the castle with cannon fire leaving the Protestants no choice but to surrender. As punishment they were taken to France and subjected to slave labor.

Lord Arran resigned as regent in 1554, but James V's widow, the Catholic dowager queen Mary of Guise, managed to secure the office in his stead. Aware of the implications, the nobles drew up a formal covenant to stand by each other in resistance to the imminent oppression. Arran led the opposition group which took the name Lords of the Congregation. In March 1557, this group wrote to their old ally Knox, who was then evangelizing in continental Europe, asking for his assistance in inciting a rebellion.

Knox returned to Scotland on May 2, 1559. On the 11th he preached a fervent sermon in Perth following which the enormous audience arose and plundered nearby Catholic churches and monasteries. Mary learned of this and sent her army to put down the rebellion. Alexander

Cunningham, the 5th earl of Glencairn, responded by directing his own army to join the insurrection. Leaders on both sides eventually met and agreed to disarm on the condition no further punishment would be inflicted on those involved. Nonetheless, only a few days after this agreement was reached the full forces of the Lords converged and launched a more ferocious attack. Perth, Sterling, and Linlithgow quickly fell whereupon the dowager queen/regent fled Edinburgh. On June 29, the Lords entered the capital in triumph.

Mary contacted her influential family in France and requested more French soldiers be sent to Scotland to quash the rebellion. The Lords, for their part, found a sympathetic ear in England where the staunch protestant Elizabeth I was similarly knee deep in reversing the religious power dynamic launched by her Catholic half-sister "Bloody" Mary, from whom she inherited the throne the year prior. Even though Scotland and England were ancient enemies and had been at war only fifteen years earlier, both the Scotch nobility and the Queen of England were willing, at least temporarily, to set aside old grudges for a common cause.

The principal lords, led by Arran and now assisted by the earls of Glencairn and Argyle along with the duke of Chastleherault, convened in the capitol on October 22, 1559. While awaiting English reinforcements, they drafted a charter proclaiming their dowager queen/regent hostile to "the glory of God, to the liberty of the realm and to the welfare of the nobles," and accordingly was "deprived from her authority by the common consent of all lords and barons here present."

Mary of Guise and assisting French troops recaptured Edinburgh; however, in January 1560 an English fleet under Thomas Howard, the 4th duke of Norfolk, finally arrived at Scotland's southeastern shire (county) of Berwick. (Howard was the cousin of the 3rd duke of Norfolk and also of the sexually charged Queen Catherine—both of whom we met in Chapter Two.) On Elizabeth's behalf Norfolk reached an agreement with the Scotch lords and, on April 2, the English army entered the foreign realm.

Mary understood the opposing alliance was more than her forces could withstand and surrendered, agreeing to the evacuation of the French troops remaining in Scotland and consigning the power of administration to the protestant aristocracy.

That autumn the Scotch Parliament enacted two laws which subverted the clergy's power. The first repealed every statute that had ever been passed to benefit the church. The second banished the saying of mass from the country.

And so it came to pass that the lords of Scotland and their ancient enemy, the kingdom of England, coalesced in improbable self-interest to eviscerate the authority of both the Scotch crown and a religious institution that had reigned supreme for over a thousand years.

♦ ♦ ♦ ♦ ♦

It is often said that the enemy of my enemy is my friend. And when it is said, it is correct, or at least could be. Competition from common enemies against whom an advantage is needed is the most frequent cause of alliances in political and military contexts. You may be reading this book because you personally feel threatened in some manner by government officials, especially those in the employ of law enforcement agencies. Perhaps you've already been wronged by them and have discovered your rights, which exist on paper, do not exist in reality. As such, you have taken an interest in alternative methods to redress your grievances. 97 to 99.9 percent of all civil rights and criminal cases in which the U.S. Government is a litigant are decided in the Government's favor. Plenty of litigants denied justice are out there. Seventy million Americans are presently saddled with criminal convictions. And anyone who has been there already knows that in this nation convictions do not arise from honest investigations, forthright testimony, and impartial judgments. When you add to these staggering numbers the sympathetic families of the oppressed, you have an abundance of potential friends.

Partnerships based on mutual self-interest are as old as life itself. Cells partner with cells. Man partners with man. Tribe partners with tribe. Man even partners with animals; whatever it takes to advance the self-interest.

Early in the 20th century African farmers began growing Cassava, a plant with edible roots native to South America. But unfortunately, a scaly insect that preys upon fruit trees, known as the mealybug, later arrived on the scene. Africans investigated the matter and found their tormentor has a natural enemy back in its native land—the carnivorous South American Wasp. Farmers imported these in large numbers and their flying, stinging allies successfully reduced the mealybug population to a tolerable level.

From 1271 to 1279 AD Mongol leader Kublai Khan finished the conquest of China started by his grandfather Genghis. As he did this he found it crucial to ally himself with local Chinese advisors who helped him adopt Chinese dress, traditions, and methods of governmental operations. Thus, with the advice of old Mongol allies in conquering territory and new Chinese ones in keeping it, he united China for the first time in several centuries.

America's Crow Indian tribe actually found their interest best served by allying themselves with Lieutenant Colonel George Custer's 7th Cavalry and against the Cheyanne and Sioux tribes for the Battle of Little Bighorn in 1876. Biologically, the Crow were more closely related to the other Indian tribes, but the longstanding feud they'd had with them pushed the Crow onto the side of the whites, whom they believed would better advance Crow interests.

Similar had taken place in 1519 when the Spaniard Hernan Cortez recruited Tlaxcalan Indians to join his army in combat against the powerful Aztec tribe and their leader Montezuma II. The latter had been extorting protection payments from the Tlaxcalan and they were happy to assist the Europeans in his deposition.

Even though Mediterranean pirates were the scourge of commerce in the first century BC, Demetrius I of Macedonia saw opportunity where his peers and predecessors saw adversity. He knew pirates were motivated by financial rewards and retained only as much loyalty as accompanied these. Thus, he recruited them into his own naval forces, deploying them as an auxiliary unit against his political enemies.

There is no need for alliances to be traditional or conform to expectations to be effective. In fact, they need not form along any particular boundaries other than self-interests and common enemies. During my time in the federal Bureau of Prisons, I formed some alliances which stand out for their diversity. I (white) partnered with Dean (black) against corrupt black inmates and officers. But I also assisted him in the overthrow of his Latino boss (The Dark One) while allying with a Latino gang against the black inmates who were persecuting me. At the end of these lengthy battles, I sought and received the aid of President Trump's Attorney General (white) in ridding the prison of those black administrators who were promoting black supremacy (Dean was not one).

Second Case in Point

The Reconstruction Acts of 1867 (U.S.) divided the defeated southern confederacy into five sections, each of which fell under the command of a federal military officer. The Acts also temporarily inactivated the states' governments and required these states to enact new constitutions which would grant black males the right to vote and hold public office.

In July 1867 liberal to moderate Texas Unionists established the state's Republican party in Houston. In so doing they allied with liberal Republicans from the northern U.S. in rejecting the ideology of Texas' conservative Democrats and working to implement Congressional Reconstruction. As part of this, they were devoted to developing projects that would improve impoverished parts of the state and raise the quality of living for former slaves. A radical faction even endorsed instituting complete civil and political rights for the freedmen.

Union general Philip Sheridan, commander of the military district in which Texas was situated, fired all key elected officials and recruited liberal minded Republicans to fill the vacancies. These new officials quickly implemented their collective agenda which included hiring former slaves to direct Reconstruction at local levels and assuring the freedmen were included in voter registration boards.

Fifty-thousand blacks voted for delegates to the Constitutional convention in February 1868. This resulted in the election of many delegates sympathetic to their and the Republican's ideas. The end product, the Constitution of 1869, in relevant part granted the right to vote and general civil rights to blacks, supported public education for all Texans, and increased the power of the governor to stop local interference with state laws.

◆ ◆ ◆ ◆ ◆

In its first official statement on a prospective World War II alliance with the Soviet Union the U.S. Department of State held "[It is] the opinion of this Government . . . that any defense against Hitlerism, any rallying of forces opposed to Hitlerism, from whatever source these forces may spring, will hasten the eventual downfall of the present German leaders and will therefore redound to the benefit of our own defense and security."

Allies need not be friends. They need not be people or groups whose company you enjoy. The main ingredient required for an alliance is merely mutual self-interest; in our case this is usually found in the form of a common enemy. Trust is important, but this is inherent in self-interests that truly are mutual. Where self-interests diverge, trust must also. People are only as trustworthy as it is in their own interest to be.

The partnership between the U.S. and U.S.S.R. was highly unlikely and we saw in Chapter Three that with it came some tension and deception. It was nonetheless necessary to preserve and advance the self-interests of both countries. Many historians believe had the U.S. (and Britain) not set smaller differences aside to cooperate with the Russians, all of Europe and perhaps all of western civilization, would be under the control of Berlin to this day.

Those who have read *Uncivilized Nation* and learned of my general disdain for law enforcement officials are often astonished to find I have allied with them. I've also collaborated with gang leaders, ambitious politicians, journalists, attorneys, special interest groups, and anyone else I can when doing so suits my purpose. As ironic as it may seem, I've often found cops of various agencies to be the best allies. One hundred percent of them are not corrupt. And the few who have integrity often loathe the corrupt majority for giving them all a bad reputation. Even cops who may not care about such matters may be interested in making a name for themselves or may have an axe to grind against the same one you are targeting.

The group protection norm (i.e. 'Blue Code') is stronger among law enforcement personnel than in most other groups, but these people are, in the words of Dr. Frank, "still subject to the same psychological laws as everyone else." (See Chapter Two.) Even for cops, interest in the self (level 1) rates higher than interest in the peers (level 4).

Alliances need not be permanent to serve their purpose. In fact, they often change in an instant as the interests of those allied change.

Psychopolitical Warfare . . . / Eric Wise

In the four major North American wars that took place from 1689 to 1763 the American colonies allied with the mother country (Britain) against France, its colonies, and allies. Holland, Spain, Prussia, Austria, and various Indian tribes picked sides when doing so suited their interests. If they had no interests at stake they abstained from involvement. Less than a decade after the American colonies helped Britain expel the French from the North American mainland, giving the British throne total control over raw materials and markets, the colonists provoked British soldiers in Boston. Eight years later the colonies were in full-blown war against the motherland and in 1778 France, still seething from defeat in the "seven years war," sided with the colonies against Britain. The next year Spain allied with France, but only so it could retain its ports on the Gulf of Mexico and reacquire Florida, which had fallen into British hands. (In the Revolutionary War American blacks sided with whomever they believed most likely to liberate them from slavey—approximately ten thousand with the British and five-thousand against them. Many Indian tribes, correctly fearing trespassed American settlers, sided with Britain.)

In our Second Case in Point liberal to moderate Texas whites allied with Texas blacks and Republicans from the northern U.S. For Texas Republicans, embracing the former slaves was simply a way to increase total membership, thus amplifying the power needed to implement their agenda. The campaign is one of many showing a collective self-interested ideology resides at a higher level than a common race or local region. It also shows what people of vastly different backgrounds can accomplish when they converge against a common enemy (in that case conservative Texas Democrats). This alliance produced a constitution historians view as an instrument that transformed the state's economic, political, and social institutions.

> If Hitler invaded Hell, I would make at least a
> favorable reference to the devil in the House of Commons.
> — Winston Churchill

Chapter Eleven

A Time to Advance and a Time to Fall Back

> I see myself as a sort of spider, lying in wait
> for a run of luck. The thing is only to be alert
> and ready to pounce at the right moment.
> — Adolf Hitler

First Case in Point

Earl Warren was a government attorney who understood the importance of timing in serving his self-interests. Like most officials, he was a born opportunist—exploiting whatever political issues were hot at the moment while waiting for others to ripen before devoting energy to them. When he determined a matter had reached the zenith of actual or potential public attention he jumped all over it—maximizing his political profit in so doing. He aptly demonstrated this skill in his rapid ascension up the governmental ladder: city attorney, deputy district attorney, district attorney, state attorney general, governor, U.S. Supreme Court Chief Justice.

Such was the case when he, as the newly inaugurated governor of California, began patiently drafting a bill to reform his state's prison system. If enacted it would: 1) create a centralized director responsible for all prisons, 2) produce a novel parole methodology, and 3) grant the governor the ability to commission special crime committees. While he had long believed an overhaul of this nature was necessary to "get away from the patchwork on our prison system and create once and for all a complete centralized system," he held fast to his belief the bill would be most apt to pass when a favorable juncture of circumstances arose. This came in November 1943 when Charles Dullea, San Francisco's chief of police alerted Warren to a situation he thought exploitable.

Two inmates of the notorious Folsom State Prison had been bribing prison officials to allow them to spend weekends in San Francisco where the inmates partied with women in local hotels. One of these was Lloyd Sampsell whose bank robbery case had received so much attention Warren himself had taken over its prosecution during his tenure as the Alameda County district attorney.

Warren had no intention to prevent the crime from recurring. Instead, he concentrated on the opportunity allowing it to recur presented. He directed Chief Dullea, "Charlie, the next time they come down, you just arrest them and give it all the publicity you can." Warren later revealed in his memoir: "The arrest of Lloyd Sampsell during his illegal sojourn away from Folsom was the exact break I needed to do something about the prison system."

After the arrest, Warren wasted no time in forming the Governor's Investigating Committee on Penal Affairs. This committee investigated, then submitted the report its creator desired only two months after its inception. Warren immediately ordered the legislature to convene for a special January session to address prison reform. By May 1944 the prison reform bill Warren drafted shortly after his inauguration had become law.

♦ ♦ ♦ ♦ ♦

Opportunism comes naturally to government officials, especially they who work in law enforcement. Their targets go about their daily lives naively engaging in questionable activities and getting away with it for so long they believe cops either don't know or don't care. There is, however, a third option. Most successful cops spend a great deal of time—weeks, months, even years—collecting evidence and building a case. Then when circumstances align by which they can maximize their political capital, they strike.

The most effective weapons can be those our opponents use against us. The Government possesses some of the planet's most powerful weapons and this includes those of the psychological and political variety. Thus, if we are wise, we will recognize these, seize them, modify them to suit our unique purpose and turn them back on the officials who oppress us. We will do unto them as they do unto us.

New Englanders of the Federalist persuasion reviled what they perceived to be President James Madison's indifference to their economic plight. But when they decided at their December 1812 convention in Hartford, CT to protest this, they couldn't have picked a worse time to do so. The Federalists had drafted a number of proposed changes to the U.S. Constitution which were designed to advance their interests at the expense of their Republican neighbors to the south. When delegates arrived in Washington to present these to Congress they discovered the capitol was caught in the midst of a heady euphoria—celebrating the peace treaty just reached in the War of 1812. Their Republican rivals exploited the opportunity by portraying the Federalists as traitors—members of an outgroup seeking to destroy the union. The Republican ploy prevailed. By calling into question a key government instrument in the height of a patriotic fervor, the Federalists forfeited moral authority and the proposed amendments failed.

Advancing when the time was right amassed Adolf Hitler an empire. But continuing to advance before circumstances were favorably aligned cost him everything.

In March 1938 Hitler took control of neighboring Austria in a coup d'état. In September he acquired Sudetenland (a Germanic portion of Czechoslovakia) at the Munich conference. Six months thence he seized most of what remained of Czechoslovakia. He easily conquered Poland (thus commencing World War II) on September 1, 1939. In April 1940 German forces plowed through Denmark and Norway, and, in May, the Netherlands, Belgium, and Luxemburg. Finally, as his crowing achievement, Hitler took France in June.

The stunned world sat watching in disbelief. And had Hitler at this point taken some time to consolidate his conquests, assimilate their citizens into the German culture and Nazi political ideology (and put down the many rebellions) they would likely still be part of the German empire. Instead, feeling overconfident, he continued advancing on too many fronts, attempting to gain the air superiority over England necessary for a ground invasion; then when that failed foraying into the Balkans, Crete, North Africa, and, most fatally, the Soviet Union.

An alliance of self-interest also proved counterproductive when German ally Japan made an ill-advised advance—bombing Pearl Harbor in Hawaii on December 7, 1941, causing the U.S. to enter the war. Hitler's final major error came on December 11 when Germany and its ally Italy formally declared war on the United States.

Second Case in Point

By the summer of 1527, Henry VIII, King of England, had grown decreasingly satisfied with his first wife—Catherine of Aragon. Seven pregnancies over eighteen years had produced only a single heir—a daughter named Mary. Not only had the aging queen been unable to bear a male heir, but it also appeared she was becoming incapable of ever doing so.[21] In Henry's mind, the only solution to this dilemma was for him to replace Catherine with a much younger wife.

Anne Boleyn first met the king when she was about fifteen years-old. Her father Sir Thomas Boleyn facilitated the introductions. Henry was instantly drawn to Anne, but she was initially only interested in flirting. The king, nonetheless, relentlessly pursued the young woman for the next seven years after which she finally acquiesced to matrimony on an obvious condition—he must first free himself from his existing state of wedlock.

Henry raised a number of spurious legal grounds in an attempt to persuade Pope Clement VII to annul the union, only to have the same declare it valid. When Catherine repeatedly rebuffed her husband's attempts to force her to agree to a divorce and concomitant reduction in status, the king took to bullying their young daughter. Mary's existence jeopardized the succession he had in mind for a legitimate male heir.

In May 1533 Henry prompted Parliament to declare all legal matters pertaining to religion would thereafter be settled in England with no input whatsoever from Rome. Consequently, an English clerical assembly voided Henry's marriage to Catherine, clearing the path between he and Anne. The two were quickly married.

The English people, however, rejected the legitimacy of the new union, loudly voicing their opinion that Catherine was the true queen and Mary the true princess. To encourage the contrary position Henry spurred Parliament to pass the Act of Succession in 1534. This removed to Anne's offspring the right to succeed Henry. The English people remained unconvinced all the same.

Henry and his men then began a series of actions which were designed, according to Imperial Ambassador Eustace Chapuys, to "cause [Mary] to die of grief or in some other way, or else compel her to renounce her rights, marry some low fellow or let her fall prey to lust, so they have a pretext and excuse for disinheriting her."

First, under orders from Henry's council, Mary's chamberlain (bedroom attendant) told her to accept that she was no longer a princess. She was then moved from her own house into one with Henry and Anne's newborn daughter, Elizabeth, who was to be recognized as the actual princess and given the seat of honor at meals.

But following the advice of her ally Chapuys, Mary, now age seventeen, had carefully protested each step of the way. With regard to her chamberlain's declaration, she had written a letter to the council stating that "Her conscience would in no wise suffer her to take anyone other than herself for princess." And after she'd received a document from the council addressed to *Lady* Mary, she wrote her father asserting that he must not have seen the order, which confused her with someone of a lower status. Mary stated she was, in fact, "your lawful daughter, born in true matrimony" and signed it "Your most humble daughter, Mary, princess."

---

[21] We now know that the sex chromosome present in the fertilizing sperm determines whether the zygote (fertilized egg) will develop into a boy or girl. Some thus argue the father has more control than the mother over the sex of the child.

When a member of the king's council had appeared at Mary's residence and personally ordered her to move in with "Elizabeth, the princess of Wales," Mary replied, "That is a title which belongs to me by right and to no one else." She then handed him a prepared statement proclaiming she had neither spoken nor acted in a manner that jeopardized her claim to the throne.

This defiance continued with Mary respectfully protesting every time Elizabeth was treated in a manner that suggested a status higher than Mary's. Following months of this, the new queen decided to talk to Mary one day when she was visiting her baby daughter, Elizabeth. Anne offered to ameliorate the tension between the rebellious young woman and her oppressive father and even improve Mary's living conditions if only the latter would admit Anne was the queen. The astute younger woman saw right through Anne's veiled attempt to advance her self-interest and, of course, the long-term implications on Mary's own self-interests. But instead of rudely spurning the "offer" Mary politely and indirectly replied, "I know of no queen in England but my mother." The king himself then offered to bestow upon Mary "a royal title and dignity" if only she would renounce her claim to the throne. The tenacious teen respectfully declined.

The situation continued deteriorating and Mary was warned that if she did not swear to uphold the Act of Succession (and therefore abjure her claim) her own father would imprison, or even execute, her. While she plotted to flee England, Mary still rejected these conditions.

A relaxation of tension finally arose when Henry recognized that Anne, like Catherine before her, was running low on childbearing years and appeared unlikely to produce the male heir Henry so fervently desired. Henry's men sought to avoid yet more succession issues and began investigating Anne. They quickly lodged false, yet believable, charges on her: she had committed adultery and had even plotted with one of her lovers to assassinate the king.

On May 15, 1536, she was convicted on the charges. Four days later Anne was beheaded on the green of the Tower of London.

Mary's fortunes immediately improved. She was relocated to a residence more appropriate to her position where she was provided servants. Later that year the Succession Act was revised to accommodate Henry's ever-changing caprice. These changes allowed the king to choose his successor. To be in line for this, however, Henry demanded Mary acknowledge her disobedience as an offense and agree to fully submit to him in the future.

With the assistance of Thomas Cromwell, the earl of Essex, the young woman scripted a letter confessing that she had offended her father in an unspecified manner and beseeching him to forgive these trespasses. She asserted she was as "sorry as any creature living" for whatever she had done to offend him.

The king did not reply so she attempted a second letter along the same lines. It also failed to satisfy him as it also failed to specify the nature of her misconduct.

Henry dispatched the dukes of Norfolk and Suffolk along with the bishop of Chester to extract the desired confession and agreement to submit. After a lengthy interrogation Mary would only repeat the positions she had already stated many times. Henry finally snapped. The king ordered his daughter be tried for treason—an offense carrying the punishment of death. But his judges, not wanting to dishonor themselves by ordering the princess' death, demurred. They came up with a last-ditch plan. Mary would be given a document proclaiming exactly what Henry wanted her to concede and only if she refused to sign would a prosecution commence. The paper, entitled, "Lady Mary's Submission," required her to recognize: 1) her parents' marriage had never been lawful, 2) she was illegitimate, and 3) the pope, who had refused to divorce her parents, retained no legal jurisdiction in England. It concluded with a request she be forgiven her willful obdurance and an affirmation that she was swearing to the statements therein, "with all her heart, inward sentence, belief, and judgment."

The document contradicted everything Mary had been asserting since she and her mother had fallen out of the king's favor in 1527. Yet, every source she trusted told her signing was her last chance to preserve her life. Even Chapuys, who had given her solid advice for years, was among those who advised her to relent. He, nonetheless, recommended she do so, then sign a second document—a denial he had written for her that would be placed only in her personal records. This was to preserve her conscience and invalidate her submission in the eyes of her creator. He convinced her that in signing the two documents she was serving a greater good by staying alive, which meant she still had the possibility to rule. And if she ruled, she could restore the "genuine faith" (i.e. Catholicism) and an honest government. She would be serving a higher purpose, he concluded, both to herself and her nation. And she believed this.

To avoid direct knowledge of what was in "Lady Mary's Submission" the young woman signed it without reading it, then signed the second document which repudiated whatever was in the first.

Seventeen years later Henry's persistent, yet patient, first born daughter, known to history as "Bloody" Mary Tudor, was crowned queen of England.

♦ ♦ ♦ ♦ ♦

Some armchair power experts advise that one should always stand up to his bullies. Make them walk away from a confrontation with some sort of injury, however trivial, the "experts" advise, so the bullies discover their victim is not an easy conquest and will stop antagonizing him. In theory it sounds good; and I have seen it work out exactly as they predict. But I've also seen, all too many times, it can make a bad situation even worse. Let's examine that.

Bullies usually have some kind of advantage. Most are well aware of this, but some sense it less consciously. If you overtly stand up to one without obtaining complete victory you may be left to deal with a number of unfavorable consequences. These are the most common:

1) The bullying continues, possibly worsening. Nearly every benefit has an associated cost. Let's say a manufacturer can sell a product for a maximum price of $40. He had previously been able to produce it for only $25, but his cost has risen to $35. Will he stop producing it for only a $5 per item profit? Unless sales are consistently very low and cannot be increased he's likely to decide the benefit still exceeds the cost and continue. Your bully may also perform a cost-benefit analysis, probably a crude intuitive one, and determine the insignificant injury you can inflict is worth the greater benefit. You have already shown you cannot defeat him; why should he stop?

2) You can get caught up in exasperating and exhausting feuds. We've already examined these in Chapter Nine (and the beginning of Ten) and have noted their high costs.

3) Your bully may severely injure or even destroy you. Bullies seldom see themselves as such. As we learned in Chapter Four, this is a matter of perspective. The bully is likely, for whatever reasons, to see himself as the good guy and you as the bad one. He may lose his patience with what he perceives to be your antagonism and take decisive action to end it once and for all.

Surviving under the rule of tyrants like Henry VIII and officials of the U.S. Government can never be compared to sleeping on a bed of rose petals. Maintaining your integrity in the face of such depraved vermin is even more difficult. In dealing with such types, you must always be attuned to every facet of the domain in which you and they operate. And while working toward a greater goal, you may need to acquiesce to the will of your overlords.

You surely noticed the extent to which timing assisted in my overthrow of the unrepentant black supremacists as described in the Prologue. When Barack Obama was president, nothing could be done to stop racial discrimination by blacks against whites in the federal BOP. In fact, over his tenure he replaced every white that stood in the chain of command between he and I with a black. This was no accident. Obama used his psychological magic to trick the American people into believing he was a color-blind champion of the little guy when in fact he was the black supremacist in chief. But with their source of power removed in 2017 I was able to manhandle the BOP's stubborn black supremacist officials just as I had many other officials who dared take their chances with me.

Henry VIII's unfortunate daughter merely craved her father's affection. But when she came to see that he viewed her as nothing more than an obstacle that stood in the way of his self-interest, she held fast to her one asset: her status as the legitimate firstborn child of the king and queen. Heeding the advice of her allies, she defended her claim in a manner designed not to raise her father's aggression.

Catherine was Spanish. She was Catholic and so was her daughter. When the pope refused to annul the marriage, Henry politically divorced England from the Vatican. But many of his people retained their Catholic faith. And Mary retained their unquestioned allegiance.

Henry must have loved his daughter. She was of his own flesh and blood. But he loved himself far more and allegiance to the king was considered unquestionable in the late middle ages. He had long retained the grounds necessary to put her to death, but he couldn't deal with her as a typical insurgent. She milked this for all it was worth. Henry was, nonetheless, a fickle and temperamental despot. As such, when she pushed him to the point he could no longer tolerate her disobedience and she believed he was ready to execute her, the young woman finally had to cave in. It was the right move for the moment. Whatever she signed under duress notwithstanding, the people and the nobles knew she was the rightful heir. And when Henry's chosen successor, Edward VI—his feeble son with Jane Seymour, died in 1553, Mary was finally given her seat on the throne.

Julius Caesar showed how intelligent he was by submitting to Cilician pirates who had kidnapped him in 75 B.C. For the thirty-eight days he was held on the island of Farmakonisi, the young Roman statesman maintained cordial relations with his captors, joining them in the games they played and amusing himself by reciting speeches to them. The high point of the entertainment, however, came when Caesar jokingly threatened to kill them all. While it may have been a laughing matter at the time, after the pirates received the ransom and released their prisoner, he avenged the abduction. Caesar and a unit of Roman soldiers tracked, captured, and imprisoned the pirates. He then crucified each and every one of them.

A weakling who opportunistically delays and withdraws, but only until his power is such that he can launch a counteroffensive is executing that to which military strategists refer as an *elastic defense*. Caesar made no attempt to resist the pirates while they held the upper hand. Instead, he bent—adapting to the reality of his circumstances, going with the flow. Once he was released the pirates no longer threatened his physical safety, but they had damaged his dignity—the esteem in which the Romans held him and in which he held himself. And he brilliantly avenged himself in deploying his own version of the strategy.

Bruce Lee, generally acknowledged as the greatest martial artist in world history, knew well when to place his gargantuan ego and cocky attitude on the backburner. As a young Hong Kong gang leader in the mid to late 1950s his paths crossed those of an older more effective fighter named

William Cheung. Bruce recognized two choices—he could either avoid William and retain his status or recognize William as the big dog, fall in under him, and improve his skills. The discerning young man chose the latter.

When one asks another for instruction, he implies his own inferiority. This flatters the target and lowers his aggression drive, leaving him in a mindset conducive to exploitation. William took the bait and Bruce was able to observe William's superior techniques and acquire his connections.

William introduced Bruce to legendary Kung Fu master Ip Man. The latter stated he was willing to accept Bruce as a pupil on the condition he first study basic techniques under Wong Shun Leung. This man was known as the King of the Talking Hands and was considered to be one of the best fighters in the city.

Bruce, in his usual flamboyance, showed up for his first lesson wearing sunglasses and meticulously sculpted hair. He was probably also chewing gum—a favorite habit. Seeing Bruce as a smart aleck Elvis wannabe, the teacher told William that Bruce lacked the serious attitude necessary and would not be accepted as a student. William broke the news to Bruce who knew what he had to do.

At their next meeting Bruce presented himself differently: he was dressed, and behaved, appropriately. And pleasantly impressed by Bruce's newfound deferential attitude, Leung changed his mind. He agreed to instruct the young man. Leung taught Bruce the fundamentals, then, according to plan, turned him back over to Ip Man who coached him in advanced techniques.

Finding the submissive attitude to be serving him well, Bruce continued to utilize it as a means to an end. A decade later in Hollywood he ingratiated himself with talented and famous actors such as Van Williams and Steve McQueen, soliciting their advice and using their connections to propel himself to superstardom.

Bruce's strategy of kowtowing to those of superior talent, of whom he was both admiring and envious, benefited him throughout his life. Every time he assumed this position of inferiority he knew it was only temporary. When his own skills surpassed those of his mentors he left them in the dust. *Enter the Dragon* has now grossed $440 million, far more than any film made by the silver screen gods who taught Bruce. In death he has become "the first and highest paid Asian star," achieving what, in life, he stated to be his "definite chief aim." Had Bruce directly challenged the superior men instead of submitting, he would've forfeited a wealth of knowledge and power. He never would've acquired his talents, fame, and fortune. In all likelihood he would've languished in Hong Kong as a hoodlum and mediocre actor, then died of his unique susceptibility to heat stroke all the same.

Many animal species have evolved instinctive knowledge of submission as a species preserving function. If a cichlid, a notoriously aggressive fish, believes a challenger has the advantage, it will turn pale (as bright colors provoke aggression), retract its fins and narrow the side of its body (to appear small). It also moves in a slow, easy manner. This is all an act designed to prevent its superior potential opponent from feeling threatened.

A rooster defeated in combat conceals its head as the bright red comb stimulates aggression and the beak is its instrument of attack. A wolf undesirous of engaging another turns away its head and offers its unprotected neck to the adversary. An inferior grackle places the vulnerable base of its skull directly under its rival's beak.

These gestures all involve two key elements of submission: 1) a turning away of the weapon (e.g. beak, teeth) and 2) a visible indication of vulnerability so the rival will not feel threatened. Note: These are cases of *intra*specific (peer) conflicts for resources (e.g. power, prestige, food, space, mates) and not *inter*specific conflicts between predator and prey.

We saw Mary speak as politely as possible to her antagonists while refusing to concede anything beyond what was necessary. Caesar submitted by joking and cooperating with his temporarily stronger captors. And instead of challenging his superior peers, Bruce Lee became their protégé. These legendary historical figures did not acquiesce because they were cowards, but because they were smart. For as I and countless others involved in psychological, political or physical contests have learned, to temporarily submit can mean surviving to conquer on a day we are better suited to do so.

> When your household overseers
> behave themselves like buccaneers
> simply do as you are bidden.
> Think your thoughts, but keep them hidden.
> — Frederick II (The Great)

Chapter Twelve

Tactical Intel

Good information, once restricted to the elite, is now available to the common man in both a greater quantity and quality than at any other time in world history. One ingests it by studying, receiving instruction, investigating, or experiencing; typically, some amalgamation of these. This information, when properly perceived and retained, becomes useful knowledge. And when this knowledge pertains to an actual or potential adversary, we call it intelligence.

Tactical intelligence concerns the processing and conversion of that which is known—often vague, incomplete, and contradictory evidence—into that which would otherwise be unknowable, for the purpose of arriving at a prudent situational judgment. Intelligence analysts who are in the employ of governments pass their recommendations on to those who decide policy, such as legislators, or they who both make and apply it, such as executives. Some individual practitioners advise governmental agencies or private clients. Others, acting on personal matters, investigate issues then arrive at and execute their own decisions.

Various means are employed in the field to fill in missing puzzle pieces and throw out defective ones. Many of these are scientific, but plenty are intuitive. Analysts employed by the U.S. Government's Central Intelligence Agency (CIA) are instructed to adhere to the scientific method. Those who do so process their information in accordance with one or more of the following models:

1. **Situational Logic Analysis**. This involves studying the facts of a case and considering them in their own right, irrespective of broader comparable events. That is to say, the analyst comes to an understanding of the particular influences active at the time and place in question and through the use of reasoning attempts to either establish the causes of an event or estimate the probable consequences of one. The benefits of this method include its applicability to nearly any situation and ability to accommodate a massive amount of pertinent information. Its chief liability is that it necessitates some understanding of the mental processes of the individuals under investigation. And as we will discuss later in the chapter, such isn't always easily discernable.

    This approach is believed best for predicting short range developments and is commonly used by analysts.

    Example: An ally brings you a federal civil rights complaint he has drafted against an oppressive official. Before he invests a large amount of time and money in the suit he wants to know its merits and the chances of a favorable verdict. First, you study the facts to be sure they are logical, consistent with each other, and consistent with the attached exhibits.

Next, you interview witnesses to be sure their testimony is logical and will match that of each other and that of the plaintiff. You then conduct some legal research to determine whether the facts smoothly fit into the requirements of the binding precedents (governing case law for the circuit). If the precedents are older cases you look into the popular political views on the matter to ascertain whether the courts may consider them ripe for change. Finally, you research the district judge for the local division to find out which president appointed him, because this is an indication of the political views by which he will interpret the law. You arrive at a conclusion.[22]

2. **Theoretical Analysis**. A theory, in *this* context, is a generalization reached by studying many examples of similar facts and events. It holds that when a certain set of circumstances develop, other certain circumstances are likely or sure to follow. Thus, when an analyst finds examples with a certain set of circumstances; that is, those that closely match the circumstances of the case he is evaluating, he can draw the conclusions that have already been determined to follow. This method acknowledges and exploits beliefs about the essential nature of people, their establishments, and their political systems. It is the most efficient approach as it allows the practitioner to focus on the important components of the case and predict future developments for which little present evidence otherwise exists. It also, however, allows the analyst to bypass evidence that actually denotes future developments and can be ambiguous as to when the anticipated developments will occur.

   Example: With respect to the aforesaid prospective lawsuit, you try a different approach. Visiting a case law database, you search your district for civil rights cases that have the same general facts and legal claims as your ally's case. You note the results of 500 cases. In 498 of them, the judge dismissed the action under Federal Rule of Civil Procedure (FRCP) 12 (failure to state a justiciable claim) or FRCP 56 (summary judgment). This translates to a 99.6 percent outcome against the plaintiff, thus establishing that when one files this type of case in your district, dismissal is highly likely to follow. You draw a conclusion and advise your ally.

3. **Historical Comparison Analysis**. One employs this approach when he strives to comprehend a present situation by comparing it to a similar event that has already transpired. In so doing he first identifies the foremost components of the situation at hand. He then searches for a suitable precedent. When he locates one he believes to be compatible, he uses the known facts of the prior event to fill in the unknown facts of the current one.

   Unlike the theoretical model, this system uses only one or a few comparable cases. It is often utilized when the analyst cannot employ situational logic, because the evidence necessary to understand a situation in its own right is deficient or he cannot employ theory because the current event has an inadequate number of historical counterparts from which general trends and facts of sociopolitical events can be inferred. This approach can fail when the analyst assumes the similarity between a historical event and a current one in some pertinent aspect means there is similarity in all respects and then falsely opines the present case will conclude exactly as did the precedent. Only when all circumstances are the same can this assumption be assured. One must further consider that conduct suitable

---

[22] The CIA uses these analytical processes to make determinations on matters such as whether a foreign leader intends to invade a bordering country or a militant group may be employing a deceptive strategy. The examples here are geared more to our purposes—protection from domestic, rather than foreign, tyrants.

to the historical context may not be to the present one (e.g. due to different customs between societies or evolving customs within one).

Unless the present and historical events have a nearly identical degree of similarity this form of analysis should not be used to draw specific conclusions. It is nonetheless effective in eliciting assumptions which can then be further scrutinized to arrive at a prediction.

This and the theoretical method are well suited to those who wish to perform their own analysis but lack the time or in-depth knowledge necessary to arrive at a detailed calculation.

Example: Analyzing the same prospective lawsuit, except via this system, you again visit a legal database. You've already noted the important elements and with this list at hand select the pertinent district to search for information. But you limit this query to the judge's name, relevant statute, governing circuit court case, and office of defendant. You find no exact matches, so you select a different district of the same state and omit the judge's name, yet otherwise apply the same query. This time you find a case nearly identical to the one your ally wishes to file. It was even adjudicated by a judge of the same political party as the judge in your division. The ruling does not issue by a higher court and cannot be considered binding, but is likely to be cited as influential if your ally does file. You scrutinize the judicial opinion and arrive at a conclusion.

A fourth method used by the intelligence community is known as "satisficing." In this the analyst merely chooses the first attractive explanation, then ignores all other possibilities while seeking to substantiate his selection. If he is able to gather and order evidence in a manner such that it fits the hypothesis, the same is accepted. While the method is not scientifically sound, and is riddled with vulnerabilities, it is believed to be the one most commonly used by American intelligence analysts.

After completing one of the foregoing assessments the practitioner crafts a number of hypotheses—assumptions about the current event made for the purpose of further examination. As we just discussed, many analysts circumvent this by embracing a favorite hypothesis and attempting to tailor the evidence to justify it. The scientific method, however, holds that it is impossible to prove any hypothesis true. This being the case we should draft many hypotheses and strive to prove each false. For its is not the one with the most evidence in its favor, but with the least evidence against it that is likely the correct one.

There are plenty of other reasons to draft multiple hypotheses. The following are two of the most important:

1. Working memory, the dimension of remembrance in which information is held while a problem is being solved, is very limited. For this reason, we have trouble even comprehending complicated problems much less arriving at the best decision to resolve them. Writing down several prospective theses helps organize and control information. It liberates the analyst to focus on the most relevant data.

2. Evidence is often consistent with multiple hypotheses. If the practitioner only drafts a single one, he will be, consciously or otherwise, inclined to seek evidence to support it rather than evidence revealing what is actually happening.

While it is far more difficult than focusing on a single thesis, pitting multiple theses against each other has been used to produce accurate judgments. For example, U.S. and British intelligence analysts practiced this in the second world war to successfully interpret Nazi propaganda, forecast the movements of German submarines, and appraise the abilities and goals of the Luftwaffe (German air force).

♦ ♦ ♦ ♦ ♦

SCENARIO

A new street commissioner for Hometown USA takes office in January. To get better acquainted with his underlings he schedules each for a brief appointment in his office. One of his first meetings is with a civil engineer named Tim. The commissioner introduces himself, makes some small talk, and tells the engineer his policy will be to improve services while adhering to policy and keeping a lid on costs. He asks for ideas to fulfill this policy. Tim replies, "If you really want to go by the book there's a few old streets in the southeast quadrant that are too narrow to comply with the updated codes. They're so narrow we can't allow cars to park on them in the winter months, because snowplows can't get through with cars on the sides. We really need to broaden them." The commissioner replies only, "That is a good idea." He then thanks the engineer for coming and asks him to send in a project manager on his way out.

Tim isn't sure how to understand his boss' response. But a few days later the commissioner holds a local TV news conference in which he announces a new policy of going by the book. He doesn't specify how this will be implemented, but concludes, "You can look forward to many improvements in your city as we start following the codes. We'll get right to work!" Watching it at home that evening, the engineer smiles. He'll get right to work on those southeast streets.

Ed, a hard working sales manager who lives in the affluent Country Club Heights subdivision of the southeast side comes home from work one July evening to the unpleasant sight of a trash pile still on his curb. It was garbage collection day, and he left the conventional household trash in his plastic cans, the recyclable materials in the blue tub, and the yard waste in the green one per policy. But he had cleaned out his garage over the weekend and also left on the curb an old tire, some pieces of metal, and chunks of concrete, none of which fit into any particular category. They'd always taken odds and ends in years gone by so he sees no reason these should suddenly be rejected.

At the office the following morning he calls the Street Department, whose duties include garbage collection. The receptionist informs him there was a retirement and a new individual took over the position of Street Commissioner in January. This one, unlike his controversial predecessor, is following the book. Ed will have to take the tire, concrete, and metal to the dump himself, she says, and pay a separate fee to dispose of each of the three types of materials.

Ed is livid. He knows a local TV station features stories of citizens who are dealt with roughly by their officials or businesses, so he calls and books a noon appointment for an interview. On his lunch break he drives home to find a cameraman and reporter waiting at his curb. The trash pile is filmed, and he explains that the previous commissioner had always taken odds and ends. He adds that he is busy working and earning the tax dollars that fund city officials' jobs. He has neither the time nor the means to transport the crap to the dump. If the new commissioner can't do the job, Ed announces, he should resign. The story airs on the evening news.

That weekend he borrows a truck, pays the fees, and disposes of the trash. Some of his neighbors have stopped by, voicing their approval of his televised criticism and encouraging him to further pursue the commissioner's resignation. They'd experienced similar frustrations with the department's performance under the new leadership: garbage cans tossed on the road and left to roll about, the street sweeper no longer tidying up. Al, a neighbor who lives one street up, complained they're widening his street for no sensible reason. A few middle blocks are closed and taking a detour up or down a block has unnecessarily added time to his commute.

Inspired, Ed starts a petition drive requesting the street commissioner's resignation. After a few weeks he's gathered hundreds of signatures and been featured again on the news. He sends copies of the petition to the commissioner and mayor via certified mail. His anger then starts to subside, and he begins to question the prudence of his campaign. The trash issue barely impacted him and now he has enemies in high places. Will there be reciprocity? Officials are known to retaliate, but they're also known to get in big trouble when they do so against the wrong person.

Ed's mind is overloaded. He's been working ten-hour days at the office and walking another three in the evening on his petition drive. During his walks he'd noticed a particular police car, #337, frequently driving past his house. Over the next week he continues observing this and comes to a conclusion: the cop is stalking him. Having reached this determination, he subconsciously descends down a rabbit hole—seeking confirmatory evidence.

Ed searches the internet for information on the street commissioner and finds that prior to his present office he worked as an actuary at an insurance company. He then searches for info on the commissioner's possible allies—the chief of police and mayor. The records of all three officials are unblemished, but Ed's record is also and if they pick on him it would be a little too obvious; especially right after he completed his petition drive.

The next door neighbor, Dave, stops over and Ed mentions the cop. Dave has noticed 337 on their street lately, but he's also noticed a police car turning from the main avenue onto the street a block north of theirs in the past. Ed dismisses this: the cop is just biding his time . . . waiting for Ed to slip. He invests considerable time and energy into altering his behavior to avoid getting caught doing anything that could remotely be considered unlawful and, to this end, even consults with a criminal attorney.

On his way home later that week he gazes in the rearview—337 is directly behind him. His heart skips a beat and he makes sure he exactly follows the letter of the traffic laws. He signals and turns off the main avenue onto his home street. 337 does the same. As he nears his house, Ed's pulse is racing. He signals, enters his driveway, and comes to a halt. Let's get it over with, he thinks. But the cop keeps on going. Ed takes a few deep breaths and makes a quick decision. He backs out and follows the cop at a safe distance. What is 337 up to? The Crown Vic turns left, then right, then into a driveway and an open garage. The cop, Ed realizes, lives on the next street up. But why doesn't he turn onto his own street from the main avenue? The cop is out of sight, so Ed whips a U-turn and heads back toward the main avenue, but he is forced to a halt—road construction is underway. He'd seen this while walking around with the petition. The neighbor on that street, Al, had even mentioned it, but with his attention focused on his mission, it hadn't dawned on him. Ed exits his Blazer and asks a worker why they are doing this construction.

The worker explains, "Some city engineer believed the hype that the new street commissioner is going by the book and was looking to impress the boss, so he ordered the street widened by a foot on each side to comply exactly with the codes. The commish really just wanted to save money and glossed it over with a pretext of by-the-book compliance; so, the engineer got an ass chewing. But we've got to finish what he started."

People have a tendency to look for a personal meaning or direct intention where there is only the interaction of random flows of energy. Actions that are actually without purpose can, and often do, appear patterned. It is possible to locate what seem to be designs in a unit of nearly anything. For example, the ancients formed and ascribed meanings to constellations, which are nothing more than stars that appear from a certain vantage point to be configured in some arrangement. And people can form an ordered story out of nearly any set of events.

Ed was correct in one respect: his political campaign against the commissioner and the presence of 337 on his street were, in fact, related events. His assumption that his campaign *led* to 337 passing his house was, however, incorrect. 337 would've passed Ed's house had he never even placed his odds and ends on the curb in the first place. This is because events can be related without one causing the other. One reason this happens is they share a common cause. In this case that common cause is the installation of the new street commissioner. Had the old commissioner not retired, the old policy would've been followed and neither event would've occurred. That is, Ed would've come home on that July evening to a clean curb and the cop would've taken his own narrow street directly home the whole time.

Cognitive errors are apt to arise in our perceptions of how others view our actions and we, in turn, theirs. On one hand, people can underestimate their contribution to the aggression of others. A good example of this is the failure of U.S. leaders to seriously perceive its country's alliance with Israel (the enemy of Palestinian Arabs) and the mere presence of American soldiers on Islamic soil infuriated a great number of Arabs, most notably Osama bin Laden. (In all likelihood had President George H.W. Bush allowed Iraq's invasion of Kuwait to "stand," the attacks of 9-11-2001 would never have occurred.)

On the other hand, people can overestimate their role in affecting the behavior of others. And this we saw in our scenario above. For when we attempt to influence someone, we retain detailed information about our own efforts to do so, but we usually lack the same as what actually caused him to act as he did. As such, we may overemphasize our impact both as a cause of his behavior and the object of it. Similarly, because people often overestimate the amount of coordination behind the activities of others they assume their actions are the deliberate product of an organized plan. Some are. Plenty, nonetheless, are attributable to impromptu situational decisions, misperceptions, confusion, errors, or accidents.

In our hypothetical, Ed perceived the cop's presence on his street was a key element of the new commissioner's well-coordinated retaliation plot. Ed believed his campaign had caused the plot and he was now the target of it. But the cop was actually there as a result of Tim's misperception of the commissioner's policy. Tim believed he had inspired his boss' televised plan to "start following the codes" and the boss wanted him to "get right to work."

With all of this in mind, let's rewind to the point to where Ed first becomes suspicious to see how he could've better handled the situation.

SCENARIO – ALTERNATE ENDING

Using the analytical tools described earlier, Ed crafts some hypotheses. He invites over next-door neighbor Dave, who suggests a few more. They debate the merits of each and narrow it down to four:

- H1. The cop is watching Ed and planning a retaliatory act on behalf of his friends at City Hall.
- H2. 337 isn't on the street any more than usual lately, but Ed is better noticing it because he is expecting retaliation.
- H3. Someone in the area has been calling for police assistance more than usual.
- H4. Environmental factors are at work.

The next day Ed sits down at his computer and uses a spreadsheet to create an array. He lists the evidence on the X axis (horizontal row) and the hypotheses on the Y axis (vertical column). He weighs each piece of evidence to determine its suitability to each thesis, then marks each cell accordingly. The end product is a diagnostic tool known in the intelligence business as an Analysis of Competing Hypotheses Matrix.

		H1	H2	H3	H4
E1	Ed carried out a massive anti-commissioner campaign.	C	C	I	I
E2	Knowledge that officials tend to retaliate.	C	C	I	I
E3	Assumption that in Ed's case retaliation would be too obvious and would lead to commissioner's downfall.	I	I	C	C
E4	History of 3 city officials is devoid of misconduct.	I	C	N	C
E5	Next-door neighbor has, in the past, noticed a police car turning off the main avenue one street up.	I	C	N	N
E6	Dave has recently noticed 337 specifically on his and Ed's street.	C	I	C	N
E7	Neighbor Al who lives one street up has to take a detour due to construction.	I	N	N	C
E8	Ed lives in an affluent neighborhood.	C	C	I	C

ACH Matrix Key: Compatible = C   Incompatible = I   Neutral = N

I should note these are subjective determinations and you may rate them differently than "Ed" and I do, but keep in mind there is no meaningful difference between ratings of compatible and neutral (or what some analysts designate "irrelevant") as we only concern ourselves with evidence *incompatible* with the hypothesis. I further note, as indicated in the table, the *absence* of an action can be substantiative as well. For example, the fact that the officials have not misbehaved in their past certainly is. The next door neighbor's sighting of 337 is relevant, but had he not seen the car, that would've been also.

Ed puts the matter out of his mind for the day. The next morning, he reconsiders the relationship between the evidence and each hypothesis. He believes he rated them correctly and makes no changes. Tallying it up, Ed ignores the Cs and Ns as they have little probative value. He is following the scientific method, not trying to prove his theses true, but trying to prove them false. He computes H1 has four Is, H3 has three, and H2 and H4 both have two. Because it is the hypothesis with the least evidence against it, rather than the most in favor of it, that is most likely correct, H2 and H4 are tied for the most likely explanations. H3 is in third place and H1 is the least likely.

Ed relaxes a bit. It turns out his own cognitive flaws (H2) and environmental factors, such as those pertaining to road conditions (H4) are twice as likely to be the cause of his 337 sightings than retaliation, which is the least likely. Knowing this, he sleeps well. After work the next day he takes a different route home and discovers the cop had been taking a detour, the same as Al, because they both live on the next street up and a few blocks of that street—between their houses and the main avenue—are under construction.

◆ ◆ ◆ ◆ ◆

The ability to retain information superior to that to which their subordinates have access is a hallmark of they who rule. (See Chapter One—Superior Resources.) And it is generally presumed that where information is concerned more is better. The U.S. Government invests heavily in the technology necessary to collect massive amounts of data. But research has shown that when one who is experienced in the practice has collected a sufficient quantity, gathering more seldom improves the accuracy of her judgment. To the contrary, it can negatively impact judgment by wrongly convincing her she has reached the correct one. That is to say it can be a factor in one of the destructive forces we studied in Chapter Three—overconfidence.

The individual practitioner seldom needs to worry about a superfluity of data when he is preparing for, or engaged in, a conflict. Be this as it may, he can, on a basis that is both economical and efficient, employ procedures to improve the quality of his analysis. Let's look at some not mentioned elsewhere.

1. **Obtain alternate viewpoints**. When conducting this sort of analysis people tend to be improperly influenced by an initial impression (based on an incomplete set of facts), a preexistent proposition, or what appears to be a single apt explanation. Further, individuals are affected by the biases we already discussed, in addition to external factors of which they may be unaware (e.g. environmental irritants such as crowding, noise, heat, humidity). Neutral parties or even "devil's advocates" should therefore be enlisted to provide different perspectives, point out possible flaws in your understanding of the information, and help to otherwise cancel out the aforesaid distorting influences.

2. **Take doubt seriously**. As we saw in Chapter Three (the space shuttles) and will see again below (WMD) and in Chapter Fifteen (Tilden's opposition to the Tweed Charter) disasters have resulted from the dismissal of dissenting voices. If you're looking for success rather than concurrence, you will be well served to thoroughly consider the reasons your position may be wrong.

3. **Note unexpected events**. In Chapter Fourteen we will examine the many ways in which unexpected factors infiltrate the execution of most strategies. This is normal. While one or even a few may be insignificant, a pattern may indicate your understanding of the situation is incorrect and requires reconsideration. If your position allows for it, there is no shame in backing off, reevaluating, and waiting for a better juncture of circumstances to execute.

4. **Do not accord inappropriate weight to certain types of evidence.** This includes:

    a. That which is clear and strongly impresses the senses when mundane, esoteric, or statistical evidence may actually have a superior value. (Those who see a photo of a horrific plane crash and then refuse to travel via commercial airlines, when this has statistically proven to be the safest method of long distance travel, err in this manner.) In Chapter Seven we discussed the psychological potency of vivid over dull evidence. Now that we're on the receiving side of the evidentiary line we must be cautious not to be misled by this.

    b. That which is consistent only because it is redundant or emanates from a small or biased group. (Those who believe a statue of the "virgin" Mary must cry tears of blood solely because several devout Catholic women attest to it fall victim to this.)

    c. That which appears to conform exactly to your view of the situation. This may indicate:

        1. Your adversary is attempting to deceive you by catering to your expectations. (See Chapter 6.)

        2. If you have received the evidence from subordinates, they are trying to please you by catering to what they believe you want to hear. (An example of this is featured on the next page.)

        3. If you are the analyst, you are falling prey to cognitive errors—preferring initially encountered evidence over new evidence and seeing what you expect. (See Chapter 6.)

5. **Thoroughly evaluate the accuracy of the evidence.** Imperfections may be attributable to many factors. Some of the most frequent are:

    a. Deception;
    b. Distortion unintentionally introduced by a chain of intermediaries;
    c. Distortion intentionally introduced by one with an interest in the matter;
    d. Time delays between evidence collection and analysis;
    e. Missing data.

An analytical decision can only be as good as the evidence on which it is based. Before arriving at one you should determine the veracity and dependability of the source of your information. And this necessitates an understanding of the circumstances in which the information was discovered and passed. In the case of informants you should assess their background information and method of access in addition to their motivation for presenting the information.

After evaluating the evidence, you may find it profitable to assign it a probability value (e.g. 70 percent likely to be accurate) instead of completely accepting or rejecting it.

6. **Hesitate to discard a hypothesis for the sole reason the evidence supporting it is lacking**. Something may exist irrespective of your knowledge of its existence. Remember, it is not the amount or strength of evidence consistent with a hypothesis that renders it the most plausible, but the scarcity of evidence against it that does so.

The ostensible political basis for the second Iraq War was the U.S. President's belief Saddam Hussein possessed weapons of mass destruction (WMD) of which he needed to be stripped. But when coalition forces scoured the country and found none, multiple investigations ensued. President George W. Bush appointed an independent committee to probe into how this false conclusion had been reached. According to Bush, his Commission on the Intelligence Capabilities of the U.S. Regarding Weapons of Mass Destruction reported primary errors were a lack of "coordination between agencies" and insufficient regard for "dissenting opinions." The commission added that analysts relied too much on a "single ambiguous source" which it characterized as "ambiguous imagery indicators." The Senate Select Committee on Intelligence found analysts had relied on "non-specific source lines," because "relevant operational data" had been withheld.

But where committee reports generalize, the former Director of National Intelligence, James Clapper, does not. Clapper imputes one source of faulty intel to an Iraqi who fled his nation and sought asylum in Germany. The man told officials of the latter he'd worked on a team that built mobile production facilities for biological agents. The German government passed the information to U.S. officials after which the CIA and Defense Intelligence Agency (DIA) confirmed it "through *another* source in the Middle East." Nonetheless, in a 2004 hearing before the Senate Armed Services Committee, CIA Director George Tenet revealed the Iraqi turned out to be a former employee of a TV station owned by Saddam's son Uday who had fled Iraq because he'd embezzled money from the station and feared the penalty. It also came to light that both the "original and corroborating sources were . . . the same person." That is, the man who provided the info to German authorities and the man who authenticated it via Middle Eastern ones were both the Iraqi who had stolen money from Uday Hussein.

Clapper also concedes plenty of personal responsibility for the faulty intel. As director of the National Imagery and Mapping Agency at the time the potential war was being planned, he states his team had secured "images of trucks arriving at WMD sites just ahead of weapons inspections to move materials before they could be found." He continues, "My team also produced computer generated images of trucks outfitted as mobile production facilities used to make biological agents." But it turned out these trucks "were, in fact, used to pasteurize and transport milk." He admits that, to support the Bush administration's objective, "we'd made some assumptions that we shouldn't have, though the circumstantial prewar evidence seemed compelling," and concludes "[we] were so eager to help [the administration] that we found what wasn't really there." Clapper had "forty years of experience in the intelligence business" at the time he made these blunders.

◆ ◆ ◆ ◆ ◆

> I long ago learned that people tend to assume that you act and think the way they would in a similar situation. They project their worldview onto you, even if you see the world very differently.
>
> — James Comey
> FBI Director (Ret.)

Earlier we learned the importance of understanding the mental processes of your subject when performing an analysis via Situational Logic. Some self-proclaimed "expert power strategists" assert this isn't as difficult as it may seem. You can get a good idea of what the person you're analyzing is thinking, they proclaim, by merely imagining yourself to be him. By walking in his imaginary shoes, they advise, you can see the world as he sees it and come to an understanding of how he would handle any situation.

In theory this sounds at least somewhat reasonable. Visualizing yourself as a great man—some hero you admire—can inject you with a shot of confidence that helps you overcome adversity. But knowing how this hero, or on a more realistic scale—the subject of your analysis, would actually handle a situation is a much more complex matter. So, this is yet another case where what sounds good in theory is not viable in practice.

The mind instinctively craves consistency. It tends to perceive that which it expects to perceive and once solidified, these perceptions resist change. Thus, when fresh information arrives, it is incorporated, even if erroneously so, into an existing mentality. (That is, a way of thinking formed by culture, experiences, mood, etc.) If this new info contradicts the existing mentality it is likely to be ignored or rejected altogether. (This is why propaganda, as we learned in Chapter Seven, is best directed at those unconvinced as to the message.)

To better understand this, let's look at another hypothetical, yet very realistic, situation.

You're in jail on a first offense. It was a crime of passion in which nobody was hurt. Other than this harmless slip of human nature, you've lived an honorable, productive life. You overcame tremendous adversity to obtain a college education (even making the Dean's List) while working at the same time. And after graduating you succeeded in your field while continuing your higher education whenever rare free time allowed for it.

As you lay on your bunk you try to imagine yourself into the head of the man who holds your life in his hands—the government's attorney. What will he do to you?

You don't know much about the man, but you briefly observed him at your initial court appearance. He's the same race, looks to be about 10 to 15 years older, and probably comes from a background similar to your own. His values, you figure, must be like yours. You see him empathizing with your situation. He's surely made some minor blunders while otherwise adhering to the rules and laws on his road to success. He will understand you're not some incorrigible anti-social career offender and you still have plenty to contribute to society. You see him making an offer of probation. This will serve justice and should satisfy his need to believe he is an honorable public servant. By doing this, you compute, he will serve his self-interest.

In reality, the prosecutor comes from a Christian family in a conservative rural area. He also worked hard to get where he is: four years of undergrad studies, another three in law school, and ten on the job. But while his broader societal culture, family background, and education may be somewhat similar to your own, this is where the similarities end. He turned down the good money in private practice to become a prosecutor because he was repeatedly victimized by bullies, thieves, and vandals during his high school and undergrad years. He hates all criminals and views his job as a platform to eradicate them. Further, over the past decade detectives and various federal agents have fed him a steady supply of cases in which they've either distorted the facts or flat out lied to make the suspects appear as evil as possible. (The more wicked a suspect appears; the more heroic law enforcement officials appear for saving the world from that "danger.")

Unfortunately for you, the detective who investigated your case is in the running for a promotion. He prepared an exceptionally heinous account and personally presented it to the prosecutor who studied it well. It is replete with inaccurate information, but he's come to assume the best in cops and the worst in suspects and sees no reason to believe otherwise in this situation. His image of you and your conduct is set.

Your attorney calls him and, in an attempt to reach a sensible plea deal, introduces a more realistic perspective. He explains that your offense was a crime of passion and fills the man in on some details of the collegiate and professional aspects of your life. You're an intelligent and productive man who has achieved success far beyond what your background would connote. He's spoken to the "victim" who was not harmed and is only reluctantly cooperating with the prosecution. Yours, the defense attorney asserts, is a life worth saving.

The prosecutor's vantage point is, however, neither yours nor your attorney's. Assimilating this new information into his preexistent mentality, he replies that your intense work ethic only gave you the energy to work harder to achieve a sinister end. Worse yet, your high intelligence supplied you with an even greater advantage over your victim. And by the way harm is presumed to flow from such actions whether it is evident or not.

Your frustrated attorney counters that the record shows you have lived a crime free life other than perhaps the incident in question. He then adds some information on your personal life to show you are not the devil the prosecutor believes you to be. But the official dismisses all of this. The notion that someone could be a good person who lived a flawless life, then slipped and committed a single serious felony does not comport with his cynical interpretations of criminal behavior. As such he assumes it is highly unlikely. You are a bad person who had probably been offending for years, he concludes, you just hadn't been caught until now.

The prosecutor will push for the maximum sentence and when he achieves this he will feel great satisfaction by serving what he perceives to be justice. And as the icing on that cake, he will appear on TV news programs. He will be recognized as a hero by his church, his bosses, and, most importantly, the registered voters. This will feed his vanity and is also likely to advance his career.

While he's not fully conscious of it, there is a subtle factor of jealousy involved as well. He's always yearned to let loose for a moment of passion, as did you, but his unattractive appearance, questionable social skills, and starchy environment have never provided an opportunity for it. Unknown for the most part even to him, he resents you for having satisfied an urge he hasn't. And he will punish you for it. Showing you no mercy whatsoever, therefore, satisfies his self-interest in many ways.

Now we'll look at an actual situation (that continues our discussion of Iraq's supposed WMD). President George W. Bush had received a great deal of information suggesting Saddam Hussein possessed WMD. The belief Hussein had these was so common, according to Bush, it was nearly universally accepted; even by Saddam's own officials.

By Bush's reasoning:

1. All of his intelligence sources (CIA, military, and foreign allies) were reporting data that led to this conclusion;

2. The fact that Saddam would not allow U.N. inspectors to establish his innocence of WMD possession further demonstrated his guilt;

3. The psychological profiles on Saddam showed he was a pragmatist who would do whatever it took to assure his own survival and that of his administration. Thus, he wouldn't risk the continuity of the regime by allowing the U.S. to misbelieve he had these weapons and remove him from power.

But after Saddam was captured by U.S. special forces in December 2003, he was interviewed by FBI agents. In Saddam's own reasoning:

1. He did not believe the U.S. would make good on its threats to depose him;

2. He was more concerned that his bordering rival, Iran, would perceive him as weak if he acquiesced to U.S. demands than he was about the threats of deposition.

Attempting to infiltrate your subject's mind is extremely difficult. And the exercise of imagining yourself in his skin may give you one perspective (yours) on how he may behave, but it is more likely to lead you astray. His genetic composition, family background, life experiences, and operational environment are not yours. There may be some similarities, but you and he are not identical. When ethnic, cultural, linguistic, and other differences are added to the calculus, the divergence only widens. It is a mistake to assume his thoughts would lead him to act as would yours in similar circumstances. Yet this assumption is common and the faulty predictions it inspires are just as much so.

> Surprise often arrives when one side assumes that the enemy or competition thinks like it does and will do what it would be likely to do in a similar situation.
>
> — Donald Rumsfeld
> Secretary of Defense under
> Presidents Gerald R. Ford and George W. Bush

Chapter Thirteen

Preparation and Execution

Chance favors only the prepared mind.
— Louis Pasteur

First Case in Point

In the late 1920s a Chicago businessman named Roger Touhy was getting his start in the illicit manufacturing and distribution of beer. When he began to achieve significant success, he caught the attention of notorious gangster Al "Scarface" Capone. The gangster recognized a challenge to his supremacy as well as an opportunity to exploit a weaker rival and summoned the up-and-coming brewer to his elegant Lexington Hotel headquarters for a meeting. (As we recall from Chapters One and Five, this is both an indication of the power differential and a tactic to widen it.)

There, the slick manipulative Capone opened the discussion by calling forth his famous charm in an attempt to lower his guest's defenses. Touhy, already well aware of Capone's methods, finally offered the cold reply, "Why'd you call me here, Al?" upon which the host finally got to the point. He asserted he was having trouble obtaining product from his usual sources and desired Touhy to supply beer for his establishments. Keeping in mind that the gangster did have an extensive customer base whereby he could increase his own revenues, Touhy offered a discount if the volume was high enough. He normally charged $55 per barrel, but at a quantity of 500, he would reduce the price to $32.50. It only cost $4.50 to produce a barrel, so he would still make a profit of over 600 percent on each. The next day Touhy delivered 500 barrels, with which his customer was well pleased. Scarface quickly ordered another 300.

The day before payment was due Capone called his supplier and pulled one of his usual tricks. He complained that fifty barrels had leaks and he was refusing to pay for them. Touhy, however, was an astute businessman. His dossier contained impressive credentials which included graduating valedictorian of his high school class, managing a Western Union office, teaching communications code to naval officers at Harvard, succeeding as an oil well speculator, and, prior to his latest venture, operating his own trucking company. This experience and a thorough study of Capone's methods had already prepared him for just such a situation. The hardened businessman calmly and confidently replied, "Forget it, Al. I manufacture those barrels myself and haven't had a leak yet." To back this up with expertise he explained that each barrel was sealed with high air pressure to assure exactly this type of problem could not occur. The powerful gangster was caught off-guard and, with no proof to substantiate his claims, relented: "Okay, Rog I'm just telling ya what I got told by the boys." Toughy triumphantly concluded the call, "I'll be by tomorrow to collect."

Capone continued his efforts to deceive and intimidate his less potent supplier into providing more for less throughout their relationship. He dispatched some of his fiercest henchmen, such as Machine Gun Jack McGurn, to talk to Toughy, but this was futile as the brewer had already planned an act for just these types of situations. Prior to the meetings he mounted an arsenal of police issue assault rifles on his office wall. Then, while the meetings took place Toughy's roughest looking truckers would storm into his office to gather weapons needed to conclude issues with enemies. During one such encounter a roughneck trucker burst into his office, venting his frustration and anger with Capone operatives. He asserted he was ready to kill any he saw. The serene Touhy merely shrugged and answered, "Do what you think is best."

Capone's chief gunman Frankie Rio, sent to negotiate at one meeting, was convinced of Toughy's resolve to handle Capone's gang with deadly force. Even the fierce Murray "The Camel" Humphries and Frank Nitti were so struck by these dramatic performances they advised Scarface to deal respectfully with Roger "The Terrible" Toughy. Capone himself, however, was not easily intimidated and undertook a mission to completely vanquish the man who had risen to become an impressive underworld rival. As part of this, the mob boss tried to frame his competitor for involvement in an operation that resulted in a police raid. But Toughy's influence on law enforcement officials, for whom he brewed a special beer, was such that he was never prosecuted. The desperate Capone then ordered his henchmen to kidnap Marty "Matt" Kolb, Toughy's business partner. After this was done, Capone called his enemy claiming he was acting as a liaison in the matter and doing Touhy a favor by trying to broker a deal between the actual kidnappers and the brewer which would result in Kolb's safe release. Touhy was furious as he had always dealt in good faith with Capone, yet Capone had responded with a relentless campaign to dishonestly disadvantage then destroy Toughy.

The next day the latter entered the office of the infamous mafia boss and dropped $50,000 in cash on his desk, asking only "Where's Matt?" Capone offered his usual smooth talk insisting he was merely a disinterested intermediary who bore no grudge against Toughy and his partner and was only trying to help. Considering $50,000 to be pocket change and the whole scheme belittling to the desperate Capone, "The Terrible" one smirked and walked away. His partner was released the following day. Shortly afterwards, Capone was imprisoned on a federal charge of income tax evasion.

◆ ◆ ◆ ◆ ◆

Roger Toughy played a dangerous game against Scarface. You play a game just as dangerous when you challenge ruthless and corrupt government officials. Like Toughy, once you have decided to engage the powerful, you must plan for every contingency and maintain a level head. Had Toughy let one wrong word slip or displayed even the slightest uncertainty, Capone wouldn't have hesitated to add the rival to his lengthy body count.

Toughy was not a killer. He had strong law enforcement and other political connections and, at heart, was merely an honest businessman who discovered he could better profit in the underworld. He was also highly intelligent, and a proficient actor well versed in the nature of inter-business and political warfare. Thus, when interacting with the notorious Capone he said as little as possible and showed no fear. Toughy had also researched Capone's network and operational methods. This gave him the insight by which he could, and did, prepare for interactions with the formidable gangster.

Whatever the Declaration of Independence and a culture of political sensitivity may theorize to the contrary, it is well known among the intelligentsia that all men are not, in fact, created equal. Some are born into power and privilege. Some have natural gifts and drives for success. By whatever means they have at their disposal the advantaged tend to ascend to positions of influence. Plenty have authority over you and I at this very moment.

There is no time like the present to begin learning. And there can be no shame in learning from superior adversaries. Where law enforcement officials are concerned, my belief is they owe this to me. They make their money off of my broken life. My pain is their profit. Thus, when I notice them successfully using a psychopolitical weapon to inflict great evil, my job is to study it, discover the source of its power, seize it, modify it to suit my own tastes and redirect it against them to protect myself from yet more abuse. Such is, in fact, the way powerful entities have always operated.

♦ ♦ ♦ ♦ ♦

Second Case in Point

Early in the third century BC the Roman army threatened to assault Tarentum, a Greek colony in southeast Italy. The people of Tarentum knew they couldn't defend themselves from the formidable foe and their leaders enlisted Pyrrhus, King of Epirus, to help.

The king arrived in Italy in 280 BC and with him a big surprise, or many as it were, awaited the enemy. Pyrrhus and his soldiers rode into battle at Heraclea not on horses, but on African Savannah elephants. The enormous animals stood approximately 13 feet tall and weighed 7 tons. They trumpeted about, terrifying the Roman soldiers and their horses. Pyrrhus masterfully exploited the confusion and, at least temporarily, had his way with the mighty Roman army.

Rome engaged general Hannibal's Carthaginian forces at Zama in 202 BC. Hannibal, as had Pyrrhus, resorted to his supply of war elephants in response. But Roman general Scipio Africanus the Elder had learned plenty from the mistakes of his predecessors. He knew Hannibal used elephants and had already studied their behavior and devised a defensive strategy. As the battle commenced, his soldiers blasted horns—sending Hannibal's skittish grey giants into a frenzy. The Romans then formed entryways into their own lines to lure the elephants in under the guise of an escape route. They took the bait, and when they passed through were pierced with Roman spears. An elephant's skin is thick enough to prevent serious injury from this, but the pain and shock drove the herd deeper into delirium. The spooked pachyderms retreated—stampeding through their own ranks, trampling and bewildering the very soldiers who employed them. The Romans handed Hannibal a crushing defeat which concluded both the Second Punic War and the imperial power of Carthage.

Adolf Hitler spent a great deal of time studying while he was ascending the path to power. In so doing he learned his enemies could be a more fruitful source of knowledge than his friends or even his heroes.

Hitler despised both Joseph Stalin and the Marxist ideological convictions on which the Bolshevik party was based. The Fuhrer was even known to erupt into lengthy tirades at the mention of either. Nonetheless, he held his Soviet counterpart in high regard—considering him to be the only leader of the period as great as himself. He confessed: "[Stalin is] a fellow of genius [for whom I have] unreserved respect." Adopting and finding success in Bolshevik propaganda and insurrectionary methods, Hitler computed: "[Marxism can] be overthrown as soon as it is confronted by a doctrine of superior truthfulness, but the same brutality in execution."

He elaborated:

> I have learned a great deal from Marxism. I admit that without hesitation. Not from all that boring social theory and materialist conception of history, not at all from that absurd nonsense . . . but I learned from their methods. Only I went about seriously doing what these little tradesmen and secretary minds timidly started.

In Chapter One we learned how Hitler—before rising to governmental power—held political demonstrations in which his private SA army was publicly displayed in a disciplined and resolute manner (e.g. marching in parades or securing Nazi party events). This was a practice he appropriated from the Bolsheviks. He also blatantly plagiarized for the Nazi flag the brilliant red from the Soviet flag as this would unify Germans under his leadership and mobilize their primal instincts. (Bright colors provoke aggression in all animal species and red does so most intensely.) Further, Hitler adopted the Bolshevik techniques of using catchy slogans, concise statements of opinion, and the implacable pursuit of public attention. (The latter is a key component of Donald Trump's success in both the private and public sectors.)

In the same respect Hitler admired a group he hated even more—Jews. While he relentlessly persecuted this people, whom he regarded as evil incarnate, he nonetheless respected their intelligence, ambition, racial exclusivity, and assuredness they were a people chosen by God; all of which were concepts embraced and promoted by the Nazis concerning the Nordic people of Germany. The Fuhrer, in fact, so admired the Jews he owned seven paintings featuring either Jewish subjects or themes, one of which he prominently displayed in the cabinet room of the Chancellery.

He believed the Jewish methodology superior to that of most European nations and theorized, "If 5000 Jews were transported to Sweden, within a short time they would occupy all the leading positions."

In his magnum opus, *Mein Kampf,* he added:

> Blood purity is a thing the Jew preserves better than any other people on Earth. And so, he advances on his fatal road until another force comes forth to oppose him, and in a mighty struggle, hurls the heaven stormer back to Lucifer.

Hitler thus acknowledged maintaining purity of blood is a means by which a race is advanced. Yet he also believed in the case of the Jews, it was only advancing the race toward doom because they had met their match. While he doesn't specify it by name, the Fuhrer also showed his understanding of what has become known as the *principle of counterailing force*—which holds that the primary check on the power drives of people and their societies is the power drives of other people and societies. And of course he propagandistically implements a dramatic biblical analogy suggesting he is God's elect who will expel the wicked enemy from heaven and return him to his father in hell.[23]

In 1940 Hitler proposed an accord with Winston Churchill, prime minister of Great Britain. When the latter rejected it, Hitler took to insulting the British people generally for their cultural inferiorities and Churchill specifically for his alcoholism. Inter alia, he stated, "It's a pity I have to wage war on account of that drunk instead of serving the works of peace." Hitler's inner admiration of the British nonetheless remained in three salient respects: 1) their leaders used some of the most

---

[23] While Hitler obviously drew inspiration from the bible (compare his statement with Luke 10:18) to hold one's own side to be the force of good and the enemy's to be the force of evil is an ancient political/military propaganda tactic. For example, after my Norman ancestors vanquished the Anglo-Saxons at the Battle of Hastings (England) in 1066, they asserted, "It took us nearly half the day to send them to the devil," to establish the Normans were God's victorious soldiers who sent Satan's inferior ones to the place such go after death.

cunning strategies he'd noted to further the kingdom's international influence; 2) they'd employed ruthless brutality to expand and protect their empire; 3) their soldiers fought with an astonishing ferocity (that Hitler personally witnessed when he was a German soldier in World War I.)

This is all to say, Hitler studied and took note of the characteristics that propelled other tribes to success. He then integrated them into his own repertoire. Whether he loved or hated the other tribes was utterly irrelevant.

No successful athlete enters a formal competition without preparation. Football coaches at every level of the sport have spies observe teams they will oppose. These spies, often assistant coaches, study the adversaries' techniques, strengths, and weaknesses then develop a strategy planned around them. Boxers have always watched films of past matches of future opponents for the same reason. Not only do athletes and coaches analyze contests of future opponents to determine what they may do, they analyze their own performance in past contests to see what they did wrong so they can avoid repeating these errors. (In the football locker room of my high school years each Monday evening was known as "film night." There was no practice—only lengthy analysis of the prior Friday's game, and recovery from injuries.)

In the same manner agents of the U.S. Secret Service study every attempted or successful assassination to discover the mistakes of their predecessors. They analyze videos in classroom settings to determine what took place, how it took place, and how it could have been avoided.

Members of the Secret Service's Uniformed Division are trained on a mock street setup at the Rowley Training Center in Laurel, Maryland. There, agents become accustomed to quickly reacting to the unexpected by traveling in a van along with a faux motorcade while ambush scenarios unfold. Agents may encounter a sniper perched atop a building, a suicide bomber barreling down the street toward their VIP protectee, or a group of assassins storming the motorcade. Sometimes smoke bombs are detonated while this is happening to acclimate agents to instantly discovering whether the bombs are themselves the threat or a diversion from the actual threat. When the situation has been handled, the entourage regroups and continues on its path, where more surprises await.

In other areas of the center replicas of Air Force One, Marine One, and Whitehouse gates and guard kiosks are installed to train agents for working in their real world counterparts.

A potent combination of preparation and overwhelming offensive strategies and tactics (e.g. deception, secrecy, surprise) has become a secret of the modern FBI's success in avoiding exactly the types of bloody bungled arrests in which its early agents all too often found themselves. (See the First Case of Chapter 3.) "What we teach is superiority of manpower and firepower to prevent incidents," James Pledger—head of the FBI's firearms training unit (Ret.)—reveals. "We have an advantage over most law enforcement because 90 percent of the time we know who we are going after, their name[s], their address[es], how they think, whether they are likely to be armed. We usually pick the time and place of the confrontation... That's why you don't hear much about the FBI getting involved in shootouts. We have the luxury of picking the time and place."

Some high level politicians now prepare for debates and press conferences using what are known in the business as "murder boards." These are composed of staff members who play devil's advocates and assault their bosses with the types of questions the latter are likely to face in the real situations for which they are preparing. This not only rehearses the politician in answering the potential question, it also accustoms her to operating under pressure so when the actual encounter is upon her she is less likely to succumb to the opponents provocation attempts and is more likely to remain calm, appear confident, and render quick intellectual decisions, rather than delayed or emotional ones.

Third Case in Point

In January 1972 Democratic presidential candidate Edmund Muskie had been deftly conducting his campaign against sitting President Richard Nixon. The challenger, a U.S. senator from Maine who was known for his good looks and speaking talents, lost a vice-presidential bid in 1968 and had since been sculpting his speeches to reflect non-controversial positions—a tactic that was proving fruitful. His personal nature, however, was about to reveal its Achilles' heel: an inclination toward impulsive, emotional decisions.

Nixon disclosed on the 25th that for the previous thirty months he had been sending advisor Henry Kissinger to Paris for secret meetings with North Vietnamese leaders. Unfortunately, the President announced, this diplomacy had failed. Instead of conducting more discussions through intermediaries Nixon now proposed via the media the most generous peace conditions yet offered by the U.S.

Muskie saw what he considered opportunity in his opponent's move. He abruptly vacated the campaign trail (as well as the moderacy that had been serving him well) and flew to Washington for an emergency meeting with his strategists. The team worked all night and the following morning Muskie delivered a critique of Nixon's peace proposal to the media at a local church. The presidential prospect pronounced Nixon's plan unacceptable and promised that upon his own election he would extend conditions far more charitable, which he then set forth.

Attorney General John Mitchell was about to take over the management of Nixon's reelection campaign. He advised the President that afternoon to ignore Muskie as any acknowledgement would only aggrandize him. While such can be an effective strategy to prevent publicizing a competing view, in this case Nixon himself, his special counsel Chuck Colson, and Secretary of State Bill Rogers recognized a more adroit defensive maneuver. Rogers briefed the press the next day—charging Muskie with sabotaging peace talks by nullifying the President's offer to the North Vietnamese. For they now had an incentive to wait out the election so they could obtain a more beneficial deal in the event Muskie was elected. And this, in consequence, meant more American costs and, worse yet, casualties. It was a devastating blow to the challenger.

In their rush, the Muskie team failed to anticipate what should have been an obvious counter maneuver by the White House; one that was broadcast from the capital of every developed nation on the globe. The senator, dazed and confused, began a rapid downward spiral making one mistake after another. He defended his position in one speech; in the next he nervously doubted it. This soon reached a point so extreme, political pundits questioned whether he had the backbone necessary to be president in the first place. As he delivered lifeless, inconsistent speeches for a nomination he believed he could no longer obtain, Muskie himself even began wondering the same.

Behavioral scientists have long believed schools of fish choose a leader simply because they notice it resolutely swimming in a certain direction, presume it must have a good reason for doing so, and follow. Sociologists call this process *social induction*. To test the thesis, a scientist removed the forebrain of a minnow. This is the location of its schooling instinct, and the only distinction of a fish so disabled is that it lacks the normal protective inhibition against separating from its own school. When he returned it to the water, the minnow confidently swam off on its own and a school instinctively followed it. Thus, by the very act of rendering it partly brainless, it became the leader.

Mayor Rudolf Giuliani and an array of New York City officials became trapped in their temporary command headquarters after Tower 2 of the World Trade Center collapsed on September 11, 2001. They had already checked the basement of the building for exits and found none; yet when an individual they couldn't even identify appeared, they trusted him to lead them to safety via an underground route. "Nobody knew who this guy was," Giuliani states, "but he seemed to know where he was going so we returned to the basement."

This, once again, is the power of perception.

In 1945, Avrell Harriman, American ambassador to the USSR, spoke of his first impression of U.S. President Harry Truman, who had just inherited the office on FDR's death: "I was disturbed during this first conversation and others that followed, because he kept saying, too often I thought, that he was not equipped for the job, that he lacked the experience and did not fully understand the issues." By contrast, Adolf Hitler understood well that if he was to convince others of the correctness of his ideas he first had to show he believed them himself. Thus, when Hitler advanced a position he did so with the strongest conviction possible and followed with reasons why it was correct; ready and able to defend against opposing views. He explained, "Not even the shadow of a doubt in the rightness of one's cause is permissible," and added, "No matter how idiotic a program is, people will believe in it because of the firmness with which it is advocated." Decades later a German historian recognized this was a secret of his success: "It was his unyieldingness and refusal to compromise that made him impressive and credible."

In 2009, U.S. intelligence agent Daniel Byman dismissed Osama bin Laden as merely a "charismatic dreamer," but a Swiss-American war reporter named Edward Girardet was one of the few westerners to actually meet Bin Laden and in 1989 near Jalalabad he debated the al-Qaeda leader for 45 minutes on the topics of war, religion, and the presence of foreigners on Islamic soil. His summation is that bin Laden was "haughty, self-righteous, and utterly sure of himself [as he] lambast[ed] the west for its feebleness and lack of moral convictions."

Donald J. Trump first discovered the power of a confident appearance in 1959 as a 7th grader attending the New York Military Academy, to which he had been sent by his strong-willed father for the correction of behavioral problems. The young Trump, like many of his peers, had a contentious relationship with a particular instructor, Major Theodore Dobias, who was formerly a Marine drill leader. Trump stated "[If] you said the wrong thing . . . you'd end up in a very negative position. This guy would come at you until you got it right." Some students dealt with this authority figure by sitting by passively. Others took the opposite approach—meeting aggression with aggression. But Donald discovered a unique approach, signaling he was not intimidated by displaying cool confidence and showing no fear. This, he found, worked better than the bipolar tactics of his peers. He held onto this psychological awakening and still employs it in tough encounters.

Legendary hotel casino developer Steve Wynn (Las Vegas' Mirage) took a memorable stroll down New York's Madison Avenue with Trump late in the summer of 1983. As a 37-year-old real estate developer who was established in the casino industry, Trump proposed Wynn ally with, rather than compete against, him in developing Atlantic City's casino industry. Mr. Wynn recalls, "It was one of the most overwhelmingly self-confident presentations any man has ever made to me." One of Trump's biographers aptly summed, "He constantly speaks with such passion and certainty that few dare to challenge him."

Displaying self-assurance was also an ingredient in Charles Lindbergh's success. After many companies declined support for his project to fly from the U.S. to France, he finally found acceptance from Harold Bixby, president of the St. Louis Chamber of Commerce. Bixby stated the factor that persuaded him to sponsor the young pilot's venture was that "all of [his] preparations were predicated on success, rather than any thought of failure." (Hitler also left himself no option but success in seeking Germany's chancellery.) This confidence, along with the dexterity with which he presented his plan, led Bixby to conclude, "Even then you could see he was a master at that game." Lindbergh thus secured the finances for his project and went on to achieve fortune and fame as the first man to fly an aircraft nonstop across the Atlantic ocean in the "Roaring 1920s."

Prospects for elected offices are well aware they must project an appearance of self-assurance, and this is why they speak to the voters as if it is certain they will be victorious. Hillary Clinton, for instance, did this by proclaiming, "You know what they say, he who takes Ohio takes it all!" after winning that state's 2008 Democratic primary election. In 2016, she similarly declared, "Labor will always have a seat at the table *when* I'm in the White House!" She was not, of course, awarded the presidency in either election, but she so impressed Barack Obama in the Democratic contest for the 2008 nomination he, as President, named her Secretary of State. This catapulted her to a position such that in 2016 she at least succeeded in securing the Democratic nomination that had eluded her eight years prior.

Not only can a confident declaration convince others, it can also convince oneself. Studies have found that when one starts promoting a view he doesn't necessarily embrace, his beliefs tend to synchronize with his words in order to avoid the incongruence we studied in Chapter Three known as cognitive dissonance.

It is seldom possible to dissect strategy into an exact prescription. Studies in experimental psychology imply people do not, as a matter of intuition, think ahead by multiple stages. That is, unless it is something they have been trained to do, they are unlikely to develop a plan for alternative actions in the event their intended action begins to go awry. And even though people tend to lay the blame on a single cause (which they often ascribe to other individuals) an amalgamation of interacting and cascading elements, plenty beyond the control of man, are responsible for most complex failures. Where intricate plans are concerned they include the interference of unforeseen influences (such as random events), unintentional delays, flaws in execution, and the contrary efforts of the adversary. (Such are collectively known in military parlance as *friction*, a topic we will examine in greater detail in Chapter 14.)

General George S. Patton opined that while, "Planning is important execution is even more so." Bruce Lee similarly advised, "The inability to adapt oneself [to changing circumstances in combat] brings destruction." To this General H. Norman Schwarzkopf, aptly added, "In battle, timing is everything . . . quick decisions make the difference between life and death." Strategy should thus be thought of less as an exact plan of action than a governing concept and sequence of possibilities that may be executable through ever transforming conditions.

War itself tends to be viewed as a series of back and forth exchanges that become increasingly modified to fit the circumstances. In some engagements this holds up, but combat is disorderly, and you are likely to find your adversary executing an offense of his own choosing while you are executing yours. You must therefore be able to react to unanticipated events as they unfold—taking advantage of opportunities and evading dangers. Further, in certain types of contests, such as brinksmanship, deterrence, and those involving confrontations short of actual combat, strategies and plans themselves may influence the opponent's strategies and plans via his perception of fundamental capabilities, interests, and intentions.

This certainly is not to say plans are useless. In fact, quite the opposite is true because in formulating them you must think through the many contingencies and permutations that may arise in execution. Then, if they do, you are prepared to instantly react. I have found it beneficial to have several alternative actions in mind before engagement begins;[24] not only so I am ready to instantly react, but also because these are usually better reactions. With this in mind, you also may wish to adopt a method now employed by the most talented military strategists and infuse into your plan specific criteria that, if not maintained or obtained, would inherently cause the operation to fail and necessitate its abortion. By dispassionately researching and reaching such determinations during the preparatory phase, you will avoid the need to make ad hoc intuitive calculations while under the confusion and pressure of execution. Research has, in fact, shown distortions in judgment are reduced when one delays intuitive judgment, and opts, in its stead, to set forth each element contributing to a possible decision, analyzes each, then arrives at a decision. Errors are further diminished when he obtains and seriously considers a second opinion. (It's no accident that Ed, our hypothetical protagonist in Chapter Twelve did both in the Alternate Ending to improve the quality of his analysis.) Nonetheless, if you don't have the benefit of planning time the outcome of decisions you've consciously made are often lodged in memory where they are available for quick automatic reactions.

It is impossible to predict exactly how an opponent will respond to a maneuver. I have repeatedly noticed the psychologists' maxim rings true: "The surest prediction of future behavior is past behavior." As we discussed in Chapter Five, most animals who feel threatened, even powerful ones like lions, prefer to flee rather than fight. They will attack only when a challenger invades a certain personal zone of safety, or they cannot flee (e.g. one is cornered or must defend its young). In a semblable fashion when most people are faced with a problem they tend to resort to either the easiest solution or one they have already successfully used. (These may be one and the same.)

In estimating how an opponent may respond to your move, you should determine, as we discussed in Chapter Six, his preoccupations, thought patterns, what the strategic nature of the situation will lead him to do and any relationships between these factors. What will be his easiest response? What will be the most effective one? On what matters are his attention focused? What has he done before in similar situations? Past behavior is the *surest* indication of future behavior, but *it is not certain.*

If you cannot obtain much evidence indicating what the enemy may do, you can get an idea of how people in general respond by studying historically similar situations or even rehearsing for the real event. He who rides the red horse of war is likely to have no shortage of hostile forces around him. He can use friendly peers to roleplay and unfriendly ones for more serious experimentation.

Edmund Muskie, the senator and unsuccessful presidential candidate we just met, surrounded himself with too many yes-men. This is a common mistake made by those in power. They (like all people) prefer to be among those with whom they are comfortable—ones who fawn over them and affirm the rectitude of their opinions. A true psychopolitical warrior needs allies but has no use for yes-men. He welcomes adversity. He may even appreciate, if only in secret, subordinates and peers who challenge him because they toughen him and prepare him for success where it counts—the high stakes contests.

I invested countless hours sparring against peers and coaches in the same club as a recreational boxer in my younger years. I wouldn't be engaging any of these friendly foes in a true match, but the practice conditioned me to techniques commonly used by boxers and exposed flaws in my own system.

In the psychopolitical arena I was forced, at least initially, to hit the ground running and learn on the go. This is certain to toughen you up and teach you a great deal very quickly, but the idea is to

---

[24] Even in the natural realm the forces of genetic mutation and Natural Selection seldom rely on a single method of issue resolution. Instead, these evolutionary forces usually call forth many means to assure the solution is effective.

minimize your losses while maximizing those of your opponents. And to this end, it is better to uncover any weaknesses in your character, strategies, or tactics before you enter the actual operations theatre.

> There is no time to think when all hell breaks loose,
> but there is plenty of time to prepare for it.
>
> — Joe Petro,
>   U.S. Secret Service Special Agent (Ret.)

Chapter Fourteen

Tales of the Unexpected

> War can trigger all kinds of unanticipated
> and unintended consequences.
> — General Colin Powell (Ret.)
> National Security Advisor to President Reagan,
> Chairman of the Joint Chiefs of Staff
> under President George H.W. Bush

First Case in Point

By the time Thomas Jefferson took office as the third U.S. President in March 1801, pirates from Africa's Barbary Coast had been pillaging America's merchant ships for decades. The routine consisted of the corsairs boarding the ship via duress, hijacking the vessel, seizing valuables, and detouring it to one of their African nations. Their captives were then enslaved, and the stolen merchandise sold. The majority of the proceeds were given to their rulers and the rest divided amongst themselves. At the time, three African countries were primarily involved in this: Algiers, Tunis, and Tripoli.

In 1803, Jefferson, who was generally considered a passive president, appointed Captain Edward Preble to command U.S. forces off of the Barbary Coast. The president was deeply disappointed in Preble's predecessor, Captain Richard Morris, who had wasted most of his service time lounging in Mediterranean countries with his family. Morris had performed so poorly that upon return to the U.S. he was convicted of incompetent leadership and expelled from the Navy.

Preble was determined not to make the same mistake. He was known to be an honorable man; a man of action.

Setting sail from Boston's Long Wharf to the Barbary Coast on August 12, 1803, Preble literally ran a tight ship: the USS *Constitution*. Weeks later he encountered the USS *Philadelphia* in the Bay of Gibraltar. Its captain, William Bainbridge, informed him that Moroccan pirates had been ordered by their new sultan to seize all U.S. assets and had already kidnapped an American crew. Morocco had thus joined its neighboring nations in piracy. Preble considered the matter and decided to split his two main forces between the two enemies he perceived to be the greatest threats. He would handle the situation in Morocco. Bainbridge would proceed to Tripoli, capturing pirate ships and assisting U.S. ships on the way.

Preble and his squadron anchored off the coast in Morocco's Tangier Harbor the first week of October. When the sultan returned a week later and beheld the exhibition of U.S. Navy weaponry—

featuring over 150 cannons—he cringed, knowing he was ill-prepared to meet the challenge. The captain and the sultan exchanged letters and the latter sent gifts to the Americans. Upon meeting, the Moroccan humbly apologized for his country's piracy, laying blame for it on a rogue official whom he promised to punish. He also vowed to honor a peace treaty his father had reached with the U.S. in 1786.

Meanwhile, the *Philadelphia*, sailing alone, happened upon a small Tripolitan ship heading for harbor. Bainbridge gave chase. When he believed it was within range he ordered the cannoneers to open fire. Because U.S. captains who had previously sailed these waters had reported erratic winds and uncharted impediments near shore, Bainbridge ordered three of his sailors to take steady depth soundings. They affirmed a drop of over forty feet, more than twice the ship's draft. Maintaining constant fire, he was unable to match the speed of the smaller private ship and as the fortress walls of the city of Tripoli came into view he abandoned the pursuit.

No sooner had he done so than his ship ran aground on a rocky reef. Its bow rose and the great ship tilted to the side. Tripolitan buccaneers in the harbor noticed *Philadelphia's* distressed bearing and began approaching. After mere cursory efforts to lighten the load and back the ship into deeper waters failed, the captain decided to render the ship useless to the corsairs and dump the weapons. He then lowered the U.S. flag in surrender.

The Tripolitans were in disbelief that he would surrender so easily and maintained their distance. To convince them of the sincerity of his surrender, Bainbridge dispatched an officer in a lifeboat who assured them the Americans were on the up and up. The astonished pirates boarded *Philadelphia* and confiscated anything of value; primarily money, jewelry, and clothes. They escorted the U.S. crew ashore and imprisoned it. The pirates, however, had been paying better attention to environmental conditions than the Americans and suspected a storm was forthcoming. They knew this would elevate the ship and lift it off the reef. By morning the storm hit. The ship was quickly loosed, and the corsairs sailed their easily won prize into the harbor.

Anchored off the Sardinian coast on November 24, Preble encountered a British ship. Its captain informed him of *Philadelphia's* capture, and he quickly headed straight to the region in which this occurred. On the way he came upon the schooner USS *Enterprise* which had already been sailing the Barbary Coast under the mission formerly commanded by Captain Morris. The two ships, sailing together, spotted a small vessel flying Tripolitan colors. Preble ordered *Enterprise* to capture it. To lower the suspicions of their target, the captain of the latter, a shrewd, young lieutenant named Stephen Decatur, Jr., replaced the U.S. flag with one of Great Britain, as that country maintained an expensive peace agreement with Tripoli.

When the captain of the little Tripolitan ship, which had been named *Mastico*, came out on deck to greet the approaching ship Decatur lowered the Union Jack and raised the stars and stripes. But there was little the pirates could do. The *Enterprise* was much larger, more heavily armed with men and cannon, and had sailed too close for escape. Preble's *Constitution*, moreover, lurked close behind. The *Mastico* was seized and would be converted into a U.S. Navy warship rechristened the USS *Intrepid*.

Preble weighed anchor just outside Tripoli Harbor in early December when he began considering a method to prevent the captured *Philadelphia* from being transformed into the world's largest pirate ship. Tripolitan divers had recovered most of the weapons Bainbridge's crew had dumped into the Mediterranean and restoration of the frigate was nearly complete. Aided with information sent in secret code by Bainbridge himself, who was now imprisoned in a castle overlooking the harbor, a plan was formulated.

Two ships would execute the operation. A small quick one would serve as the advance ship and a large one would act as a mother ship, luring protectively behind to provide reinforcements. The *Intrepid*, which had been reconfigured with shorter masts and triangular sails to give the appearance of a local ship, would be the former. It would be captained by Decatur. The USS *Syren*, a newly constructed battleship that had just arrived from the states would be the latter. And it too was disguised. A coat of paint indicative of Tripolitan ships was applied. The gun ports were closed, and the highest masts removed. At dusk on the designated day, teams of sailors from the *Syren* would depart on its lifeboats to accompany *Intrepid* into the harbor. Under cover of the night these men would board *Philadelphia*, set it ablaze, and evacuate.

On February 16, 1804, the operation launched and immediately ran into trouble. *Intrepid* was a speedy ship, perhaps too much so. It approached the harbor before the sun had set, rendering it visible. Knowing shortening the sails could arise suspicion that it was not a merchant vessel, the crafty captain instead ordered his men to create a drag line out of buckets, spars, and miscellaneous debris. This effectively slowed its progress. Lt. Decatur could allow only six men on deck; seventy-five remained hidden below in tight quarters.

A related issue arose as the sluggish *Syren* fell far behind its smaller counterpart and was unable to sufficiently bridge the lost distance in time for the 10:00 p.m. attack. After considering the matter, Decatur concluded his crew could carry out the plan alone and boldly sailed on.

City lookouts likely spotted *Intrepid* but because it was disguised found no cause for alarm. When the little ship approached the massive *Philadelphia* a Tripolitan onboard the latter ordered the former to back off. Preble had already planned for such a situation, employing a Sicilian who spoke the native tongue. His man was on deck and ready. The ship had lost its anchors in a storm, the Sicilian asserted, and just needed a place to tether for the night. He would purchase new anchors ashore in the morrow. The Tripolitan then asked the name of the ship lurking in the distance. It was, of course, the *Syren* incognito, but Preble prepared the Sicilian for this question as well. He answered that the ship was named *Transfer*—a British warship the Bashaw (ruler) had recently purchased from the crown. Its arrival had been greatly anticipated. With the Tripolitans appeased, boats were dispatched to fasten *Intrepid* to *Philadelphia*.

As the smaller boat was drawn to the larger, a Tripolitan noticed something awry and shouted, "Americans! Americans!" But it was too late. Decatur, completely unruffled, gave the order to board and the assault began. Following plan, U.S. sailors quickly slaughtered the pirates, using swords and knives. Gunshots, Decatur knew, would alert enemy reinforcements. Some of the pirates nonetheless escaped and swam to shore.

With assistance from Bainbridge, Preble and Decatur were already aware of the large ship's layout and had planned accordingly. Candles that had been soaked in turpentine were passed up from *Intrepid* to teams of three, each of which possessed lanterns. One team descended to one berth deck and forward storeroom. Another team entered the cockpit and rear storeroom. Yet another handled the wardroom and steerage. When Decatur gave the order, they set their respective areas ablaze, then raced back to deck and jumped down to *Intrepid* in a precisely calculated order. A problem, however, awaited.

The huge fire was consuming air, and wind would not fill the small ship's sails. Decatur quickly ordered men to board one of the adjacent smaller boats and use oars to tow *Intrepid* into open water. When air filled its sails they made their getaway. Belated gunfire from the shore of Tripoli proved ineffective, striking only *Intrepid's* upper sails.

By the next morning the pirates' proudest capture was reduced to ash. The crews of *Intrepid* and *Syren* related the good tidings to an elated Commodore Preble at Sicily's Syracuse Harbor two days thence.

A battery of U.S. ships bore up Tripoli Harbor in early June 1804. At the designated point they barricaded the port. Preble, on board his USS *Constitution*, hoped the Americans had adequately demonstrated their military muscle and the Bashaw would be willing to negotiate peace. On the 13th he dispatched Richard O'Brien, former captain of USS *Dauphin*, to conclude a deal. Preble had authorized generous terms—a $40,000 ransom for the imprisoned *Philadelphia* crew and a $10,000 gift (bribe) to the Bashaw. But the ruler, instead of feeling either intimidated or cooperative, was still fuming over the destruction of *Philadelphia* and refused to even meet with O'Brien. As it tends to do, the absence of face-to-face discourse only intensified the tension and on August 3 it erupted.

When hidden Tripolitan boats emerged from behind a protective barrier of rocks Preble's armada moved into position and opened fire. The ensuing battle lasted 2-1/2 hours. In the end the only U.S. gains were six captured gunboats and about fifty dead pirates. Decatur's brother, Lt. James Decatur, was killed in action.

Four days later the commodore received a letter from Washington informing him he was being relieved of his command. His replacement, who would soon arrive, was Commodore Samuel Barron, captain of the USS *President*. Preble felt a deep need to redeem himself and that night his fleet attempted to pummel the city into submission by cannon fire. Unfortunately, most of the cannon balls landed well short of their targets and one of the previously captured gunboats exploded—killing ten U.S. sailors. On the night of the 24th, a squadron of small gunboats Preble dispatched to attack the city produced zero enemy casualties. The 28th saw yet another bungled night assault which produced only the sinking of one small enemy boat. These were hardly the sort of results that would intimidate the Bashaw into a settlement.

With Barron about to supplant him, Preble grew increasingly desperate. He had accomplished a few notable feats, especially in the destruction of *Philadelphia*, but the bottom line remained: he was leaving a stalemate in his successor's hands. His anxious mind conjured up a fresh idea. He would create and deploy the mother of all military weapons at the time—an "infernal machine."

Preble's plan involved sending the *Intrepid*, which had served his team so well, on a final mission. First, his men loaded an astonishing five tons of gunpowder below deck. Then they piled fifty 9 inch shells next to the hundred 13 inch shells on the deck. They tipped this off with iron scraps and ballast to act as shrapnel. The commodore personally supervised the conversion of his small ship into a sailable bomb. This, he believed, would show both Washington and the stubborn Bashaw the stuff of which he was made.

Master Commandant Richard Somers and a crew of five sailors boarded the supercharged *Intrepid* and departed toward Tripoli Harbor on the evening of September 3, 1804. Preble had been waiting for perfect weather and that of this slightly breezy moonless night, he decided, was exactly it. He ceased his heavy bombardment of the capitol for the evening.

The length of the fuses was selected to afford Somers and his crew a full eleven minutes after lighting to board an attached lifeboat and row to the USS *Nautilus*, which would trail a safe distance behind *Intrepid*.

The men aboard *Nautilus* watched hopefully as *Intrepid* slipped slowly into the darkness. Two shots, likely from the Tripolitan battery, pierced the silent night. But at 9:47 p.m. a blinding flash irradiated the harbor. A deafening blast that shook the US fleet instantly followed. Even the commodore's *Constitution*, which hovered a full six miles out to sea, was rocked.

Afterwards, sailors on the *Nautilus* deck prayed to see their comrades aboard lifeboats rowing safely toward them—yet only the still of the night replied.

Preble was informed at sunrise that the enemy had sustained no damage. Sometime later, a sailor spotted a wooden object lodged outside the harbor's rocky barrier. It was the charred keel and ribs of *Intrepid*. The floating bomb, which had probably been ignited by enemy fire, had detonated long before reaching its target.

Later that day, the Bashaw smugly invited the imprisoned Captain Bainbridge to view the remains of "six persons in a most mangled and burnt condition lying on the shore."

Commodore Barron arrived five days later. The crestfallen Preble struck his pennant and sailed back to America.

◆ ◆ ◆ ◆ ◆

No fact or event occurs in a state of isolation. Anything that has taken place through the history of the universe is the product of an inconceivably complex conflation of factors. To fully comprehend how it came to pass we would need a substantial amount of information. In the case of an event in human history this would pertain to the lives of the people involved, the cultural ideas implanted into their minds early in life, and the life stories of their parents, grandparents, and ancestors.

The principles involved in analyzing events and their ancestry are known as *causality*, *determinacy*, and *predictivity*. Such were central components of the career of German physicist Werner Heisenberg. The scientist concluded that if we fully understood the present, we could predict the future. Yet he also found the premise on which such a notion was based faulty, because "as a matter of principle we cannot know all determining elements of the present."

With respect to the individual, every characteristic one manifests results from an elaborate amalgamation of genetic, embryonic, and environmental influences. The genetic elements are those one has biologically inherited from one's family line. Embryonic factors act upon one in the primitive stages of prebirth development—when tissues and organs are forming. Environmental influences are the product of 1) biological interactions; that is, mutual actions and effects among living organisms and 2) abiological components, which are those pertaining to geography, climate, soil chemistry, altitude, and water salinity.

A person, therefore, is not merely a being whose life is the product of voluntary choices. Each of the useful complicated mechanisms of his body results from billions of years of natural selection and genetic mutations. And similar is true of instinctive and learned behavior. Much of his social behavior, unbeknownst to him, arises from rituals imposed by his ethnic and cultural heritage. The person who stands before you today is, in fact, merely the latest commodity in a line derived from a series of circumstances and events over which he had no control.

What one perceives to be in his best interest is influenced internally by his personality, attitudes, beliefs, family background, etc. It is also influenced by external factors such as social pressures, ethical and legal strictures and other inducements. The service of self-interests, as we've already seen, is the primary factor motivating human behavior, but many elements beyond this also contribute to the causes of an event in which one or more people are involved. Most noticeable are the environmental factors. An array of them awakened as the events transpired in the previous case. Some, the historical figures involved were able to anticipate; others, they could not. Let's look at the more obvious of such instances.

Captain Bainbridge had been informed the Tripoli Harbor region featured unpredictable winds and uncharted obstacles, so he took precautions. He reduced speed and his crew diligently conducted depth soundings; but 140 years before sonar was invented they could only discover the depth of the water through which the ship was then traveling. There was no way for the captain to exactly foresee the underwater reef he approached. He disclosed, "After giving up the chase in pursuit of the cruiser, striking on the rocks was as unexpected to me as if it happened in the middle of the Mediterranean Sea." He also failed to expect a storm that would bring an enormous influx of wind and rain, raising the sea and lifting the ship above the reef. The barometer and hygrometer had both been invented over a century earlier. With those and his lengthy experience he should've been able to detect the forthcoming atmospheric assistance as did the pirates. There was no pressing need to surrender. His enemy wasn't pushing for it and initially couldn't believe he was seriously considering it. High Admiral Murat Rais, leader of the Tripoli Navy, observed: "Who, with a frigate of 44 guns and 300 men, would strike his colors to solitary gunboats must surely be a coward or a traitor." Had Bainbridge merely waited a few hours instead of so emphatically cowering before the pirates, disaster could have been avoided.

When, on the mission to burn the easily captured *Philadelphia*, the weather unexpectedly changed, Lt. Decatur adapted—slowing his craft and making a quick calculation to go in without the support of the lagging *Syren*. Tripolitan pirates knew U.S. naval forces were in the region. They also must've known the same wanted the frigate either returned or neutralized. They should have, but did not, anticipate the approach of a disguised U.S. naval crew. The operation took place at night. The Tripolitans were probably groggy—their senses and mental acuity dulled. They failed to perceive that with only a slim crescent moon, lighting was so dim they needed to maintain a higher degree of vigilance. The corsairs thus noticed nothing amiss until it was too late.

Preble anticipated a colloquy would take place as *Intrepid* approached *Philadelphia* and accordingly hired a man who spoke the native tongue to communicate with the adversary. He also kept informed on current naval events and was aware the Bashaw had purchased a British ship whose arrival was expected at that time. This knowledge came in handy in stalling suspicions when his representative was questioned as to the identity of the ship hovering in the distance.[25] And while he and Decatur perhaps should've foreseen the conflagration robbing *Intrepid* of sailing air, Decatur quickly adapted to his circumstances—using a rowboat to tow the sailboat to open sea.

Finally, numerous unforeseen factors doomed *Intrepid's* final mission. The most evident, of course, is that it was simply a bad plan. It involved far too much risk. First, the U.S. fleet had been sporadically bombarding Tripoli until the night *Intrepid* sailed. And with the *Philadelphia* scuttling four months earlier, sneaky nighttime attacks could no longer fully surprise. America's naval officers knew or should have known the city's watchmen would be on full alert. Further, sailing a manned bomb into an enemy port, where that enemy can with a single distant gunshot detonate it more safely than the party aboard, must be regarded as borderline, if not absolute, asininity.

German philosopher Georg Hegel observed, "What experience and history teach us is this—that people and governments never have learned anything from history or acted on principles deduced from it." As we just determined, it is impossible to precisely predict the future. We also noted we would have to know everything about how the past became the present in order to do so. But while it may be beyond our capabilities to know all of the facts of the past, we can know some.

---

[25] We observed Preble and Decatur successfully employing deception in four instances: 1) swapping U.S. flags with British ones to present a friendly image to *Mastico's* commander, 2) disguising *Intrepid* and *Siren* to present a friendly image to the Tripolitans guarding *Philadelphia*, 3) hiding the larger part of the *Intrepid* crew below deck on the approach, as to not arouse the enemy's suspicions, and 4) employing someone who spoke the local tongue so that person could mislead the enemy. Note: The latter is an ancient technique of strategic military deception. U.S. Navy SEALs utilized it to lure Osama bin Laden's son from a hiding place so they could kill him, clearing the path to bin Laden himself. (In addition to the obvious benefit of facilitating communication, speaking a common language increases trust.)

And if we study these we see the general circumstances in which individuals and governments find themselves tend to recur. The primary reason for this is that human nature has not changed.

You and I are not like the people Hegel describes. We study the past. And we learn from it. Then we apply that knowledge to our actions. This alone gives us a tremendous advantage over our less prepared adversaries. Be this as it may, before we conclude the stupidity of Preble's final operation is so obvious it could never happen again, we find that 140 years later, in fact, it did.

The young Navy officer Jack Kennedy had received a tremendous amount of publicity for rescuing most of his crew after a Japanese destroyer plowed through their patrol torpedo boat in the Blackett Strait near Kolombangara in August 1943. While his older brother Joe Jr., a Navy pilot, was proud of Jack, he was also jealous. He knew he had to top Jack's accomplishment to please their demanding father and a year later volunteered for a mission so dangerous not many of his peers were competing for it: flying a PB4Y Liberator bomber airplane filled with explosives from England into enemy territory. Kennedy was, of course, supposed to eject before the flying bomb reached its target—the primary German V-1 rocket launch site on the coast of Belgium. But just as the *Intrepid* had detonated before the sailors could jump ship, so did Joe Jr.'s plane. And as with *Intrepid* the precise cause of the premature detonation remains unknown.

The case of the *Intrepid* was in the military history books of the 1930s and '40s. As an officer, Joe must have, or at least should have, studied these and been aware of it. (The same is true of the officers who planned and approved the mission.) Yet with desperation clouding sound judgment, he and the other officers failed to appreciate the lesson. He would not live long enough to achieve what his brothers would.

♦ ♦ ♦ ♦ ♦

Second Case in Point

The campaign for the 1796 U.S. presidency was suffused with an ambiance of suspicion. The aristocratic federalist party, which favored a strong militant government, and the agrarian Republican party, that preferred a limited national government, became increasingly bitter toward each other. As tensions escalated, factions began forming within the Federalists and they were unable to agree on a candidate. Most influential members believed John Adams was the aspirant most likely to prevail over Thomas Jefferson, the Republican nominee. One prominent Federalist, however, had an agenda of his own. Alexander Hamilton, the single most powerful figure in the party, was President George Washington's Secretary of the Treasury. He did not want Adams to be president. He alleged this was because Adams was not best suited for the office, but secretly he disfavored Adams because the latter was a mentally strong man whom he, Hamilton, couldn't control. Hamilton wanted a party puppet. And he believed Thomas Pickney would be exactly that. The descendant of a wealthy South Carolina family, Pickney was employed as the U.S. ambassador to Spain a year prior. He earned great accolades when he apparently extracted from Spain a number of favorable concessions. These include the opening of the southernmost section of the Mississippi River to U.S. merchants, the right for these merchants to store merchandise in New Orleans absent duty payments, the establishment of a U.S./Spain border on the northern boundary of Florida, and a commitment to abstain from Indian affairs. Unbeknownst to Americans at the time, however, Spanish officials had received information, the misinterpretation of which led them to believe the U.S. had already allied with Great Britain to acquire by force Spain's North American territory. Spain only offered the conditions to avoid a war that hadn't even entered the minds of American leaders.

In an attempt to assure this man would be the next president, Hamilton schemed with Federalist electors who would have otherwise cast one ballot for Adams and one for Pickney. If properly executed the ploy would cause Pickney to receive more votes than Adams and be elected. All went well until New England party members who were loyal to Adams, caught wind of Hamilton's machinations. They informed Adams and abandoned Pickney entirely. As a result, Adams was elected to be the 2nd U.S. President and Republican rival Thomas Jefferson Vice President.[26]

Once sworn into office Adams repeatedly retaliated against Hamilton and his haughty High Federalists by thwarting their military agendas. He ignored their proposed officer commissions and denied their request to ask Congress to declare war against France; thus, leaving the U.S. with an expensive idle standing army. Hamilton, in turn, refused to support Adams when he was up for reelection in 1800, again trying to supplant him with Pickney, and again failing. With the party divided, two Republicans were elected: Thomas Jefferson as the 3rd President and Aaron Burr as his Vice President.

♦ ♦ ♦ ♦ ♦

The ensurance of secrecy in covert plans and operations is known in military doctrine and espionage tradecraft as *operational security*. While it is beyond the scope of this text to elaborate on the matter, it has been my own experience that when fewer records are created, fewer eyes and ears have access to secret information, and fewer steps are involved in execution, the operation is less likely to be discovered. To this day the U.S. Government still hasn't shown its awareness of this, which is the reason why the news regularly features stories of some politician, CIA operative, FBI agent, military contractor, or soldier being prosecuted for distributing classified information to unauthorized recipients.

Political maneuvering can, and often does, go awry. Moreover, it sometimes backfires entirely—producing results antithetical to those intended. And Alexander Hamilton aptly demonstrated for us how the machinations of even the most powerful of men, when executed under the wrong circumstances, can cause the worst possible effects. His 1796 scheming violated the trust of both Adams and the greater membership of the Federalist party. Instead of thrusting Pickney to the presidency, it created sects of divided interests which inadvertently propelled the opponent's candidate to the vice-presidency. His continued maneuvering over the years succeeded only in weakening the party to the point both the vice presidency and presidency were won by Republicans. As the wound grew deeper and festered, it led to the demise of the party altogether late in the 19th century.

Hamilton was killed in a duel by his Republican rival Aaron Burr in July 1804. Shortly before his death Hamilton had branded Burr, "The most dangerous man of the community." Yet, by his own refusal to adequately check his operational security and thoroughly consider the possible consequences of his action—right up to his last one—Hamilton showed he was the most dangerous man to his party and even himself.

♦ ♦ ♦ ♦ ♦

Third Case in Point

Karate champion Chuck Norris was on a run of good luck in the summer of 1968. He was scheduled to defend his title in the Long Beach International Karate Championship tournament on August 4, and on the 5th he would film his big screen debut in *The Wrecking Crew*, a spy satire starring

---

[26] At the time, the candidate with the most electoral votes became president and the runner-up vice president. This changed in 1804 with the 12th Amendment of the U.S. Constitution.

Dean Martin, Sharon Tate, and Elke Sommer. Norris' part was miniscule—he would play Sommers' bodyguard. This required him to speak only one line, followed by a high kick to Martin, who played a James Bond type of character. Norris, nonetheless, viewed the bit as an opportunity and wanted his first film appearance to be flawless.

In the locker room before the match, the champ approached his opponent, Skipper Mullins, who was ranked Number 3 nationally. The two had become friends over the years and Norris thought Mullins might be willing to do him a favor. "I have my first part in a movie tomorrow," he explained, "so beat on my body, but try not to hit me in the face. I don't want to go on set looking like I've been in a brawl." The challenger insidiously agreed, "Okay, but you'll owe me one."

The two entered the ring and bowed. Mullins launched the action with his trademark roundhouse kick which Norris expected and blocked. Mullins instantly followed with a backfist to Norris' face. The champ, believing his opponent would leave his face unscathed, hadn't expected that. The surprise punch shook Norris physically, and worse yet, psychologically. He immediately began worrying about the condition of his face. Would it be ruined for his movie debut? Would this finish his movie career? After having to fight much more intensely than he had expected, the long battle finally concluded with a physically and mentally exhausted Norris retaining his title by only a single point.

On the next day, the make-up artist had to spend two full hours concealing the champ's blackened eye region. Still shaken, the nervous Norris flubbed his scene, barely able to croak out his four-word line.

◆ ◆ ◆ ◆ ◆

In Chapter Three we discovered the many mistakes made by authority figures and the key reasons for them. In Chapter Five we learned surprising powerful adversaries is nearly always more profitable than warning them. The fact is, in most cases throughout recorded history, surprise attacks have only succeeded because the target was remiss in considering the available indications and tocsins, then preparing and reacting accordingly.

Before one hits, there is usually some evidence (often plenty) revealing it is on the way. Signals are received but dismissed. Suggestions are heard but misinterpreted.

JFK and his staff received warnings from allies that Dallas was not a city he should visit while he was planning his November 1963 trip to the city. UN Ambassador Adlai Stevenson telephoned presidential aide Aurthur Schlesinger, Jr. and earnestly requested Kennedy be dissuaded from going. He advised that he, Stevenson, had just given a speech in Dallas where bestial Texans had cursed at and spat upon him. J. William Fulbright, chairman of the Senate Foreign Relations committee, had called the President himself and told him, "Dallas is a very dangerous place. I wouldn't go there. Don't you go." Not only did Kennedy ignore this sound advice, he insisted on riding in an open convertible and prohibited his protective Secret Service detail from riding on the car's rear running boards.

Throughout the spring and summer of 2000, U.S. intelligence officials intercepted messages numbering in the thousands specifically stating the Navy ship USS *Cole* would be attacked in Yemen. Because threats against American assets are common, the officials ignored them. In October, the ship was sunk by a boat loaded with explosives. Seventeen sailors were killed and 39 injured in the bombing, for which al-Qaeda would claim responsibility. (One of the many reasons U.S. intel failed to predict the 9/11 attacks is that reports of assaults on the American mainland were discounted amid the noise of greater reports pointing to attacks on targets overseas.)

Earlier we noted how Germany's perception of the conditions of the Treaty of Versailles provoked that nation's wrath and led to World War II. While that is the primary motive for Hitler's actions there seldom is a single cause for a war; in its stead an interaction among many factors. In the case of the second world war some blame can be attributed to the victors of the first world war (primarily Britain and France) for failing to preserve the peace. Had those nations more seriously considered and responded to developments in Germany[27] the latter would have been prevented from launching any major military operation.

Donald Rumsfeld, secretary of defense from 1975-77 and 2001-06, very aptly advised:

> Given the reality of surprise time and again, it's worth considering what we may be missing at any given decision point. It is a useful mental exercise to carefully think through the what-ifs. What might we wake up to tomorrow that we hadn't anticipated? What are the dangers that we are focused on, but may seem likely only because they are familiar? How might we expand our imaginations to break through the 'poverty of expectations' that enabled surprise attacks like Pearl Harbor and 9/11 to be so stunningly successful?

Note: "Poverty of expectations" is an expression he apparently borrowed from the economist Thomas Schelling, which encapsulates the fact that, to their own impairment, people tend to "confuse the unfamiliar with the improbable" and limit themselves to preparing for what they expect. We examined this lightly in Chapter Seven and comprehensively in Chapter Twelve.

I'm fond of an observation by Dean Rusk, secretary of state under Presidents Kennedy and Johnson: "Only one-third of the world is asleep at any given time and the other two-thirds are up to something." While this is relevant to anyone, in our field we must be constantly scanning for, and evaluating, information pertaining to those forces that may be working contrary to our interests. Some omens may be overt, but often they must be deduced from the character of the situation and human nature itself.

Relationships often have multiple aspects and while they may be harmonious in one respect, they can be discordant in another. So, as soon as we detect a hostile element in an otherwise amiable alliance, we must be on guard. Mullins may have been Norris' friend outside the ring, but inside of it business is business. In the pre-match locker room conference the champ surely also evoked a little envy he should have, but did not, expect, by revealing he was about to film his first big screen appearance. Thus, when "Achilles" revealed his "heel," Mullins was happy to note it and, the instant the opportunity arose, strike it as hard as possible.

Norris should've kept his mouth shut. (See Chapter 8.) His lack of foresight in disclosing his weakest point to an envious self-interested rival nearly cost him his title and future acting career. Fortunately, his part in the movie was so insignificant the director considered it acceptable, and, at any rate, the actor would never be widely associated with it.

◆ ◆ ◆ ◆ ◆

Societies of the modern day are far more complex than those of antiquity; perhaps incomprehensibly so. Every element of a person's life is entangled in interdependent systems of other people. And those systems are, in turn, intertwined with others involving yet more people. Malfunctions in any of the components involved can instigate catastrophic effects on other

---

[27] These include the fall of the weak Weimar Republic and rise of the militant Nazi regime, the rearmament of the Rhineland, the sudden and massive rebuilding of the military, and the content of Hitler's speeches.

components or the system(s) as a whole. For our purposes this means actions can cascade and lead to unintended and drastic consequences. It seems hard to believe that the inattentiveness of an Austrian chauffeur on June 28, 1914 would affect you or I. But it likely has, in some way, impacted the majority of humans presently living on the planet. As you may recall from Chapter Six, that driver's attention lapse as to the safe route to take out of Sarajevo enabled a teenaged rebel to assassinate Archduke Franz Ferdinand, which provoked World War I. The Treaty of Versailles ended that war, but the conditions it imposed on Germany were perceived by that nation to be so oppressive they provoked World War II. While there were countless other factors involved, the fact remains that our lives would probably be different in many respects had that driver thought clearly. We may not even exist in our present form.

Many forces affect our daily lives. The self-interests of other people, effects of nature, and various random interactions can drastically impact your plans in a situation that is not even adversarial. And you can be sure this will only worsen in one that is. Processes interact with each other. Some are cumulative and perpetuate themselves. War, like any competition, is often a series of interactions. Side A acts. Side B reacts. A reacts to B's reaction. B reacts to A's reaction and so on. That is to say each reaction is dependent upon the previous action of the opponent. And the rapid, fluid nature of combat, when conflated with the numerous environmental and random influences, render it difficult to compute prior to our opponent's action what our reaction should be. Worse yet, as mentioned in the previous chapter, you are likely to find neither side willing to wait to see what the other may do as both execute offensive actions simultaneously.

In Chapter Twelve, *Tactical Intel*, we examined the formal methods taught by CIA instructors to predict the outcome of events. My own experience, however, is that while these (especially the ACH matrix) have proven highly accurate in revealing the unknown, I seldom have the opportunity to sit down and calculate such analyses. In these situations, I apply intuitive judgment, experience, and principles of human nature to arrive at an impromptu decision. You will likely find yourself doing the same.

The surest simple indication of how someone will behave in a certain situation is how he has already successfully behaved under similar circumstances. People tend to develop philosophies and ways of dealing with others and they're likely to fall back on these when confronted with problems to which they perceive these solutions are relevant. We saw an excellent example of this in Chapter Six as Coke Stevenson, under heavy political fire from LBJ, reverted to his lifelong philosophy of refusing to address negative attacks and allowing his record to speak for itself. By the time his campaign strategists finally convinced him to forsake his philosophy and respond, Stevenson's political fate had already been sealed.

If you can determine which path affords your target the least amount of resistance to an objective, you have another indication of how he may behave. (This is particularly true when you give him a problem he must solve.) If, for example, you want to know what path an official will take on his way to the office so your process server can surprise him with a summons, the most likely is the one that will permit him to arrive in the least amount of time, which is probably the same route he has taken in the past. If he runs errands on his way (e.g. dropping the kids off at school or grocery shopping) he is still going to take the path of least resistance to each point. And it's unlikely to be any different once he's at the office working, especially when confronted with whatever political issues you may drop on his lap.

As we've already discussed, you also may be able to discern his intended action by examining what the strategic nature of the situation requires. If, for example, your research affirms your opponent must win the majority of the labor vote in order to be elected and the polls indicate his support from that group is presently deficient, you can infer he will prepare and act in a manner necessary to improve that.

You can always be sure perceived self-interest will be the number one factor determining behavior. In many cases, however, your target will, consciously or otherwise, perceive that doing what he has successfully done before and/or taking the path of least resistance is what best serves his self-interest. If you want him to do something different, he will need to perceive that doing so best advances or protects this interest.

Even with absolute conformity to the scientific method and a thorough knowledge of science and history, it is impossible to exactly predict how an adversary will initially act or respond to your actions. It is also difficult to precisely foresee how other forces will play into the situation, and ultimately, what the final outcome will be.

The "Pyrrhic victory" is one where the costs of triumph turn out to exceed the benefits originally expected. It is a common result of every type of war. (Where the military variety is concerned Operation Iraqi Freedom comes to mind.) In battling against the U.S. Government, I have often found unpredicted effects result from successfully forcing its mighty hand. But as hard as it may be to believe, nature itself is even more powerful than the Government. In fact, it appears to be the only thing that is. And it is because nature (human nature in our case) is so powerful that we must learn to understand and exploit it in order to protect ourselves from aggressive, opportunistic officials looking to advance their interests at our expense.

Powerful forces do not appreciate interference. And unintended consequences nearly always arise from tampering with them. Think of the long list of side effects that are listed with the information sheets accompanying prescription medication: e.g. headaches, sleepiness, drowsiness, excitability, rashes, itching, colored urine, dry mouth, dizziness. The list seems infinite. (Sumatriptan, a medicine used to treat migraine headaches, has actually been found to turn the blood green.) Some info sheets even list as side effects the very symptoms the medicine is intended to relieve. There is, in fact, no drug which treats only a single symptom. Each and every one has side effects.

My decades of headbanging against the powers that be remind me of a 1990's horror movie entitled *The Wishmaster*. It featured a demonic character known as a djinn which was inspired by the genies of legend.[28] Upon being freed these genies grant their liberators three wishes. The djinn of the movie does this as well, but as it is a sinister being, incorporates a harmful element into fulfillment. For example, when a fashionable young sales clerk wishes to be beautiful forever, the djinn turns her into a statue. The story is, of course, fictitious, but where our purposes are concerned, contains an element of reality. When you coerce powerful forces into doing your bidding, you can count on undesired side effects. The end product is often a nefarious distortion of what you originally sought—a "Pyrrhic victory."

Human nature is such that when one expects something positive and doesn't receive it, this frustrates and angers him beyond what it would had he never expected it in the first place. It is wise to maintain an awareness that unexpected forces will arise in battle and unexpected results await when it is complete. But just as you should try to defensively anticipate the unexpected, you should offensively deliver it to your opponent as well.

---

[28] In Islamic mythology, the djinn were evil or mischievous spirits with bodies of flame or vapor who often appeared in the forms of animals. They were capable of controlling dreams and interfering with actual human affairs. One served King Solomon by transporting the Queen of Sheba's throne from her palace in Southern Arabia to Jerusalem. Another warned him of her demonic aspect.

Psychopolitical Warfare... / Eric Wise

>No war ever showed the characteristics we expected.
>
>— Dwight D. Eisenhower,
>   U.S. President, Five Star General,
>   Commander of Allied Forces
>   in the European Theatre

Chapter Fifteen

The Power of Perseverance

> As long as the Earth turns around the sun, as long
> as there are cold and warmth, fertility and infertility,
> storm and sunshine, so long will struggle continue
> among men and among nations . . .
> What mankind has become, it has become through struggle.
> — Adolf Hitler

First Case in Point

During the mid 1800s rural areas of New York state had controlled the city of New York from the capital in Albany. The Democrats of New York City, represented by the faction known as Tammany Hall, decided to revolt against this outside rule. When the legislature convened in January 1870, State Senator William "The Boss" Tweed, chairman of the legislature's Committee on Municipal Affairs, immediately set out to return control of the city to the city. His colleague Peter Sweeny had recently been elected district attorney. Sweeny drafted a charter which would intercept state dominion over public safety, public schools, judgeships, docks, and the city's budget. A committee of four city officials: the mayor, comptroller, and commissioners of parks and public works would be in charge of the aforementioned areas. The bill however would not only terminate state control, it also called for a transfer of power from the city's elected aldermen to the committee and further held three of the four positions would be appointive, rather than elective, with the elected mayor alone determining who fills the other three seats. Mayor "Elegant" Oakey Hall and Comptroller Richard Connolly were already members of Tammany's inner circle, and it would be easy for the former to fill the remaining two offices with other members; specifically, Sweeny and Tweed.

To secure passage of the bill, Tweed and his lobbyist handed out hundreds of thousands of dollars in bribes—to Republicans and fellow Democrats alike. Tweed supplemented this by promising jobs or business assistance to the same or their friends.

On the evening prior to the final vote, Chairman Tweed convened a formal hearing. There, six city leaders addressed concerns with the charter. The chairman answered these and most of the people present were satisfied. One, however, was not. Samuel Tilden, chairman of the New York Democratic party was a wealthy attorney who had made his money in railroad litigation. At least outwardly, he was opposed to the opportunities for corruption inherent in the bill. He and his faction, known as the Swallowtails, for the long-tailed suit jackets they wore at formal gatherings, despised the gritty inner city Tammany Hall crew and their mostly illiterate Irish working class supporters.

Tilden issued a lengthy dissertation of his opposition to the article, during which Tweed interrupted, "I'm sick of the discussion of this question." Tilden then summed up his argument: the bill nullified the power of the voters and their legislators by transferring it to a semi-permanent committee of four. Once the mayor appointed the other three, even he could not remove them until their terms of six to eight years expired. "It is in the stagnation of bureaus and commissions that evils and abuses exist," he concluded. This, of course, was the whole purpose of the charter. But Tweed had already worked his magic and Tilden's dissent was brushed aside. (See Chapters 3: *Fallible Officials* and 12: *Tactical Intel* (Dismissal of dissenting voices as a leading cause of mistakes in organizations.)) The next day, April 4, 1870, the bill passed by a vote of 116 to 5. Tilden immediately predicted Tweed would "close his career in jail or exile."

Mayor Hall appointed Sweeny head of Parks and Tweed head of Public Works. And the new committee wasted no time in advancing the interests of its four members.

Sweeny and Tweed initiated an informal policy of refusing to pay the bills of contractors unless the latter had first "padded" them. If a member of the committee, for example, received a bill from a plumber for $3,000, he just filed it away. When the plumber complained about non-payment, the official replied that he should increase the bill to $15,000. The plumber complied, upon which he was paid the $3,000 actually due. The remaining $12,000 was deposited into a complex series of accounts designed to conceal both its origin and destination. Ultimately, it ended up in the personal account of a committee member. In most actual cases, this was Tweed.

George Jones, the Republican publisher of the *New York Times*, had grown resentful of Tweed and his Tammany Democrats. Two years prior, Comptroller Connolly had refused to pay an advertising bill for $13,761 based on a political motive. And when the committee formed, it completely discontinued city advertising in the *Times*.

After one day too many of walking to work past City Hall and what he believed to be the epitome of graft and corruption, the new county courthouse, Jones reached a decision. He would begin publishing a series of articles that questioned how the big four had become wealthy when they ostensibly were mere public servants. He had no specifics to support allegations of corruption and could only imply it. (We noted this Chapter 6: *The Faces of Deception*.)

About this time a cartoonist named Thomas Nast inferred the same thing: the committee members were dishonestly enriching themselves at the public's expense. But as he, like Jones, lacked hard evidence could also only imply it. He did so by drawing a series of political cartoons for *Harper's Weekly* magazine. One of the first, entitled "Tweedledee and Tweedledum" depicted caricatures of Tweed and Sweeny raiding the public treasury and passing out money to citizens. The caption read "Let's blind them with this and then take some more [for ourselves]."

A friend for whom Tweed had done a favor reciprocated with the gift of a $15,000 diamond pin.[29] (We examined quid pro quo in Chapter 2: *The Official Motivation*.) Nast perceptively featured it on the chest of Tweed's character. To this he added another irritating quality. At the time, only those who did not perform manual labor and could afford excessive food could accumulate extra weight. Thus, obesity was associated with wealth. While Tweed was overweight, both the size of the diamond and Tweed's girth were grossly exaggerated to amplify the public's jealousy of, and disdain for, him. (See Chapter 7: *Propaganda and Persuasion*.)

The psychopolitical techniques began to sink in and fester.

---

[29] For those who would like to do the math $1 in 1870 is worth approximately $21 today.

Some New Yorkers questioned how, in fact, honest politicians could have become so wealthy. Others steadfastly stood by Tweed and his crew. To these, the so-called "Tweed Ring" remained the hometown heroes who had returned local rule to the city. And Tweed himself, after all, had a long productive political career under his large belt as alderman (1852), U.S. representative (1853), school commission member (1856), county supervisor (1858), and deputy street commissioner (1861) prior to his present positions as state senator and public works commissioner. He had famously sponsored bills chartering the Metro Museum of Art, the Brooklyn Bridge, the fancy new county courthouse, and even the New York Stock Exchange. The Boss had also pushed through funds to support the Mt. Sinai and Presbyterian hospitals as well as the Shepard's Fold orphanage. His administration had widened and paved streets all over Manhattan and invested between $10 and $20 million in Central Park, causing real estate in the adjacent wards to triple in value from 1856 to 1866. Not only did this keep happy the owners of said properties, but it also returned millions in tax revenue to the city treasury.

This being the case many New Yorkers took issue with Jones' and Nasts' unsupported accusations. But through their respective publications, the two kept hammering away. They knew that if they whipped up a big enough storm the evidence would eventually surface.

By March 1870, Sheriff Jimmy O'Brien and his deputies, all of whom were Tammany members, had an axe to grind with Tweed. First, they had enforced a ballot box fix that produced important victories for Tammany candidates in the 1868 election. Second, Comptroller Connolly was refusing to pay some of O'Brien's expenses in operating the sheriff's department. Third, O'Brien and his faction, who called themselves the Young Democrats, clearly saw Tammany was positioned to take over the city and state and they craved a bigger chunk of the power pie.

Several back room meetings between Tweed and Young Democrats took place, but when they were unable to come to a lasting agreement, rebellion broke out. O'Brien's faction demanded a meeting of Tammany's general committee. With 174 members they believed themselves strong enough to overthrow Tweed, who was now Tammany's Grand Sachem (chief). Tweed granted the request, but when the Young Democrats arrived for the meeting The Boss had a surprise in store: 800 NY City police officers blocking the entrance. (Chapter 14: *Tales of the Unexpected*) Privately, Tweed had phoned his friend, the Metropolitan Police Commissioner and indicated a riot may take place at the meeting without additional security. Publicly, Tweed claimed he too was surprised to learn of the blockade.

The attempted coup failed, and the Young Democrats were, according to the ways of war, punished. (See Chapters 1: *Psychological Aspects of Authority* and 9: *The Brazen Rule*.) They were denied their potential share of kickbacks and O'Brien was expelled from the general committee. Soon he would even lose his job. (Chapter 11: *A Time to Advance and a Time to Fall Back*.)

Before his fall, however, O'Brien had gotten a friend named Bill Copeland placed in the comptroller's office. In the sweltering summer of 1870 this man, who worked as a bookkeeper in the Auditing department, approached O'Brien asking for advice. He noticed all manner of irregularities in the city's account ledgers and didn't know how to politically handle the problem. O'Brien, sensing the opportunity for revenge and redemption, instructed his friend to keep quiet, secretly copy the ledgers, and bring the copies to him. O'Brien would handle the matter from there.

That fall Jones noticed the city had not filed its annual financial statement and computed there must be a good reason for this. The *Times* asserted Connolly was deliberately keeping the public ignorant because he could not account for millions of dollars. He dared the Ring to produce the report.

Instead of publishing a full fiscal account, Connolly employed a slick evasive tactic. A month before the election he assembled an investigative commission composed of six of the city's most respected financial titans—all allies. They included John Jacob Astor, grandson of NY's largest landowner; Moses Taylor, president of City Bank; and steamship baron Marshall Roberts.

On the eve of Election Day, the Astor Commission published its report. It pronounced the city's finances healthy. "We . . . certify the account books of the department are faithfully kept, that we have personally examined the securities of the department and sinking fund and found them correct. We have come to the conclusion and certify that the financial affairs of the city under the charge of the comptroller are administered in a correct and faithful manner." Timing this as such assured: 1) the info would be fresh in the public's mind as they went to the polls and 2) The *Times* would be unable to issue a response before the vote.

After the Astor Commission's announcement, the *New York World* labeled the *Times* an "unscrupulous incompetent libeler." Publisher George Jones was shunned by his associates. Even his staff began to question his decision to pursue the Tweed Ring. The months had passed, and he still had no concrete evidence of Ring wrongdoing. But Jones knew where there was smoke there was fire. He kept at it.

Through intermediaries, the Ring had been threatening Jones: a consortium of New York's wealthiest men, including Sweeny, Tweed, Taylor, and railroad tycoon Jay Gould may instigate a hostile takeover of the *Times*. Jones' former partner Henry Raymond had died a year earlier, and Jones knew Raymond's widow could easily be persuaded to relinquish her 33 percent of company stock. This, along with the motive and immense wealth of the prospective buyers, made the threat credible. (Chapter 5: *Mind Games*)

Nast, through his publisher Fletcher Harper, was also threatened. Harper produced and sold to the city's schools tens of thousands of textbooks each year. If Harper and Nast didn't back off, the city's Board of Education would refuse any business with the company and further, would discard all Harper books presently in stock. Mayor Oakey Hall also threatened to prohibit sales of *Harper's Weekly* at city-licensed newsstands.

Nast, however, was achieving great fame and fortune. Because of his cartoons, *Harper's Weekly* was also selling at an all time high. He and his publisher were undeterred.

One of Nast's most effective cartoons featured a giant's hand reaching down from the sky. The huge thumb was squashing NY City while adjacent New Jersey placidly operated without such interference. Emblazoned on the giant's cufflink was the name "William M. Tweed." The caption read "Under the Thumb. The Boss: 'Well, what are you going to do about it?' " Tweed never actually said this, nor did Nast directly quote him as such. He merely implied Tweed, whose nickname was The Boss, said it. The pseudo quote was repeatedly cited and eventually the public came to believe Tweed had arrogantly come right out and admitted he had the city under his thumb and dared the people to do something about it. It was an absolutely brilliant maneuver. New Yorkers became increasingly incensed by the haughty challenge Tweed presumably issued and more importantly became increasingly agitated to "do something about it." (Chapter 6: *The Faces of Deception*)

Cracks began forming in the Ring. European investors who owned city bonds voiced concern over their value. The enthusiasm of potential investors also cooled, and the city started having difficulty selling its bonds.

Nast and Jones plowed ahead, ridiculing Tweed and his gang as wealthy, imperious thieves. A Nast cartoon depicted a typhoon about to sweep the big four ring members away as they cling to the city's treasure chest. Tweed's character, always wearing the glittering diamond pin, grew fatter with each cartoon.

In July 1871 another of Connolly's disgruntled bookkeepers, this one named Matthew O'Rourke, decided to revolt. He visited George Jones at the *Times* building and informed him the city was engaged in some outrageous financial transactions. It had, for instance, spent $85,500 to rent an uninhabitable and thus unused drill room for the National Guard. It had also paid $36,000 per year to rent the top floor of Tammany Hall as office space when it could have spent only $3,600 for comparable space elsewhere. Jones was all too happy to publish this information and even listed the addresses of the properties so readers could inspect them and draw their own conclusions as to the propriety of the expenditures. (This constitutes the provision of credible support for an argument, the necessity of which we affirmed in Chapter 7.)

The Ring meanwhile was trying to prove true the slogan "You can't beat city hall." It had city attorneys investigating the title to the property on which the *Times* had constructed its building. If they found any flaws, perhaps in the zoning or the transfer of ownership from a church group to the newspaper in 1857, it would serve as a basis to evict the business or otherwise terminate its operations. Tammany thugs followed the *Times'* managing editor, Louis Jennings, as he walked the streets. Some made ambiguous threats, but one stormed into his office and made a very clear threat—he would cut out the editor's heart. And soon after the aforementioned exposé on excessive spending was published, police began arresting Jennings on bogus charges.

By this time Jimmy O'Brien was no longer the sheriff. But he still had in his custody a weapon far more powerful than any service revolver. His friend at City Hall, Bill Copeland, had fully copied and turned over the questionable ledgers. O'Brien had taken the evidence to nearly every newspaper in town and none would touch it. Most leaned Democratic. Others simply wanted nothing to do with crossing the Tweed Ring. O'Brien finally accepted that only one paper would vindicate his humiliation.

While Jennings and Jones were no friends of any Tammany associate, the fact is O'Brien's status, and interests, had changed. He paid Jennings a visit late one night in July 1871. Without an invitation the former sheriff entered the editor's office, made some small talk, dropped a large, heavy envelope on his desk, and quietly departed.

Jennings and Jones were thrilled to have stronger evidence to substantiate the allegations they'd long been making. Only one problem remained—ownership. Wrongly assuming Jones would be swayed by a threat, the Ring had unwisely advertised its interest in a hostile takeover. This gave Jones the opportunity to prevent it. (As we noted in Chapter 5, surprise is usually more profitable than warning.) To this end, he visited an old friend, E.B. Morgan of the Wells Fargo Stagecoach Co. Morgan quickly made Henry Raymond's widow an offer on her *Times* stock she couldn't, and didn't, refuse. Jones and his ally Morgan then held 82 percent of the company, enough to block any takeover by the enemy.

On July 19 Jones announced Morgan's purchase. And three days later he made a much more explosive announcement.

"The Secret Accounts—Proofs of Undoubted Frauds Brought to Light," blared the headlines of the *New York Times* on July 22, 1871. The most inculpatory account statements taken directly from the comptroller's ledgers were depicted below.

Among the entries were plastering and other repairs to the courthouse at $2.9 million; cabinets and furniture for city buildings at another $2.9 million; and armory chairs at $170,000. The *Times*, knowing it needed to translate this into meaningful information, explained that the courthouse had just been opened and questioned how it could already necessitate $2.9 million in repairs. As to the cabinets and furniture it showed that for such an amount the city could've purchased enough of the same to supply "nearly 300 houses on Fifth Avenue." Regarding the chairs the *Times* showed that for the money the city could've purchased "314,145 chairs, and if placed in a straight row these would have reached . . . about seventeen miles."

By calling the account "secret" in the headline Jones and Jennings shrewdly enticed the public's curiosity. That is, the people were now getting a forbidden glimpse at information not intended for their eyes. And to say the least it called into question the integrity of city officials.

To further drive home the point, each day the following week Jones issued editorials repeating the message (a propaganda tactic) and further asking the wealthy businessmen of the Astor Commission how they could've overlooked this. No answers were forthcoming from City Hall. And only later would the Commission assert it hadn't been shown all of the ledgers. In fact, it had only given them a cursory inspection—six hours.

The *Times* had already tipped off the likeminded Nast, whose resultant cartoon appeared in *Harper's Weekly* the same day. (We note several powerful alliances of self-interest, as discussed in Chapter 10, in this Case.) It depicted the heads of the three key Astor Commission members mounted on the bodies of mice which were running for cover. A knife labeled "Sharp Editorials" cut off their tails, which signified "Prestige." The caption read "Three Blind Mice! See how they run! The Times cut off their tails with a carving knife!"

Shortly thereafter, Nast too received uninvited visitors who attempted to stay his pencil. One showed up at his house on a Sunday offering him a half-million dollars to "study art abroad." When he replied he had already made up his mind to put Ring members in jail, the visitor grimly concluded, "Only be careful that you do not first put yourself in a coffin."

While the city's working class stood behind its Tammany allies, opining the "secret" ledgers proved nothing, the ruling class believed otherwise. And it panicked. Its members were the ones who owned real estate and whose money primarily filled the treasury. Thus, they were the ones from whom the Ring had stolen. They could lose millions if the fraud led to a fiscal implosion. Bankers had already started denying the city credit and when it offered $40,000 in bonds, it did not receive a single bid. The Berlin Stock Exchange even prohibited the trading of New York City and County bonds.

To protect their interests, New York's aristocrats allied themselves in opposition to the Ring. (We already learned in Chapter 1 what this foretells.) In the last week of July nearly a thousand merchants signed a petition requesting City Hall answer for its spending. They also vowed they would pay no property taxes until it does so. The German Democratic Union met on August 28. Its members passed a series of resolutions denouncing Tweed. Another group, the City Council of Political Reform, convened on September 2 to raise the money necessary to fight the Ring in court.

Two days later, the largest meeting yet of New York's elites took place. Several thousand of the city's most influential citizens convened at the Cooper Union Hall for the sole purpose of condemning the city's leaders. A special seat of honor was given to George Jones, the *Times* publisher who had suffered greatly for the cause. Several speakers elicited enthusiastic responses by declaring Ring members to be morally wrong and unfit for civil service. But the convention peaked when former mayor William Havemeyer worked the crowd into a frenzy then shouted to it Tweed's supposed challenge: "What are you going to do about it?!"

A group of wealthy reformers filed a lawsuit seeking an injunction to prohibit the city from raising, borrowing, or spending any money unless such is first approved by a new board of apportionment. A hearing was held on September 17, 1871. To the astonishment of all, George Bernard, a judge Tweed himself had placed on the bench, granted the injunction. But he did this out of no concern for justice. Bernard merely recognized that without the support of the elite the rulers were doomed and saw nothing to gain for himself by siding with a losing team. (In the

Prologue and Chapter Two we noted the principal motivation of a government official is to protect or advance his own interests.)

Nast released another propagandistic cartoon. The big four were depicted running for cover at the *Times* disclosures. It was impossible to reasonably portray the slender mayor as overweight, but he could easily be shown as justifiably terrified, and this is exactly how Nast represented him. The other three were drawn regally dressed and obscenely obese. Tweed's character, as always, wore his enormous sparkling diamond pin. In guilty hysteria Connolly had fallen onto his enormous belly. Their hair was frizzed into a mess, and they wore the expressions not of imposing statesmen but of maniacs.

Reporters harassed Tweed. Strangers, recognizing him from Nast's cartoons, laughed at him. Friends distanced themselves.

The big four began fighting among themselves—a sign of weakness. (Chapter 4: *The Realm of Psychopolitical Warfare.*) One needed to resign to ease the pressure. The most likely candidate was the comptroller. These were, after all, financial problems and he was the supervisor of all public expenditures. Connolly, nonetheless, demurred— believing resignation to be tantamount to admission of guilt.

After one such meeting, Tweed was cornered by a news reporter asking for an interview. The writer, curious as to his interviewee's thoughts on the injunction, asked a series of questions on the matter. At first, Tweed replied in a cool, vague manner as politicians are coached to do. (Chapter 8: *Anything You Say.*) But talented reporters know how to get under a man's skin and this one artfully hurled Tweed's supposed challenge back at him: "What are you going to do about it?" The Boss' thoughts, already scattered from the heated meeting, were thrown into further disarray. He started to come unglued. Like a good attorney, the more the reporter noticed this, the harder he pressed. The questions culminated in a series strongly implying the newspapers were working up a lynch mob. Finally, he asked, "You don't seem to be afraid of a violent death. Are you?" Tweed finally snapped. Stomping his foot and clenching his fists, he vented, "Well, if they want to come I'll be there . . . If this man Jones would've said the[se] things . . . twenty-five years ago he wouldn't be alive now . . . I would've killed him!"

Every paper in New York printed the interview. Tweed had spent decades cultivating his image as a polished unflappable dignitary, but he now appeared a frightened child cracking under the stress. He looked weak. He looked guilty. (We discussed deceptive provocation in Chapters 6 and 8.)

The injunction itself only exacerbated the matter. Unable to borrow money or issue paychecks, construction on city projects halted. Contractors pleaded for payment. Thousands of city laborers clamored.

Comptroller Connolly was beside himself. His pigheaded wife didn't want him to resign, but nearly everyone else insisted on it. In desperation, he imprudently solicited the advice of former mayor Havemeyer—the same man who had so fervently spoken out against him and his three peers at the September 4 convention. Havemeyer "advised" Connolly not to resign. He knew the comptroller was in a weakened state and could be manipulated to further his, Havemeyer's, own purposes. (Chapter Two) Instead of resigning, the former mayor advised Connolly to seek an experienced attorney. And there was none more suitable than Havemeyer's ally Sam Tilden.

Tweed's old nemesis seized the opportunity to enter back into the fray. (Chapters 11: *A Time to Advance and a Time to Fall Back* and 13: *Preparation and Execution.*) The upstanding "Swallowtail" and Democratic party chairman could never represent a politician so crooked. But he also recognized Connolly could be of value and offered to quietly "mentor" him behind the scenes. After some research, he came up with a plan. The comptroller could invoke an obscure legal provision allowing him to remain in office while transferring power to a deputy. This was enacted to provide temporary leadership in the event a department head became sick or took a vacation. Naturally, Tilden already had just the man in mind to be acting comptroller—his ally Andrew Green. Tilden met with Connolly again and convinced the confused official that by abdicating to Green he was returning to the path of righteousness and the authorities would thus show leniency toward his sins. With Havemeyer, Tilden, and his own attorneys present, Connolly signed on.

In mid-September 1871 Green took office. A mountain of work awaited the new acting comptroller. The presidents of New York's ten wealthiest banks were well aware of their own risk in the present financial uncertainty. These men met with Green, whose reputation was impeccable, and agreed to loan the city the money necessary to pay its employees. Green also wasted no time in issuing orders banning political mischief by workers under his command and firing scores of employees who were receiving pay without showing up for work. Then he opened up all of the city's financial records to the public.

In early October a city contractor named John Keyser alleged endorsements on his city paychecks had been forged. Green informed Tilden. The *Times'* ledgers suggested city officials had cheated the taxpayers, but they failed to show an exact crime by an exact official. Perhaps, Tilden thought, he could be the one to pin the crime on the official. He recruited some allies and began a massive investigation into Keyser's allegation.

After analyzing warrants, spreadsheets (the paper variety), ledgers, and deposit slips, the team discovered Tweed's clerk at the County Board of Supervisors had been endorsing checks and depositing the funds into his own account. After this, the funds were directed into a long, murky series of transactions that eventually filtered down to none other than Tweed himself.

Tilden laid out the evidence in a straightforward chart showing how the money paid to contractors worked its way down chains of intermediaries to Tweed's personal account. His assistants presented the chart to the governor, who, in turn, sent his attorney general to meet with Tilden. The chart was also sent to the like-minded *New York Times*. (We discussed flaunting the misconduct of officials before higher officials and the public in the Prologue and Chapter 4.)

On October 26, 1871, the *Times* devoted an entire section of its paper to displaying and commenting on this new chart. Two days later Tweed was arrested on charges he had neglected his legal duty to audit contractors' claims and had corruptly abused his authority. He remained free on payment of a $2 million bail bond.

Connolly finally resigned as comptroller on Halloween. Two weeks later, Mayor Hall, accepting reality, appointed Green permanent comptroller. Connolly was arrested just before Thanksgiving Day. After spending most of December in jail, he bonded out and fled to Canada, then Europe. He lived the remainder of his life in Egypt, Switzerland, and France. He accepted civil liability for $8 million in December 1877, but would never pay it. By this time, he had developed Bright's disease and approximately two years later he expired in Marseilles, France.

Oakey Hall survived an attempted impeachment by the city's aldermen. A March 1872 criminal proceeding resulted in a mistrial. A second trial ended in a hung jury.

Tweed resigned his post as Commissioner of Public Works on December 28, 1871. A January 1873 criminal trial produced a hung jury. In November he was retried, convicted, and finally incarcerated. A lengthy series of civil and additional criminal prosecutions ensued. In December 1875 he escaped to Cuba. He then fled to Spain where he was identified from one of Nast's cartoons and, in early September 1876, arrested by Spanish police. Tweed was quickly extradited back to New York City where he was reincarcerated. The old boss died in prison on April 6, 1878.

William Havemeyer replaced Oakey Hall in 1873, thus reacquiring the mayoral office. (We examined the power of perception and rewards for success in Chapter 1.)

Samuel Tilden was elected governor of New York in 1874. He lost a bid for the U.S. presidency to Rutherford Hayes in 1877.

Jimmy O'Brien, whose copies of the ledgers uncovered the Ring's corruption, was elected to the U.S. House of Representatives in 1874.

Thomas Nast was honored by President Ulysses Grant at a February 1872 White House dinner. Leaders of both the House and Senate also invited him to the floor where they recognized his achievement.

George Jones' articles on the Ring catapulted newspaper sales and bottom line revenue. But in 1884 he switched from the Republican to Democratic party after which his GOP readers deserted the paper. He died in 1891 and his business was purchased by Adolf Ochs who resurrected the newspaper and propelled it to its current lofty status. Its founder, Jones, is nonetheless recognized as the first to assume the role of an honest publisher who served his own interest by serving the public's. His determination to do what he believed to be right, notwithstanding immense pressure by government officials, is legendary.

> There is no substitute for victory.
>
> — General Douglas MacArthur

♦ ♦ ♦ ♦ ♦

It often takes incredible tenacity to become a leader in either the public or private sector. These people don't rise to the top easily and neither do they come down easily. Before you lock horns with them you must be aware that you are making a substantial commitment to resources such as time, energy, mental peace, and probably money.

As I described in the Prologue, I was warned by a powerful U.S. Senator that federal BOP officials were likely to retaliate against me for my war against cigarettes and drugs. I plunged into it anyway and as it dragged on, his prediction proved correct. Surrender, however, was an option that never even entered my mind. Eventually victory came and that war transformed into a greater war against unredeemable inmates and crooked officials. Success in some battles came more quickly than others, but absolute conquest took a solid nine-and-a-half years.

The contest does not always go to the contestant who appears to hold the upper hand. We've certainly seen that the most potent officials are not invincible. As we discussed in Chapter 3, powerful people are often arrogant people. And arrogant people are apt to err. Error, however, doesn't necessarily cause them to just drop like flies from their lofty echelons the moment it is discovered. "Power," in the words of Henry Kissinger, "is the ultimate aphrodisiac." Thus, just like the dope fiend who will do whatever he must to obtain his next high, officials cling to the thrill only power can provide.

One seldom breaks a powerful adversary's will in a single strike. Doing so can necessitate a lengthy, sustained effort, often increasing in intensity (a favorite *modus operandi* of five-star general Dwight D. Eisenhower). Your enemy's zeal is fervent and his strength of endurance likely is too. Expect a substantial effort to convert his errors into your victory.

Second Case in Point

In the late 1700s the illustrious music composer Wolfgang Amadeus Mozart was widely considered a talent far superior to Ludwig Van Beethoven. Mozart's father Leopold, also a musician, had been teaching Wolfgang since he was a small child. Mozart also possessed an innate musical aptitude far beyond that of his peers. And with seventeen years of age on Beethoven, he had a huge head start. So, as the two contended for glory in Vienna (Austria), it appeared Mozart's brilliant star would fully eclipse the dimmer one of his young rival.

Beethoven, nonetheless, had resources of a different variety. He may have lacked the early training, encouraging father, and natural talent, but he still retained high standards, a strong work ethic, and an insatiable drive to excel—what he summed up as his "active fiery temperament." While Mozart scripted a perfect piece of music in a single setting—making no corrections—Beethoven constantly revised, adding texture and refining melodies. He had to work much harder, but it was work he was willing to do. To assure a superior musical product he also undertook a comprehensive study of counterpoint—the blending of multiple melodies into a harmonious whole. Ludwig went so far as to seek out and hire the great Franz Joseph Hayden to be his mentor on the subject. His immense effort eventually produced a quality of work so high he could charge three times more than his peers for a concert.

In the spring of 1787 Beethoven performed in Vienna. The frail Mozart, who was nearing the end of his life, was present. The older composer was so impressed by his younger peer he turned to some bystanders and conceded, "Mark that young man; he will make a name for himself in the world." And, in fact, by the time Beethoven's own life drew to a close in 1827, the less naturally talented, but more determined, composer's name had risen to even greater heights than Mozart's.

> Success comes from pursuing one's
> thing with dogged determination.
> — Bill Gates

Third Case in Point

A man whose name is equated with triumph itself was once an underdog. Having soared to the heights of success in New York's heady 1980's real estate market, his fortune crashed after his heavy ill-timed investments in Atlantic City's hotel-casino business coincided with a recession late in 1990.

What he recounted as "by far the worse day in my life" unfolded on March 26, 1991 when both the *Wall Street Journal* and *New York Times* published front page stories flaunting the man's failure. Without a doubt, the newspapers opined, his career was finished. The humiliation continued the following year as a March issue of *Business Week* magazine declared: "Donald Trump. The name is a punchline now associated with the worst of 1980's extravagance, egomania, and greed. Once the world marveled at the scope and mastery of Trump's megabuck deals. Today, he is widely regarded as a washed-up real estate mogul who has been stripped of his once lustrous possessions." He had, in fact, $975 million in personal debt at the time.

His enthusiastic admirers grew silent. Reporters no longer called. Associates had no need for his advice. Trump was down . . . but he would not be counted out.

Banks foreclosed on loans in these situations, and this is exactly what everyone believed would happen. Trump, nonetheless, could see this would not be in the bankers' best long-term interests. He called them to a meeting, showed them the folly of foreclosure, and made an unheard of proposal—a five-year moratorium on loan payments. The business world was amazed when it learned the bankers had agreed to Trump's plan.

By 1993, he had reduced his personal debt to $115 million. Two years later, he was no longer in debt. Another two years later he was worth $3 billion, and in 2016 and again in 2024 he was elected President of the United States.

Donald Trump is not exceptionally gifted. He is endowed with neither high intelligence nor outstanding oratorical talent. What he has instead is confidence and tenacity. He is known for his ability to undertake massive projects and bring them in on time and under budget.

In 1986, he embarrassed New York City officials, who had spent seven years bumbling around on the construction of a skating rink. They had already invested $20 million in the rink and had little to show for it. In July of that year Trump took over control of the project. With a mere $3 million investment and four months of work not only did he appear a hero to the citizenry when he opened the rink in time for the winter skating season, he also accomplished this $750,000 under budget.

◆ ◆ ◆ ◆ ◆

The power of perseverance requires an almost superhuman will. Many people simply don't have it. And to those I say: don't get involved in psychopolitical warfare. To the rest I say: prepare for failure. While your adversary (or jealous naysayers) may punish you for an unsuccessful challenge, you should feel no shame in this. If you succeed too easily, opportunities for mental strengthening and the trial and error whence learning arises are forfeited. The lives of many great men, some mentioned herein, are littered with failures; often so many it's nothing short of miraculous they finally hit paydirt.

> I tell veteran boxers the experiences we've had in life are practically unique. We have learned to conduct ourselves in our profession in such a way we can't afford to lose our temper. If we do, we get our heads knocked off. We pay for it immediately. We learn to put up with pain, push pain aside, disregard it entirely. Very, very few people realize what that is. They suffer from headaches, from stomach pains, from sore muscles, and they have a lot of imaginary sufferings that they could just push aside if they'd had these experiences we've had. We know how it is to carry on in the face of pain. I fought seven rounds with a broken rib. I fought four rounds in Madison Square Garden with a sprained ankle. I've fought for years with a broken right hand. I didn't let it affect my ability. How many people in the world have gone through this kind of an experience? Here we are regarded by a great many people with a contemptuous attitude, because they figure we're brutal, we're rough, we're tough, we're going to smash our way through everything.
> — Tommy Loughran
> Light-Heavyweight World Champion
> October 1927 to August 1929

If you're going through hell, just keep going.

— Elon Musk

Appendices

Appendix 1

U.S. Department of Justice

Federal Bureau of Prisons

Federal Correctional Complex

Office of the Warden

P.O. Box 90026
Petersburg, Virginia 23804

June 13, 2017

Eric Wise
Reg. No. 01382-449
Federal Correctional Complex
P.O. Box 1000
Petersburg, VA 23804

Dear Mr. Wise:

Your correspondence dated March 31, 2017, to Jeff Sessions, Attorney General, has been forwarded to my office for response. In your correspondence, you complain of racial discrimination at the Federal Correctional Complex Petersburg. Specifically, you claim there is favoritism shown to the black inmates at the institution and you assert these inmates are given special privileges and authority over "white" inmates. You have requested for the issues to be addressed in compliance with the Constitution, Codes of Federal Regulation, and Program Statements.

Staff conduct is governed by Bureau of Prisons' Program Statement 3420.11, <u>Standards of Employee Conduct</u>. Employees perform their duties as directed by policy to ensure the safety and security of the inmate population, institution, and the public. Allegations of staff misconduct are taken seriously, because of the potential to jeopardize the safety of all individuals incarcerated and/or working at this institution.

A review revealed several allegations made by you were forwarded to the Special Investigative Section (SIS). However, during the investigative process you failed to provide adequate information to support your allegations. Therefore, no further follow-up could be conducted. Additionally, a review of the Administrative Remedy Program revealed you have requested a formal review of several issues to which you have received a response in accordance with policy.

Sincerely,

Eric D. Wilson
Warden

Appendix 2

THE WHITE HOUSE

WASHINGTON

Eric R Wise

NOTICE DATE: April 29, 2021
NOTICE NUMBER: 1444-C (en-sp)

My fellow American,

On March 11, 2021, I signed into law the American Rescue Plan, a law that will help vaccinate America and deliver immediate economic relief to hundreds of millions of Americans, including you.

A key part of the American Rescue Plan is direct payments of $1,400 per person for most American households. With the $600 direct payment from December, this brings the total relief payment up to $2,000. This fulfills a promise I made to you, and will help get millions of Americans through this crisis.

<u>I am pleased to inform you that because of the American Rescue Plan, a direct payment of $1,400.00 was issued to you by paper check/debit card. If you haven't received your payment within 7 days of receiving this letter, please check the status of the payment by visiting the IRS website or calling the IRS phone number listed at the bottom of this letter.</u>

There may be other parts of the American Rescue Plan that will help you as well. For example, there is aid for small businesses, an expanded child tax credit for families, and resources to reopen our schools safely. The American Rescue Plan also extends unemployment insurance and helps reduce your health care premiums if you have a plan through the Affordable Care Act.

To learn more about this law and how it will work for you, please visit wh.gov/arp.

When I took office, I promised the American people that help was on the way. The American Rescue plan makes good on that promise. This bill was passed to provide emergency relief to millions of Americans. I want to be sure you receive all the benefits that you are entitled to.

This has been a long, hard time for our nation. But I believe brighter days are ahead. We are on the path to vaccinating the nation. Our economy is on the mend. And our children will be back in school. I truly believe there is nothing we can't do as a nation, as long as we do it together.

President Joseph R. Biden Jr.

For information on your direct payment, please visit IRS.gov/coronavirus or call 800-919-9835.

Appendix 3

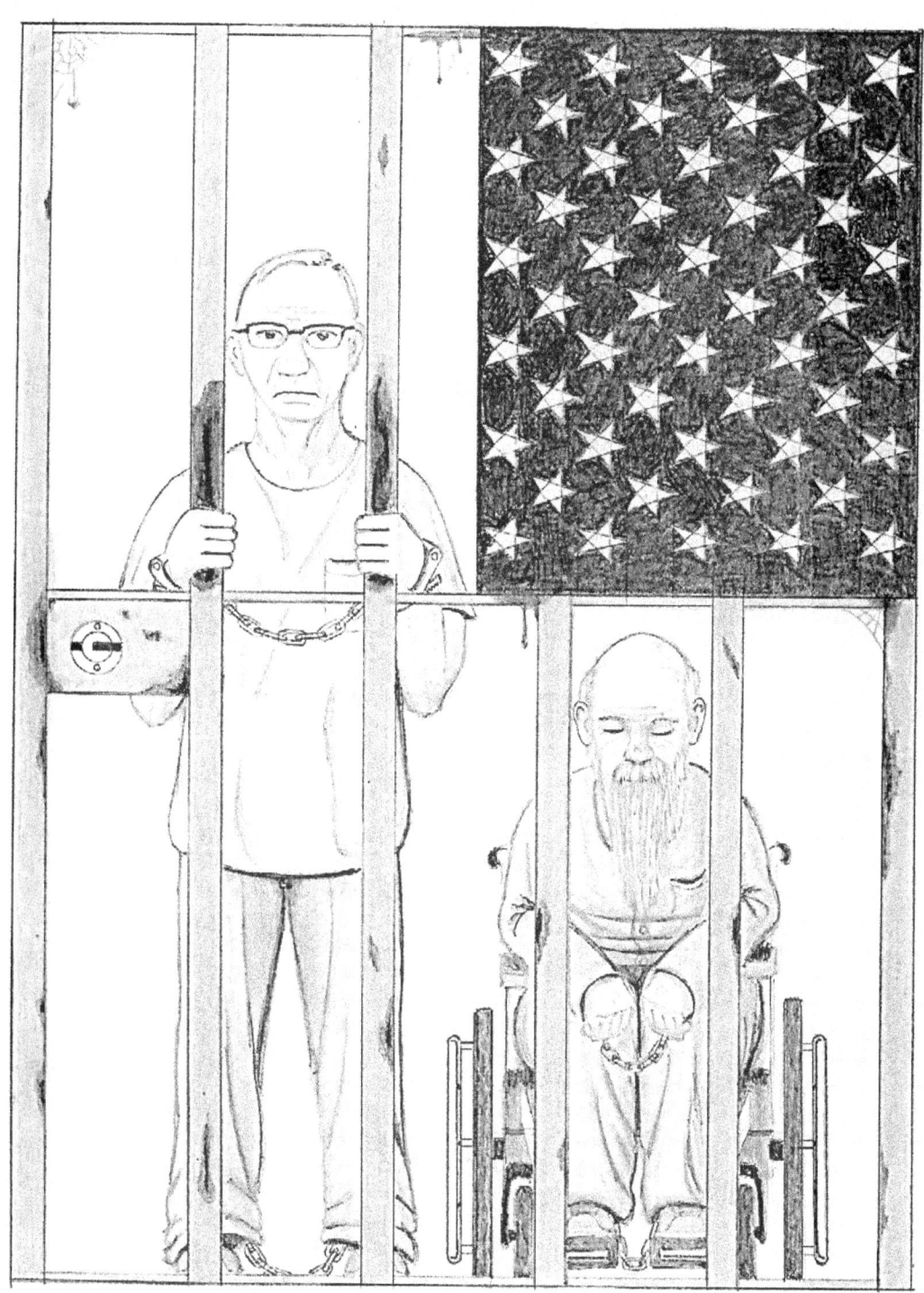

Stars And Bars. Will you be America's next Victim?

Appendix Four
Legal Minutiae

1. Suspect's conviction (under Nevada law) for refusing to disclose name held not violative of Fifth Amendment as disclosure of his name presented no reasonable danger of incrimination. (Suspect was convicted of "willfully resisting, delaying, or obstructing a public officer in discharging any legal duty of his office" and fined $250. He had refused to provide his name when he was drunk and acting belligerently.) *Hiibel v. 6th Judicial*, 524 U.S. 177 (2004). See also *Johnson v. Nocco*, 83 F. 4th 896 (11th Cir. 2023).

2. The privilege against self-incrimination generally is not self-executing and a witness who desires its protection has to claim it. A witness does not invoke the privilege simply by standing mute. Petitioner's Fifth Amendment claim failed because he did not expressly invoke the privilege against self-incrimination in response to the officer's question. *Salinas v. Texas*, 570 U.S. 178 (2013). Accord *U.S. v. McClain*, 2024 U.S. Dist. LEXIS 1823 (N.D. Il. 2024).

3. As chief of the State Attorney's office for Montgomery County, Maryland, Andrew Sonner and his staff had grand juries subpoena those who had already been convicted of crimes, after which they forced the convicts to testify against conspirators. Sonner states he chose this strategy because "The courts have consistently held that the Fifth Amendment protection against self-incrimination vanishes after conviction." Sonner, Andrew. *A Maryland Prosecutor*, Rockville, MD: HL Books, 2019.

4. Courts ruled situation in which defendant repeatedly refused to give iPhone passcodes, then was arrested and gave them, mandated evidence obtained thereby be suppressed from criminal cases as it was compelled contrary to the Fifth Amendment right to be free from self-incrimination. Nonetheless, because defendant's parole conditions required him to "truthfully answer all questions and follow all written and verbal instructions from parole officer," his parole officer was authorized to arrest him for a parole violation. *U.S. v. Sanchez*, 2018 U.S. Dist. LEXIS 155591 (N.D. Ga. 2018). See also *U.S. v. Saechao*, 418 F.3d 1073 (9th Cir. 2005). Accord *U.S. v. Watson*, 2023 U.S. Dist. LEXIS 184812 (D. Id. 2023).

5. Inculpating evidence suppressed because defendant produced documents after U.S. probation officer told defendant that if he did not provide the documents he would tell the court. *U.S. v. Singleton*, 2010 U.S. Dist. LEXIS 103527 (N.D. Ga. 2010).

Appendix Five

ADVANCED STUDIES IN MIND CONTROL

A Condensed Example and Analysis of Suggestive Questioning and the Implantation of False Memories

Example:

Therapist:	Let's start by taking some time to relax.
Patient:	Ok.
Therapist:	How was your day?
Patient:	Fine. Well, I had an argument with some girls at school who want to start trouble.
Therapist:	You're so pretty that they're probably jealous of you.
Patient:	That's what my friend Jacy says.
Therapist:	I bet a lot of people tell you that.
Patient:	Well yeh . . . I guess so.
Therapist:	You're so pretty that men may want to take advantage of you also.
Patient:	Maybe. I don't know. Men like me. I like them.
Therapist:	Maybe too much. But what we're talking about here is abuse, not love. You're too young to know what love is. Do you know that?
Patient:	Um . . . ok.
Therapist:	And you show signs of sexual abuse. Do you know that?
Patient:	Um . . . ok.
Therapist:	I read your statement to the police. You were scared when talking to them, weren't you?
Patient:	Yeh.
Therapist:	Did that cause you to hold back some things?
Patient:	Yeh.
Therapist:	It's ok. This isn't your fault. Let's go back to the events of January 2003.
Patient:	Ok.
Therapist:	Just relax and focus on what I'm saying. You can trust me. Now, let go and open up your mind. Imagine yourself standing in the hotel room beside the bed with the assailant.
Patient:	You mean my boyfriend?

Therapist: You can't think of him in those terms. Again, this is abuse.
Patient: Ok.
Therapist: Ok, now we're just trying to get a general idea of what took place.
Patient: Ok.
Therapist: Visualize yourself standing beside the bed with the assailant. He kissed you, but you weren't really comfortable with that, were you?
Patient: Um . . . I guess not.
Therapist: Then he reached over and unbuttoned your jeans and slid them and your underpants to the floor?
Patient: Didn't I do that myself?
Therapist: Remember not to get bogged down in precise details. We're visualizing, getting a general idea.
Patient: Ok.
Therapist: So he slid your pants down, then pushed you onto the bed?
Patient: Um . . . yes?
Therapist: And you protested when he inserted himself into your body?
Patient: Yes.
Therapist: Of course. You're a good girl!
Patient: Yeh . . . I know.
Therapist: And you cried and begged him to stop, but he kept going until he was satisfied, right?
Patient: Yes! Yes!
(The patient starts to cry and the therapist hands her a Kleenex and comforts her.)
Therapist: That's ok. Just let it all out. Let it all out. It's not your fault.
(Several minutes pass.)
Therapist: Now let's just go over it again together a couple more times. Then you can describe the events back to me on your own.
Patient: Ok. Ok.

Analysis

Memories can be changed after the receipt of false post-event information. This is known as the *misinformation effect*. One's confidence in a memory is flexible and exposure to new information can exaggerate her assurance of its accuracy, an effect known as *confidence inflation*. Exposure to new misinformation can, therefore, act upon both the recollection of a memory and the assurance it is correct. (Loftus and Doyle 1997 and 2005)

The first step is for the therapist to establish a rapport with the patient. (Female therapists are usually used for this as women and minors, who tend to be the targets, are more comfortable around them.) This rapport lowers the patient's resistance, opens her to the suggestive influence, and encourages cooperation. (Leo 2008) The therapist asks the patient to imagine, not recall, the scene—perhaps even stating this doesn't need to be exactly how it happened. For merely imagining a past event can lead to the belief it really took place. (Seamon, Philbin, and Harrison 2006) This phenomenon, which is often called *imagination inflation*, occurs in part because visualizing something stimulates brain areas similar to those activated when actually experiencing it. (Gonsalves, et al. 2004).

The therapist then leads the patient into a series of suggestive questions. That is, the wording of the questions is such it elicits the desired answer. Experimental research psychologists report that misleading and suggestive information can erode actual memory. (Ornstein, Ceci, and Loftus 1998) And questions containing hidden assumptions elicit twice as many "memories" of nonexistent events as do questions without them. (Loftus and Zanni 1975) Further, people often adjust what they say to please their listeners. As the listener here is an authority figure, this is even more likely to be the case. (Manis 1974, Tesser 1972, Tetlock 1983) Convincing the patient she is blameless and giving her positive feedback increases her confidence. (Douglass and Steblay 2006; Jones 2008; Wright and Skagerberg 2007) (I've read enough transcripts of these sessions to infer this is an essential tactic in sex cases.)

Finally, retelling the story cements it in the patient's memory and also commits her to that version of it. She eventually becomes convinced it is the true memory of an actual event. (Bergman and McAllister 1982; Wells, Ferguson, and Lindsay 1981)

Note: Some therapists still administer the "truth serum" amobarbital, aka sodium amytal, a crystalline compound used as a sedative and hypnotic agent, to ease the process along. See e.g. *Coleman v. McCormick*, 874 F.2d 1280 (9th Cir. 1989) (State administered injection and interview to alter defendant's memory, causing him to reverse his testimony. Where he had previously stood by his innocence, he suddenly declared his guilt.)

Psychopolitical Warfare . . . / Eric Wise

Appendix 6

UNITED STATES DEPARTMENT OF JUSTICE
FEDERAL PRISON SYSTEM

AFFIDAVIT
* * * * * * * *

State of Virginia)
) ss:
County of Prince George)

I, Eric Wise, 01382-449, at the Federal Correctional Institution, Petersburg, Virginia make this statement freely without any promises or assurances:

I began to observe odd behavior between staff member ~~Hendrickson~~ and the Mexican inmate with tattoos on his head (~~_____~~ Reg. No. ~~_____~~) and notified the SIA. The officer work recreation on September 10, 2016, flirting with the inmate. She told the inmate "I used to sit out there on the fuckin C-South steps smoking my fucking cigarettes!" It was almost if they were on a date. They were there on the recreation yard together from 7:10 p.m. until 8:30 p.m. I observed them together on 10/21/16 around 10:00 a.m. in the F unit stairwell. The inmate is not assigned to F unit and therefore should not have been allowed to have been there. I observed the officer on two other occasions meeting with the inmate and having a conversation. The inmate shirt was pulled up just a little as if he was going to put something in or take out of it. I have never seen her give the inmate anything but she has ~~always~~ gone out of her way to see him. EW

Page: 1 of 2   AFFIANT's INITIALS: EW   DATE: 10-27-16

Appendix 7

From: ^!"WISE, ^IERIC RICHARD" <01382449@inmatemessage.com>
To:
Date: 10/29/2016 8:20 AM
Subject: ***Request to Staff*** WISE, ERIC, Reg# 01382449, PEM-A-N

To: .
Inmate Work Assignment: .

ATTENTION

Please cut and paste the message indicator below into the subject line; only this indicator can be in the subject line.
848bc251-c281-4fd9-80b9-719a11544e24
Your response must come from the departmental mail box. Responses from personal mailboxes WILL NOT be delivered to the inmate.

Inmate Message Below

The management of the A-N housing unit [(b)(6); (b)(7)(C)] are intentionally subjecting inmates who they dislike, [(b)(7)(F)] violations. Earlier this year they placed a large, mentally ill black inmate [(b)(6), (b)(7)(C), (b)(7)(F)] newly imprisoned white inmates [(b)(6), (b)(7)(C), (b)(7)(F)] threatened them and demanded [(b)(6), (b)(7)(C), (b)(7)(F)] who, along with the others, all asked Unit Team to be moved. These requests were denied and they were abused more [(b)(6), (b)(7)(C), (b)(7)(F)] nearly being choked to death.

The same unit management has recently moved an old black pimp [(b)(6), (b)(7)(C), (b)(7)(F)] as a younger white [(b)(6), (b)(7)(C), (b)(7)(F)] where the former pays the latter [(b)(7)(F)]

This unit team further arranged a naive younger white inmate [(b)(6), (b)(7)(C), (b)(7)(F)] [(b)(6); (b)(7)(C)] with an old Puerto Rican [(b)(6), (b)(7)(C), (b)(7)(F)] An officer named [(b)(6), (b)(7)(C), (b)(7)(F)] caught [(b)(6), (b)(7)(C)] in the act of raping a mentally challenged inmate [(b)(6), (b)(7)(C), (b)(7)(F)] less than 2 years ago.

FOI EXEMPT

SOUNDTRACK

This manuscript was composed under the influence of the following:

Radio:
    101.1 WRR—Classical, Dallas
    95.7 KNET—"Hits from the 70s and 80s!"   Palestine
    91.7 KXT—"Where Deep Album Tracks Go to Live,"   Dallas

iPad:

Song	Artist
March into Hell/Arrival/Grinding Wheels of War	Fallen Angel
Hell Patrol	Judas Priest
Poor Girl	Tobruk
Stay With Me	Megan Jennings
Give Me a Sign	Damien
Season of the Arrow	Damien
I'd Rather be Wasted	Cara Paige
I Can See the Lightning	Summon the Elders
Over You	Ashlee Nikole
Ashes in the Sky	Loudness
Pendulum	Machinae Supremacy
The Headless Children	W.A.S.P.
Sowilo Rune	Agalloch
Even Your Blood Group	Devilment
The Burden and the Grief	Tormentor
Chronicles of Death	Metal Force
The Unknown	Metal Force
Perfect	Amanda "the Panda" September
Time and Space (Part 1)	Avian
Kingdom	Super Toxic Snake
Nightmare	Super Toxic Snake
All the Good Ones	Chloe Adams
Blade	Rearview Mirror
Behind the Gun	Leatherwolf
Grey Matter	Zora
Deja Vu	Zora
Last Breath	Heavyquake
The Weight of the World	Inciter

The ancient knightly family of Wise is one of the oldest in western England. This surname derives from the Norman "le Wyse": a nickname for *the wiseman*, an intelligent or learned person. Naturally, out of the nine bearers recorded in the *Rotuli Hundredorum*, eight were found in Cambridgeshire and Oxfordshire, and were likely graduates of the respective universities in those counties. The family first became established in Devon, England where they were Lords of the Manor of Greston.

In 1400, King Henry IV granted arms of achievement to the family:

ARMS: Sable, three chevronels argent charged with ermine.

CREST: Demilion rampant gules guttee d 'eau sprinkled with water wielding in the dexter paw a regal mace.

WREATH OF THE COLORS: Argent streaked with sable.

> – The "Book of Wise"
> (Compiled in the 1970s by the
> author's paternal great aunt.)

Wise